THE GOLDEN AGE OF CHRISTMAS MOVIES

Thomas A. Christie

Other Books by
Thomas A. Christie

Liv Tyler: Star in Ascendance

The Cinema of Richard Linklater

John Hughes and Eighties Cinema

Ferris Bueller's Day Off: The Pocket Movie Guide

The Christmas Movie Book

Notional Identities

The Shadow in the Gallery

The James Bond Movies of the 1980s

Mel Brooks: Genius and Loving It!

The Spectrum of Adventure

A Righteously Awesome Eighties Christmas

Contested Mindscapes

John Hughes FAQ

THE GOLDEN AGE OF CHRISTMAS MOVIES

Festive Cinema of the 1940s and 50s

Thomas A. Christie

To Eddie,

With festive best wishes!

Tom

E**X**TREMIS *publishing*

The Golden Age of Christmas Movies: Festive Cinema of the 1940s and 50s by Thomas A. Christie.

First published in Great Britain in 2019 by Extremis Publishing Ltd.,
Suite 218, Castle House, 1 Baker Street, Stirling, FK8 1AL, United Kingdom.
www.extremispublishing.com

Extremis Publishing is a Private Limited Company registered in Scotland (SC509983) whose Registered Office is Suite 218, Castle House, 1 Baker Street, Stirling, FK8 1AL, United Kingdom.

A CIP catalogue record for this book is available from the British Library.

ISBN: 978-1-9996962-0-7

Typeset in Goudy Bookletter 1911, designed by The League of Moveable Type.

Printed and bound in Great Britain by IngramSpark, Chapter House, Pitfield, Kiln Farm, Milton Keynes, MK11 3LW, United Kingdom.

Front cover artwork is Copyright © Suat Gursozlu at Shutterstock.
Back cover artwork from Pixabay.
Cover design and book design is Copyright © Thomas A. Christie.
Author image is Copyright © Eddy A. Bryan.
Incidental illustrations are Copyright © Fabio Pagani at Shutterstock / Pixabay.

The copyrights of third parties are reserved. All third party imagery is used under the provision of Fair Use for the purposes of commentary and criticism.

While every reasonable effort has been made to contact copyright holders and secure permission for all images reproduced in this work, we offer apologies for any instances in which this was not possible and for any inadvertent omissions.

This book is dedicated to
my beloved brother

Robert Christie

Gone but never forgotten

Contents

Also in This Series:

A Righteously Awesome Eighties Christmas

Festive Cinema of the 1980s

THOMAS A. CHRISTIE

'No man is a failure who has friends.'

Clarence Odbody,
It's a Wonderful Life **(1946)**

Foreword

WHEN I was asked to write the foreword for this book, I pondered the differences between the period in which these movies were created and today's world. So much has changed during the last 80 or so years.

One thing that hasn't is the innocence and the God-centered heart of most people. I see this every year as a professional Santa Claus, when children of all ages come to me with hope in their eyes and longing in their hearts. Some dreams cannot be measured, and while the material things seem all important to many, one can hear the deeper desires if they look and listen carefully.

You also see on social media and hear from friends how they cannot wait for the Christmas movie season to begin. Many posts exalt the Hallmark Channel and their choice of Christmas titles, along with other stations and their marathon showings of seasonal favorites.

The movies from this era focus on, and bring to light, those inner feelings we try to emulate better than any other cinematic period. A perfect example of this is *The Bishop's Wife* where the bishop, played by David Niven, is convinced he must build a massive cathedral to pay glory to God. However, he ends up helping his fellow man with the assistance of an angel played by Cary Grant. The bishop's goals were misplaced, but his heart was not.

Such was a central theme during the making of these classic movies. People frequently miss the whole point of Santa Claus, and fewer still know the descendant of St Nicholas on whom Santa is based. St Nicholas did whatever he could to take care of his fellow man. He did this because he knew in his heart this is what God wanted him to do. Many of these movies center on helping others, especially under challenging circumstances. Often a good dose of humor is thrown in.

Movies like *Christmas in Connecticut*, *It Happened on 5th Avenue*, and the immortal *It's a Wonderful Life* all demonstrate how helping others gives the greatest gift to ourselves, even if the gift was not originally planned or appreciated at first. Some of these movies show that even characters with a nefarious nature and seemingly few redeeming qualities can do wonderful things for people. *We're No Angels*, *Three Godfathers*, and *The Lemon Drop Kid* all show that even with questionable motives, people have a tendency toward good if given half a chance to let the good in them shine.

There is no better example of this than the numerous productions of Charles Dickens's classic *A Christmas Carol*. From a very young age, we are brought up on various versions of this story showing how even the most miserly and inward-looking person can be taught to appreciate and take care of others. Perhaps so many alterations of this story, such as *Scrooge*, have been produced to continuously remind us of this fact. Similarly, the film *Christmas Eve* shows how three very inward-looking men return to the aid of the foster mother in her time of need, even when it is not in their best interest to come home.

These Christmas themes teach us time and again to look beyond our own small and centered world to see those who have bigger needs and fewer resources than we do. Some of these movies are purely entertaining like *White Christmas*, but even here the central motive is to help their former general who has fallen on hard times after retiring from the service.

Many of these movies are standards we watch year in and year out and for extremely good reasons. For instance, *Meet Me in St Louis* made in 1944, that takes place around 1904 and the World's Fair, has been deemed 'culturally significant' by the Library of Congress and fifty years after its creation was selected for preservation in the United States National Film Registry. Made up of a series of short stories, each vignette centers around the hopes and heartaches of the Smith family and, well, I'll let Tom tell you more about it, as that is the point of this book.

Our point is for us to keep watching these gems of our own consciousness, and to take away the morals and lessons they try to teach us.

I hear a lot from people that we have turned a corner and could never return to the days of a more gentle heart. But I am here to say that as a Santa Claus and fellow author, nothing could be further from the truth. I see wonderful examples every day of people helping and reaching out to others. We just need to make up our minds to do it, and these movies make us mindful that we only need to take the first step.

So enjoy this wonderful trip down memory lane as Tom Christie unwraps each of these movies like a Christmas present for you to enjoy. But do not lose the lessons they teach or the understated meaning of these and other Christmas movies. Perhaps a little bit of Santa Claus will surface in you, too.

Santa Joe Moore
Author and Professional Santa Claus

The North Pole Press
Maryville, TN
http://thenorthpolepress.com

THE GOLDEN AGE OF CHRISTMAS MOVIES

Festive Cinema of
the 1940s and 50s

Introduction

THE Christmas movie is a genre that is as old as cinema itself, and themes and settings inspired by the festive season have enjoyed a unique and often surprisingly dynamic relationship with the international film industry over the years. While Christmas is a time of year that has become synonymous with the various cultural traditions which have developed around it, these customs have come to transcend the religious (and, more recently, commercial) significance of the holiday season, creating some truly memorable big screen experiences in the process.

Over the past few centuries, the month of December has brought us everything from annual greetings cards and bestselling yuletide songs to turkey dinners and tinsel-strewn plastic fir trees propped up in living rooms across the Western world. Yet for all the instantly-recognisable traditions that have come to be associated with the celebration of this fondly-anticipated season of the year, the Christmas film has gradually established numerous tropes of its own which have become equally familiar to audiences. Festive movies have proven to be every bit as adaptive as other cinematic genres during the rapid social changes of the twentieth century, and – for a number of reasons – movies in this category still perform convincingly with critics and at the box-office in the present day.

Over the decades, the themes and styles of festively-themed motion pictures have continued to develop – radically so, during some periods – in order to remain relevant to contemporary audiences. Sometimes the premise of more modern takes on the Christmas film will prove to be highly inventive, and on occasion they may be distinctly offbeat. But more often than not they can still be seen to retain some distant reflection of the optimistic, life-affirming foundations of the genre which were laid down during its golden age in the 1940s and 50s.

In this book, I will be taking a look at the themes and conventions which became established in Christmas cinema throughout its formative years. While festive topics had been addressed in a number of films prior to the 1940s – not least in features such as *Babes in Toyland* (Gus Meins and Charles Rogers, 1934) and *A Christmas Carol* (Edwin L. Marin, 1938) – Christmas-based premises and settings remained relatively few and far between until the period of the Second World War and its aftermath, when the key themes of the festive movie were laid down more explicitly and the Christmas movie – as the distinct category of film that has come to be recognised today – began to take shape.

Due to the long-term artistic influence of the films in this seminal genre which were being produced during the forties and fifties, themes of family, friendship, community and personal transformation would become synonymous with the Christmas movie in ways which would see these themes being revisited, reinvented, subverted – and ultimately honoured – for many years to come. Today it is difficult to imagine Christmas without a lengthy list of beloved films from our respective childhoods, with every generation treasuring particular entries in the genre from the time of their own youth. But it would be in festive cinema's golden age that these central conventions were first recognised and explored, inspiring so many memorable motion pictures in the decades which followed.

It may, perhaps, be advantageous to explain the use of the term 'Christmas film' as it appears in the context of the analysis to come. It is now generally considered that there are three discrete categories of Christmas movie. First, and most pertinent to this study, is the film that deals with themes relating to Christmas as its central subject matter, considers issues deriving from the festive season, or which somehow examines the social, cultural and/or religious conventions of Christmas. The second category, which is also referred to occasionally throughout the book, is the film which is set at Christmas, either principally or in part, but which may or may not directly address topics directly related to Christmas. These include comedies and dramas set during the festive period, but which usually lack a specific or dominant Christmas theme even if they feature a prominent yuletide backdrop. The third category, which is not covered by the remit of this book, refers to the films which are regularly shown by television networks over the course of the festive period (especially in the United Kingdom), but which otherwise have no direct connection with Christmas. Features in this category typically include cinematic classics and epic blockbusters such as *The Great Escape* (John Sturges, 1963) and *The Wizard of Oz* (Victor Fleming, 1939), popular musicals like *The Sound of Music* (Robert Wise, 1965) and *Chitty Chitty Bang Bang* (Ken Hughes, 1968), and the appearance of at least one entry from Eon Productions' perennially successful *James Bond* film series. Such films have formed a degree of nostalgia amongst audiences due to regular December screenings, but do not otherwise offer a direct association with the holiday season.

3

It should also be noted that this book discusses films which have been produced for, and exhibited upon, the big screen. There is no examination of any festive features which were produced by television networks during the period under consideration, simply for reasons of space – though as we shall see, many classics of Christmas cinema have subsequently gained a dedicated audience due to TV broadcasts many years after their first appearance in theatres. While the collection of specific films which I have chosen for discussion in this book may not necessarily please everyone, they have each been carefully selected in order to give the broadest possible analysis of the different themes addressed by directors and screenwriters in Christmas motion pictures during the course of the vitally important period of time that is under examination. Taken together, the choice of films in this book has been employed as a springboard for a broader assessment of how they have come to fit into the wider tapestry of Christmas movie subgenres, and to discuss the range of conventions and premises that have been established as time has passed.

By employing a chronological frame of reference, the evolution of the canon of Christmas films will be charted from 1940 until the end of the 1950s, and the changing styles – and attitudes of critics and audiences – will be addressed as well as the universal themes which emerged and have since remained more or less constant within the genre. Christmas movies have not only been enjoyed by vast audiences over the years, but have also proven to be deeply influential, inspiring directors and screenwriters in profound and occasionally unusual ways. Sometimes these films are intended to promote seasonal themes of peace, mutual understanding and goodwill, while others slyly provide satirical comment on culture and society at the time of their production. On more than a few occasions

4

both approaches have been employed simultaneously, and to great effect.

As this study will explore in some detail, the Christmas film has come to mean a great many things to a great many people over the years. For some it is the Nativity story which originally inspired the holiday, for others it is an account of Santa Claus and his Christmas Eve visits, and for many it is the notion of peace, hope and goodwill to every adult and child... or, at the very least, simply a heart-warming diversion to pass the cold winter months. But whatever specific element springs to mind when people think of festive movies, this cat-egory of cinema has come to span a very wide variety of dif-ferent genres over the years, from fantasy and horror to com-edy and drama. Yet given how acutely Christmas films are often concerned with the preservation of tradition, it is also intriguing to note just how dynamic and adaptable the genre has proven to be as the decades have passed. Although the content of festive cinema has inevitably been affected by changing social attitudes, many aspects have tended to remain largely impervious to the influence of contemporary stylistic movements within the world of film; the genre has largely been inclined to march to its own drumbeat rather than being shaped too pliably by the development of other cinematic trends that were evolving around it over the years. This has been due, at least in part, to the way in which many Christ-mas films encompass a certain nucleus of recurrent subject matter that are concerned with embracing certain archetypes and/or mythological areas integral to the traditional festive season: the legend of Father Christmas, Christian symbolism and iconography, and the recognised customs of the modern Christmas which have been established since at least the nine-teenth century.

But while this understated revolution in festive film-making has inspired warm nostalgia and thoughtful good cheer, we must never forget that it found its genesis in the darkest hour of modern world history. Emerging from the dark shadows of wartime like a freshly-lit beacon of hope, films with a Christmas theme were to reflect some aspect of the national and international climate of the time, moving from the bleak struggle of the war years to the austerity and quiet optimism of the period immediately following the conflict, and then on to new purpose and idealism during the fifties. Taken cumulatively, this developmental period was to form perhaps the single most interesting, significant and influential era in the genre's long history.

It seems certain that as long as there is a holiday celebration every December, there will also be a thriving market in Christmas films: continuing box-office success and a persisting audience appetite for festive cinematic fare remain undiminished in the modern age, with viewer enthusiasm not lessened even by an ever-more-intimate familiarity with the time-honoured conventions of the genre. But while time alone will tell if Christmas films will ever again reach the heady heights of critical acclaim which saw the genre showered with Academy Award nominations in the 1940s and 50s during their silver screen heyday, the fact remains that the movies of the festive season have proven to be among cinema's great survivors: a category of film-making which has demonstrated both endurance and adaptability, as well as inspiring wistful reminiscence. The Christmas film continues to appeal to the idealist in all of us, encouraging hope that even in a world of uncompromising realities and moral complexity, there may yet be a chance for each of us to achieve a happier life and pursue a brighter tomorrow, in friendship and in harmony.

Early Christmas Movies

1897-1939

THERE is no question that Christmas films have been with us, in one form or another, since the very birth of cinema. The development of the genre which we have come to identify as the Christmas film, however, has been a gradual one which has come to take form over a number of decades. Although the foundations of what we now recognise as key archetypes of Christmas film-making were laid down in the genre's golden age during the Second World War and its aftermath, movies with a Christmas setting had been produced as far back as the concluding years of the nineteenth century, with many silent films and early 'talkies' being situated in a festive locale or incorporating aspects of Christmas iconography into their narratives.

There is growing consensus amongst many commentators that the first Christmas film to be exhibited to the general public was the American Mutoscope Company's *Night Before Christmas* (1897), a short feature which centred upon a group of children hanging up stockings in their family home on Christmas Eve before heading for bed in anticipation of a visit from Santa Claus. The directorial credit for this film is generally attributed to American Mutoscope's famous founder, William Kennedy Dickson, and it was to form the first instalment of a cycle of four interrelated Christmas features, all of which were released later in the same year. (The other short films in the cycle, in order, were *Santa Claus Filling Stockings*, *Christmas Morning*, and *The Christmas Tree Party*). American Mutoscope's famous cycle has come to be known collectively by the title *Christmas Eve* (1897) and also *The Visit of St Nicholas* (1897), though perhaps the most significant other Christmas film of the late nineteenth century was a British feature, *Santa Claus* (1898), which had a running time of around one minute in duration and was produced by George Albert Smith Films. Directed by Smith himself, this feature was remarkable in a number of ways: it was one of the first films to include an opening title screen which contained alphabetic lettering, it used iris-masking of the camera lens in order to produce a fantasy sequence which played out over the main action, and it was also to utilise some pioneering visual effects (for the time) such as stop-motion jump-cuts. It, like Dickson's film, featured a brief appearance from Santa Claus as he visits a family home with gifts on Christmas Eve.

The dawn of the twentieth century brought with it a boom in new silent features, with an eager public appetite for new works in all kinds of different genres. The Christmas film was no exception, and the opening decades of the new century were to bring a wide variety of entries in this incipient category of moviemaking. Amongst the most prominent works to see release in this period included the heart-warming family scenes of *A Holiday Pageant at Home* (1901), *The Night Before Christmas* (Edwin S. Porter, 1905) – which included some inventive effects work – and the spirited *A Winter Straw Ride* (D.W. Griffith, 1906). Rather more serious in tone was *A Trap for Santa* (1909), which dealt with themes of alcoholism and petty crime over the festive season, and Harold M. Shaw and Bannister Merwin's *A Christmas Accident* (1912), an early tale of yuletide redemption. Burglary and mistaken identity featured in *The Adventure of the Wrong Santa Claus* (1914), where an opportunistic felon receives his comeuppance when caught during some Christmas Eve thievery, while *Santa Claus Versus Cupid* (Will Louis, 1915) shares the moral theme of criminality and its ramifications but concludes its narrative positively thanks to the timely intervention of Father Christmas himself. Mr and Mrs F.E. Kleinschmidt released their independent production *Santa Claus* (1925) some years later, where Jolly Old Saint Nick recounts his numerous activities beyond his annual Christmas Eve travels around the globe, while shortly afterwards popular comedian Charley Chase was to star in *There Ain't No Santa Claus* (1926), an offbeat tale which featured the unlikely combination of romantic gestures, Christmas gifts and overdue rent money.

By far the most prominent yuletide feature in the cinema of these decades was, perhaps not surprisingly, a string of adaptations of Charles Dickens's influential 1843 festive tale, *A Christmas Carol*. Among the best-remembered of these early festive outings was Walter R. Booth's *Scrooge, or, Marley's Ghost* (1901), a five-minute silent British feature which is generally considered to be the earliest surviving filmed version of the story. This was followed by Essanay Studios' *A Christmas Carol* (1908), filmed in Chicago with Thomas Ricketts as Scrooge, and another silent version, also entitled *A Christmas Carol* (J. Searle Dawley, 1910), produced for Edison Studios and starring Marc Dermott as the famous Dickensian miser. The short film *Scrooge* (1913) (also known as *Old*

Scrooge from the time of its American screening some years later) starred Sir Seymour Hicks, who had played Ebenezer to great acclaim in stage productions in years gone by, while a few years later there was the release of Rupert Julian's famous *The Right to Be Happy* (1916), featuring Julian himself in the role of Scrooge, which was the first adaptation of *A Christmas Carol* to run to feature length. Also held in critical esteem was Edwin Greenwood's *A Christmas Carol* (1923), a British production which presented Russell Thorndike as the penny-pinching Victorian anti-hero.

Another recurrent feature of this early period of Christmas film-making were the many adaptations of Peter B. Kyne's 1913 novella *The Three Godfathers*, which proved to be almost as popular a source of inspiration in these formative years as Dickens's ground-breaking story had been. Cinematic versions of the tale began with Edward LeSaint's *The Three Godfathers* (1916), which was remade a few years later by John Ford under the title *Marked Men* (1919). Both films starred Harry Carey, and featured a story which centred upon three bank robbers who accidentally stumble upon a newly-born infant child in the desert – a scenario which is presented with various stylistic overtones of the Nativity. The film was remade by William Wyler as *Hell's Heroes* (1930), the first film that he had directed which was to feature a sound track, and then it was to be adapted again by Richard Boleslawski in 1936 (once more with the title *The Three Godfathers*) before John Ford returned to the story to create what has become widely regarded as the definitive version, in 1948 (q.v.), starring John Wayne, Pedro Armendáriz and Harry Carey Jr.

The era of the talkies brought with it a new wave of Christmas-related features, albeit with a very broad range of subject matter which meant that some dealt with the themes of the festive season more closely than others. *Turkey Time* (Tom Walls, 1933), an adaptation of Ben Travers's stage play, was a Christmas-situated comic family farce, while *Babes in Toyland* (Charles Rogers and Gus Meins, 1934) – sometimes known in later years by the alternative title *March of the Wooden Soldiers* – was a comic fantasy which made good use of its legendary stars Stan Laurel and Oliver Hardy. Based on

Babes in Toyland (1934): Hal Roach Studios/Metro-Goldwyn-Mayer

Victor Herbert's 1903 operetta of the same name, *Babes in Toyland* is one of the few films of this vintage which remains readily available on the commercial home entertainment market; it has been colourised more than once, and was remade by Jack Donohue for the Walt Disney Company in 1961. Henry Edwards's *Scrooge* (1935) was a British feature-length version of Dickens's story, with Sir Seymour Hicks reprising his role as Ebenezer Scrooge following his earlier appearance in the 1913 silent adaptation. Edwards' version is considered to be the first version of the tale to feature sound, but its reputation has been dwarfed in subsequent years by Edwin L. Marin's *A Christmas Carol* (1938), a glossy MGM production which starred Reginald Owen as Scrooge. The Marin version is perhaps the best-known feature-length adaptation of the Dickens text prior to Brian Desmond Hurst's legendary 1951 film (q.v.), which introduced Alastair Sim in the title role. George B. Seitz's (now rather obscure) comic crime fantasy *The*

Three Wise Guys (1936) also made its debut in this decade, as did *Bachelor Mother* (Garson Kanin, 1939), a well-received comedy of manners set around the festive season which starred David Niven and Ginger Rogers.

A number of other films emerged throughout the 1930s which either featured a festive theme or yuletide setting. *The Bill of Divorcement* (George Cukor, 1932), which starred John Barrymore and was the film debut of Katharine Hepburn, was an adaptation of Clemence Dane's stage play of the same name. With a narrative which commenced on Christmas Eve, this mature and thought-provoking drama centred on the subject of a marriage which had been dissolved on grounds of insanity, and raised numerous thoughtful questions about mental health, emotional attachment and domestic life. The cosy festive setting acts as a jarring contrast to the challenging emotional and psychological issues that the film address-es throughout. *Baby Face* (Alfred E. Green, 1933) starred Barbara Stanwyck and George Brent, as well as featuring a young John Wayne (only twenty-five years of age at the time) as one of the supporting char-acters. The film was one of the most notorious features of Pre-Hays Code Holly-wood, with a frank explora-tion of how sex appeal can be used to climb the social ladder. *Baby Face* features a

A Christmas Carol (1938): Metro-Goldwyn-Mayer

pivotal scene set on Christmas Day, but is otherwise largely unconcerned with the festive season. *The Thin Man* (W.S. Van Dyke, 1934), adapted from the Dashiell Hammett novel, starred William Powell and Nora Charles as unconventional spouses – a retired private eye and a well-to-do socialite. The mystery at the heart of the film's storyline, which is a tightly-plotted whodunit, takes place in New York City over the Christmas holidays.

Movies with yuletide connections continued to appear towards the end of the decade. *Stella Dallas* (King Vidor, 1937) was based on a novel by Olive Higgins Prouty, and starred Barbara Stanwyck and John Boles. A tale of social mobility and complicated romances, the film's festive connections rarely run deeper than its famous Christmas tree outfit scene – one of its most instantly-recognisable sequences. *Grand Illusion* (Jean Renoir, 1937) was a French war film which focused upon the complex social relationships existing between incarcerated officers of the French armed forces who are plotting to escape from a prisoner of war camp during the First World War. Starring Jean Gabin, Marcel Dalio and Erich von Stroheim, the movie is now considered one of the finest works of French cinema ever produced, and features one of Renoir's most celebrated scenes – a Christmas Eve celebration where escapees from the camp find shelter at a remote farm and thank the owner by quickly (and skilfully) improvising a Christmas tree and model Nativity scene.

Holiday (George Cukor, 1938) is a remake of Edward H. Griffith's 1930 film of the same name, starring Katharine Hepburn and Cary Grant, and was adapted from a stage play by Philip Barry. A romantic comedy full of eccentric characters and high society situations, the film's festive credentials concentrate around a Christmas Day scene at the Seton family mansion which has pivotal ramifications for its two young lovers. *Love Finds Andy Hardy* (George B. Seitz, 1938) starred a young Mickey Rooney in the title role, and was one of a series of sixteen *Andy Hardy* movies based on characters created by Aurania Rouverol. Also starring Fay Holden, Judy Garland and Lana Turner, the film features the complicated romantic entanglements of the eponymous teenager as he attempts to juggle the affections of three separate suitors. Key to the plot is the local high school's Christmas Eve dance, and Hardy's difficulties in choosing a date for the event.

The Old Maid (Edmund Goulding, 1939), based on Zoe Akins's Pulitzer Prize-winning stage play (in turn adapted from Edith Wharton's 1924 novella of the same name), was an American Civil War-based drama starring Bette Davis, Miriam Hopkins and George Brent. A convoluted story of family relationships, its brush with Christmas is meaningful but slight, and its profile has since been dwarfed by its proximity to the release of almost certainly the most prominent movie to deal with the Civil War during this era of moviemaking, *Gone with the Wind* (Victor Fleming, 1939). The latter film, famously starring Clark Gable, Vivien Leigh and Leslie Howard and adapted from the 1936 novel by Margaret Mitchell, itself features a prominent seasonal sequence where – following the tumultuous Battle of Gettysburg – Leigh's Scarlett and Howard's Ashley share an impassioned Christmas Day kiss before the latter returns to his wartime duties.

As the above summation demonstrates, a reasonable number of films had been released between the turn of the century and the outbreak of the Second World War which had made use of a Christmas setting, but relatively few of them had dealt directly with the nature of the festive season itself. Although producers, directors and screenwriters had employed Christmas to achieve a variety of functions – from providing an atmospheric backdrop for domestic dramas to framing outlandish comic situations – not many were inclined to consider the season in depth, in order to examine (as Dickens had done with such panache) exactly what it was about that fateful, wintry period in December that wielded the power to transform attitudes and mould new hope and optimism from despair and broken dreams. All of this was soon to change, as the West entered a period of intense self-consideration and cultural reflection during – and especially after – the events of World War II. The Christmas film was about to enter its golden age: an era which would define the themes of the genre, and forever change expectations about how this most unique time of year was depicted on the big screen.

1

The Shop Around the Corner (1940)

Metro-Goldwyn-Mayer

Director: Ernst Lubitsch
Producer: Ernst Lubitsch
Screenwriter: Samson Raphaelson, from a play by Miklós László

THE Christmas movie, as we have come to recognise the term today, may well have been around from the very earliest days of the cinema industry, but the conventions of the genre – as well as the emergence of its numerous subgenres – were not to fully emerge until the arrival of the 1940s. In some ways, the bleakest hour of the twentieth century may have seemed an unlikely point for the traditions of the Christmas film to emerge; the shadow of fascism had fallen across Europe, and the United States would shortly enter the Second World War in the aftermath of the Pearl Harbor attack of 1941. Yet sometimes it takes the darkest conditions for a light to shine most brightly, and the tropes which would come to characterise Christmas movies – such as family, community and positive transformation – would be particularly relevant to a free world that was fighting for its very survival against tyrannical, totalitarian forces.

While the Christmas movie would not truly enter its golden age until the period immediately following the war's conclusion, the early forties would nonetheless play host to a number of prominent features which used festive settings and situations as a backdrop for their action. Many of these films were nostalgic in nature, with the uncertainty of world geo-politics inclining audiences towards the comforting memories of less desperate times, and this was certainly true of Ernst Lubitsch's celebrated romantic comedy-drama *The Shop Around the Corner*. As Artemisia D'Ecca has remarked, the film subtly presaged the later Christmas movie theme of communal goodwill overcoming avarice and materialism: '*The Shop Around the Corner* nicely evokes a sense of time and place; and the small specialized world in which it is set becomes the whole world. [...] Although its values are those of the world of commerce, somehow it makes you feel that the commercial side of Christmas is not all bad'.[1]

Taking place in Hungary in a deliberately hazily-defined pre-war period, *The Shop Around the Corner* was adapted from Miklós László's 1937 play *Parfumerie* and drew heavily upon Lubitsch's own experiences of working in retail during his formative years (specifically in his father's tailoring business, S. Lubitsch of Berlin). While romance has always been a major theme in Christmas moviemaking, even in its earliest years, *The Shop Around the Corner* was to make explicit the connection between the festive season and the realisation of true love by uniting the two unwitting participants in a budding relationship on Christmas Eve – a precept which would be revisited many times in the decades to come.

Ernst Lubitsch (1892-1947) was a major figure in Hollywood at the time, with his trademark thematic sophistication and refined characterisation marking him out for critical praise and audience appreciation. So considerable was his contribution to the cinema of the thirties and forties in particular that no brief summary could possibly do even a cursory level of justice to his work. Initially becoming an actor in his native Germany, the youthful Lubitsch joined the Deutsches Theater in 1911 and would appear in films until 1920; as a well-regarded director even while performing in front of the camera, he decided to concentrate solely on his directorial career from 1920 onwards. He eventually formed his own production company, and after a professional visit to the United States in 1921 he made a move to Hollywood in 1922. Initially directing silent films, he built a solid reputation through the urbane comedies of manners that would define his career. However, it was for *The Patriot* (1928) – his biopic of Emperor Paul I of Russia – that he would receive his first Academy Award nomination for his direction. He made a move into the 'talkies' the following year with *The Love Parade* (1929), which saw a further Academy Award nomination conferred on him, and he would go on to great success with many later films which included romantic comedy *Trouble in Paradise* (1932) and adroit satire *Ninotchka* (1939) – which featured a screenplay co-written by Billy Wilder and a starring role for Greta Garbo – as well as the later *To Be or Not to Be* (1942), a topical black comedy based around an acting company trapped in Warsaw, with Poland then occupied by invading Nazi forces. Nominated on three occasions for Best Director, for his prolific professional contribution to the world of cinema Lubitsch was presented with a Special Academy Award in March 1947, only a few months before his death in November that same year. Lubitsch's films were often promoted as exhibiting his famous 'Lubitsch Touch', which Scott Eyman has described thus: 'With few exceptions Lubitsch's movies take place in ⟦...⟧ a place of metaphor, benign grace, rueful wisdom ⟦...⟧ where the basest things are discussed in elegant whispers;

of the rapier, never the broadsword'.[2] There is little doubt that his trademark stylistic elegance, erudite dialogue and subtle characterisation were all very much on display throughout *The Shop Around the Corner*, one of his most enduring cinematic achievements. As Jeffrey M. Anderson has observed, 'this might be Lubitsch's gentlest work: sweetness mixed with a genuine sadness'.[3]

***The Shop Around the Corner* (1940):** Metro-Goldwyn-Mayer

Matuschek & Company is a high-class store in Budapest ('just around the corner from Andrassy Street, on Balta Street', as the opening caption helpfully informs us) which specialises in leather goods and luxury items. In the years leading up to the outbreak of World War II, the shop is under the management of its owner, the permanently over-anxious Mr Hugo Matuschek (Frank Morgan). Though his larger-than-life presence is constantly felt – and often feared – throughout the store, Matuschek retains a healthy respect for Alfred Kralik (James Stewart), his best salesperson, who he looks upon as a kind of surrogate son. Other employees of the store include the kind-hearted Mr Pirovitch (Felix Bressart), dapper but duplicitous Ferencz Vadas (Joseph Schildkraut), prim Flora Kaczek (Sara Haden), glamorous Ilona Novotny (Inez Courtney), and a self-motivated – if somewhat outspoken – delivery boy named Pepi Katona (William Tracy).

A notorious perfectionist, Matuschek rules the store with an iron fist, and the staff members are permanently aware of his fluctuating moods. The professional, highly proficient Kralik has become the older man's protégé, and his rising star in the company is reflected by the respect with which he is treated – alone among the employees, he is invited to a private dinner party at the Matuschek family residence, for instance. Though admired by his colleagues, Kralik must fend off constant aspersions and insinuations from the smarmy Vadas, always keen to stir animosity to further his own ends.

Kralik confides to Pirovitch in the store's stockroom that he has been privately corresponding with a woman who put a classified advertisement in a Sunday newspaper. Her responses suggest that she is knowledgeable and refined, and Kralik clearly finds her appealing. He resolves to continue writing to her, even though – as the correspondence address is a post office box – he has no idea of her true identity or location.

Strain begins to develop between Matuschek and Kralik. The former is keen to source a line of musical cigarette boxes and asks Kralik's opinion on the matter, but the salesman is deeply sceptical and admits that they are of low quality and will be an awkward fit with the shop's existing stock, irritating Matuschek. Vadas unctuously tells the shop-owner that the cigarette boxes are a work of genius, but Kralik's personal integrity is such that he refuses to back down. Eventually the dealers telephone Matuschek and try to pressure him into a sale, but when pushed he resentfully takes Kralik's side and refuses to stock the cigarette boxes. This bruises his ego, leaving him in a filthy mood.

A young woman named Klara Novak (Margaret Sulla-van) arrives at the shop looking for employment. Kralik, knowing that business at the shop has been slow, tells her that no positions are presently available, but she continues to pursue the matter with increasing determination. Eventually Matuschek himself tells her that the company is taking on no new staff, but when he later witnesses Klara selling the sample model of the cigarette box at a healthy profit – by telling the customer it is actually a candy box – he is impressed by her initiative and agrees to employ her, much to Kralik's palpable chagrin.

Six months later, winter has set in and Christmas is on the way. Matuschek's big plans for the cigarette/candy boxes have not borne fruit – the shop is now selling them at a heavily discounted price just to get rid of them. Pirovitch and Kralik note that Matuschek has become distant and unsociable, with Kralik admitting that he is no longer invited to social occasions with the boss. There is constant conflict between Kralik and Klara, with the pair bickering incessantly. Kralik tells Pirovitch that he is at least thankful that the woman he corresponds with is benevolent and sophisticated, unlike the argumentative Klara. He is keen to move the relationship into new territory and has arranged a dinner date with his mysterious, anonymous friend that night – though he admits to Pirovitch he is worried that neither person will be able to meet the other's expectations.

In spite of Matuschek's inclement mood, Kralik resolves to ask him for a raise – eager to move into better accommodation in the hope of an eventual marriage proposal. However, Matuschek continues to behave in an aloof manner, and in spite of Kralik's best efforts he is unable to discern the reason behind the older man's standoffish attitude. Kralik's dinner date plans are also thwarted when Matuschek tells the staff that they must stay late to redress the shop windows after work. Not realising Kralik's personal plans, Klara also has arrangements for a date at the exact same time and tries to ingratiate herself with Kralik in the hope that she can persuade him to give her the night off. However, he proves immune to her charms.

Keen not to miss dinner with his mystery suitor, Kralik asks Matuschek if he may be excused from the overtime work, but the owner flies into a rage in front of the other staff. Kralik and the others are stunned at the irrationality of his anger, but Matuschek implies that his former protégé is deserving of his ire – much to the younger man's confusion. Matuschek's wife calls to request the urgent delivery of a large sum of money, though Matuschek refuses to allow Kralik to deliver it to their home and requests that Vadas does so instead.

That night, the staff joylessly festoon the shop with Christmas decorations – constantly under the surly Matuschek's steely gaze. Out of the blue, Matuschek asks Kralik to meet him in his office, where he abruptly fires him without explanation. Kralik is stunned as Matuschek grants him a month's salary as severance pay and sends him on his way with a letter of reference. The other staff members share Kralik's shocked confusion as he leaves the shop, amazed at the seemingly-bizarre lack of reasoning behind Matuschek's decision. His callousness seems particularly hard to understand given the fast-approaching festive season. None of them realise that Matuschek suspects his wife of having an extramarital affair, nor that he believes Kralik to be the culprit.

Shortly after Kralik's departure, Matuschek receives an enigmatic phone call and suddenly sends the staff home without warning. Seeing the chance to make her dinner date after all, Klara races off, but the compassionate Pirovitch stays for a while longer in an attempt to change Matuschek's mind about Kralik's dismissal. However, his efforts are in vain. Once the staff members have all left the premises, a private investigator (Charles Halton) arrives to meet with Matuschek. The detective is able to confirm Matuschek's suspicions that his wife is having an affair, but the shop owner is thunderstruck to discover that the guilty party was not Kralik but Vadas. Distraught at his spouse's infidelity and wracked by guilt at his unjust treatment of Kralik, Matuschek withdraws to his office after the investigator leaves and attempts to commit suicide by shooting himself with a handgun. Only the timely arrival of delivery boy Pepi – who is unaware of recent events – interrupts Matuschek's actions and indirectly saves his life.

Pirovitch has managed to persuade the dejected Kralik to go to the Café Nizza in town to make the long-arranged dinner date with his mystery correspondent. Upon arrival, however, Kralik discovers that the woman he has been writing to for months is, in fact, Klara. Crestfallen, Kralik moves to leave but eventually decides to talk to her – though he conceals his identity as her mystery correspondent by claiming to be at the restaurant to meet with Pirovitch. Kralik struggles to mentally resolve the fact that his argumentative work colleague is also the smart, urbane author of the letters they have exchanged. Privately, he hopes that somehow a romance may still be possible in spite of the antipathy which exists between him and Klara. However, Klara – unsuspecting of the fact that Kralik is her own mystery correspondent – rudely dismisses him from the café, believing that his presence may ruin the planned dinner with her unidentified date.

Thanks to a phone call from Pepi, word reaches Kralik of Matuschek's suicide attempt. A hospital doctor (Edwin

Maxwell) confides in Pepi that Matuschek is physically unharmed but that he is going through a nervous breakdown. Kralik rushes to Matuschek's bedside, where the older man explains that he had received an anonymous letter tipping him off about his wife's affair and had jumped to the wrong conclusion. Apologising to Kralik, Matuschek reinstates him and gives him a promotion to shop manager (as well as a longoverdue raise), handing him the keys to the store. The ailing owner also promotes Pepi from errand boy to clerk, much to the fast-talking youth's delight. Matuschek asks Kralik to fire Vadas, but to do it as quietly as possible in order to minimise any possible scandal.

The next morning, Kralik's colleagues are thrilled at his reinstatement, though Klara calls in sick, obviously distressed at believing that her mystery admirer has stood her up at the restaurant. Vadas insincerely congratulates Kralik on his promotion and shows off a new diamond ring, which he claims is a gift from an elderly relative but is quite obviously the reason why Mrs Matuschek required delivery of the money earlier. Kralik delights in ordering the sycophantic salesman to perform meaningless labour-intensive chores, while Pepi – newly arrived on the sales floor in his promoted role – fills in the other staff members with regard to the previous night's astonishing events. Kralik soon has his fill of Vadas's obsequious platitudes and fires him, pushing the salesman through a display of musical cigarette boxes and making clear his disdain for his two-facedness. Vadas threatens legal action for unfair dismissal, to say nothing of assault, but flees the premises with a month's severance pay before Kralik can forcibly eject him.

Klara visits her rented post office box, but is disconsolate that no letter has arrived from her anonymous correspondent to explain his non-appearance at the Café Nizza. She then calls in at work to speak to Matuschek and is shocked to discover Kralik reinstated and in the role of manager. Initially she refuses to believe it and suspects that her old adversary is playing a trick on her, but when he takes a phone call and makes clear his new professional status she faints and lands on the office floor. Later, Kralik visits Klara at home to check on her condition, and finds that she is feeling very emotionally brittle as a result of recent events. Klara resents his paternalistic tone and emphasises that Kralik should not hold himself responsible for the way events have unfolded – the fault lies with the apparent disappearance of her secret admirer. However, Klara's Aunt Anna (Mabel Colcord) arrives with a letter, having just checked the post office box on Klara's behalf. The young woman is overjoyed to hear from her unknown correspondent again, and reads the letter's contents out aloud – never suspecting that Kralik is actually its author. Accepting the explanation within (that the 'mystery writer' had seen Kralik at the restaurant with Klara and had lost the courage to approach her, wrongly assuming that they were a couple), Klara assures the new manager that she will be back at work the following day.

Some weeks later, Christmas Eve has arrived and trade at the store under Kralik's management is booming. As Pepi lords over the firm's jittery new errand boy Rudy (Charles Smith), Kralik rallies the staff to make the most of the festive season in order to maximise profits. He adds that according to the hospital, Mr Matuschek is now feeling much better – news which delights his gathered colleagues. Klara is confused by Kralik's newly-supportive behaviour, and divulges to Pirovitch that she hopes by presenting her mystery admirer with a Christmas gift, she will receive one of her own – an engagement ring. Pirovitch cleverly manages to dissuade her from giving him a musical cigarette box, instead suggesting that she should choose a wallet instead. (She never suspects that this strategy has been cooked up between Pirovitch and Kralik, who has always detested the boxes.)

As hoped, the day is a great commercial success, with Matuschek & Company being packed with customers in search of a last-minute Christmas purchase. Newly discharged from hospital, Mr Matuschek arrives at the shop and watches in appreciative awe as the staff sell a steady stream of products. He is further buoyed when a passing policeman (Charles Arnt) on the beat confirms that the store is conducting a roaring trade in comparison with its competitors. When business is over for the day, Matuschek and the staff members are all overjoyed to discover that the shop's sales figures are unprecedented. Genuinely moved, Matuschek assures his workforce that they are all more than just his employees – as he has worked at the shop for most of his life, he considers them his family.

Matuschek hands out Christmas bonuses to each of the staff before leaving for the holidays. Feeling rather self-consciously solitary after the breakdown of his marriage, he then tries to encourage various colleagues to join him for dinner at an exclusive restaurant in the city but soon discovers that they already have Christmas plans of their own in place. Eventually he ends up persuading seventeen-year-old delivery boy Rudy to join him for a luxury festive meal; as the teenager lives alone, he happily agrees, ensuring that neither is left feeling lonely during the holiday season.

With only Kralik and Klara left in the shop before it closes for Christmas, the pair discuss their plans for the festive season. Klara reveals the wallet that is intended for her admirer, and Kralik produces an ornate necklace which he asks

Klara to model for him. Klara admits that she had feelings for Kralik when they first encountered one another, but rationalises them away by saying that she had simply been too credulous a person at that point. Realising that Klara is anticipating an engagement, Kralik affects that he has encountered her anonymous correspondent and has discovered that he is flabby, has a receding hairline, and is out of work. Once he has playfully spun his tall tale at her expense, Kralik puts a red carnation into the buttonhole of his lapel and finally confesses that he is, and always has been, the secretive author of the letters. They kiss, both now realising that their fantasies of romance have met with reality at last.

While the mid-European setting (complete with Hungarian signage) of *The Shop Around the Corner* may have seemed a reasonably unusual departure for a Hollywood romantic comedy, the nostalgic warmth of Lubitsch's depiction of this locale must have seemed all the more poignant to the audiences of the time who would have been all too aware of the horrors that were affecting the continent throughout the early forties. The superb craft of Lubitsch's direction, along with Samson Raphaelson's beautifully-observed screenplay, creates a feature that is packed full of memorable moments. Edwin B. Willis's immaculate set design is a joy to behold, with every nook and cranny of the Matuschek & Company store taken up with period goods, and this busy environment forms the perfect backdrop for many astute character observations. A scene-stealing Joseph Schildkraut excels as the snake-like Vadas, the character's oily charms proving just as entertaining as his treachery, while Frank Morgan's Matuschek is a revelation, temporarily interrupting himself in mid-rant to serve a customer with total professionalism before seamlessly returning to his tirade as soon as they have departed. From

Kralik desperately trying to convince Klara to buy her 'mystery admirer' a wallet instead of one of the hated musical cigarette boxes to Felix Bressart's Pirovitch rapidly making himself scarce every time the overbearing Matuschek looks for 'an honest opinion' (knowing that there is never a 'safe' answer to offer), it is the acute observation of each character's quirks and individual qualities which makes each of them come alive. There is also much to enjoy when the Café Nizza's resident band strikes up a rendition of 'Ochi Chërnye' (literally 'Dark Eyes', a romantic Russian song from the nineteenth century), mirroring the tinny tones of the musical cigarette boxes which recur as a running gag (and useful plot device) throughout the film. The balance of comedic moments and dramatic incidents is perfectly honed, with the supporting performances being given just as much opportunity to shine as the film's stars. As Dave Kehr has noted: 'Interwoven with subplots centered on the other members of the shop's little family, the romance proceeds through Lubitsch's brilliant deployment of point of view, allowing the audience to enter the perceptions of each individual character at exactly the right moment to develop maximum sympathy and suspense'.[4]

The success of *The Shop Around the Corner* lies in Lubitsch's determination to keep the focus of the film rigidly on the staff of Matuschek & Company and the relationships between the store's members of staff. Hugo Matuschek's complex mixture of paternalism and imperiousness is masterfully articulated by Morgan, who at that time was prominent in the public consciousness for having played the title role in *The Wizard of Oz* (Victor Fleming, 1939) the previous year, and so much of the film revolves around the various employees' reactions to Matuschek's shifting disposition and caprices.

As Lubitsch himself mentioned at the time of the movie's premiere:

> I have known just such a little shop in Budapest. [...] The feeling between the boss and those who work for him is pretty much the same the world over, it seems to me. Everyone is afraid of losing his job and everyone knows how little human worries can affect his job. If the boss has a case of dyspepsia, better be careful not to step on his toes; when things have gone well with him, the whole staff reflects his good humor.[5]

Yet rather than overtly emphasising the film's stage-based roots, concentrating on the dynamics of day-to-day existence within the store allows Lubitsch to rewardingly tease out the chemistry which exists between the various characters. Thus we see the kindly peacemaker Pirovitch trying to use diplomacy to smooth over conflicts, just as the aspersive Vadas does exactly the opposite, deliberately agitating disagreements to meet his own ends (his constant mendacities providing convenient cover for his own indiscretions). Similarly, there is much satirical potential in the way that the ambitious, quick-thinking Pepi manages to contrive an unlikely route up the company's social ladder, only to subsequently act like a martinet towards his successor as delivery boy, the hapless Rudy. Thus while the film has of course become best-known for its central romance between James Stewart's Kralik and Margaret Sullavan's Klara, its enduring appeal has arguably derived from the relatable way in which its cast of characters are presented, offering audiences a kind of universality that this slice of life tale always excels at articulating. As Eyman has remarked:

The Shop Around the Corner is immensely ingratiating, but it never condescends to its characters
or to us. Part of its strength is its concentrated unity. Lubitsch rigorously excludes everybody outside
the immediate family of Matuschek and Company;
we never see the home life of Pirovitch, we never
see the duplicitous Mrs Matuschek. Ernst [Lu-
bitsch] gives the people at Matuschek and Company the full measure of his respect and affection.
Through the dignity with which he treats them,
the film becomes a celebration of the ordinary,
gently honoring the extraordinary qualities that lie
within the most common of us.[6]

The film's setting does, of course, guarantee a certain
degree of pathos – although events appear to have a happy
(or at least bittersweet) ending for each of the characters, audiences of the early forties would know only too well that the
tumultuous conflict that had engulfed Europe would not spare
Hungary. Lubitsch was, of course, acutely aware of the terror
that was sweeping the continent – and much further afield –
and would engage with the need to counter the far-reaching
threat of fascism in his later filmography (most famously in *To
Be or Not to Be*). As David Parkinson alludes, the febrile nature of geopolitics of the time was reflected through the
themes and social attitudes that were presented throughout
the course of *The Shop Around the Corner*: 'With Europe
already at war, this was an unashamedly nostalgic film about
maintaining the status quo. The clerks tolerated the indecision
and impoliteness of the customers for fear of alienating Mr
Matuschek, who himself dreaded the discovery of his wife's
long-suspected infidelity, lest it damage his reputation and
authority. Even Alfred and Klara resist the temptation to

meet their epistolary sweetheart, in case their romantic illusion was shattered by cruel reality'.[7] These uncertainties – whether of the emotional tenderness of budding romance or the internal politics of a small, well-regarded business – were of course relatable enough in nature to transcend their geographical and historical setting. Yet there was undeniable admiration at the time for Lubitsch's loving recreation of pre-war Budapest, with its exactingly-detailed exteriors and painstakingly accurate costumes. As Frank S. Nugent noted in his January 1940 review of the film for *The New York Times*:

> A pretty kettle of bubbling brew it makes under Mr Lubitsch's deft and tender management and with a genial company to play it gently, well this side of farce and well that side of utter seriousness. Possibly the most surprising part of it is the adaptability of the players to Mr Lubitsch's Continental milieu whose splendid evocation is one of the nicest things of the picture. But they all have become natural figures against a natural background – even Mr. Stewart, who, on the face and speech of him, hardly could be called the Budapest type, and Mr Morgan, who plays a benevolent dictator (in leather goods) with scarcely a trace of the comic fluster and bluster that have established him as one of Hollywood's most standardized funny men.[8]

As Nugent suggests, the meticulous recreation of the styles and manners of Budapest before the war aids the film's charm immensely, but is never allowed to get in the way of its dramatic objectives. For instance, only Morgan and Schildkraut lend their characters mid-European accents, with most of the other cast members retaining their own American intonations, and while the currency and signage which appears throughout the film is in authentic Hungarian, the shop's pre-Christmas window display – which is dominated by a notice declaring the vast reduction of the musical cigarette boxes' retail price – is printed in English, to avoid any doubt about this significant plot point. Certainly the efforts of Schildkraut and Morgan to not just lend a degree of regional realism to their characters' speech, but also in their deft balance of comic traits and dramatic depth, have led to their efforts being praised even by contemporary commentators; Wesley Lovell, for instance, writes that '*The Shop Around the Corner* has a number of charming elements and the secondary characters, despite falling into heavy stereotypes, are quite entertaining. Morgan and Joseph Schildkraut stand out best from the rest. They manage to coax enough charm and wit out of their characters that belie the underwritten nature of the parts'.[9] Indeed, one of the great pleasures of *The Shop Around the Corner* is the fact that it contains so many immaculately-perceived character moments which delight in isolation, but also make the movie considerably more than the sum of its parts. This has an overall effect, as Andrew Wickliffe observes, that the film 'requires the viewer pay a lot of attention to the details in dialogue. Samson Raphaelson's script – adapted from a play, which accounts for the big jump in time (director Lubitsch beautifully turns act breaks and scene breaks into gentle resets for the viewer with fade outs) – always has a lot of talking and many of the details become important. It's all so well-written and so well-performed, you get the important details because you don't want to miss even disposable dialogue'.[10]

It says much for the talent of the film's supporting cast that although *The Shop Around the Corner* is so acutely concerned with the circuitous route of its central romance, there is still plenty of time for the secondary figures to emerge as appealing and well fleshed-out individuals. There is much to admire about the unconventional path that Kralik and Klara's nascent relationship follows – from suspicion and distrust to open hostility, then to a gradual meeting of minds – and James Stewart and Margaret Sullavan both bring a considerable level of complexity to their performances, never trivialising the hopefulness of either character as they realise that their idealised mystery partner is actually rather more familiar than either of them had anticipated. The interesting chemistry between Klara and Kralik may well have been aided by the fact that Sullavan and Stewart knew each other well from previous years and were said to share a healthy professional and personal respect, having both performed with the University Players – an intercollegiate stock company based in West Falmouth, Massachusetts – in the years prior to pursuing their respective careers in cinema. Such is their absolute dedication to their roles that the audience is able to mentally paper over the cracks of some of the narrative's more glaring leaps of logic (for instance, does Klara truly never notice the similarity of her anonymous suitor's handwriting to that of Kralik's during all the months she spends working at Matuschek & Company?). The upright, morally-refined Kralik is also a highly effective counterpoint to the cunning philanderer Vadas; when the newly-minted manager shoves his two-timing nemesis through a pile of the infamous musical cigarette boxes, it is a low-key moment of triumph for all present to see the self-regarding sales clerk receiving his deserved comeuppance. The juxtaposition of the all-American figure of

Stewart (albeit in the role of a Hungarian everyman) and the vaguely Germanic tones of Schildkraut's debonair character is one which has relevance, as Neil Young points out: 'Though set in a moderately fancy Budapest store specialising in suitcases and luxury items – it's never *quite* clear how one should classify Matuschek and Co., which is part of its slightly disorderly charm – the characters all speak English, nearly all of them American-accented English, with the exception of the distinctly mittel-European Vadas (Austrian actor Joseph Schildkraut). And it's surely no accident that, in a film made at the start of the World War 2, the latter turns out to be the most deceitful and despicable individual on view – part and parcel of a movie that has no shortage of sourness, even nastiness, alongside its underlying sweetness'.[II] At a point when the United States was viewing the growing European conflict with increasing concern, though before it became directly involved in the war, Lubitsch's well-grounded apprehensions seemed timely. (Star James Stewart famously enlisted with the US Army Air Corps a year or so later, in March 1941, before the United States had entered World War II; a highly proficient pilot, he would become a decorated veteran of the conflict.) However, *The Shop Around the Corner* was to make its social observations only with great subtlety, and while Lubitsch's concerns about the war are indisputable, the film is, at heart, one which is much more directly concerned with the impact of interpersonal relationships on lives – both individual and collective – than it ever is with geopolitical commentary. This degree of intricate sensitivity was ideally suited to Lubitsch's approach to film-making, as Jaime N. Christley discerns:

Radiating perhaps even more brightly than the burgeoning romance between Alfred Kralik

(James Stewart) and Klara Novak (Margaret Sullavan), employees at a modest Hungarian gift shop,
is Lubitsch's sense of the shop itself, no longer ap-
plying his famed 'Lubitsch touch' on thinly concealed sexual flirtations between the likes of Mau-
rice Chevalier and Miriam Hopkins, or Herbert
Marshall and Kay Francis, but, without a hiccup,
using his legendary intuition to recreate the delicate organism of a small business and the men and
women who subsist on it. [...] Its characters are
temporarily unable to believe that a curved road is
actually straight, that good people are actually
good, that bad people are not so great, or, to para-
phrase Blake, when the doors of misperception are
eventually cleansed, everything appears to Lu-
bitschian heroes as it is: wonderful.[12]

Perhaps because of its early wartime release, *The Shop
Around the Corner*'s towering reputation as a romantic comedy-drama set in a then-recent past – one which was already
seeming like a distant memory of a more innocent time –
sometimes overshadows its credentials as a Christmas film.
Yet given that the majority of the action takes place in December, in the snowy approach to the festive season – a hugely significant and potentially lucrative time for retailers –
there is no denying the fact that Christmas themes feature
prominently throughout the film. From Kralik's resolve to
maximise pre-Christmas profits to Pirovitch's determination to
enjoy a family get-together, the sharing of gifts between Kralik
and Klara's anonymous alter-egos, and even the loneliness experienced by Matuschek and Rudy on Christmas Eve, the film
certainly does not shirk from its exploration of how the festive
season affects different people in different ways – especially

poignant given Matuschek's realisation that his employees are really more like kinfolk than staff to him. As Laura Grieve remarks: 'The stories in most Christmas movies evoke warm, positive feelings. It also doesn't hurt that many Christmas films are simply exceptionally good movies, and one of the very best is *The Shop Around the Corner*. [...] Except for scenes in a restaurant and Klara's bedroom, the entire movie is set at the shop, which lends to the feel that the movie creates a cozy little world of its own, in Matuschek's; as Mr Matuschek says, the store is where he spends most of his life, and the staff are family'.[13]

Made particularly palpable due to the traditional Christmas preoccupation with hearth and home, the stress placed on Matuschek & Company by Matuschek's abortive suicide attempt does not diminish the festive appeal but instead forces an opportune re-evaluation of what makes Christmas so potentially significant to individual lives. (As Philip French sagely notes, 'it anticipates (in its Christmas setting, painful revelation of adultery, attempted suicide, shy secret lover and a cast sharing the same workplace) a much darker comedy by a Lubitsch admirer, Billy Wilder's ⟦1960 film⟧ *The Apartment*'.[14]) With the twitchy, neurotic Matuschek forced to take care of his health under the watchful eye of medical professionals, and the poison of the devious Vadas now purged from the shop's delicate ecosystem, the staff members are given space to breathe and are thus able to look forward to relaxing over the festive season, when the frantic pre-Christmas sales period is at last behind them.

In intriguing ways, the Christmas setting for the film is almost as significant as its chronological situation in the years leading up to the Second World War. Owen Van Spall, for instance, notes that: 'Director Ernst Lubitsch's *The Shop*

Around the Corner is perfect seasonal fare. [...] Viewers coming to this film for the first time might find the setting odd – the aforementioned shop is on a small street in pre-War Budapest – given the starring role of American actor James Stewart. But this wintry, old European backdrop adds a quaint air of romance to the picture, almost as though the audience is being invited to view a last hurrah of innocence before the storm clouds of war'.[15] Thus just as Lubitsch capitalises on the mannerly etiquette and behaviours of the interwar period to present a very particular time and place in recent history, particularly in contrast to a more brutal and unstable present, so too does he use the comforting conventions of Christmas to explore his characters' sense of community, their hopes and friendships, and also the way in which they perceive the festive season not just as one of commercial consequence but also personal reflection. In this sense, as John Lingan observes, we can perceive that even something as everyday as putting up Christmas decorations can have hidden import in the hands of Lubitsch and his performers: 'One of the movie's greatest shots occurs when [Kralik and Klara are] forced by the store owner to work late, and thus both miss the date that would have brought them together, perhaps prematurely. Too annoyed and self-pitying to even bother fighting, they're made to decorate a window-display Christmas tree together, and Lubitsch employs a rare zoom-in two-shot to frame James Stewart and Margaret Sullavan both scowling at their respective decorations and lost in thought'.[16]

Ultimately, *The Shop Around the Corner* is a film of skilful contrasts; while it uses the genteel social certainties of the pre-war period as a counterpoint to the cruelties and inhumanity facing Europe in the early 1940s, it also compares the impossibly high romantic expectations of its two lead characters to the rather more humdrum realities facing them, and even presents Christmas as a complex melange of mercantile duties and exciting possibilities. Running throughout the film seems to be Lubitsch's suggestion that life is really only ever what we choose to make it. Klara and Kralik can lament the fact that their exhilarating, mysterious romantic correspondents are in fact just colleagues whose jobs compel them to encounter each other every working day, or they can instead reconsider their connection and work towards a better future together. Similarly, Matuschek has the option to see his world solely in terms of profit and commercial opportunity, or to embrace his employees as living, breathing people who each have their own aspirations. Even Christmas itself is shown to mean a range of disparate things to the people who work at the store: for Kralik and Klara, an exchange of presents eventually provides the impetus for them to reveal their true feelings for one another; for Pirovitch, it offers the chance to enjoy the company of his loving family away from the hustle of working life; and for Matuschek and Rudy, who exist at diametric opposite ends of the shop's hierarchy, an unlikely friendship offers an opportunity to avoid loneliness at the festive season. As Ed Howard is correct in observing, the film's engagement with Christmas conventions is one which exhibits numerous dimensions, none of which are ever squandered:

Ernst Lubitsch's *The Shop Around the Corner* is a rich, moving love story, a very warm film despite its snowy Christmastime setting. [...] The film is about the ideal of love as contrasted against the more prosaic but also more tangible reality: it's telling that before Kralik can reveal himself to [Klara], he must adjust her expectations downward by shattering the fantasy of the letters, preparing her not only for the revelation that he's her great love, but that her great love is only a flesh-and-blood man after all. Lubitsch also has a wonderful feel for the anxieties of money, for the pressures of the working class life and the fear of losing a job, and the film makes great use of the Christmas setting for its subtle commentary on consumerism and salesmanship. It's a beautiful, funny, emotionally complex masterpiece with so much heart, so much beauty, in every image and every line that, despite its modest, unassuming surface, it winds up being an almost overwhelming experience.[17]

The legacy of *The Shop Around the Corner* was to continue long after its initial release. The film was remade as a musical, *In the Good Old Summertime* (Robert Z. Leonard, 1949), where the action was shifted to Chicago at the turn of the twentieth century. It was also remade, many years later, as *You've Got Mail* (Nora Ephron, 1998), which adapted the story for modern-day New York City (with appropriately updated correspondence technology, as the film's digital age title suggests). As was often the custom for motion pictures of the time, a number of abridged dramatisations were produced for radio. The Screen Guild Theater was to broadcast a half-hour adaptation on 29 September 1940, with James Stewart and Margaret Sullavan reprising their roles from the film, and Lux Radio Theater transmitted a one-hour dramatisation on 23 June 1941 with Don Ameche and Claudette Colbert. Later, The Screen Guild Theatre would broadcast a new adaptation on 26 February 1945 starring Van Johnson and Phyllis Thaxter, as well as featuring Felix Bressart who reprised his role as Pirovitch. A Broadway musical adaptation, *She Loves Me*, followed in 1963, with the book by Joe Masteroff, lyrics by Sheldon Harnick and music by Jerry Bock. The film's source material – Miklós László's original play, *Parfumerie* – has additionally been performed and reinterpreted many times since its 1937 debut. As Young notes, *The Shop Around the Corner* was also to form a loose inspiration for David Croft and Jeremy Lloyd's long-running, department store-based BBC television situation comedy *Are You Being Served?* (1972-85).[18] However, arguably the film's most enduring attainment has been its preservation in the United States National Film Registry by the Library of Congress in 1999, in recognition of its significance to cinema.

The Shop Around the Corner was broadcast on television from the 1950s onwards (debuting on Chicago's WBBM on 11 April 1957), and has earned a reputation not only as one of Ernst Lubitsch's best-loved films but also as one of the finest possible examples of an early Christmas romantic comedy, standing out even amongst well-regarded features of the period such as *Remember the Night* (Mitchell Leisen, 1940). Though it was not to be the most famous festive movie to star James Stewart in the lead role, *The Shop Around the Corner* has nonetheless won many admirers for the moving nature of its central romantic premise, its subtle meditation on loneliness even in well-populated urban areas, and its emphasis on the support of the community being preferable to the self-centredness of the individual. It remains among Lubitsch's most beloved and accessible contributions to American cinema, and its many skilful performances and exacting production values have ensured that it is still being enjoyed by audiences even in the present day.

REFERENCES

1. Artemisia D'Ecca, *Keeping Christmas Well* (Dublin: Phaeton Publishing, 2012), p.377.

2. Scott Eyman, *Ernst Lubitsch: Laughter in Paradise* (Baltimore: Johns Hopkins University Press, 2000) [1993], pp.15-16.

3. Jeffrey M. Anderson, 'Secret Santas', in *Combustible Celluloid*, 26 May 2006.
   <http://www.combustiblecelluloid.com/classic/shoparound.shtml>

4. Dave Kehr, '*The Shop Around the Corner*', in *The Chicago Reader*, 27 November 2007.
   <https://www.chicagoreader.com/chicago/the-shop-around-the-corner/Film?oid=1051445>

5. Ernst Lubitsch, in Cátia, '12 Days of Christmas: Day 9: *The Shop Around the Corner*', in *Back to Golden Days*, 22 December 2015.
   <http://back-to-golden-days.blogspot.com/2015/12/12-days-of-christmas-day-9-shop-around.html>

6. Eyman, p.279.

7. David Parkinson, '*The Shop Around the Corner* Review', in *Empire*, 26 June 2006.
   <https://www.empireonline.com/movies/shop-around-corner/review/>

8. Frank S. Nugent, 'The Screen in Review: Ernst Lubitsch Offers James Stewart and Margaret Sullavan in a Genial

and Tender Romance in *The Shop Around the Corner* at the Music Hall', in *The New York Times*, 26 January 1940.
<*https://www.nytimes.com/1940/01/26/archives/the-screen-in-review-ernst-lubitsch-offers-james-stewart-and.html*>

9.   Wesley Lovell, '*The Shop Around the Corner*', in *Cinema Sight*, 22 November 2010.
<*http://www.cinemasight.com/review-the-shop-around-the-corner-1940/*>

10. Andrew Wickliffe, '*The Shop Around the Corner*', in *The Stop Button*, 28 December 2014.
<*https://thestopbutton.com/2014/12/28/shop-around-corner-1940/*>

11. Neil Young, 'July Briefs: *Senna & The Shop Around the Corner*', in *Neil Young's Film Lounge*, 5 July 2011.
<*https://www.jigsawlounge.co.uk/film/reviews/july2011/*>

12. Jaime N. Christley, 'Review: *The Shop Around the Corner*', in *Slant*, 22 December 2014.
<*https://www.slantmagazine.com/film/the-shop-around-the-corner/*>

13. Laura Grieve, 'Tonight's Movie: *The Shop Around the Corner*', in *Laura's Miscellaneous Musings*, 28 November 2017.
<*https://laurasmiscmusings.blogspot.com/2017/11/tonights-movie-shop-around-corner-1940.html*>

14. Philip French, '*The Shop Around the Corner*: Review', in *The Observer*, 12 December 2010.
<*https://www.theguardian.com/film/2010/dec/12/the-shop-around-the-corner*>

15. Owen Van Spall, '*The Shop Around the Corner*', *Eye for Film*, 20 November 2010.
<https://www.eyeforfilm.co.uk/review/the-shop-around-the-corner-film-review-by-owen-van-spall>

16. John Lingan, 'Take Two #16: *The Shop Around the Corner* (1940) & *You've Got Mail* (1998)', in *Slant*, 29 March 2011.
<https://www.slantmagazine.com/film/take-two-16-the-shop-around-the-corner-1940-youve-got-mail-1998/>

17. Ed Howard, 'Films I Love #55: *The Shop Around the Corner*', in *Only the Cinema*, 19 October 2011.
<https://seul-le-cinema.blogspot.com/2011/10/films-i-love-55-shop-around-corner.html>

18. Young.

2

Meet Me in St Louis (1944)

Metro-Goldwyn-Mayer

Director: Vincente Minnelli
Producer: Arthur Freed
Screenwriter: Irving Brecher and Fred F. Finklehoffe

IF *The Shop Around the Corner* had been produced in the early years of the Second World War, before the United States had become directly involved in the conflict, *Meet Me in St Louis* was to be released to a very different American audience. With the country now fully committed to opposing the Axis Powers in both the European and Pacific theatres of war, there was a surge in patriotic film-making which accentuated the general mood of nationwide dedication and love for freedom that epitomised American sentiment during the long-running hostilities. Yet it was also a period of battle-weariness, with the public acutely aware of the mounting casualties in all fields of conflict and the great sacrifice of the Allied armed forces across the globe. With this in mind, there was a growing appetite for nostalgic entertainments which hearkened back to simpler, more innocent times – providing a welcome evocation of a now-departed world that was untouched by the horrors of modern international warfare.

Produced by Metro-Goldwyn-Mayer, *Meet Me in St Louis* was a glossy, Technicolor musical whose bright, bold hues and emotive songs proved to be just as popular with audiences as was its evocative setting in 1903-04, prior to both World Wars. In the style of numerous other films of the period, such as *Holiday Inn* (Mark Sandrich, 1942) and *The Bells of St Mary's* (q.v.), the events of *Meet Me in St Louis* are informed by a seasonal structure which gradually advances the action – in this case, from summer 1903 through to spring 1904. Though this does, of course, mean that the film is not entirely focused upon the festive season, its Christmas sequence has proven to be especially memorable and remains one of its best-known sections, meaning that for many people it remains one of the most noteworthy Christmas experiences in early 1940s cinema. As Philip French notes, *Meet Me in St Louis* is 'a movie that defines perfection, as it captures the spirit of hope and anxiety that informed the last years of the Second World War, when it was made. It's a film whose four parts cover the seasons from summer to spring but is truly a film for all seasons and all time'.[1]

Meet Me in St Louis became one of the best-known features in the filmography of its director, Vincente Minnelli, and also his first to be filmed in colour. With extensive experience of theatre (he had worked as a set designer and costume designer before becoming a stage director), he seemed tailor-made for the director's chair and was offered a job at Metro-Goldwyn-Mayer by Arthur Freed in 1940. Though his first movies – *Cabin in the Sky* (1943) and *I Dood It* (1943) – are no longer as widely viewed, the meteoric commercial success of *Meet Me in St Louis* (only his third film) would destine Minnelli for a prolific and highly-regarded directorial career with features which would include *Father of the Bride* (1950),

46

The Band Wagon (1953) and *Brigadoon* (1954). *An American in Paris* (1951) and *Gigi* (1958) were both winners of the Academy Award for Best Picture; the former film also saw him nominated for the Best Director Academy Award, an accolade which he would later win for his work on the latter movie. Additionally, Minnelli has a remarkable claim to fame in that he directed no less than seven different actors in performances that would lead to them being nominated for Academy Awards. His reputation as an *auteur* also garnered him considerable critical attention from academics and commentators, not least in the legendary journal *Cahiers du Cinéma*.

The story of *Meet Me in St Louis* was adapted by Fred F. Finklehoffe and Irving Brecher from a series of semi-biographical short stories written by Sally Benson, who was a prolific prose writer as well as an accomplished screenwriter (who would later work with Alfred Hitchcock, amongst other leading figures in the industry). Benson's short fiction was initially published in *The New Yorker* magazine, in a cycle of eight vignettes entitled *5135 Kensington* which appeared between 14 June 1941 and 23 May 1942. Benson later compiled these eight stories,

Meet Me in St Louis (1944):
Metro-Goldwyn-Mayer

along with a further four, into a novel-length work entitled *Meet Me in St Louis* (1942). In a manner similar to the film, the chapters are based on months of the year during the 1903-04 period, forming a twelve-month period in total. Minnelli, Brecher and Finklehoffe skilfully evoke the wistful nostalgia of Benson's work, recreating the community-oriented society of turn-of-the-century rural America in a manner which appealed greatly to the audiences of the time. It is a film in which, as Raphael Samuel observes, '1900s picture postcards were used to frame the action and reaffirm the worth of small-town America',[2] and yet – far from being satisfied with conjuring up a sentimental evocation of times gone by – the movie is one which demonstrates considerable creative confidence and artistic ambition on the part of its director. As Noel Murray has not been alone in noting: 'This glorious musical was only Vincente Minnelli's third film, and his first in color. But it showed a remarkable instinct for the form and remains one of Hollywood's most astonishing achievements in Technicolor'.[3]

The film follows the lives of the various members of the Smith family, a well-to-do household who are based in St Louis, Missouri. Lawyer Alonzo 'Lon' Smith (Leon Ames) and his wife Anna Smith (Mary Astor) have a large family consisting of daughters Rose (Lucille Bremer), Esther (Judy Garland), Agnes (Joan Carroll) and the spirited young 'Tootie' (Margaret O'Brien), as well as son Lon Junior (Henry H. Daniels, Jr.). The story begins in the balmy summer of 1903. Esther persuades Katie (Marjorie Main), the family's good-natured maid, to prepare dinner an hour early; though reluctant, Katie makes arrangements as requested, as Esther explains that eldest sister Rose is awaiting a long-distance call from New York City that she is keen to ensure the other family members do not overhear. (As the telephone is in the dining room, the only way to avoid eavesdroppers is to ensure that the call takes place at a time other than dinner.) Esther tells Katie that Rose's caller is her admirer Warren Sheffield (Robert Sully), and that the expectation is that he will be proposing over the telephone that night – or, at least, that Rose can somehow motivate him to do so.

Rose isn't the only sister with romantic ambitions; Esther is besotted with their new neighbour, John Truett (Tom Drake), and is frustrated that he seems oblivious to her best efforts to catch his eye. Rose consoles her by emphasising that he has only lived there for a handful of weeks, and that there will be plenty of time to attract his attention. By contrast, five-year-old Tootie is more excited about the fact that the World's Fair will be coming to St Louis the following year – a major event that she doesn't want to miss.

Lon returns after a bad day at work and insists on having dinner at the appointed time, meaning that the meal coincides with Rose's phone call from Warren. She feels humiliated when he not only doesn't propose as expected, but also nimbly deflects any prompting in the direction of matrimony. He does, however, promise to write a letter to her later. Rose's mortification is amplified by the fact that the entire family are in the dining room overhearing the conversation. However, she puts a brave face on her embarrassment.

In September, Lon hosts a house party in celebration of Lon Junior being accepted to study at Princeton University. At Esther's instigation, John Truett from the house next door is invited as a guest, which finally gives her the opportunity to speak with him. After a night of musical entertainment and dancing, the party eventually winds up and Esther sees the chance to talk with John at greater length when extinguishing the gas lamps once all the other guests have departed, leaving

the house cast at a more romantic level of illumination. However, in spite of her high expectations John doesn't appear to
reciprocate her dreamy-eyed attentions; in particular, she is
affronted when he casually notices that she wears the same
perfume as his grandmother. In time he begins to warm to her
advances, but squanders any goodwill by complimenting her
on the strength of her uncommonly firm handshake.

The following week, Esther and some friends take a
ride on a trolley from the city to the location of the World's
Fair – currently still a construction site. Esther, remaining
hopeful that romance may develop with John (in spite of their
somewhat uneven first meeting), is disappointed when he
doesn't turn up for the streetcar before it departs. However,
her mood brightens when it transpires that he is simply late
and appears from nowhere, racing along the road to catch up
with the trolley.

Autumn arrives, and with it Halloween. Agnes and
Tootie go trick-or-treating, but Tootie is upset when she is
considered too young to be involved in the other kids' construction of a bonfire. Keen to assert herself, she offers to
knock on the door of a family that are considered particularly
fearsome, much to the consternation of her peers. Somewhat
overcome by the occasion, she steels herself and throws flour
at the hapless homeowner (who is not nearly as formidable as
she had feared), and wins the respect of all the neighbourhood's children in the process.

Later, Esther and Rose are admiring the perceived virtues of local man Colonel Darly (Hugh Marlowe) when
Tootie can be heard screaming. The family comes racing to
her aid, and Tootie tearfully explains that John is to blame for
her dishevelled state. As a doctor arrives to examine her, Esther slips away and races next door, assaulting John in the

belief that he has struck the little girl. However, she gives him no time to defend himself. By the time Esther returns home, Agnes gets back from the trick-or-treating session and explains that she and Tootie had stuffed a dress to look like a dead body, leaving it on a road track in the hope of derailing a streetcar. It transpires that John had caught the pair in the act and had dragged them away from the scene, to protect them from police enquiries. Ashamed, Esther realises that her attack on John was unfounded and returns to his house to apologise. Thankfully her neighbour is agreeable about the misunderstanding, and the pair kiss for the first time.

Later, Lon arrives home from work with some pressing news – he is to be appointed the head of his legal firm's New York office. He will be going there on a business trip in the near future, and then the entire family will be relocating in the coming year. Lon is over the moon about his professional advancement, but Anna is downcast at this sudden development, bemoaning the fact that life in the big city will be so different from their current, rural existence. While Agnes and Tootie are initially excited about the prospect of the move, Rose and Esther are confounded by the news; not only do they have educational commitments at their local school, but they will be leaving behind all of their friends – to say nothing of the fact that their respective romantic ambitions will be disrupted. However, Lon believes that the increase in income will be essential for the family – and especially his children, as they come of age – and firmly resists any calls to reconsider the move.

A few weeks later, Christmas is on the way. Snow has fallen, and the Smith daughters have been busy building snowmen (and snow-women). Lon Junior, back home for the holidays, is feeling emotionally tender because his intended date for the Christmas Eve ball – Lucille Ballard (June Lockhart) – will be attending the event with someone else. Meanwhile, Rose's own feelings are bruised because the object of Lucille's affections is none other than Warren Sheffield, who she feels has unfairly rebuffed her. Katie suggests that Rose and Lon Junior accompany each other to the dance in order to avoid missing out on the event entirely. Though they fear that they will be a laughing stock, they eventually capitulate and agree to do so.

The evening of the ball arrives, and John arrives with some bad news – he has been unable to rent or buy a tuxedo for the night, meaning that he can't accompany Esther as her date. Esther bravely tries to brush aside the matter, telling John that she will simply stay at home and pack for the fast-approaching house move, but is unable to contain her disappointment at missing her last Christmas ball in St Louis. Thankfully her grandfather (Harry Davenport) offers to accompany her instead, meaning that she still has the opportunity to attend.

At the ball, Rose and Esther find themselves enjoying the evening more than either had expected. Both have dance cards filled with the names of eligible men. Warren and Lucille arrive, and Rose and Esther hatch a plan to ruin their evening by filling Lucille's dance card with gawky and graceless dance partners. However, to their consternation Lucille explains that Warren only has eyes for Rose, and then goes on to express a romantic interest in Lon Junior. This turns the sisters' plans on their head, and they feel even more guilty when Lucille – obviously keen on becoming friends when the Smiths get to New York – promises to arrange a party in their honour when they move to the city. Esther quickly switches her own dance card with Lucille's, meaning that Lucille gets to dance with the skilled partners while she is left with the clumsy ones.

After an evening of dancing with lumbering and socially-awkward bores, Esther is ecstatic when John appears – having somehow managed to acquire a tuxedo. The pair dance the rest of the night away, but Esther later becomes upset as she realises that this will be her last Christmas dance in her home town. John asks Esther to marry him, and she happily accepts the proposal, but neither of them know how their matrimonial plans can play out with the Smiths due to move to New York in a matter of a few days. They embrace as the church bells mark the arrival of Christmas Day.

Back home, Esther finds Tootie waiting for the arrival of Santa Claus. The younger sister is concerned that with their imminent move to the big city, Santa may not know about their change of residence and may be unable to deliver their presents. Esther does her best to reassure Tootie, but her attempts are unsuccessful; distressed at the prospect of leaving behind everyone and everything she has ever known, Tootie races out into the garden and destroys the snowmen and snow-women that they had built earlier. (This is presumably prompted by Esther's off-the-cuff comment that the snow figures are just about the only possession the family will be unable to take with them when they leave the house.) Neither of them realise that their father is watching Tootie's outpouring of emotion with concern from one of the upstairs windows.

Lon is deeply moved by Esther's impassioned statement that whether the family is based in St Louis or New York, all that matters is that they remain together. Looking around the house, where Christmas decorations jostle for space alongside packing crates, he comes to an abrupt decision and calls for the other members of the family to join him. With new determination, Lon tells everyone that he has decided against accepting the promotion to New York – he will explain to the senior partners that he plans to remain in St Louis, which he predicts will be brimming with new opportunities as a result of the World's Fair. The Smiths are overjoyed, but they have barely begun to celebrate when Warren unexpectedly bursts into the house and audaciously proclaims his undying love for Rose, avowing that they must marry as soon as possible. The family realise that with his change of heart, Lon has given them the best Christmas present they could have dreamed of.

A few months later, spring has arrived and the Smiths are heading in horse-drawn carriages for the newly-opened World's Fair. Joined by John, Warren and Lucille, the family take in the sights and watch in wonderment as hundreds and hundreds of lights illuminate the exhibition's pavilions, realising that they are seeing history being made right there in their home town of St Louis.

Vincente Minnelli had a long and highly-regarded career in filmmaking, and *Meet Me in St Louis* continues to stand out as one of his best-loved features amongst audiences. The film's mix of childhood antics and gentle romance proved to be a winning combination which has appealed to cinemagoers ever since its initial release. While the social attitudes now seem hugely outdated (with daughters Rose and Esther endlessly preoccupied by finding the most eligible bachelor as a future spouse, and Leon Ames's fatherly Lon Smith trying – and mostly failing – to assert patriarchal authority), and the sentimental air to proceedings may likely feel too saccharine to suit modern sensibilities, the film's warm nostalgia for a more innocent, bygone past was just what audiences of the late forties were seeking as an antidote to the dark geopolitical environment they were living in. The genteel world of turn-of-the-century Missouri seemed a world away from the harshness of modern warfare and the horrors of fascism, even if its evoca-tion unconsciously reinforced the fact that this idealised, high-ly socially stratified way of living was now destined to remain in the past for good. In this sense, as Peter Bradshaw astutely comments, 'you could see the entire film as a brilliant show-case for its sensationally melancholy song: "Have Yourself a Merry Little Christmas", which Judy Garland sings in the presence of her sobbing sister, with her eyes upturned like a secular, sorrowing saint. Only now do we realise the song is a comment on the war: the sisters are sad that the family will be torn apart by moving to New York. Of course, audiences would have understood the subtext: that they are torn apart, spending Christmas apart from their loved ones'.[4]

While the film's exquisite use of Technicolor, Roger Eden's admirable original score and the many memorable songs (including Hugh Martin and Ralph Blane's 'The Boy Next Door' and 'The Trolley Song') have long been admired by commentators, what is of particular interest is the way in which *Meet Me in St Louis* has earned its place within the pantheon of golden age Christmas cinema when its events feature the festive season only briefly. This may, in part, be explained by the crucial importance of the film's Christmas scenes, which not only bear witness to the triumph of the family unit over commercial concerns (as Lon abandons his promotion to the New York office in order to remain in St Louis, knowingly causing himself economic impairment and possibly professional damage in the process), but also sees the Smiths reconnect with the community rather than being sev-ered from it. Colin Jacobson, for instance, has not been alone in asking: 'Is 1944's *Meet Me in St Louis* a holiday film? It appears to be regarded as one, though only a small section of the flick actually takes place during the Yuletide period. However, the movie boasts a classic song via "Have Yourself a Merry Little Christmas", and that appears to trump logic – a holiday picture it is! ⟦...⟧ The movie's warm view of Americana can delight. It may be absurdly unrealistic, but I think it provides some fantasy pleasure as it shows a world in which doors are never locked and no one ever seems particularly perturbed about much'.[5] Here the film performs perhaps its most delicate balancing act: conjuring up the warmth and innocence of an inviting Christmas setting whilst remaining mindful that for contemporary audiences, family members and other loved ones may well have been displaced to the fields of combat, fighting for liberty and their own lives even as others are forced to celebrate the festive period without them. This is, of course, highlighted by the Smiths' own attempts to maintain a sense of normality over their exchange of Christmas presents while most of their belongings are packed up and ready to be shipped out to New York. Eric Henderson notes that 'the standard "Have Yourself a Merry Little Christmas" actually reveals itself to be a bitterly ironic lament for the unreliability of everything, even the holiday spirit. Because of its modern take on the seductive but naïve binds of nostalgia, *Meet Me in St Louis* remains one of the most vital of musical films'.[6]

The melancholy of celebrating Christmas even as the Smith family contemplate being uprooted from their friends and local neighbourhood was to be an effective metaphor for the film's broader concerns about the demise of a simpler, less worldly way of life and the turmoil and complications of the then-present day of the mid-1940s. In this regard, its engagement with the festive season makes perfect sense, using this most family-oriented time of the year to delineate the changes that are being experienced not just by the Smiths, but by America at large. As Dennis Schwartz observes:

The Christmas chapter [is] the most memorable – many even calling this period film perfectly suitable as holiday fare. [...] The personal changes among the coming-of-age family members hints at the end of an era and the simple ways of country life. There's a hidden fear about a more complex world that's about to descend that will make it impossible for them to continue their uncomplicated existence, which frames the film around a good way of life vanishing and gives the genial film a somewhat darker edge than what might be perceived at first.[7]

While Christmas is used to striking effect near the conclusion of the film, the most recurrent motif throughout *Meet Me in St Louis* is, of course, the World's Fair of 1904. This real-life international exposition took place in St Louis from 30 April to 1 December 1904, and received around $15 million in funding. Known formally as the Louisiana Purchase Exposition (and initially conceived to celebrate the centenary of the Louisiana Purchase in 1803), it comprised exhibition spaces maintained by 62 countries and 43 (of the then-45) American States. Covering an area of 1,270 acres, it was attended by nearly 20 million visitors and contained over 1,500 buildings in total. The event had a huge impact on science, technology, the arts and culture, and was similarly beneficial for the city of St Louis which was greatly popularised as a result of its staging. It is thus no surprise that the characters in the film are so excited about the approach of the World's Fair, even though the celebratory song that many of the Smith family regularly perform – 'Meet Me in St Louis, Louis' by Kerry Mills and Andrew B. Sterling – would not be published until 1904 (meaning that as most of the film takes place in 1903, they are actually depicted singing it a year early). Because so much of the film surrounds the building anticipation as the characters approach the opening of the World's Fair, as well as the Smiths' growing dread at the prospect of leaving St Louis, the motif of the changing seasons proves to be more than simply an attempt to mirror the vignette format of Sally Benson's original prose source material. This almost elegiac recognition of the futility of any attempt to hold back progress, and the way in which human experience is essentially always in flux due to the ebb and flow of socio-cultural phenomena, is made only subtly via the film's gentle treatment of its subject matter. Rick Altman, for instance, discerns that:

At the end of the credits in *Meet Me in St Louis* we see an old-fashioned black-and-white tintype image of the Smith mansion. As we track in toward this house this ornately framed vision from the past, brown with age, slowly takes on the bright colors of summer and the activity of small-town life. This device sets up a number of relationships which guide our viewing of the film. Taken, as it were, from the family album of the American heritage, the discolored picture defines the entire film as a memory, a recollection of those wonderful days when life was still a family affair. When we dissolve to a Technicolor shot of the mansion, however, that past suddenly becomes a virtual present, a reality characterized by clarity, color, and movement, rather than by the washed-out static quality of an old postcard. Minnelli's introductory device thus defines his film as both memory and present reality, both artistic stylization of experience and realistic reproduction of that experience. The film's style thus depends on a merging of memory and observation, of art and reality.[8]

The skilful use of colour throughout *Meet Me in St Louis* is especially noteworthy in the demarcation of the seasons; summer sequences are full of vibrant green lawns and bright floral displays, whereas winter scenes contrast the cold snowy exteriors with the warmth of hearth and home. The autumnal hues of Halloween, as the *Time* magazine reviewer noted at the film's time of release, capture the excitement of the trick-or-treating neighbourhood kids and the flickering flames of their bonfire: 'Technicolor has seldom been more affectionately used than in its registrations of the sober mahoganies and tender muslins and benign gaslights of the period. [...] To the degree that this exciting little episode fails, it is because the Halloween setup, like the film as a whole, is too sumptuously, calculatedly handsome to be quite mistakable for the truth'.[9] Yet Minnelli is also unafraid to turn expectation on its head in surprisingly subversive ways. The performance of Hugh Martin and Ralph Blane's song 'Have Yourself a Merry Little Christmas' – now a festive staple thanks to its performance by a plethora of recording artists, not least Frank Sinatra – is used to juxtapose Tootie's excitement at the Christmas Eve arrival of Santa Claus with her growing despair at the prospect of her departure from St Louis in the new year. This eventually results in a scene that strangely manages to be more disturbing than anything that the Halloween sequence had to offer, as Matthew Sorrento describes: 'With news of the move [to New York] upsetting Tootie, Garland's

Esther sings "Have Yourself a Merry Little Christmas" to pacify her sister and make holiday music history. The moment does little for Tootie, resulting in the film's ⟦...⟧ horrifying sequence, when she raids her snow-covered backyard at night, hacking at snowmen (another seasonal festivity proving monstrous)'.[10]

Though Judy Garland's winningly wide-eyed performance as Esther is arguably its best-remembered, *Meet Me in St Louis* also contains many excellent supporting performances such as Margaret O'Brien's Tootie and her enchantingly offbeat taste for the macabre, Harry Davenport's sprightly, droll Grandpa, and Chill Wills' dryly witty turn as Mr Neely the local iceman. Garland was already very well-known to the audiences of the time for her appearances in films such as *Love Finds Andy Hardy* (George B. Seitz, 1938) and most especially as Dorothy Gale in *The Wizard of Oz* (Victor Fleming, 1939), but O'Brien had also, by this point, become one of the most popular child actresses in America with appearances in films such as *Journey for Margaret* (W.S. Van Dyke, 1942) and *Jane Eyre* (Robert Stevenson, 1943).

Edwin B. Willis's set design and the art design by Lemuel Ayers, Cedric Gibbons and Jack Martin Smith are also immaculately realised throughout, as was the work of the film's other crew, as Emanuel Levy observes: 'From first frame to last, *Meet Me* is a delectable, beautifully evoked entertainment. For the first time in musical history, nostalgia was used in the service of art. The industry showed its appreciation with four Oscar nominations, including Irene Sharaff's costumes and George Folsey's luminous cinematography'.[11] Enormous care and attention went into maintaining the authenticity of the film's period detail, including the production team reportedly consulting clothing catalogues from the era to ensure that even the most minor aspect of realism was not overlooked. It was this concurrence of national reminiscence, appealing characterisation and flawless production values which, as James Naremore has suggested, has led to the film's lasting influence:

> Set in the 'gateway to the West' at the turn of the century, [*Meet Me in St Louis*] celebrates the foundation of an urban Eden in the wilderness – a place where capitalism makes the lawns spacious and the weather perfect, and where a giant exposition of commodities has been built on a swamp. [...] This theme would recur with only minor variations in several postwar musicals, including *State Fair*, *Centennial Summer*, *Summer Holiday*, and *In the Good Old Summertime*; none of these later pictures, however, were able to suggest so many ironies and ambiguities while sustaining an air of lighthearted simplicity, and none were so formally elegant or artful.[12]

At the time of the film's release, *Meet Me in St Louis* received generally favourable reviews, many of which were to praise the quality of its production. Bosley Crowther of *The New York Times*, for instance, was to note that: 'The Smiths and their home, in Technicolor, are eyefuls of scenic delight, and the bursting vitality of their living inspires you like vitamin A. [[...]] We would confidently predict that *Meet Me in St Louis* has a future that is equally bright. In the words of one of the gentlemen, it is a ginger-peachy show'.[13] Modern appraisals of the film have remained positive, with critics such as Christopher McQuain noting that the film's longevity has derived not only from the catchiness of its songs but also its admirable restraint from drifting into all-out sentimentality: 'Even if you've never seen *Meet Me in St Louis*, you've undoubtedly heard at least some of Hugh Martin and Ralph Blane's songs for the film, if only "Have Yourself A Merry Little Christmas" during the holiday season. [...] They've become a part of the American songbook, and though they're unfailingly perky and ebullient, they never cross that line into the sickly sweet, thanks in part to their fairly seamless integration into the story'.[14] Others, such as Noel Murray, have praised the veracity of the film's period setting for its lasting sense of charm: 'In the middle of WWII and the heart of the lighter, revue-musical era, director Vincente Minnelli made *Meet Me In St Louis*, an ambitious nostalgia piece with a broad emotional palette. [...] The set's dirt streets and horse-drawn carriages add a mild twist to what could pass for a '50s TV sitcom suburb, full of friendly neighbors and manicured lawns. Minnelli frequently frames his characters through windows, which, along with the shallow depth of field, creates a diorama effect, boxing up the past like a Christmas window display'.[15]

Interestingly, even more sceptical appraisals of the film have been reasonably muted in their criticism. John J. Puccio, for instance, makes the observation that 'you'd better like the music here because there's precious little plot to enjoy. Fortunately, the songs are memorable, the characters charming, and the romance sweet. Together, they're more than enough to carry the day and make MGM's 1944 production of *Meet Me in St Louis* one of Hollywood's first important modern musicals, one that directly tied its music to the action of the story'.[16] Raymond Knapp, by comparison, takes note of the film's relatively conservative range of songs and musical sequences: 'Most remarkably, perhaps, given its credentials as a sterling representative of its genre, *Meet Me in St Louis* runs its course, structurally and thematically, as a musical gone sour, whose initial optimism is fully spoiled and extravagantly lamented before being restored in the final sequences, in the meantime managing almost to forget, save for its stylish exaggerations, that it is a musical at all'.[17] However, Glenn Erickson may perhaps provide the most incisive assessment of the film's endurance in popular culture, emphasising its universal call to acknowledge the importance of home, family and community:

Meet Me in St Louis is one of the pillars of the old MGM. For the record, it's considered the first of the classic Arthur Freed era of Technicolor musicals. The film in which Judy Garland blossomed into a full-fledged star is a triumph, an example of what the ritziest studio could do even in the middle of a world war. [...] In 1944 the Smith family of 1903 *St Louis* was immediately recognized as a picture of an idealized America worth fighting for, the one on the cover of *The Saturday Evening Post*. That's why the actual business of the film – teenage dates, parties, a foolish Halloween night – is secondary to the overall theme of the film, the conservative but attractive idea that staying home and staying the same is a great ambition.[18]

Meet Me in St Louis proved to be enormously popular at the box-office in 1944, and eventually became the second-largest grossing film of the year (after Leo McCarey's *Going My Way*), eventually establishing itself as one of the most popular films to be produced during the Second World War. The film's glossy production values would have a huge impact on later MGM musicals, and indeed on the musical film in general, and was deemed culturally significant by the Library of Congress in 1994, being preserved in the United States National Film Registry. *Meet Me in St Louis* was later adapted into a one hour radio adaptation which was broadcast on Lux Radio Theater on 2 December 1946. Judy Garland, Tom Drake and Margaret O'Brien were all to reprise their roles from the film in the radio production. Television adaptations followed in 1959 and 1966. Many years later, the movie was also adapted for stage; opening on Broadway at the George Gershwin Theater on 2 November 1989, the stage version contained additional songs in comparison to the cinematic original and would be nominated for a number of Tony Awards in 1990.

Though today it is perhaps best-known as one of Vincente Minnelli's most charming features, and among the most appealing performances of Judy Garland's early career following her famous appearance in *The Wizard of Oz*, *Meet Me in St Louis* has become one of the most prominent movies to deal with a Christmas setting during the war years, and this lavish production – with its appealing evocation of the yuletide scenes of years past – would play an important part in informing the festive nostalgia of countless films in decades to come. With so many later Christmas films of the forties evincing a sense of strident modernity, the wistful charm of *Meet Me in St Louis*'s longing reminiscence would win it generations of admirers and has ensured that it remains amongst the most fondly appreciated of all American cinematic musicals.

REFERENCES

1. Philip French, '*Meet Me in St Louis*: Review', in *The Observer*, 18 December 2011.
    <*https://www.theguardian.com/film/2011/dec/18/meet-me-st-louis-review*>

2. Raphael Samuel, *Theatres of Memory: Volume 1: Past and Present in Contemporary Culture* (London: Verso, 1994), p.350.

3. Jeffrey M. Anderson, 'Clang, Clang, Clang', in *Combustible Celluloid*, 12 April 2004.
    <*http://www.combustiblecelluloid.com/classic/meetstlouis.shtml*>

4. Peter Bradshaw, '*Meet Me in St Louis*: Review', in *The Guardian*, 15 December 2011.
    <*https://www.theguardian.com/film/2011/dec/15/meet-me-in-st-louis-review*>

5. Colin Jacobson, '*Meet Me In St Louis*', in *DVD Movie Guide*, 2 December 2011.
    <*http://www.dvdmg.com/meetmeinstlouisbr.shtml*>

6. Eric Henderson, 'Review: *Meet Me In St. Louis*', in *Slant*, 8 April 2004.
    <*https://www.slantmagazine.com/film/meet-me-in-st-louis/*>

7. Dennis Schwartz, '*Meet Me in St Louis*', in *Ozus' World Movie Reviews*, 28 November 2005.
    <*http://homepages.sover.net/~ozus/meetmeinstlouis.htm*>

8. Rick Altman, *The American Film Musical* (Bloomington & Indianapolis: Indiana University Press, 1987), pp.77-78.

9. Anon., 'The New Pictures', in *Time*, 27 November 1944. <*http://content.time.com/time/subscriber/article/0,33009,7 96926,00.html*>

10. Matthew Sorrento, 'Essential Film Performances 2013 Update: Part 7', in *Pop Matters*, 6 August 2013. <*https://www.popmatters.com/174230-essential-film-performances-2013-update-part-7-2495734419.html*>

11. Emanuel Levy, '*Meet Me in St. Louis*: Minnelli's Classic Musical and First Masterpiece, Starring Judy Garland', in *Cinema 24/7*, 14 March 2007. <*http://emanuellevy.com/review/meet-me-in-st-louis-1944-3/*>

12. James Naremore, *The Films of Vincente Minnelli*, Cambridge Film Classics series (Cambridge: Cambridge University Press, 1993), pp.71-72.

13. Bosley Crowther, 'The Screen: *Meet Me in St. Louis*, a Period Film That Has Charm, With Judy Garland and Margaret O'Brien, Opens at the Astor', in *The New York Times*, 29 November 1944. <*https://www.nytimes.com/1944/11/29/archives/the-screen-meet-me-in-st-louis-a-period-film-that-has-charm-with.html*>

14. Christopher McQuain, '*Meet Me in St Louis*', in *DVD Talk*, 13 December 2011. <*https://www.dvdtalk.com/reviews/51997/meet-me-in-st-louis/*>

15.   Noel Murray, '*Meet Me in St Louis*', in *AV Film*, 20 April
       2004.
       <https://film.avclub.com/meet-me-in-st-louis-1798199532>

16.   John J. Puccio, '*Meet Me in St Louis*', in *Movie Metropolis*,
       2 December 2011.
       *<https://moviemet.com/review/meet-me-st-louis-blu-ray-
       review>*

17.   Raymond Knapp, *The American Musical and the Perfor-
       mance of Personal Identity* (Princeton & Oxford: Princeton
       University Press, 2006), p.94.

18.   Glenn Erickson, '*Meet Me in St Louis*', in *DVD Savant*, 27
       November 2011.
       <https://www.dvdtalk.com/dvdsavant/s3740meet.html>

3

Christmas in Connecticut (1945)

Warner Bros. / First National Pictures

Director: Peter Godfrey
Producer: William Jacobs
Screenwriters: Lionel Houser and Adele Comandini,
from a story by Aileen Hamilton

C HRISTMAS *in Connecticut* was one of the last festively-themed movies to be released during the Second World War, appearing mere days before the sur-
render of the Japanese Empire and the conclusion of the conflict. A comedy which strikes a very different tone to the understated melancholy of earlier wartime Christmas features
such as *The Shop Around the Corner* (q.v.) and *Meet Me in
St Louis* (q.v.), arguably the main strength of *Christmas in
Connecticut* is the way in which it articulates the changing
national mood of the time; the exultation of victory and celebration of liberty, tempered by the knowledge of past sacrifice.

Though it features no shortage of quick wit and amusing situations, *Christmas in Connecticut* is nonetheless a film
which never leaves its audience less than aware of the time of
its production. Beyond its reputation as a screwball romantic
comedy, the exuberance of its many farcical situations conveys
a tangible sense of excitement and liveliness which accompa-

nied the end of a long and impossibly brutal period of global warfare. Yet while it acknowledged the sheer relief of the Allied nations in nearing the end of hostilities, it also recognises the depth of loss which had been required in order to reach this point; the film clearly identifies the suffering that armed service personnel had undergone during the conflict as well as the reverence with which their efforts were held by the general public, and also touches upon the national sense of tension and anxiety that had so greatly affected families across America as they waited patiently for the final victory that would secure an end to hostilities.

The film is today perhaps best-known as a vehicle for its star, Barbara Stanwyck, who was one of the most prominent actresses in Hollywood throughout the 1930s and would eventually be nominated for the Best Actress Academy

Christmas in Connecticut (1945): Warner Bros./
First National Pictures

Award on no less than four occasions. She would later be presented with an Honorary Oscar in 1982, though she also received innumerable awards over the years for her work in cinema and, latterly, on television. Moving into cinema after a brief but highly acclaimed career on stage, by 1944 she was recognised as the highest-paid woman in the United States and had established an illustrious filmography with roles in many well-known movies such as *Ladies of Leisure* (Frank Capra, 1930), *Baby Face* (Alfred E. Green, 1933) and *Stella Dallas* (King Vidor, 1937). She would, over the course of her long career, collaborate with legendary directors such as Fritz Lang and Cecil B. DeMille, while her later television performances in series such as ABC's *The Big Valley* (1965-69) and *The Thorn Birds* (1983) ensured that she would remain in the public eye for decades to come. Widely acknowledged for her incredible versatility and flawless professionalism, Stanwyck would bring her talent for immaculate comic timing and understated emotional articulation to her appearance in *Christmas in Connecticut*, ensuring that the end result would be a success with critics and the general public. It was, as Briallen Hopper has noted, a film that would have special significance both for Stanwyck and for Christmas cinema in general: '*Christmas in Connecticut* is a very different kind of holiday war movie. Released just three days before V-J Day, it is maybe the only classic Christmas movie to begin in the middle of an actual battle. [...] Like *White Christmas* and *It's a Wonderful Life*, *Christmas in Connecticut* is about managing the specter of irrecoverable loss. [...] The end of *Christmas in Connecticut* and the end of World War II simultaneously mark the end of Stanwyck's easy-and-funny era of exuberant comedic heroines, the newspaperwomen and card sharks and gangster's molls who write and cheat and talk their way to the top'.[1]

Christmas in Connecticut was helmed by veteran British director Peter Godfrey, who had initially come to fame as a stage director when he founded London's influential Gate Theatre Studio in 1925. Initially an actor in repertory theatre, he continued to perform on stage and later on screen, but it is for his directing that he would find enduring recognition. Following his directorial debut *Down River* (1931), he would be responsible for numerous films on varied subjects such as action adventure *The Lone Wolf Spy Hunt* (1939), crime drama *Highways by Night* (1942) and wartime thriller *Hotel Berlin* (1945). He would go on to later, high-profile success with features including *The Two Mrs Carrolls* (1947), *The Woman in White* (1948) and *The Great Jewel Robber* (1950), amongst many others.

The action of *Christmas in Connecticut* begins with the sight of a Nazi U-Boat torpedoing a US Navy destroyer in the North Atlantic. American Quartermaster Jefferson Jones (Dennis Morgan) and his shipmate Seaman Sinkewicz (Frank Jenks) abandon the sinking ship and take to a lifeboat, where they drift for weeks on the freezing cold seas and become ravenously hungry due to a lack of rations. They are eventually rescued and taken to a military hospital to convalesce, but Jones is disappointed that due to the condition of his health (having been starved for eighteen days), solid food is off the menu. He looks longingly at a copy of *Smart Housekeeping* magazine showcasing a mouth-watering collection of Christmas recipes created by Elizabeth Lane (Barbara Stanwyck), who is being promoted as 'America's Best Cook'. Eventually, he manages to persuade nurse Mary Lee (Joyce Compton) to provide him with some hospital food, but he laments the fact that he isn't enjoying one of Elizabeth Lane's famous seven-course meals. Mary is attracted to Jefferson and encourages him to propose marriage but he is reluctant, claiming that his itinerant lifestyle before the war as an artist and painter have made him averse to settling down.

Reasoning that if Jefferson could experience a happy domestic life, he would become more amenable to the idea of marriage, Mary writes a letter to Alexander Yardley (Sydney Greenstreet), the publisher of *Smart Housekeeping*. Mary had previously nursed Yardley's granddaughter following an outbreak of measles, and uses this familiarity to explain to him about Jefferson's knife-edge escape from the ship he had been serving on. As it happens, when Yardley receives the letter in New York City he simultaneously discovers that his daughter and granddaughter are unable to join him for Christmas, and the realisation that he will be spending the festive season alone makes him all the more emotionally affected by Mary's account of Jefferson's bravery. Yardley contacts the magazine's editor, Dudley Beecham (Robert Shayne), and asks him to arrange a meeting between himself and Elizabeth Lane. The publisher is bemused when Beecham appears highly reluctant to set up the meeting, and demands that it take place later that same day.

While Elizabeth's public profile is one of a perfect home-maker, spouse and mother, her tales of life on her un-spoiled Connecticut farm are completely fictional. In reality she lives in a cramped inner-city apartment in New York over-looking an urban vista, has never married, has no children, and is unable to cook. It transpires that her mouth-watering recipes are actually the work of her good-natured friend, mid-dle-aged Hungarian chef Felix Bassenak (S.Z. Sakall), who runs a restaurant nearby. In the past, Elizabeth helped his business financially when it was struggling, and although he eventually paid her back in full they remain the best of friends. Elizabeth is celebrating the arrival of a new mink coat – an early Christmas present to herself – when a panicked Beecham arrives. He explains that Yardley has received a letter asking if returning war hero Jefferson might be invited to spend Christmas at Elizabeth's picture-perfect rural home. The only problem with this request, of course, is that no such farm actually exists. Worse still, as Yardley insists on the high moral conduct of his staff at all times, he is sure to fire them both if he realises that the high circulation figures of one of his flagship magazines have been based on a lie.

Elizabeth despairs, believing that her career is on the brink of disaster, but Beecham persuades her to spin Yardley a yarn and wriggle out of hosting the convalescing sailor. At first she is resistant to the idea, but eventually changes her mind when she realises that Beecham's livelihood is on the line as well. Their conversation is interrupted by the untimely arrival of Elizabeth's unctuous friend, architect John Sloan (Reginald Gardiner). When he hears of her predicament, he immediately senses the chance to attempt another of his marriage proposals, but it is obvious that Elizabeth has no intention of accepting. What's more, she has clearly already rebuffed many such previous requests by him to tie the knot.

At Yardley's palatial mansion, Elizabeth tries in vain to pretend that her 'child' is ill and that she cannot possibly accommodate Jefferson as a house guest over the Christmas period. But the overbearing publisher steamrollers over her attempts to evade the prospect; it turns out that he is a huge fan of her writing and is determined that as his employee, she must take care of Jefferson as a patriotic act. On a less altruistic note, he also mentions that having the recuperating sailor on her farm is bound to have a positive effect on the sales of *Smart Housekeeping*, meaning that he will not take no for an answer. Even his offer of a bonus does little to ameliorate Elizabeth's sense of growing panic, but things go from bad to worse when he then invites himself to Christmas dinner in Connecticut as well.

A dejected Elizabeth meets with Sloan and Beecham at Felix's restaurant. When her editor hears the news, he is deflated and withdraws to tell his wife that he will soon be looking for a new job. Sensing that Elizabeth's self-confidence is at a low ebb, Sloan sees yet another opportunity to propose. While Elizabeth emphasises that her feelings toward him have only ever been platonic, Sloan assures her that she will develop genuine affection for him in time. Believing her career to be in ruins, and reasoning that she has nothing to lose, she finally accepts his offer of marriage. However, when Beecham returns and hears the news of their engagement he quickly hatches a plan. Sloan owns a farm in Connecticut, which has been the fictional basis of Elizabeth's prose descriptions for her magazine articles. He suggests that as Elizabeth and Sloan are now engaged, they should somehow 'borrow' a baby for the duration of the holidays and pretend to make her illusory rural idyll a reality – if only temporarily, for the sake of fooling Yardley and Jefferson. Both are reluctant to comply, but the prospect of Beecham losing his job just before Christmas – and the devastating effect this would have on his family – persuades them to accept his outlandish idea. However, Elizabeth agrees only on the condition that Felix should accompany them to the farm; as she is unable to cook, they will need a top chef on the premises to keep up the pretence that she is capable of creating sumptuous gourmet meals.

Elizabeth, Sloan and Felix arrive by horse-drawn carriage at the farm in the Connecticut countryside, where Christmas Eve has arrived and a thick blanket of snow has already fallen. They meet housekeeper Norah (Una O'Connor), who is far from enthusiastic about the prospect of Felix taking over her kitchen for the festive season. (Felix, for his part, is similarly less than keen about being away from the city and his beloved restaurant at such a lucrative time of year.) At Sloan's instruction, Norah has meticulously ornamented the farmhouse with Christmas decorations, ensuring that it exactly matches the description Elizabeth had given in her Christmas magazine feature. John has also arranged for the accommodation of another 'house guest' – the baby of local woman Mrs Wright, who is being looked after by Norah while both parents are occupied by the war effort. This will complete the illusion of the perfect nuclear family unit.

Felix and Norah's bickering over cookery preferences is interrupted when they are required as witnesses at Elizabeth and Sloan's wedding; Sloan has arranged for local magistrate Judge Crothers (Dick Elliott) to come to the farm and legalise their marriage with a civil ceremony. However, the formalities are unexpectedly disrupted by the early arrival of Jefferson. Sloan hurriedly vacates the judge from the room while Elizabeth welcomes Jefferson to the farmhouse. The pair are immediately attracted to each other, and Jefferson is clearly amazed to find that Elizabeth isn't the matronly figure he had assumed from reading her magazine articles.

The crying of the baby in an adjacent room leads Jefferson to deduce that it must be time for the child's bath. This leads to some awkwardness as Elizabeth, who has no experience of child-care whatsoever, tries to bathe the infant capably without giving herself away. Thankfully Jefferson has spent time looking after his sister's children, and volunteers to step in quickly enough to obscure Elizabeth's inexperience. She also manages to quickly sidestep further embarrassment when, having introduced the baby as a boy, Jefferson discovers that she is in fact a girl; Elizabeth rapidly interjects that the sailor must simply have misheard the name 'Robert' for 'Roberta'.

Sloan senses the chemistry between Elizabeth and Jefferson, and rapidly tries to reattempt the marriage ceremony as the judge is still on the premises. However, this plan is interrupted by the sudden arrival of the overbearing Yardley, who is keen to ensure that everything goes smoothly. He is delighted to see that the farmhouse is exactly as described in *Smart Housekeeping*. Sloan keeps the imperious publisher entertained while Felix (who is posing as Elizabeth's uncle) surreptitiously ensures the unseen exit of the affable Judge Crothers. Yardley meets Jefferson and the baby, and compliments Elizabeth on having created the perfect Christmas hideaway.

As Sloan bores Yardley with excruciatingly detailed accounts of his architectural prowess, followed by a less-than-riveting game of dominoes, Jefferson reveals hitherto-unsuspected musical talents on the farmhouse's piano while Elizabeth decorates the Christmas tree. Yardley reveals to Sloan that Elizabeth's column is hugely valuable to his publishing interests, as it gives his company the edge over its competitors. Noting that when Elizabeth wrote about the birth of her child, the magazine's circulation increased dramatically and attracted many advertisers, Yardley implores Sloan to consider persuading his 'wife' to have another child; if she falls pregnant in the near future, the magazine can beat its nearest rival who plans a similar exclusive the following autumn. As Sloan mulls the implications of this, the judge telephones and explains that he will be arriving within the next fifteen minutes to reattempt the marriage ceremony. Sloan thus rounds everyone up and explains that they favour having an early night in the countryside; once all the guests have retired to bed, Sloan and Elizabeth await the judge's return. But their plans are yet again disrupted, this time when Yardley sneaks downstairs to put Christmas presents under the tree and encounters Jefferson, who has sneaked into the kitchen for a midnight snack. Sloan rushes the judge and Elizabeth into the study to keep them all out of sight, but then realises that they have no witnesses to the ceremony. Elizabeth slinks out to find Felix and Norah, but ends up interrupting the amiable conversation between Yardley and Jefferson. One of the farm's cows comes to the kitchen door, and Jefferson offers to escort Elizabeth as she returns it to the barn. On their stroll in the moonlight, the attraction between the pair becomes undeniable, though their flirtatious exchange comes to an abrupt halt when the cow manages to evade them and needs to be searched for. Sloan is irked that Elizabeth's nocturnal ramblings with Jefferson have delayed the wedding ceremony yet again; while they eventually find the cow in the barn, Jefferson and Elizabeth are covered in snow following an avalanche from the building's roof. The judge decides to return home rather than wait around any longer, but states that he will be back on Christmas morning to finally formalise the marriage.

The next day, Felix hurriedly gives Elizabeth a primer on cooking breakfast, as Yardley has expressed a desire to see 'America's best cook' in action. The doorbell rings, and a neighbour arrives to drop off her baby to be cared for while she is working; however, it isn't Mrs Wright, and the child is a boy rather than a girl. As the mother is in a hurry to get to work for her shift, Elizabeth has no time to protest. But before the implications of this infant swap have begun to sink in, Sloan arrives to sweep her off into the study, where the judge has returned – yet again – to conduct the marriage ceremony. Yardley arrives on the scene unexpectedly, and the spouses-to-be swiftly concoct another falsehood, explaining that they renew their wedding vows on the morning of every Christmas Day to commemorate the occasion of their marriage. With one witness now in place, Sloan heads off to find Felix, but finds the chef panicking – while he was looking after the newly-arrived baby, he tried to distract him with his watch only for the child to accidentally swallow it. Yardley becomes highly suspicious when he discovers that the infant is now blonde, having been dark-haired the previous day, but Elizabeth manages to shoo him from the room before he can ask any further questions. Felix privately reveals to Elizabeth that the child is perfectly fine; realising that her true feelings lie with Jefferson, Felix had fabricated the tale of him swallowing the watch simply to send the judge back home and postpone the wedding to Sloan once more. It is clear that Felix does not approve of the relationship, much less the prospect of his dear friend marrying the wrong man. However, the judge is now losing his patience and warns that if he doesn't marry the couple on his next return to the farmhouse, they will have to wait until the New Year to tie the knot.

Sloan is also tiring of the endless deceit and decides to finally confront Yardley with the truth. But before he can explain what has been happening, the publisher makes an unexpected announcement of his own; he is seeking a new editor for a magazine section which will specialise in homebuilding, and he believes that someone with Sloan's architectural expertise would be an invaluable asset. Yardley emphasises that Sloan's honesty and upright character made him realise that he would be ideal for the job, thus ensuring that Sloan immediately changes his mind about revealing the situation behind his sham marriage to Elizabeth – especially when he realises that Yardley's job offer will lead to a handsome salary and widespread recognition as an expert in his field.

Later, a representative of a local community group arrives and invites the household to the Christmas dance at the town hall; they are keen to honour the courage of Jefferson, who is hailed as a war hero for surviving the destruction of his ship. They agree, and everyone attends the dance later that day. The attraction between Elizabeth and Jefferson continues to grow, while Sloan is now fully committed to the idea of working for Yardley, regaling him with endless ideas of how to promote new building materials and construction practices. Yardley warns Sloan that appointing him as editor will be entirely contingent on Elizabeth falling pregnant in time to boost his magazine circulation figures as early as possible, thwarting the designs of his rivals. Sloan is growing increasingly amenable to the idea, but Yardley becomes highly suspicious when he notices Jefferson and Elizabeth in an obviously affectionate embrace on the dancefloor.

Elizabeth and Jefferson collect their coats from the cloakroom and head out into the snowy night. Neither realises that Yardley has noticed their absence and is watching them intently from inside the town hall. Jefferson reveals that he must leave the following day to return to his duties. Elizabeth is disappointed by the news and suggests that they go for a walk to mark his last night in Connecticut, but the snow is too deep for her choice of footwear. Jefferson spots a nearby horse-drawn carriage and suggests that they have a seat in the stationary cart to converse in comfort, but the horse hasn't been restrained and thus begins to canter into motion. As they disappear off into the distance, an increasingly distrustful Yardley sets off in pursuit, but he accidentally falls into a roadside ditch before he can catch up with the carriage. Elizabeth leaves Jefferson in no doubt that if she were not 'married', she would be keen to start a relationship with him. Jefferson reveals that he feels exactly the same. Their romantic interlude is eventually interrupted by the arrival of the horse and carriage's owner, as well as the town sheriff who takes the couple into custody for attempted theft and joyriding.

Back at the farmhouse, Norah heads off to spend the evening of Christmas Day with her sister, but informs Felix (who has not attended the dance) that the baby's mother will be arriving later than expected to pick up her young son. However, by the time the woman appears Felix has fallen fast asleep in front of the fireplace and is unaware of her entrance. Yardley arrives back at the farm just as the mother is leaving with her baby, and deduces that the child is being kidnapped. Alarmed, not least by what the infant's abduction could mean to the sales figures of his magazine, Yardley gets on the telephone and summons state troopers. When they arrive, along with press reporters, he proclaims that he will offer a $25,000 reward for the child's safe return, but has difficulty providing a description because the appearances of the two different babies were so markedly dissimilar.

The sheriff returns Elizabeth and Jefferson to the farmhouse early the next morning, the earlier misunderstanding now ironed out. They are confused to find the living room full of slumbering reporters, but when Elizabeth wakes them up Yardley promptly takes the focus off her late arrival and emphasises the trauma she must feel at her missing child. As soon as the reporters have gone, however, he fumes at her callousness in having been out all night with Jefferson, inadvertently putting her child in danger. At last, their deceit un-ravels as Yardley discovers that Sloan and Elizabeth were never married in the first place; the arrival of Mrs Wright and her friend from the war plant – along with their two, marked-ly different babies – hammers home the point that the entire domestic situation at the farmhouse has been completely fab-ricated. Incensed at having been lied to, in addition to the amount of professional damage he fears that his publishing empire will now face, Yardley fires Elizabeth on the spot.

Although she now faces the killing blow to her career that she has always feared, Elizabeth remains buoyant because she can at least explain to Jefferson that she is single and available. However, his fiancée Mary arrives, leaving Eliza-beth confused and despondent – she had no idea that he was even engaged. Devastated, she withdraws to pack her belong-ings and leave the farmhouse. As Felix goes to prepare food for Mary, she confesses that she has actually married Jeffer-son's friend Sinkewicz – a fact which immediately gives him an idea. Leaving Mary in the study, Felix goes to the kitchen and begins to cook kidneys: a particular favourite of Yardley, who is immediately enticed by the aroma. Cunningly, Felix manages to persuade Yardley that the owner of his great rival, *American Housekeeping* magazine, has already been in touch to poach Elizabeth now that she has left his employ. Outraged at the audacity of his competitors, Yardley declares that in order to thwart their plans he will not only overlook Eliza-beth's string of deceptions, but also intends to offer her back her job – and double her salary into the bargain.

When Yardley approaches Elizabeth with his business proposal she angrily rebukes him, telling the pompous pub-lisher that she has had her fill of being browbeaten and ma-nipulated. Yardley is stunned at her attitude, never having

realised that someone would be resistant to his towering professional influence. However, her sense of desolation is challenged when Jefferson arrives. While she deplores the idea of
him being engaged – not realising that his intended fiancée is
now actually married to another man – she is also oblivious of
the fact that Felix has told Jefferson the full story of what has
been going on, meaning that he is now aware of the fact that
she is not married to Sloan. After all of the misunderstandings
have finally been ironed out, the couple declare the full extent
of their feelings for one another, and they decide to summon
back Judge Crothers to carry out the wedding at last – only
this time for a ceremony between Elizabeth and Jefferson.

   Christmas in Connecticut is an enjoyably light knocka-
bout comedy where plausibility is very much left to one side
for most of the proceedings in favour of eccentric situations
and an infectious sense of fun. Barbara Stanwyck's comic talents come to the fore in very satisfying ways; while the timing
of her reactions is impeccable, so too does the dramatic content of her performance never endanger her wittily insightful
approach to the role by overshadowing its sharply-defined
drollness. Because Elizabeth is clearly a smart and independent
character with abundant talent, the audience knows that her
search for a loving partner is one of personal choice; she is
obviously more than capable of being successful on her own,
but seeks to share her life with someone that she can relate to
on an emotional level as well as an intellectual one. Crucially,
as MaryAnn Johanson suggests, this depth of characterisation
ensures that Elizabeth is not scorned or demeaned by the
screenwriters as a result of the journalist's efforts to replicate
the level of domestic perfection that she regularly conjures up
through her writing:

Though we are treated to the continuing spectacle of a hopelessly undomestic Liz trying to live up to Yardley's image of her as 'the finest, most exemplary wife and mother', the film's point of view does not belittle her. Many a comedy – and particularly those made in our supposedly more enlightened times – treat women lacking housekeeping and cooking skills as objects of ridicule or, at best, pity. Here, if anything, living up to the fantasy Liz creates in *Diary of a Housewife* is shown to be an impossibility – it's the pursuit of an unrealizable domestic nirvana that generates the humor here.[2]

Reginald Gardiner and Robert Shayne both make the most of the comedic content of their roles. The oily Sloan is clearly absorbed with furthering his own interests, happy to dispense with Elizabeth as soon as she seems to become a liability to realising his ambitions, and Gardiner brings remarkable insight to the role by making this thoroughly opportunistic character still seem charming and ingratiating enough to be a smooth operator. Shayne, on the other hand, provides a masterclass in understated scheming as the put-upon magazine editor Beecham, quietly manipulating Elizabeth into going against her better interests in the hope of preserving his livelihood. In a manner similar to Sloan, the character of Beecham could well be considered self-serving and mercenary were it not for the easy charm of Shayne's portrayal, which emphasises the professional ordeal of a beleaguered family man who is simply doing his best to keep everyone as happy as possible.

The film greatly benefits from the comic characterisation of its many supporting figures. S.Z. Sakall's kindly, blustering Felix is well balanced against the straight-talking practicality of Una O'Connor's straight-talking Irish housemaid

Norah, while the subtle aspirations of Frank Jenks's Sinkewicz and Joyce Compton's self-motivated Mary Lee perfectly foreshadow the characters' marriage. However, Sydney Greenstreet steals the show, cast against type to great effect as the imperious, morally upright Alexander Yardley. Greenstreet was a Kent-born British actor who, in spite of a long career on the stage, did not emerge into the world of cinema until the age of 61. He then enjoyed a run of highly successful appearances in films such as *The Maltese Falcon* (John Huston, 1941), *Casablanca* (Michael Curtiz, 1942) and *Passage to Marseille* (Michael Curtiz, 1944), usually playing menacing crime bosses with a speciality for intimidation. (The script of *Christmas in Connecticut* even pays an ingenious tribute to his earlier gangster roles; Felix, who dislikes the pompous Yardley, repeatedly mutters 'fat man' under his breath when he encounters him, alluding to Greenstreet's earlier role as the villainous Kasper Gutman in *The Maltese Falcon*, who was known by the alias of 'The Fat Man'.) As Yardley, Greenstreet seems to take great enjoyment from subverting audience expectation; because he was so immediately recognisable from his appearances as threatening and sinister characters, there is a palpable sense of him wringing every ounce of comic value from this domineering publisher as he strong-arms and steamrollers over everyone around him without a second thought. Much humour is generated from the fact that although Yardley continually affects a tendency towards high-minded moralism, his own ethics are questionable at best because they are completely driven by an insatiable profit motive and an obsession with the wholesomeness of his brand. As Jacqueline T. Lynch observes, this tendency makes the juxtaposed motivations of Yardley's character one of the film's most significant thematic dichotomies:

Christmas in Connecticut (1945) gives us a nostalgic wartime Christmas, but in curiously modern wrappings. Its charm is its coy look at exploitation, of the holiday, of the war effort, and of human nature. Never was cynicism presented so cheerfully. [...] The movie successfully gets away with winking at self-serving human nature while celebrating the possibility of the best of human nature, including our resilience to adversity. It is funny that Sydney Greenstreet keeps referring to his employees as his possessions and calls the baby (or babies) *The Smart Housekeeping Baby*. Here we have an actual magazine ad for Mennen baby lotion using the images of Stanwyck, Morgan, and that sweet, good-natured baby from *Christmas in Connecticut* to sell a product. Art imitating life? Or just the American way?[3]

While the film's far-fetched scenarios would win no prizes for believability, director Peter Godfrey and screenwriters Lionel Houser and Adele Comandini (working from an original story by Aileen Hamilton) demonstrate a keen eye for humorous situations and sight gags, perhaps best epitomised by the dozens of rocking chairs which have been sent to Elizabeth by her adoring readers after she made an off-the-cuff mention in an article about looking to buy a new one. So many are delivered to her apartment that she is forced to start storing them in the building's basement, and thus the film perfectly presages the near-inevitability of Jefferson's arrival at the farmhouse being accompanied by the gift of a rocking chair – which, in a genius twist, bears the letters MGM as a subtle wink in the direction of the great studio rivals of Warner Bros., Metro-Goldwyn-Mayer.

Naturally the main thrust of the film's comedy is generated by Elizabeth's self-confessed hopelessness as a cook, mother and home-maker. While the character is constantly being hyped as America's best-regarded purveyor of home-cooked meals and inviting domestic environments, she immediately runs into a brick wall when faced with the reality of preparing connoisseur dishes and the many challenges of caring for an infant. While there is a certain predictability surrounding misunderstandings over the baby's gender and appearance throughout the film (Elizabeth eventually abandons all pretence of accuracy regarding whether the baby is a boy or a girl, and begins referring to the infant(s) simply as 'it'), the conceit is never overplayed and is even used to foreshadow Jefferson's growing enthusiasm for a family unit of his own – a prospect which, we are subtly led to understand, Elizabeth is also gradually warming to. It is perhaps germane to note that while this scenario may seem rather outmoded to modern audiences, it was actually acknowledged as appearing a trifle passé by critics even in the mid-1940s; as *The New York Times* considered it: 'There's not much sense going into all the plot convolutions here; they are pretty obvious anyway. Let's just say that [Elizabeth] manages the problem admirably, though not without a great deal of complications, some more hectic than funny. [...] It takes something more than a polished production and a script with some naughty intentional clichés to carry off successfully old jokes like the one about the baby boy who turns out to be a girl. Oh, well, the snowscapes are refreshing anyhow'.[4]

Elizabeth's status as a professional 'domestic goddess' and her serene rural dream home have led some to surmise that the character was based on Gladys Taber, a popular writer for *Family Circle* magazine and *Ladies' Home Journal* who lived on a Connecticut farm and recounted her country-side experiences for readers. Certainly the kind of homestead popularised by Taber's writing is fully on display in Elizabeth and Sloan's fabricated paradise; there is much to admire in Casey Roberts's impeccable set design, which beautifully conjures up the very kind of fairy-tale rural Christmas retreat that perfectly epitomises the fastidiously-decorated country-side utopia of Elizabeth's articles. The same farmhouse set had previously appeared – sans holiday decorations – in an earlier screwball comedy, *Bringing Up Baby* (Howard Hawks, 1938), starring Cary Grant and Katharine Hepburn.

While the success of *Christmas in Connecticut* is entirely contingent on a healthy suspension of disbelief, some eyebrows have been raised in more recent years with regard to exactly what kind of message its events may be conveying to audiences. Like so many screwball comedies of the era before it, a relatively simple premise is blown up to hilariously absurd proportions through a confluence of unexpected events and unwise decisions. Elizabeth and Beecham know that Yardley, who insists on principled moral conduct, demands that all of his staff members are upstanding and honourable. Thus when their subterfuge involved in projecting Elizabeth's public persona is on the verge of discovery, they decide to create a plethora of vaguely plausible lies in order to obscure the original deceit that caused the problems in the first place. Except, of course, the vast network of duplicity necessary to maintain the pretence soon becomes so unworkable that even the characters who are 'in' on the falsehood eventually seem to have difficulty working out who is supposed to know what at any given time. While some may find it objectionable that, in the end, the characters all somehow manage to prosper as a result of their elaborate ruse – subverting the old adage that 'honesty is the best policy' – the out-and-out preposterousness of the film's situations surely goes some way to inoculating it against accusations that it is somehow encouraging dishonesty as a legitimate means to get ahead. Elizabeth and Beecham hatch their scheme not as a deliberate plan of subterfuge but rather as an act of desperation in order to save their jobs from an employer who proves himself next to impossible to reason with, while Felix and Sloan's part in proceedings is merely to help their friends (in the former's case, for unselfish reasons; for the latter, to further his own self-interest). Thus if the film is a proponent of any moral strategy, it is arguably that of taking the timeworn cliché of 'fake it 'til you make it' and exaggerating it to farcical effect. As Dennis Schwartz perceptively puts it, the film is a 'delightfully cheerful screwball comedy that is especially suited for the Christmas holidays. It's winsome despite being so predictable and the dialogue not as snappy as a film of this sort requires. But it's always entertaining and Barbara Stanwyck gives an outstanding performance, making her manipulative heroine's part somehow appear endearing if you don't think about what she stands for twice'.[5]

While the golden age of the festive movie would not truly start in earnest until the post-war era, *Christmas in Connecticut* features many characteristics which typify the best of the genre. As J.P. Roscoe has stated, the film fits comfortably into the canon of other 1940s Christmas cinema: 'Directed by Peter Godfrey, *Christmas in Connecticut* is a classic Christmas film. The movie airs frequently during the holidays and was part of the whole classic romance style from the time period. *Christmas in Connecticut* is one of those movies that you could start the plot and tack on "hijinks ensue" at the end. The set-up feels very modern in the idea of this elaborate plan to pull one over on the poor soldier and editor just so

[[Elizabeth]] can keep her job... [[...]] As you can see, this is a classic set-up, but the absurdity of the plot isn't that crazy in the long standing of plays and film'.[6] Although the movie has never quite achieved the legendary status of later Christmas features of the forties, such as *It's a Wonderful Life* (q.v.) and *Miracle on 34th Street* (q.v.), it has, nonetheless, carved a niche for itself as one of the most wittily sophisticated movies of the period. Marc Fusion is not alone in observing that the satirical content of the screenplay – deriding both the apparent perfection of Elizabeth's fictional domestic existence and Yardley's single-minded fixation on corporate prosperity – elevates it above the norm: 'The writing in *Christmas in Connecticut* is a great example of humor that is wild and sometimes over the top, but also very intelligent. A lot of the humor in the movie is fueled by the characters, so the jokes and humorous situations have more weight, it isn't often just one off lines or random jokes. This really elevates the material and helps it land stronger, as well as just be a richer comedic experience. The character driven humor is bolstered by a gifted cast that embraces the material and has some terrific chemistry as an ensemble'.[7]

Even though many of the social attitudes depicted throughout the film have naturally become very dated given its age, other aspects have weathered the passing decades with admirable credibility. Styles of gift may have changed dramatically over the years, but some expectations about the festive always remain constant – not least the desire to create the ideal domestic environment in which to celebrate Christmas, even given the logistical nightmare involved in attempting to make this pipedream into reality. Laura Grieve, for instance, ventures the opinion that '*Christmas in Connecticut* is a fun film – not a great one, but a very pleasant way to spend a December evening. The performers are pleasing and the film is well paced. In many ways the movie is still quite topical – for instance, six decades later visions of the perfect home are still being sold by lifestyle magazines'.[8] In its surprisingly unsentimental take on Christmas, constructing a faultless yuletide environment while (entirely due to circumstance) exhibiting precious little of its festive cheer with any degree of sincerity, the film portends other, far more riotous and contrarian films in the genre which would follow in later decades. (Ironically, the action only ventures headlong into the more familiar Christmas territory of hearth and home in the closing minutes, once the last vestiges of Elizabeth and Beecham's grand deceit have been swept away.) Commentators such as Michael Reuben have made the point that the film was not only creditably modern in its attitudes and approach, but can actually be seen to be somewhat ahead of its time:

I doubt that its makers intended this, but the 1945 holiday comedy *Christmas in Connecticut* has a slyly subversive streak. If one leaves aside the relatively recent phenomenon of cynical anti-Christmas films like *Bad Santa*, Yuletide fare generally centers on family. From *It's a Wonderful Life*, to any iteration one may choose of *A Christmas Carol* (including Bill Murray's modern version, *Scrooged*), to the slapstick chaos of *National Lampoon's Christmas Vacation*, to the aptly titled *The Family Man*, both Christmas and Christmas movies are about surrounding oneself with family, either literally or by adoption (as Scrooge adopts the Cratchits). But not *Christmas in Connecticut*. The film's central character is a career woman who has steadfastly rejected family life, while spinning idyllic (and totally fraudulent) tales of a Norman Rockwell country existence as a housewife and mother to boost the circulation of a ladies' magazine. When her secret is threatened with exposure one holiday season, screwball comedy ensues.[9]

Not all appraisals of the film have been quite so enthusiastic, however, with its oddball charm not proving to be to every taste. Comedy is always a highly subjective area, and no less so within a festive framework, meaning that the boisterous antics and eccentric situations of *Christmas in Connecticut* have proven to be something of an acquired taste among some critics. Some, including Jeffrey M. Anderson, have made the observation that the film may seem over-reliant on the extensive talents of its star to carry the day, opining that 'Barbara Stanwyck uses every acting muscle in her body to redeem this silly holiday romance in which characters run themselves ragged to keep up a ridiculous deception'.[10] Others have instead lamented the film as something of a wasted opportunity, noting that many themes and situations are elaborately set up but not fully mined for either their comedic or dramatic potential. Stuart Galbraith IV points out that '*Christmas in Connecticut* almost but doesn't quite come off. The picture takes an awful long time to get started, with a long, clumsy, and contrived sequence at a naval hospital that the picture would have been better without. (And, in retrospect, is completely unnecessary anyway.) [...] Another curious aspect is how little the Christmastime and country setting impact the story and its characters. The potential for Stanwyck's hardened city girl, Greenstreet's domineering publisher, etc. to somehow be transformed by life in country is barely scratched, and the fact that these disparate characters find themselves together on Christmas is scarcely mentioned'.[11] Another criticism levelled at the film is that its momentum has been considered by some reviewers to dissipate the closer it gets to reaching its climax, squandering the plot's capacity for anarchic chaos in favour of an overly neat conclusion to events. Josh Medcalf is among the commentators who have observed that this surprisingly languid method of wrapping up such inspired pandemonium may be seen as something of a disappointment: '*Christmas in Connecticut*, starring the lovely Barbara Stanwyck, is a charming, enjoyable little comedy that's not quite Frank Capra and not quite Billy Wilder, but ventures into either territory on more than one occasion and is welcomed with open arms. [...] My only problem is that the climax is too easy. It just fizzles out, like air out of a balloon. I won't spoil how the secret is finally let out of the bag, but the actual event leaves much to be desired, considering the energy of the first two acts'.[12]

If *Christmas in Connecticut* has earned itself a place in the pantheon of festive film-making, it is almost certainly for the way in which it makes such a virtuoso use of its wartime setting. The movie was, in many ways, an impeccable blend of Christmas charm and post-war exhilaration, juxtaposing the comfort and familiarity of festive traditions with the exhilaration of a United States nearing the end of four years of constant, bloody conflict to striking effect. But as *Back to Golden Days*' reviewer Cátia has remarked, the holiday season is employed not just as a suitably uplifting backdrop but rather as a means of reminding the audience of what it truly means to be free in a world where the shadow of totalitarianism had been determinedly pushed back by the forces of freedom and independence: 'The festive season serves as a means of bringing Elizabeth and Jeff together and transforming them into a post-war couple. Their romance is the result of sharing traditional Christmas activities: trimming the tree, singing carols and riding on a sleigh through a picturesque snowy landscape. [[...]] In a way, *Christmas in Connecticut* was the perfect wartime Christmas film: it offered traditional Christmas activities that worked as a "comforting ideal" for a nation recovering from the heartaches and anxieties of wartime, as well as the reassurance that post-war readjustment need not be punitive or stifling'.[13] The film has thus come to form, in more recent years, an appealing time capsule of post-war euphoria within a determinedly festive setting; it celebrated not just everything that was positive about Christmas, but also extolled the virtues of a pastoral existence in rural America – a traditional kind of life which had been fiercely protected and was now considered safely preserved, if only due to the sacrifice of countless defenders. As Greg Orypeck comments, to capture this heady mix within a creative work was essentially to catch lightning in a bottle at a very particular point in the history of the United States:

> *Christmas in Connecticut* was being filmed during the closing months of World War II and released in the U.S. August 11, four days before Japan surrendered. [...] Many seasonal and popular songs are at the ready, both as source music and as part of the soundtrack, including 'Jingle Bells', 'O Little Town of Bethlehem', 'The Wish That I Wish Tonight' and 'Turkey in the Straw'. Although the main title credits the music to Frederick Hollander, the score consists of much stock music by Adolph Deutsch and Max Steiner. All the negatives and silliness considered, *Christmas in Connecticut* makes for a pleasant evening's viewing

should some of the more polished seasonal movies be unavailable. With a bowl of hot popcorn and some eggnog, it goes well with the season. The film is a snapshot of a time gone by, of another, more innocent age. It is a warm reminder of those slapstick movies of the '30s and '40s.[14]

Although it was released in the August of 1945, meaning that it was considerably out of season for a festively-themed movie, *Christmas in Connecticut* was highly successful at the box-office and went on to considerable popularity from television screenings from the mid-1950s onwards. As was so often the convention at the time, *Christmas in Connecticut* was later adapted for radio presentation and was broadcast on *Stars in the Air* on 20 March 1952 as a half-hour dramatisation starring Phyllis Thaxter and Gordon MacRae. Many years later, the film was remade for television – with the same title – in 1992, directed by none other than eighties action legend Arnold Schwarzenegger. The TV movie, which was aired by TNT, updated the action to the modern world of the nineties and starred Dyan Cannon as Elizabeth, Kris Kristofferson as Jefferson and Tony Curtis as Yardley. Moving the action away from the original wartime setting led to a number of narrative changes, such as Jefferson no longer being a Naval war hero but instead a heroic forest ranger whose log cabin home has been destroyed by fire. Elizabeth, by contrast, is no longer an icon of the magazine world but rather the presenter of a TV cookery show, who must make dinner for Jefferson live on air while desperately trying to conceal the fact that her culinary skills are, in reality, sadly lacking.

Like *The Shop Around the Corner* (q.v.), *Christmas in Connecticut* was an early exponent of the romantic subgenre of the Christmas movie, laying the groundwork for a plethora of other such features in the years to come. Yet in other ways, it was much more than simply an upbeat romantic comedy with a yuletide setting. While it provides just about every visual element required to tick all the requisite boxes of festive cinema – a sleigh-ride along a snowy country lane, a decorated Christmas tree next to a roaring log fire, traditional Christmas carols sung with gusto, to say nothing of a deeply unconventional family unit being brought together by the holidays – the film was also, in an understated way, establishing the foundations of a new era of the genre. With the Second World War now over and the West taking stock of a new and very different global environment, films such as *Christmas in Connecticut* offered reassurance that even though the geopolitical composition of the world had altered radically – with power shifting profoundly and unpredictably as a result – the consoling, heartening traditions of Christmas still remained constant. Just as the festive season had offered much-needed succour in times of international conflict, as it had in *Meet Me in St Louis* (q.v.), so too would it continue to provide reassurance and solace in a post-war world that was beginning to emerge from the mid-forties onwards.

REFERENCES

1. Briallen Hopper, '*Christmas in Connecticut*', in *NotComing.com*, 25 December 2010.
    <*http://www.notcoming.com/reviews/christmasinconnect icut/>*

2. MaryAnn Johanson, '*Christmas in Connecticut*', in *Flick Filosopher*, 11 December 1999.
    <*https://www.flickfilosopher.com/1999/12/christmas-in-connecticut-review.html>*

3. Jacqueline T. Lynch, '*Christmas in Connecticut*', in *Another Old Movie Blog*, 10 December 2007.
    <*https://anotheroldmovieblog.blogspot.com/2007/12/chris tmas-in-connecticut-1945.html>*

4. Anon., 'The Screen: *Christmas in Connecticut*, With Barbara Stanwyck, Opens at Strand', in *The New York Times*, 28 July 1945.
    <*https://www.nytimes.com/1945/07/28/archives/the-screen-christmas-in-connecticut-with-barbara-stanwyck-opens-at.html>*

5. Dennis Schwartz, '*Christmas in Connecticut*', in *Ozus' World Movie Reviews*, 26 December 2004.
    <*http://homepages.sover.net/~ozus/christmasinconnecticu t.htm>*

6. J.P. Roscoe, '*Christmas in Connecticut*', in *Basement Rejects*, 30 November 2012.
    <*http://basementrejects.com/review/christmas-in-connecticut-1945/>*

7.   Marc Fusion, '*Christmas in Connecticut*', in *Marc Fusion: King of Twitch*, 20 December 2017. <*https://marcfusion.com/2017/12/20/christmas-in-connecticut-1945/*>

8.   Laura Grieve, 'Tonight's Movie: *Christmas in Connecticut*', in *Laura's Miscellaneous Musings*, 27 December 2007. <*https://laurasmiscmusings.blogspot.com/2007/12/tonights-movie-christmas-in-connecticut.html*>

9.   Michael Reuben, '*Christmas in Connecticut* Blu-Ray', in *Blu-Ray.com*, 9 November 2014. <*https://www.blu-ray.com/movies/Christmas-in-Connecticut-Blu-ray/109472/#Review*>

10.   Jeffrey M. Anderson, 'Holes in the Holidays', in *Combustible Celluloid*, 25 December 2009. <*http://www.combustiblecelluloid.com/classic/chrisconn.html*>

11.   Stuart Galbraith IV, '*Warner Bros. Classic Holiday Collection*', in *DVD Talk*, 8 November 2005. <*https://www.dvdtalk.com/reviews/19068/warner-bros-classic-holiday-collection-boys-town-men-of-boys-town-a-christmas-carol-christmas-in-connecticut/*>

12.   Josh Medcalf, '*Christmas in Connecticut*', in *The Parallax Review*, 17 December 2010. <*http://www.theparallaxreview.com/on_cable/christmas_in_connecticut.html*>

13.   Cátia, '12 Days of Christmas Films: Day 5: Christmas in Connecticut', in *Back to Golden Days*, 18 December 2015. <*http://back-to-golden-days.blogspot.com/2015/12/12-days-of-christmas-films-day-5.html*>

14.   Greg Orypeck, '*Christmas in Connecticut*', in *Classic Film Freak*, 15 December 2012. <*https://www.classicfilmfreak.com/2012/12/15/christmas-in-connecticut-1945-barbara-stanwyck/*>

4

The Bells of St Mary's (1945)

Rainbow Productions

Director: Leo McCarey
Producer: Leo McCarey
Screenwriter: Dudley Nichols, from a story by Leo McCarey

T HE seasonal anthology film has had a close relationship with festive cinema right from the inception of
the genre, with films such as *Holiday Inn* (Mark Sandrich, 1942) and *Meet Me in St Louis* (q.v.) being considered
virtually synonymous with Christmas even though their engagement with the holiday season is actually often comparatively brief. *The Bells of St Mary's* may thus seem like a
slightly contentious choice of film to regard as an exemplar of
the Christmas movie genre. Although it has come to be comfortably embedded within this category of film over the years,
and indeed is now one of the most regularly-cited Christmas
features of the period immediately following the Second
World War, on first glance the film actually appears to spend
very little time focusing its action upon the festive season itself. However, with its prominent messages of faith and
goodwill, *The Bells of St Mary's* was to present the viewer
with many of the themes which have subsequently come to be
associated with the pantheon of Christmas films in general.

Nor indeed should we allow the film's somewhat fleeting dalliance with the festive season to distract us from its underlying purpose: when Ebenezer Scrooge promises at the end of *A Christmas Carol* that he promises to keep Christmas in his heart the whole of the year round, he could have done far worse than to look to *The Bells of St Mary's* for a blueprint of how he might achieve that ambition.

The film, in its depiction of organised religion, actually proves to be something of a peculiarity in the broader canon of Christmas films. On the face of it, this may seem like an unusual fact given the historical and spiritual origins of Christmas celebrations. Although later features would occasionally dip into traditional religious iconography, calling upon elements ranging from angels to the Virgin Birth, *The Bells of St Mary's* centres firmly upon people of faith and the manner in which their belief in a supreme being can bring about events which would otherwise seem impossible. While many other subsequent Christmas films would draw upon the vital importance of having faith in one's fellow human being, few others – even during this period which preceded multi-faith (and now secularist) society – were to deal with the perceived significance of religious belief in a higher power quite so directly. This interesting clash between the spiritual and the practical would later be explored by Henry Koster in *The Bishop's Wife* (q.v.), and of course George More O'Ferrall's *The Holly and the Ivy* (q.v.), albeit in very different ways.

The Bells of St Mary's was directed by long-time industry veteran Leo McCarey, who also acted as producer as well as providing the storyline for the film's screenplay. McCarey had been active as a director since 1921, having helmed a wide variety of features including *Let's Go Native* (1930), *The Awful Truth* (1937), *Make Way for Tomorrow* (1937) and *Love*

Affair (1939). Throughout his distinguished career, he had worked with such legends of early Hollywood as Laurel and Hardy, Mae West and Eddie Cantor, in addition to directing one of the Marx Brothers' best-known films, *Duck Soup* (1933) and Harold Lloyd's famous boxing-themed comedy *The Milky Way* (1936). His characteristic blend of subtle, under-stated comedy and sentimental human observation was argua-bly to reach its apex with *Going My Way* (1944), the film which was to introduce audiences to the popular character of Father Charles 'Chuck' O'Malley as portrayed to great ac-claim by Bing Crosby. The plot centred upon the arrival of O'Malley at the parish of St Dominic's, where he energetical-ly attempts to modernise the church's appeal to the wider neighbourhood in order to better serve the com-munity in which it is based. The film was a huge hit at the box-office and did exceptionally well with critics, going on to win seven Academy Awards (including Best Picture, Best Director and Best Actor) and being nominated for a further three.[1] The massive suc-cess of *Going My Way* would lead to a much-anticipated sequel the following year – a pro-duction which was to reunite McCarey and

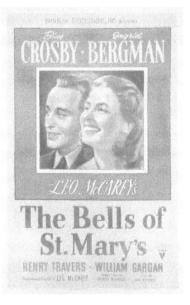

The Bells of St Mary's (1945): Rainbow Productions

Crosby: *The Bells of St Mary's*. As J.P. Roscoe has explained: 'There is no need to see *Going My Way* to enjoy this film, and the movie was actually planned to be the first film with Father Chuck O'Malley. The film is often considered a holiday film, but the only Christmas reference is a segment that has the children performing a Nativity play. With this and the spiritual aspect of the characters, I guess it could be considered a Christmas film, but you don't have to wait until Christmas to watch it'.[2]

Father Charles O'Malley (Bing Crosby) has been assigned by the church to support the nuns who administrate a ramshackle inner-city parochial school named St Mary's. The building is dilapidated and, in spite of recent emergency structural repairs, is heading towards dereliction. O'Malley learns that the children face a cross-town journey to another educational establishment if St Mary's is condemned, though the sisters of the school – led by the devoted Sister Mary Benedict (Ingrid Bergman) – are adamant that the power of prayer will solve their problems. His brief is to advocate whether St Mary's still has the ability to function as a working school building, or whether the church's responsibility instead lies with closing it down and moving the children to a better-equipped learning facility.

A modern office building is being constructed next to the school, on the playing fields which have had to be sold in order to fund the repairs to St Mary's. Sister Benedict believes that they must all put their trust in God to persuade the new building's owner, curmudgeonly businessman Horace P. Bogardus (Henry Travers), to donate the office block to the church so that it can be used as a new school with modern facilities. However, she greatly underestimates Bogardus's stubbornness: the crotchety mogul is determined to buy the crumbling St Mary's itself for a token sum so that he can demolish it and turn the area into a car park for his new workforce. If the church refuses to sell the school, Bogardus is fully prepared to use his influence with the city's planning council to close it down compulsorily.

As the film progresses, the viewer follows Father O'Malley and Sister Benedict through a year of trials and tribulations at St Mary's. In that time, the staid Sister Benedict must instruct one of her bullied young students in the noble art of boxing, and Father O'Malley manages to repair the ailing marriage of estranged couple Joe and Mary Gallagher (William Gargan and Martha Sleeper) while helping to buoy the damaged self-confidence of their daughter Patsy (Joan Carroll). The school staff even manage to squeeze in a heavily improvised Nativity play in December, enacted by the infant members of St Mary's, which culminates in a rousing rendition of 'Happy Birthday to You' as the baby Jesus makes His way into the world.

While O'Malley's influence has an immediate and positive impact on the students, he often finds himself at odds with Sister Mary Benedict with regard to teaching methods and general issues of administration. This kicks off when, as his first duty as the school's *de facto* headteacher, he declares that the children are on holiday for the day. He believes that this will make an instant impression on the student body, while Mary Benedict sees only the complications this will cause given the unplanned nature of the decision, the school's duty of care to the children in their charge, and so on. As the year progresses, they remain at odds on many subjects, but their shared professional respect is such that they are able to overcome their disagreements amicably while still acknowledging that they tend not to see eye-to-eye.

As the end-of-term graduation nears, time is beginning to run out for St Mary's. O'Malley attempts to talk Bogardus into giving St Mary's a reprieve, but the older man simply won't accommodate the idea. However, upon later discovering that the business leader is suffering from a heart complaint, O'Malley succeeds in convincing Bogardus's doctor (and, eventually, Bogardus himself) that by performing selfless deeds he has the potential to improve his physical wellbeing as well as his spiritual welfare. This message takes a while to filter through to Bogardus, but eventually he begins to consider O'Malley's instruction more seriously. After a period of prayer at his local chapel, Bogardus takes into account the many benefits that his new building could bring to the children who attend St Mary's. He tells Sister Benedict that – in spite of the considerable cost of the office block's construction – he has decided to donate it to the church in order to allow the students to have access to modern facilities. The sisters are overjoyed that their prayers have been answered, just in the nick of time.

While the new school is outfitted with up-to-the-minute equipment, Dr McKay (Rhys Williams) informs O'Malley that he has discovered during a routine chest X-ray that Sister Benedict is suffering from the early stages of tuberculosis. He implores O'Malley to keep the news from Sister Benedict herself, in the hope that her generally optimistic outlook will speed a recovery if she is unaware of the potential seriousness of her condition. O'Malley arranges with the church to transfer her across the country to a warmer, drier climate in the expectation that her health will improve as a result of the more favourable environment, but Sister Benedict is devastated by the news that she will no longer be able to head up the new St Mary's building when it opens for the first time. She initially believes that O'Malley has recommended her removal, given their constant disagreement over so many issues during their time working together, and although she leaves her post without complaint she is distraught at having to do so. Just as she is set to depart the premises, however, O'Malley finds that he is unable to let her go without a frank explanation of her situation, and relates the circumstances more fully. Now seeing the full picture, Sister Benedict is elated – not only does she realise that there is no bad blood between O'Malley and herself, but there is also a real possibility that she can return to St Mary's once the condition of her health picks up. Satisfied with the direction of her life once more, she leaves the school willingly and contentedly.

The Bells of St Mary's presents a disarmingly idealised depiction of contemporary life, where it seems that all problems can be overcome with little more than a kind heart and unwavering faith in a higher authority. Any naïveté that this may imply to modern eyes must be considered in the context of the general moral climate of the time. As Bruce Babington and Peter William Evans have observed, the effectiveness by which the film achieves its aims can be seen to lie in the fact that no matter how lofty the issue of spirituality may seem, the characters' goals are inevitably practical and functional, benefiting ordinary people and working to the advantage of the community at large:

The Bells of St Mary's [is] the film that, beyond any specificities of sectarianism, most speaks for a populist American religious optimism. [...] As Father O'Malley, Bing Crosby acts out a secularisation of religious impulses into mundane sentiments touched with a faint religious numinousness

– life lived (as his jaunty straw boater affirms) with a practical, but not wholly unidealistic, ease, summoning up all the vaguer pelagian securities without religion's more stringent demands. [...] Equally, the problems solved by O'Malley and Sister Mary are ultimately secular, not those of an estranging realm of the religious but concerned with the preservation of a charitable capitalism (re-achieved in the *Christmas Carol* 'conversion' of the Scrooge-like Bogardis [sic]) and the restoration of the family (O'Malley's search for and re-domesticising of Mrs Gallagher's wandering husband and his rescuing her from prostitution).[3]

It is testament to McCarey's breezy direction that the film does not linger overduly upon incidents which, though unashamedly sentimental, always stop short of having a quality of out-and-out saccharine. While the requisite bullying and needling takes place between the schoolkids of St Mary's from time to time, everyone always somehow manages to achieve rapprochement in the end with their heads held high. This, of course, is similarly true of the administrative discord which brews between O'Malley and Mary Benedict, as Sanderson Beck notes: 'This spiritual drama reflects the difficulties of religious schools in the modern world but suggests that miracles of human charity are still possible. The priest and the sister superior found that they could disagree and still respect each other.'[4] Thus the gentle yet meaningful differences of opinion between the earnest but demure Sister Mary Benedict and the progressive, cheery Father O'Malley are fully resolved by the film's conclusion, where the best of all possible resolutions has been established.

Horace Bogardus, the hardest of hard-nosed business-men, has no time for the intrinsic value that the sisters of St Mary's place on their school, and yet is somehow able to be talked around by a combination of divine intervention and O'Malley's smooth-talking. In this respect, his transformation from uncaring mogul to altruistic benefactor is very much in keeping with the central tropes of festive cinema, as this theme of personal rehabilitation during, and as a result of, Christmas (first popularised, of course, in Charles Dickens's novella *A Christmas Carol* in 1843) would be revisited per-haps more than any other in the decades that followed. While the film's yuletide credentials have sometimes been questioned by more sceptical commentators, there is little denying the fact that the hopeful optimism of *The Bells of St Mary's* would situate it quite comfortably within the wider auspices of the Christmas film genre. As Jeffrey Kauffman has explained, 'the 1945 Leo McCarey opus *The Bells of St Mary's* really isn't even that "Christmasy", though it was originally released in December and contains a sweetly nostalgic and humorous Christmas Pageant done by some cute kids in an urban paro-chial school which is overseen by Father O'Malley. [...] *The Bells of St. Mary's* is a simple, heartfelt paean to a simpler time, when the United States was just emerging from the depths of World War II, the lines between good and evil were clearly drawn, and there was an inherent hope for a brighter, more peaceful, future'.[5]

It is easy to see why *The Bells of St Mary's* became so popular with the audiences of the time. The film's cheerful, buoyant sense of moral conviction must have seemed particu-larly welcome to cinemagoers after the intense dramas and propaganda features which had populated theatres during the war years. Although its actual Christmas content extends only so far as the brief, aforementioned sequence where the school's infants enact a (somewhat radically adapted) stage version of the Nativity, the film's December release in cinemas did seem particularly appropriate. This is a feature which exudes goodwill and mutual understanding, such that it transcends its underlying message of the power of religious faith to extend into a rather more broadly-encompassing narrative which centres on considering the common good over one's own personal goals. Though the film is not entirely without concession to material needs alongside the spiritual, this materialism is largely passive in nature. The desire for a new school building, for instance, not only saves the children from a long journey to another educational facility elsewhere in the city, but also retains the sisters' sense of purpose and pride in their instructive and developmental roles. (It is also strongly hinted that Bogardus is more than rich enough to avoid financial ruin by donating his prized office block – and, indeed, he receives a valuable trade-off in the greater feeling of self-worth and generosity of spirit that his noble benevolence achieves.) In this regard, as Bill Weber clarifies, McCarey observes a particular kind of cultural and spiritual perspective that was specific to the age of the production: 'Aside from his slapstick interludes with cats and a dog that recall his roots in silent comedy, and a sweetly humble Christmas pageant staged with six-year-olds delivering lines with natural hesitation, McCarey made the film as a tribute to Sister Benedict's namesake, an aunt who died of typhoid. It's certainly a time capsule of a mid-century, masculine Irish Catholic worldview, as when Benedict secretly coaches a bullied boy on dispatching his rival in a fistfight after studying up on "pugilistics"'.[6]

A slightly more contentious issue is that of Father O'Malley's proactive behaviour in reconciling Joe and Mary

Gallagher. Although separated from his wife for many years (though not actually divorced), O'Malley tracks down wayward musician Joe who eventually recognises the need to reconcile with his estranged spouse and start afresh. O'Malley's actions are in part motivated by a desire to recreate a stable home life for the couple's daughter, Patsy: a bright student whose intense emotional turbulence is causing her to fail at school. The importance of the family unit is a perennial theme that would be emphasised by many later Christmas films, but rarely is its significance quite so profoundly indicated as it is throughout *The Bells of St Mary's*. However, credibility is stretched to near breaking point by the way in which the couple instantly reintegrate into each other's lives, striking up a largely-effortless reconciliation in spite of being separated for so long that their daughter doesn't even recognise her father. Yet this in turn provides additional drama when the sensitive Patsy – who, through a misunderstanding, believes that her mother is seeing another man – is thrown into such turmoil that she fails her end-of-year exams. Patsy's poor performance in class leads to a standoff between Sister Benedict, who believes that qualificational standards must be maintained at all costs, and Father O'Malley, who suggests that perhaps bending the rules might be admissible in order to avoid the ruinous effect on Patsy's self-esteem if she isn't somehow allowed a decent chance at passing the final paper. That both characters' views seem so reasonable is laudable even though, in the serendipitous tradition of the rest of the film, a mutually-agreeable resolution is eventually arrived at.

McCarey makes full use of his star cast, with Bing Crosby, Ingrid Bergman and Henry Travers all delivering excellent performances. Crosby was of course a highly successful performer by the mid-1940s, his vocal talents and likeable acting style ensuring that he quickly became well-known for his appearances in popular musical features including *Pennies from Heaven* (Norman Z. McLeod, 1936), *Rhythm on the River* (Victor Schertzinger, 1940) and of course Mark Sandrich's festive *Holiday Inn* (1942), as well as appearances in the hugely successful *The Road To* film series (1940-62) where he appeared alongside Bob Hope and Dorothy Lamour, and his aforementioned, Oscar-winning role in McCarey's *Going My Way* in 1944. Crosby's performance as Chuck O'Malley allows ample opportunity to display his renowned aptitude for singing throughout the course of the film, though this was no mere attempt to harness his vocal talents to fulfil the purposes of a cinematic star vehicle; as Kristine Butler Carlson has observed, music was of vital importance to the film: 'Song in *The Bells of St Mary's*, from singing the old school song to intoning a Christmas hymn, is equated with the artless joy of living and with a simple, somewhat nostalgic unfailing Christian faith in the future'.[7] In this sense, O'Malley fulfils his leadership role admirably in encouraging song throughout the course of the movie – both on his own and occasionally in concert with others – which reflects the priest's propagation of traditional faith values for the benefit of those in his charge and the wider community beyond the confines of the school. Crosby's effortless charm in the role of O'Malley works well in emphasising the understated on-screen chemistry he shares with Ingrid Bergman's Sister Mary Benedict. Bergman, who had appeared in films in her native Sweden from 1932, shot to fame in Gustaf Molander's *Intermezzo* (1936), later remade by Gregory Ratoff in 1939 as *Intermezzo: A Love Story*. Although she had enjoyed great success for performances in films as diverse as *For Whom the Bell Tolls* (Sam Wood, 1943), *Gaslight* (George Cukor, 1944) and

Spellbound (Alfred Hitchcock, 1945), it is almost certainly her appearance as Ilsa Lund in Michael Curtiz's *Casablanca* (1942) that had gained her a full measure of cinematic immortality. In *The Bells of St Mary's*, Bergman creates a multifaceted character which belies Sister Benedict's prim and slightly stolid exterior; whether teaching a bullied student the subtleties of boxing or reviving her youthful passion for baseball, the viewer is left in little doubt that this nun is a character who seeks to embrace society and improve the lives of others in practical and positive ways, rather than simply aiming to shy away from a rapidly-changing world that lies outside her cloistered existence.

Bergman and Crosby create a fascinating on-screen duo, a pairing made all the more interesting by the fact that – due to their characters' devout religious faith – there is never any clichéd reliance on romantic tension, but rather the development of a professional friendship which, in spite of their frequent differences of opinion, endures the ups and downs of their demanding situation. However, as Nick Zegarac has explained, the firm grounding of the two characters' chaste religious principles gave Crosby and Bergman the opportunity for some light-heartedness during filming: 'During production, the Catholic League of Decency sent a representative to ensure that the due austerity of religion was preserved. Although McCarey assured a sterling adherence to those guidelines, Crosby and Bergman decided to have some fun with the representative. During the final moment in the film, in which Sister Benedict forgives Father O'Malley, Crosby and Bergman suddenly embraced in an unscripted passionate kiss, sending the representative into a momentary tizzy'.[8]

The film's central roles are well supported by a talented cast of supporting actors, including Ruth Donnelly as a quietly refined Sister Michael and Rhys Williams as the jocular Dr McKay, but particular praise is due for Henry Travers as the oft-bewildered Horace Bogardus. A British-born character actor who had been active in film since 1933, usually playing amiable or eccentric parts in films such as *Wyoming* (Richard Thorpe, 1940), *High Sierra* (Raoul Walsh, 1941) and perhaps most notably William Wyler's *Mrs Miniver* (1942), Travers brings dignity and more than a touch of humour to Bogardus, managing to make his improbable transformation of character appear as plausible as the narrative will allow. Evolving from a pitiless industrialist into a slightly baffled philanthropist throughout the course of the film, the dextrous Travers works hard to imbue Bogardus with a credible internal motivation as the befuddled businessman tries to rationalise the unconventional logic that O'Malley sets loose upon him. Yet of course, Travers's role as Bogardus was not by any means his most prominent performance in a Christmas film, for only a year later he would make his famous appearance (almost certainly the best-known of his career) as the affable angel Clarence Odbody in Frank Capra's *It's a Wonderful Life*.

The Bells of St Mary's was a smash hit at the box-office, eventually becoming the highest-grossing film of 1945 and – has been widely noted – the most profitable feature in the history of RKO Pictures, the studio which distributed the film. Its huge commercial success was reflected in its performance at awards ceremonies. Although it failed to replicate the massive achievement of *Going My Way* at the Academy Awards, the film nonetheless received an impressive seven nominations for Oscars (including Best Actor in a Leading Role, Best Actress in a Leading Role, Best Director and Best Picture), and won an award for Best Sound Recording. The film also won a Gold Medal at the 1946 Photoplay Awards, while Ingrid Bergman's performance as Sister Mary Benedict earned her a Golden Globe Award and a New York Film Critics Circle Award in the same year. The film has contin-ued to prove popular with reviewers, with many citing its unremitting positivity and faith in the goodness of the human spirit as its most appealing characteristics. John Sinnott, for instance, praises the guileless charm of *The Bells of St Mary's*, noting that 'directed by the immensely talented Leo McCarey (the man who told Stan Laurel and Oliver Hardy that they should team up) [[...]] the film has many memorable moments, from Sister Benedict teaching a boy to fight to Patsy's paper on "The Six Senses" but the one that's most enjoyable is the Christmas play that the 1st graders put on. They wrote it themselves, and though they change it every time they prac-tice, it's priceless'.[9] Others, such as Jeffrey M. Anderson, have compared it less favourably with its illustrious predecessor but acknowledges its undeniable success with the audiences of the time:

Overall, this odd sequel is less balanced and streamlined than its predecessor, and seems a bit less planned out. It has the same balance of humor and hokum that drove the first film, and yet it all still works. [...] The movie's biggest asset is no doubt McCarey's skill, which seems at once easy-going and high-pitched, funny and maudlin, goopy and streamlined. He was as skilled as [Frank] Cap-ra was at turning in this kind of laugh-cry crowd-pleaser, and he did it, I think, with a lightness of heart and an overall focus on the comedy to draw people in and lower their defenses, put them at ease. Though the various irregular pieces of this movie make it one of McCarey's least satisfying movies on an artistic level, it's totally understandable as to why it's his most popular.[10]

Of course, the secular world we live in today is quite different from the cultural environment of the mid-1940s, and as such various critics have noted aspects of *The Bells of St Mary's* which have dated badly as a result of changing attitudes. Kauffman, for instance, discerns that: 'What may strike some modern day cynics as at least a little eyebrow raising is how decidedly dated and maybe even politically incorrect the film is at times. [...] There's a Priest pretty much congratulating one little boy for beating up another one (telling Sister Mary Benedict "it's a man's world out there" in the process – yikes!), while a nun then goes on to promote bodily harm as the story progresses. One of course has to view these plot points through the prism of 1945 society'.[11] Similarly, the film's enthusiastic endorsement of spiritual beliefs and religious instruction – while very much in keeping with the society of its production – have put it at variance with the material rationalism so prevalent in the present day. This has led some critics, such as José Arroyo, to opine that the film has lost relevance to the modern world of the 21st century: 'How is *The Bells of St Mary's* in any way acceptable? It's false through and through and offensively so: hip priests and cute nuns, pretending to be all self-sacrificing and cheerful, solving all the world's problems, manipulating everyone with prayer, conning an old man out of his building. [...] Yes, there's Ingrid Bergman, gloriously radiant, enraptured in a halo of faith that is beautiful to see; Bing sings skilfully in that marvellous baritone of his; McCarey is great at staging the comedy in a low key, famously improvised manner; the actors are excellent; but excellent in the service of what?'[12] Ultimately, however, the film's good-natured approach to its subject matter and the unrelenting exuberance of its premise have continued to win it fans even now, even among those who have identified aspects of it which have since become outmoded. Brian Koller perfectly sums up this viewpoint with his observation that 'it is a family movie made to warm the hearts of its viewers. The good news is that it does so with such skill that even the occasional cold-hearted critic that takes a swipe at it has to admit that it is a pretty good film at that'.[13] Indeed, the light-heartedness of McCarey's methodology is key to the film's success, ensuring that – even as an exponent of social attitudes which now seem less applicable to the mainstream of everyday experience – it still retains charm and appeal both as a period piece and as a Christmas film. As Nathan Rabin sagely comments:

To its credit, *The Bells of St Mary's* seems to view its plot as a minor distraction it's happy to work around. For a blockbuster starring two of the biggest movie stars in the world, *The Bells of St Mary's* is shockingly, consistently low-key. McCarey and his cast and crew are never afraid to take their time and let scenes meander at a leisurely pace. [...] *The Bells of St Mary's* hearkens back to a more innocent era, where the inspirational-priest movie wasn't just a palatable subgenre, but a massive commercial force. It'd be impossible to imagine a film like *The Bells of St Mary's* being made today, both because popular conceptions of priesthood have changed so dramatically, and because we lack a famously public Catholic like Crosby to make all that stern, unyielding morality go down smoothly – with a wink, a smile, and a catchy song.[14]

The movie's enduring resonance with audiences at the time of its release led Crosby and Bergman to reprise their roles for two separate radio adaptations of *The Bells of St Mary's*. Both were broadcast as part of The Screen Guild Theater radio programme, with airdates of 26 August 1946 and 6 October 1947 respectively. (Bing Crosby had earlier performed as Father O'Malley, along with Barry Fitzgerald and Paul Lukas, in an adaptation of *Going My Way* which was similarly broadcast on radio under The Screen Guild Theater banner on 8 January 1945.) Additionally, a television remake of *The Bells of St Mary's* was produced by CBS in 1959; directed by Tom Donovan, it starred Robert Preston as Father O'Malley, Claudette Colbert as Sister Benedict, and Charles Ruggles as Horace Bogardus. Later still, author George Victor Martin adapted the screenplay into a novel in 1966, published by New York's Bantam Books.

Although *The Bells of St Mary's* featured a number of songs, the rendition of the title song has become far and away the best-known. Composed by A. Emmett Adams with lyrics by Douglas Furber, it was first published in 1917 but became greatly popularised by the success of the McCarey's film. It has since been re-recorded many times by artists as diverse as Perry Como, The Drifters, Andy Williams, Connie Francis, Vera Lynn, Jimmy Preston and Sheryl Crow. Additionally, Crosby was to record no less than four songs from the film as singles which were released by Decca Records and later compiled onto a double-record 78rpm album entitled *Selections from the Bells of St Mary's* (1946). The songs which featured on the compilation were 'Aren't You Glad You're You?', 'In the Land of Beginning Again', 'The Bells of St Mary's' and 'I'll Take You Home Again, Kathleen'. The album was released as an LP in 1949.

At one memorable point in *The Bells of St Mary's*, Father O'Malley makes mention of the generosity of spirit that comes uniquely from Christmas, and indeed the film's rapid succession through that one particular period in the school's long life shows clearly how McCarey is suggesting that the values and goodwill of the festive season can be applied to wider existence outside of a single week in December. As mentioned earlier, the film has remained among the most overtly spiritual of films associated with Christmas, its status challenged only perhaps by Henry Koster's *The Bishop's Wife* (q.v.) or a handful of later features such as *The Juggler of Notre Dame* (Milton H. Lehr, 1970) and *The Nativity Story* (Catherine Hardwicke, 2006). Yet for a film about religious faith, its approach somehow manages to be just secular enough in application to satisfy mainstream tastes. Indeed, so wide-ranging is the human scope of McCarey's canvas that we are left in no doubt that irrespective of the viewer's own religious beliefs (or even lack of them), this film articulates with unwavering precision the director's message that every member of society carries within themselves the capacity to improve the lives of others; irrespective of the scale of these efforts, we are clearly shown that all individuals are significant in their own way and always have the potential to encourage the most profound of personal transformations. As we will see, however, *The Bells of St Mary's* would be far from the last or the most prominent Christmas film of the 1940s to deal with such a far-reaching theme of self-improvement.

REFERENCES

1. Anthony Burke Smith, 'America's Favorite Priest: *Going My Way* (1944)' in *Catholics in the Movies*, ed. by Colleen McDannell (New York: Oxford University Press US, 2008), pp.107-126.

2. J.P. Roscoe, '*The Bells of St Mary's*', in *Basement Rejects*, 29 November 2012.
   <*http://basementrejects.com/review/the-bells-of-st-marys-1945/*>

3. Bruce Babington and Peter William Evans, 'Theorising the Biblical Epic', in *Biblical Epics: Sacred Narrative in the Hollywood Cinema* (Manchester: Manchester University Press, 1993), 1-24, pp.18-20.

4. Sanderson Beck, '*The Bells of St Mary's*', in *Movie Mirrors*, 2005.
   <*http://san.beck.org/MM/1945/BellsofStMarys.html*>

5. Jeffrey Kauffman, '*The Bells of St Mary's* Blu-ray Review: Going Their Way', in *Blu-ray.com*, 19 November 2013.
   <*https://www.blu-ray.com/movies/The-Bells-of-St-Marys-Blu-ray/84798/#Review*>

6. Bill Weber, 'Blu-Ray Review: *The Bells of St Mary's*', in *Slant Magazine*, 18 November 2013.
   <*https://www.slantmagazine.com/dvd/the-bells-of-st-marys/*>

7. Kristine Butler Carlson, '1945: Movies and the March Home', in *American Cinema of the 1940s: Themes and Vari-*

ations, ed. by Wheeler Winston Dixon (Piscataway: Rutgers University Press, 2006), 140-61, pp.158-60.

8.   Nick Zegarac, 'Classic Holiday DVDs', in *DVD Beaver*, 23 September 2003.
      <*http://www.dvdbeaver.com/film/DVDReviews19/holida y_dvds.htm*>

9.   John Sinnott, '*Bells of St Mary's*', in *DVD Talk*, 19 November 2013.
      <*https://www.dvdtalk.com/reviews/62052/bells-of-st-marys/*>

10.   Jeffrey M. Anderson, '*The Bells of St Mary's*', in *Combustible Celluloid*, 19 November 2013.
      <*http://www.combustiblecelluloid.com/classic/bellsmarys.s html*>

11.   Kauffman.

12.   José Arroyo, '*The Bells of St Mary's*', in *First Impressions*, 15 July 2015.
      <*https://notesonfilm1.com/2015/07/15/the-bells-of-st-marys-leo-mccarey-usa-1945/*>

13.   Brian Koller, '*The Bells of St Mary's*', in *FilmsGraded.com*, 21 April 2008.
      <*http://www.filmsgraded.com/reviews/2008/04/bellso. htm*>

14.   Nathan Rabin, '*The Bells of St Mary's*', in *The Dissolve*, 19 November 2013.
      <*http://thedissolve.com/reviews/381-the-bells-of-st-marys/*>

5

It's a Wonderful Life (1946)

Liberty Films

Director: Frank Capra
Producer: Frank Capra
Screenwriters: Frank Capra, Frances Goodrich and Albert
Hackett, with additional scenes by Jo Swerling,
from a story by Philip Van Doren Stern

ALMOST certainly the most recognisable of all modern Christmas stories, *It's a Wonderful Life* has become a true classic of cinema – a motion picture which has genuinely stood the test of time, not just at Christmas but at all times of the year. Faithfully screened every festive season around the world, it has come to epitomise everything that is heart-warming and meaningful about the Christmas spirit, and all that is positive and life-affirming about small town America. And yet it is indisputably true to say that *It's a Wonderful Life* has become much more than simply a festive cinematic favourite. Beloved of academics and media commentators for decades, Frank Capra's complex narrative and multiple layers of subtext have ensured that the movie has become one of the most thoroughly discussed American films of the post-war period.

In many ways, *It's a Wonderful Life* has become the quintessential Christmas film. Its enduring popularity over the years is testament to the universal nature of its key themes and its evocation of the positive effects of community spirit and human kindness. Although it faced a relatively lukewarm critical and commercial reception on its initial release in 1946, the film has now come to be regarded as an all-time classic ever since its unexpected revival on television networks throughout the 1970s. Yet as Frank Thompson has observed, its enduring appeal was far from certain during its mid-forties run in cinemas: '*It's a Wonderful Life* was a resounding flop, and Capra's career never fully recovered. [...] But in the early seventies, a strange phenomenon occurred. New generations discovered the delights of *It's a Wonderful Life* through repeated television broadcasts. The film had slipped into the abyss of the public domain; television stations played it endlessly without having to pay a licence fee, and in the eighties the picture became available from a dozen different home video distributors. *It's a Wonderful Life* became a national treasure, and Capra, in his old age, was toasted by film students and movie buffs'.[1] Released repeatedly on VHS video, DVD and now Blu-Ray, including a number of attempts to colourise the film (with varying degrees of success), *It's a Wonderful Life* has now entered into the public consciousness so profoundly that for generations it has become synonymous with Christmas at the movies. So ubiquitous is its presence that, as James Berardinelli and so many others have noted, 'every year around Christmas, there are two stories guaranteed to show up somewhere, sometime on television: *A Christmas Carol* (of which there are several good versions) and *It's a Wonderful Life* (of which there is only one). [...] In fact, it was the expiration of *It's a Wonderful Life*'s copyright that transformed it into a Christmas staple. Once the film began showing with such frequency during the month of December, a whole new generation of movie-lovers discovered (and fell in love with) the previously-obscure release'.[2]

It's a Wonderful Life marked an interesting point in the careers of both its director, Frank Capra, and its star James Stewart. For the multiple Academy Award winner Capra, the film's lack of pulling power at the box-office dealt his career an unfortunate blow, meaning that he was never again to reach the dizzying heights of his earlier successes with acclaimed films such as *It Happened One Night* (1934), *Mr Deeds Goes to Town* (1936), *You Can't Take It With You* (1939), *Mr Smith Goes to Washington* (1939) and *Arsenic and Old Lace* (1944). (Capra filmed *Arsenic and Old Lace* in 1941, but it would not be released until the play upon which the film was based had completed its Broadway run three years later. By the time of its eventual appearance in cinemas, Capra was serving as an officer in the US Army Signal Corps where he was stationed throughout America's involvement in World War II.) Yet it must be emphasised that *It's a Wonderful Life* was not the dismal failure that urban myth has come to suggest: while it did record a substantial loss for RKO Pictures – its commercial performance falling short of breaking even at the box-office against strong competition in 1946 – it is difficult to reconcile any tales of a universal critical panning with the fact that *It's a Wonderful Life* won Capra a Golden Globe for Best Director in 1947, and the same year was to see the film being nominated for five Academy Awards in prominent categories (including Best Picture, Best Director, Best Actor in a Leading Role, Best Sound Recording and Best Film Editing). One of these nominations, the Best Actor Award, was reserved for James Stewart, and though he did not win in

It's a Wonderful Life (1946):
Liberty Films

the 1947 Awards (he had earlier been the recipient of an Oscar for his part in George Cukor's acclaimed 1940 drama *The Philadelphia Story*), the role had been among his best-regarded since his appearance in *It's a Wonderful World* (W.S. Van Dyke II, 1939) and his earlier pre-War collaborations with Capra, most notably in the title role of *Mr Smith Goes to Washington*. Prior to his wartime service, Stewart had risen through a variety of supporting and leading roles from the early thirties to become one of the pre-eminent acting talents in Hollywood, and following his remarkable performance in *It's a Wonderful Life* he cemented a post-war return to acting with great aplomb, paving the way for a glittering future career that would see him headlining several prominent Westerns, occupying the starring role in a number of Alfred Hitchcock's best-regarded thrillers, and – perhaps most memorably – appearing as the lovable eccentric Elwood P. Dowd in Henry Koster's *Harvey* (1950), an adaptation of Mary Chase's Pulitzer Prize-winning play. Yet *It's a Wonderful Life* has continued to be praised as one of Stewart's career-defining roles not simply on account of the undeniable quality of his acting, but also due to the fact that with George Bailey

he brought to life one of the great defining everyman characters of post-war American cinema. As *Urban Cinefile* has so
sagaciously considered the performance:

> Stewart, a national hero after aerial combat duty
> in WW2, is perfectly cast as the everyman who
> stays in the small town he wants to leave but never
> can while there are good folks who need help and
> injustices to be fought. The magic ingredient of the
> drama is not George Bailey's kindness but the dark
> side of his character. He's shown to be angry and
> even violently frustrated at being stuck in a Noth-
> ingsville like Bedford Falls. It's what makes him
> human and makes us in believe in everything the
> film champions – the value of the individual and
> the strength of community ties. [...] A film is only
> as old as it seems and *It's A Wonderful Life* trans-
> cends the times because it believes in all the good-
> hearted dreamers before and after George Bailey.[3]

The inspired plot of *It's a Wonderful Life* has long
since passed into the annals of cinematic legend. In the small
American town of Bedford Falls on the Christmas Eve of
1945, the family of George Bailey are praying for him, sensing
that he is upset and in a turbulent state of mind. In the heav-
ens, senior angels hear the prayers that have been offered up
and decide to despatch Clarence Odbody (Angel, Second
Class) to visit Earth and convince George that his life is
worth living. If Clarence is successful, not only will he have
saved George and answered his family's prayers, but he will
also have earned his angel wings in the process.

Through the briefing which Clarence (Henry Travers)
receives prior to his arrival on Earth, we are led through the

life of George Bailey (James Stewart) from his youth until the present day. Starting in a wintry 1919, where young George (Bobbie Anderson) saves the life of his little brother Harry (Georgie Nokes) who is drowning in an icy pond – even though George subsequently becomes deaf in one ear due to a resulting infection – we see the beginning of a life of sacrifice which is endured for the benefit of other people. After returning to his part-time job as a delivery boy at the town drugstore, George discovers that pharmacist Mr Gower (H.B. Warner), racked with grief and remorse over the recent death of his son from flu, has accidentally given a sick child the wrong prescription. In so doing, he saves Gower from a potential manslaughter charge.

George graduates from high school in 1928 and regales an admirer, his childhood sweetheart Mary Hatch (Donna Reed), with his dreams of travelling widely and becoming an architect, designing structures all over the country. However, his ambitious plans are derailed by the impact of other events which are closer to home. He decides to assist with the family business, Bailey Building and Loan, until Harry (Todd Karns) has completed high school, following which George will be able to belatedly attend college to gain his required qualifications. However, nobody foresees the sudden stroke that is later suffered by his father, which leaves George unexpectedly in charge of the building and loan company – an act of altruism made all the more necessary by the scheming of local financier and property developer Mr Potter (Lionel Barrymore), who is determined to persuade the organisation's board of directors that their provision of home loans for low-income earners is financial folly.

George decides to gift the savings he had put aside for his education to his brother Harry, so that at least one of them can attend college. However, his belief that Harry will take over the reins of the building and loan company following his graduation – thus allowing George a late opportunity at further education – is sunk when Harry returns with a new wife, and the news that his father-in-law has offered him a good post in his business. George is disappointed that his ambitions have once again been curtailed, but doesn't have the heart to persuade Harry to turn down the offer of employment because he knows that his brother's future prosperity will likely rest upon it. George resignedly begins to realise that his own fate is unavoidably intertwined with that of his building and loan business.

Marrying Mary, George and his new bride are in the process of leaving town to go on honeymoon when there is an entirely unanticipated run on the town's bank, which leaves the building and loan company teetering on the brink. In order to ward off Potter's attempts to extort money from those who can least afford it through crippling loans, George agrees with Mary to use their $2,000 honeymoon fund to lend the people of Bedford Falls the money they need to get by. The crisis thus passes with the building and loan company still intact, but Potter is infuriated that George's self-sacrifice has once again won the day. He is no happier with George's later formation of the Bailey Park housing project, which entices residents away from the chronically high rate of rent they had to pay in order to live in Potter's properties. Desperately trying to disrupt George's plans, Potter offers him a job with a drastically higher salary. However, George firmly declines Potter's proposal, remaining contemptuous of the older man's obvious derision towards the people of the town. Profit may be the only thing motivating the malign Potter, but George has demonstrated time and again that he recognises the importance of social responsibility.

Years later, the Second World War breaks out. George, who now has a family with Mary, is unable to enlist in the war effort on account of being hard of hearing following his childhood rescue of Harry. He has no choice but to remain in Bedford Falls as an air raid warden while Harry serves his country with distinction, becoming a fighter pilot in the U.S. Air Force. His bravery is recognised by the government, and Harry is awarded the Medal of Honor for his military service. Back in Bedford Falls, George and Harry's jovial Uncle Billy (Thomas Mitchell) is on his way to the bank on Christmas Eve with savings from the building and loan when he meets Potter. Full of pride and satisfaction that his nephew's courage in the defence of the United States is to be recognised by the authorities, Billy shows Potter a newspaper article outlining Harry's achievements, but is so caught up in the moment that he accidentally misplaces the $8,000 that he was due to deposit. The amount is later discovered in full by Potter, but the malevolent old man decides to keep the money for himself rather than alerting George and Billy to its whereabouts, knowing all too well the havoc this unseen criminal action will wreak.

George is driven to distraction by Billy's carelessness; a banking inspector is due to visit the building and loan company later, and the vast shortfall in funds will mean a certain end to the business. He frantically hunts around the town in search of the missing $8,000 but – as Billy clearly has no idea of its whereabouts – he is at a loss as to where he should even start to look. George becomes unbalanced due to the worry he feels, upsetting his family and a number of the townsfolk in the process. Eventually, he is compelled – as a final act of utter hopelessness – to approach Potter for a loan to make up the deficit facing the building and loan company. As collateral, he offers his life insurance policy, though it is worth only $500 in equity. Never letting on that he is in possession of the missing funds, Potter smugly berates George before denying him a loan with the greatest of self-satisfaction.

Now totally despondent, George drives out to a remote bridge on the outskirts of town. Crashing his car into a tree, he staggers over to the bridge with the intention of committing suicide. This, he reasons, will solve the problem, as his life insurance policy will pay out to the tune of $15,000 in the event of his death – thus ensuring that the company will go on, even if the price of its survival will be his own demise. However, as he is set to jump into the icy water he is shocked to see a stranger drowning in the river beneath him – Clarence. Diving in to save him, George is bewildered when the elderly man introduces himself as George's guardian angel. George finds it difficult to take this revelation seriously. Deeply resentful at the impending demise of the building and loan, he indignantly tells Clarence that the world would likely have been a better place if he had never been born in the first place. Calling his bluff, Clarence decides to show George exactly what the town would look like if this had in fact been the case.

In an instant, George finds himself in an alternate reality where he soon discovers that he is, in fact, an unknown bystander in a world where he has never been born. The warmly inviting Bedford Falls has long since ceased to be, and in its place is a grim collection of slums named Pottersville. In this town, without George's philanthropy to act as a brake on Potter's greed, the inhabitants are dark and twisted shadows of their true selves. At every turn, he finds himself faced with suspicion and hostility in a world where generosity and altruism seem to be virtually non-existent. Mary, having never met George, is now a fearful, unmarried librarian who is deeply distrustful of the world around her. The pharmacist Mr Gower was arrested for his accidental poisoning of a young boy – the tragic error which the adolescent George wasn't around to stop – and after a lengthy spell in prison he is reduced to alcoholism and begging in order to survive. Bailey Park was never built and is now a graveyard, while the Bailey Building and Loan is a run-down dance hall. Things go from bad to worse when George realises that as he hadn't existed to save Harry, not only did his brother drown in youth but also the many people who Harry was subsequently to save during the war have also died on account of the young man's early demise. Even the easy-going Uncle Billy has been declared medically unable to function in society, and is now confined to a mental institution.

George is stunned at how one single man's actions – his own – could have had such a vastly transformative effect on the community in which he lives. Appalled at the horrifying state of Bedford Falls in his absence, he begs God to return him to life again so that his actions will once more have consequence. His prayer granted, George finds himself back at the exact point in time that he had met Clarence on the bridge. Racing home, now jubilant at his newly-found sense of worth and purpose, George is elated to discover that the town has returned to normal. Of course, this inevitably also means that the banking inspector is present and seeking answers with regard to the missing funds from the building and loan company. However, before George can be prosecuted for fraud, the townsfolk and his family – including the recently-returned Harry – rally around and reveal that they have raised the necessary funds to rescue George from being taken into custody, as well as saving the building and loan from collapse. George is stunned that, after so many years of selfless concern for his neighbourhood, the community has now come to his own aid instead. As the gathered assembly break into a heartfelt rendition of 'Auld Lang Syne', George hears a bell ringing on his Christmas tree and remembers Clarence's earlier revelation that whenever a bell rings, an angel is being granted his or her wings. Mindful of all that his guardian angel has done for him, George realises that – in spite of the difficulties that have faced him over the years – he really has had a wonderful life after all.

It's a Wonderful Life seems so firmly and centrally embedded in the framework of the cinematic Christmas experience that it is difficult to believe that throughout the fifties and sixties it had drifted into near-total obscurity. Only with its lapse into the public domain in the seventies, which led to many subsequent screenings on American television, did the film achieve cult notoriety and – soon after – mass appeal. In an ironic twist, what had been considered one of Capra's less successful films was turned into his most iconic, and today it is almost certainly his best-remembered. Yet as mentioned earlier, the film has become much more than a fondly regarded seasonal classic, for it contains themes both subtle and bold which have led to it being studied and discussed at great detail over the past few decades. Most contentious among these, inevitably, was the film's depiction of the unscrupulous banker Potter and his unabashed theft of funds from George's Building and Loan which is the central cause of conflict in *It's a Wonderful Life*. There was alarm in some quarters of officialdom at the time that Bedford Falls' most prominent banker, a role which would have been considered one of the archetypal pillars of society at the time, should be considered as an antagonist – particularly one so ruthlessly venal and immoral. As Will Chen has pointed out, while the film's themes may seem to perfectly epitomise the spirit of Christmas cinema, in the forties the geopolitical climate surrounding its release gave rise to certain ideological anxieties: 'I love *It's a Wonderful Life* because it teaches us that family, friendship, and virtue are the true definitions of wealth. In 1947, however, the FBI considered this anti-consumerist message as subversive Communist propaganda. According to Professor John Noakes of Franklin and Marshall College, the FBI thought *Life* smeared American values such as wealth and free enterprise while glorifying anti-American values such as the triumph of the common man'.[4] However, Lionel Barrymore's superb, gleefully malevolent performance is one of such skill and distinction that we are left in little doubt that Potter's actions are borne more of malice than simple capital gain – his antipathy towards George (and the citizens of Bedford Falls in general) has less to do with commercial competitiveness than it does with spite towards the town's nominal philosophy of mutual co-operation. Indeed, it is even more difficult to consider the film as being generally negative towards capitalism when the protagonist himself, with all of his virtue and altruism, also works in the banking industry and actively uses this position to make life better for those around him. This, as Kat Eschner suggests, means that the principal concerns of *It's a Wonderful Life* were considerably more social in nature than they were political: 'Ironically, it is the very aspects of the film that put it under suspicion that have helped to make it a Christmas favorite. [...] George Bailey's central question of whether his life, good or bad, has been worthwhile, is the kind of thing a person might wonder in the dark of the year. It's a question that transcended the FBI's concerns'.[5]

Whereas *The Bells of St Mary's* (q.v.) had depicted a specifically (and traditionally) Christian approach to social responsibility and working towards the common good of the community, the moral thrust of *It's a Wonderful Life* appears much more secular, quite in spite of its memorable evocation of angels and divine intervention. The film displays a more universal approach to its subject than Leo McCarey's film had done, stipulating clearly the need for individuals to support each other for the greater good of their neighbourhood and, by extension, society at large. As Clarence so memorably observes, nobody who has friends around them can truly be considered a failure in life, and it is this simple but all-encompassing promotion of mutual support which has really become the film's greatest and most lasting legacy to later Christmas films. George Bailey's unstinting selflessness echoes all the way down his life, from the sacrifice of his hearing to save his brother through to the abrogation of his *wanderlust* in order to support his family's business, but it takes the goodwill of the festive season (and the near-tragedy which occurs during it) to highlight just how much his community appreciate him and the way in which he has forfeited his dreams in order to support the town he loves so much. In this sense, there is much more to be said about the film's recreation of small town life, and Capra's staunch defence of the self-determination of individuals, than the film's rather ambiguous approach to the febrile political realities of the time. In this sense, as Patrick McGee has argued, the central message of promoting social responsibility over uncontrolled material acquisitiveness is inevitably problematised by the undeniable fact that the film is a commercial enterprise in and of itself:

It's a Wonderful Life virtually negates its own promise as a commodity of the culture industry. Life, it says, is not so wonderful after all. Furthermore, analysis has the effect of subverting its commodity form, which is reflected in the Christmas-card quality of the framing images. Though over the last half-century the film's commodity form has probably dominated the mode of its reception as a Christmas movie that reaffirms the humanist values of capitalist culture, analysis reveals that another mode of reception is possible and perhaps has already taken place. It reveals in the work a tendency towards autonomy which offers resistance to the pressures of the culture industry that would reduce the film to an object completely subsumed by the profit-making calculations of business.[6]

Intriguingly, the genre characteristics of *It's a Wonderful Life* have also become a hotly-contested issue. Based upon Philip Van Doren Stern's 1939 short story 'The Greatest Gift', the screenplay of the film went through numerous revisions and many drafts before the story we recognise today began to take shape. Capra bought the script from RKO Pictures, who had initially planned to use it in order to develop a film which would have starred Cary Grant, and worked in collaboration with a succession of screenwriters including Frances Goodrich, Albert Hackett, Jo Swerling, Michael Wilson and Dorothy Parker to develop the characters and plot that would eventually reach cinema screens. While varying accounts have suggested that the script's development was a somewhat fraught process, it is also noteworthy that Capra's overall intent was not to produce a film that was specifically festively-themed, but rather to focus upon the importance of healthy community life in post-war America. Roger Ebert, for instance, has stated that: 'Frank Capra never intended *It's a Wonderful Life* to be pigeonholed as a "Christmas picture". This was the first movie he made after returning from service in World War II, and he wanted it to be special – a celebration of the lives and dreams of America's ordinary citizens, who tried the best they could to do the right thing by themselves and their neighbors'.[7] While the film succeeds admirably as a drama as well as having become one of the single greatest Christmas movies ever made, there has been additional dissention amongst critics with regard to whether it may also be considered a fantasy feature, or even have a place within the annals of science fiction. While opinions have been advanced on both sides of this argument, commentators such as Germain Lussier have wisely drawn attention to the fact that as Capra himself seemed less intent on genre considerations than he did with concentrating on the accessibility of the film's characters and situations, categorising *It's a Wonderful Life* is less important than enjoying the overall experience of the film and considering what it has to tell us about determining what is important in life: 'The movie isn't about its genre elements, it's about the human spirit. But those elements are in there, they're important, and it's obvious once you spell it out. Mostly, it's just that Capra's tone and filmmaking never focus on it. Instead, everything in *It's a Wonderful Life* feels grounded, simple, and heartwarming. Still, there's no denying that the whole film hinges on an event that could never actually occur, unless created by scientific innovation or mystical beings. Which, my friends, are pretty much the textbook definitions of science fiction and fantasy'.[8]

In the film's imaginative sequence set in the dystopian slum of Pottersville, we see first-hand the nightmarish social drudgery which thrives in a world where George had never been on hand to aid the lives of those around him. The lurid excesses of Potter's corrosively negative effects on the community are made all the more immediate given Capra's painstaking build-up to their depiction, showing the audience detailed snapshots of George's interactions with the denizens of Bedford Falls during his life up until that point in order to heighten the emotional impact when we are introduced to the same characters in the harsh neon light of Pottersville. (The same technique was later used to excellent effect in the creation of the bleak, uncompromisingly grim parallel version of Hill Valley, corrupted by the spiteful manipulations of the antagonistic Biff Tannen character, in the second act of Robert Zemeckis's *Back to the Future: Part II* in 1989.) So skilful is Capra's gradual, unrelenting accumulation of the difficult – and eminently relatable – issues that beset George and make him question the worth of his very existence, the character's grim resignation in the face of his apparent fate makes the sudden revelation of Pottersville and its attendant shocks all the more affecting. This continued relevance, as Jamie S. Rich suggests, is a major reason why the film has continued to influence audiences even in the present day: 'Despite its ubiquitous presence every holiday season and the years where it seemed like every TV station on the planet had a print of the film, *It's a Wonderful Life* has never lost a shred of its power. [...] Frank Capra tempers his unflinching optimism with a healthy cynicism about how low human nature can sink. George doesn't end up on that bridge easily, it's a building weight, the accumulation of failures and defeats'.[9] But just as we are given a bitter taste of hopelessness in viewing the direct consequences of a world without George, where greed and exploitation have been allowed to predominate unchecked in Bedford Falls, so too can we share in George's elation at his return to normality and – in his beatific realisation that his life has not been lived in vain after all – savour the film's triumphant conclusion. In this sense, the film transcends even Capra's intention to celebrate the virtues of small town America and manages to embrace an even more universal concern, as Daniel J. Sullivan suggests: 'The American Dream in its deepest dimension is not exclusively "American" at all; it is a universal dream attainable by all men in every conceivable circumstance. The central prerequisite is loving your neighbor. To combat the disillusionment of postwar America, Capra used Bedford Falls and George Bailey to show how regular people doing common-place things could lead extraordinarily "rich" lives'.[10]

Some have considered Capra's preoccupation with the dark mirror-image of Bedford Falls to be a wider comment on the potential dangers facing America in a time of intense social and cultural flux. This may, in fact, be part of the reason why he labours George's virtues so extensively, for the voracious covetousness represented by Potter is so potentially all-embracing that Capra seems eager to delineate just how acute the underlying danger of unrestricted acquisitiveness can be to the fabric of society, if it is not continually constrained by the bulwark of personal and social responsibility. Capra's intent to demonstrate the transformative effects of just one life on the condition and development of a community is absolutely at the heart of the film, for just as George's self-sacrifice comes to unite Bedford Falls, so too does Potter's overly-materialistic malevolence threaten to destroy it. As Raymond Carney has observed, the monstrously covetous Potter has become so consumed by raw greed that his very self appears to have been eroded by the corrosiveness of his base impulses, making him the diametric opposite of the altruistic, community-minded George:

> Potter holds out the possibility of surviving (and even thriving) by repressing all merely human compassion, sexual impulses, and familial connections, all emotional, social, and biological intimacies and responsibilities. In the Calvinistic-acquisitive form of capitalism that he represents, Potter has cut his links not only with his family, friends, and relatives (he has none) but even with his own body and the life of his senses. [...] (He has apparently severed himself even from the biological processes of aging, appearing as shriveled and old in the first scenes of the film as in the last, thirty years later.) He has, in effect, given up his body and almost all practical bodily functions and biological impulses and gratifications for the sake of the denatured accumulation of capital.[11]

Unlike Horace Bogardus in *The Bells of St Mary's*, no Damascene conversion is possible for Potter – he cannot be guided, manipulated or reasoned with, and thus he seems incapable of any kind of constructive development with regard to his moral outlook. And yet, as Leonard Quart and Albert Auster have remarked, *It's a Wonderful Life* is so intensely concerned with the promotion (and fragility) of small town life – and those who help to make it what it is – that the film actually marked a comparative departure from Capra's earlier deep anxieties concerning more clearly-defined contemporary social developments in films such as *Mr Deeds Goes to Town* and *Mr Smith Goes to Washington*: 'Capra's usual mythic, tranquil, small town, Bedford Falls, is destroyed by selfish materialism and turned into a raw, industrial, neon-lit Pottersville (a fantasy possibly inspired by the squalid boom towns that grew up across America in the wake of the wartime industrial explosion). Even his archetypal common man, George Bailey (James Stewart), is beset with feelings of self-doubt and resentment. Nevertheless, Capracorn and the spirit of Christmas eventually do triumph [...] and the significance of each man's life, no matter how ordinary, reaffirmed'.[12]

It is worth noting that Capra entirely manages to avoid allowing the film to descend into the predictable Manichaeism of an overt morality tale; while the audience can remain in no doubt of his social and cultural concerns, *It's a Wonderful Life* is every bit as focused on the small, everyday joys of life in a close-knit community as it is with the sudden precariousness of such an existence. Yet while Capra presents his universal concerns within a framework of a modestly-sized local community, he clearly intends to use this neighbourhood as a canvas upon which to project these relatable anxieties in a way that can be readily consumed by a much wider audience. As Chris Cabin astutely suggests in relation to the film's events: 'We're talking about a narrowly averted tragedy based on an upper-middle-class white bank manager who finds himself in a fight with the town's major financial leader; when you get right down to it, these are ultimately midrange concerns at worst. But to say the path is an easy one is more than a bit dismissive and shows a curious lack of empathy, especially when the film in question largely condemns capitalism and boasts something approaching a quasi-socialist fantasia that's hard-won by Bailey. [...] To claim that Capra ignores the real pains of the sacrifices he asks his protagonist to accept suggests a sort of secular tunnel vision'.[13] It is here that the film's supporting cast members are allowed to shine, both in their Bedford Falls and Pottersville guises. Donna Reed sets the screen alight as the spirited Mary Hatch, later to become the supportive, family-oriented Mrs Bailey. Yet while her energetic performance as George's independent-minded soul-mate stays in the memory, so too does her portrayal of Mary's nervy, withdrawn alter-ego, cast adrift in a dystopian existence where she met neither George nor any other romantic partner. Whether depicting members of George's family like Thomas Mitchell's affable Uncle Billy and Beulah Bondi's motherly Mrs Bailey, or larger-than-life town characters such as Frank Faylen's taxi driver Ernie and Ward Bond's Bert the policeman, Capra's film succeeds like few others in weaving a tapestry of a small town where all individuals have worth and meaning, and then subverting that same diorama to lay bare just how delicate the status of their largely-contented existence actually is. Affably overseeing proceedings is the genial angel Clarence, unforgettably played by Henry Travers. The diametric opposite of his earlier portrayal of the belligerent Horace Bogardus, Travers invests much warmth and wistfulness in his depiction of this trainee guardian angel, and it is of little surprise that the character – appearing as he did in the twilight of Travers's career – would come to be regarded as the most recognisable of his entire filmography. Clarence is unwaveringly certain of the positivity and purposefulness of George's existence, and will stop at nothing to convince the beleaguered banker that he must not throw away the potential that the rest of his life may still afford him. So profound is the pathos of Clarence's success in his task that it is hard to imagine anyone in the audience who does not share, to some extent, in the satisfaction of his achievement. (Eagle-eyed viewers will no doubt spot the fact that *The Bells of St Mary's* appears on the marquee of the local cinema in Bedford Falls; this was not just a way of indicating the Christmas 1945 setting of *It's a Wonderful Life* by alluding to the wildly successful Leo McCarey box-office hit of that same year, but also a visual tribute to Travers who had prominently featured in that earlier film.)

For all the multitude of memorable performances in *It's a Wonderful Life*, the film belongs primarily to James Stewart and his legendary lightness of touch. The most remarkable thing about George Bailey is that for all of his supreme self-lessness, he remains an identifiable figure. He is virtuous, yet he is not saintly. He may be honourable, undoubtedly, but he is also vulnerable. And while he is just and unselfish, he is also all too human – when pushed to the furthest of extremes, we see him come close to the ultimate breaking point. Yet it says a great deal for Capra, and the distinctive character he creates, that George's would-be suicide on the bridge is not depicted as the last desperate attempt of a broken man to escape the consequences which face him, but rather as an act of supreme sacrifice: we are left in no doubt that George's genuine intention is to willingly give his life in exchange for the life insurance that could secure the futures of those close to him. The amiable Jimmy Stewart appears absolutely tailor-made for the role of the folksy, well-intentioned George Bailey, and it is little surprise that he repeatedly named the role as his favourite performance among all of his many cinematic appearances. *It's a Wonderful Life* was to make George one of the most immediately-recognisable characters in Christmas cinema, and Stewart one of the actors most closely associated with the genre's golden age. This is all the more remarkable when we consider the fact that although George manages – with the help of his friends and the local community – to overcome the seemingly-insurmountable difficulties that face him, there is no clichéd happy ending beyond the recognition that a healthy, mutually supportive civic life exists for the betterment of all. This challenging moral reality is delineated by MaryAnn Johanson thus: 'George deferred and eventually lost all his dreams in order to help other people fulfill their dreams. A noble cause, surely, and helping others is certainly something we should all be doing... to an extent. But who's gonna help poor George realize his dreams? It bothers me, too, that Potter – whose sneaky act is finally what drives George to suicide – gets no comeuppance and suffers no consequences as a result of his contemptible act. Sure, we're supposed to see Potter as a loser because he has no friends – unlike George, beloved by the entire town – but Potter seems quite happy with himself'.[14] Perhaps controversially, some have raised the possibility that the lack of justice for Potter's crime of theft would become symbolic of the fact that the idealised rural world of Bedford Falls (and all too many other small towns in the same mould) would, in later decades, come to be swept away by the unstoppable tides of modern commerce in a manner that would no doubt have delighted the graspingly materialistic character. As Gary Kamiya has put it: 'We all live in Pottersville now. Bedford Falls is gone. The plucky little Savings and Loan closed down years ago, just like in George's nightmare. Cleaned up, his evil eyebrows removed, armed with a good PR firm, Mr Potter goes merrily about his business, "consolidating" the George Baileys of the world. To cling to dreams of a bucolic America where the little guy defeats the forces of Big Business and the policeman and the taxi driver and the druggist and the banker all sing "Auld Lang Syne" together is just to ask for heartbreak and confusion when you turn off the TV and open your front door'.[15]

It's a Wonderful Life was a noteworthy feature for other reasons – many of them quite unexpected. Among the most interesting facts behind its production was the fact that the film won an Academy Award for Technical Achievement, on account of Russell Sherman and the RKO Radio Studio special effects department who had developed an entirely new method of simulating falling snow on the set of a motion picture. The reason for this innovation was that previously, films had generally used white-painted, toasted cornflakes to mimic snowfall. However, the process tended to be very noisy in practice, meaning that dialogue in such scenes had to be redubbed in post-production. As Capra preferred to record a film's dialogue live, a quieter process had to be created, and eventually this was arrived at by using a mixture of soap, water and the fire-fighting compound foamite. This amalgam was then injected through a wind machine at very high pressure, generating the effect of falling snowflakes which were as silent as the real thing.

Other surprising details about the film included the fact that the huge Bedford Falls set took two months to construct, and at that time was one of the longest sets ever to be assembled for a motion picture. Crafted at the Encino Ranch in California, which was owned by RKO Pictures, it eventually covered four acres, with the main street set alone being the length of three city blocks (around 300 yards). The set also included a residential area, the town's slums, an industrial zone, and no less than seventy-five buildings including commercial stores. Capra was particularly eager for the town to look authentic and went to great effort to ensure that it appeared 'lived in', even allowing cats and birds to roam the set.

Yet for all the film's festive realism, it was actually recorded during a heatwave meaning that the cast had to feign braving the cold of winter in exterior shots. Even James Stewart's triumphant race along the main street at the conclusion of the movie was filmed on a sweltering day in July. The set had to be highly adaptable given that scenes were set in different decades and seasons, and Capra even had oak trees transferred onto location for the sake of faithfulness to the visual qualities of a real small town. Remarkably, filming took place entirely within Capra's anticipated ninety-day production schedule, starting on 15 April 1946 and concluding on 27 July of the same year.

The reviews of *It's a Wonderful Life* were mixed at the time of its release. *Time* magazine, for instance, lavished praise upon the film and was comprehensive in its critical approval: '*It's a Wonderful Life* (Liberty Films; RKO Radio) is a pretty wonderful movie. It has only one formidable rival (Goldwyn's *The Best Years of Our Lives*) as Hollywood's best picture of the year. *Wonderful Life* is a triumphant Hollywood homecoming for two efficient ex-soldiers. Producer-Director Frank Capra (*It Happened One Night*, *Mr Deeds Goes to Town*), ex-Signal Corps colonel who bossed the making of such outstanding wartime documentaries as *San Pietro*, has lost none of his civilian cunning at whipping up top-drawer entertainment. He is still one of Hollywood's most talented moviemakers'.[16] On the other end of the scale, Kate Cameron of *The New York Daily News* was much more sceptical of the movie's quality, stating that 'the film is too sprawling in extent, too noisy as to background music and voices and much too obvious in the application of its social significance notes. But while it isn't the best picture to come out of Hollywood this year, nor is it Capra's masterpiece, it tells a good story and its conclusion has a heart-warming effect on the audience. [[...]] The picture would have been greatly improved by some judicious editing. It turns too long for its own good'.[17] In spite of the fact that positive appraisals of *It's a Wonderful Life* outnumbered the negative when it first appeared in cinemas, the film faced extremely stiff competition and, as such, its commercial performance was underwhelming. Michael Willian takes note that 'although *It's a Wonderful Life* received largely favorable reviews upon its release in December 1946, the film did not exactly take the box office by storm. According to *Variety* magazine, *It's a Wonderful Life* failed to crack the top 25 grossing films for 1947, coming in on the last tied for 26th at $3.3 million, compared to $11.5 million for the top grosser, *The Best Years of Our Lives*'.[18] Thus while the film would later go on to become arguably Capra's most enduring work, its initial box-office takings were to have a detrimental effect on his cinematic career at the time. As Mark Eliot has observed, *It's a Wonderful Life* 'was initially a major disappointment and confirmed, at least to the studios, that Capra was no longer capable of turning out the populist features that made his films the must-see, money-making events they once were'.[19]

With every passing decade, Capra's film continues to grow in stature, and as such it is almost impossible to overstate the cultural influence of *It's a Wonderful Life*. There are very few who would now argue the fact that it is near-impossible to find fault with any element of the film, from Dimitri Tiomkin's unforgettable score to Emile Kuri's brilliant set decoration (including the many impressively period-accurate products displayed in Mr Gower's drugstore), which brings alive the comforting charm of Bedford Falls just as effectively as it underscores the nightmarish wantonness of Pottersville. As a result, modern criticism of Capra's movie has been far more fulsome in its approval, with many commentators lauding it for its landmark contribution to the Christmas film genre – as well as to American cinema in general. Jonathan Munby, for instance, acknowledges that the film was somewhat ahead of its time, declaring that '*It's a Wonderful Life* has assumed the status of *the* Christmas movie. ⟦...⟧ Of interest here is how a story that is in many ways an American reworking of Dickens's *A Christmas Carol* did not resonate with its original audience, yet has since become an essential part of the American Christmas viewing ritual. ⟦...⟧ In 1946, the film's more fantastic elements would have been understood as just that. An analysis of the contemporaneous contexts of reception will reveal that *It's a Wonderful Life* could not have been consumed as a holiday movie that seamlessly affirmed the regenerative features of what Paul Davies describes ⟦in *The Lives and Times of Ebenezer Scrooge*⟧ as the *Carol* as "culture-text"'.[20] James Agee concurs with the Dickensian correlation but is sceptical of what he perceived to be a level of moral ingenuousness, remarking that 'this story is somewhere near as effective, of its kind, as *A Christmas Carol*. In particular, the hero is extravagantly well played by James Stewart. ⟦...⟧ But mistrust, for instance, any work which tries to persuade me – or rather, which assumes that I assume – that there is so much good in nearly all the worst of us that all it needs is a proper chance and example, to take complete control. I mistrust even more deeply the assumption, so comfortably stylish these days, that whether people turn out well or ill depends overwhelmingly on outside circumstances and scarcely if at all on their own moral intelligence and courage. Neither idea is explicit in this movie, but the whole story depends on the strong implication and assumption of both'.[21] Others, such as Martin Liebman, have instead focused on James Stewart's central performance as being one of the main reasons behind the film's enduring success:

> *It's a Wonderful Life* took a turn for the wonderful over the years, emerging not as merely a 'good' or even 'memorable' film, but an unmistakable classic not only because of its Christmas setting (at least in the final act) but because of its enduring message on what it truly means to be alive. [...] Stewart shifts gears at the drop of a hat (or the plunge of an Angel, as the case may be) to transform his character into a man at first on the verge of doing the unthinkable, and later, as a man lost in time and place, confused, physically disheveled, and spiritually broken. It's a fabulous effort all around, and his uncanny ability to cover not only the range of emotion but sell the meaning of the movie at the end truly makes it a hallmark performance in the history of cinema, as treasured as the film itself.[22]

In 2006, the American Film Institute cited the film as the most inspirational motion picture ever to be produced, and indeed this auspicious legacy now seems to be safely cemented within the annals of popular cinema forever. With the singular exception of *A Christmas Carol*, it has become the most regularly parodied and pastiched of all festive stories. Many long-running television series across the world have used the film's memorable premise of the conflict between altruism and individualism as the basis for one of their episodes (often, but not exclusively, set at Christmas), and throughout the passing years the warm sentimentality of the original has occasionally been subverted into a thinly-veiled attempt to satirise the issues of the day. Effective spoofs have ranged from sophisticated political farces such as the 'It's a Soaraway Life' sketch from the BBC's *A Bit of Fry and Laurie* (broadcast on 12 February 1995) all the way through to Mike Judge's darkly humorous – and predictably surreal – 'It's a Miserable Life' Christmas special of MTV's infamous animated series *Beavis and Butthead* (shown on 19 December 1995). Clips from the original Capra film have also appeared in numerous later movies and TV features (usually being shown as part of a television broadcast or cinema screening being witnessed by the characters) as varied as the 'Christmas Cheers' episode of NBC's famed situation comedy *Cheers* (first broadcast on 17 December 1987), Italian drama *Cinema Paradiso* (Giuseppe Tornatore, 1988), PBS's festive *Sesame Street* TV movie *Elmo Saves Christmas* (Emily Squires, 1996), celebrated horror comedy *Gremlins* (Joe Dante, 1984), and – perhaps most memorably – in the wildly successful, yuletide-situated family comedy *Home Alone* (Chris Columbus, 1990) and its sequel *Home Alone 2: Lost in New York* (Chris Columbus, 1992).[23]

It's a *Wonderful Life* was remade for television by Donald Wrye in the seventies, as *It Happened One Christmas* (first broadcast on 11 December 1977). Although it has become a rather obscure feature in recent years, this TV movie – based, as *It's a Wonderful Life* had been, on Philip Van Doren Stern's short story 'The Greatest Gift' – was nominated for two Primetime Emmy Awards in its day, and featured none other than the legendary Orson Welles as the nefarious Henry Potter. Starring Marlo Thomas as Mary Bailey Hatch and Wayne Rogers as George Hatch, *It Happened One Christmas* relates a new version of the original film's events which this time centres around Mary rather than George, complete with an affable female angel named 'Clara Oddbody', played by the inimitable Cloris Leachman. In spite of its talented cast and decent production values, *It Happened One Christmas* has now largely vanished into a state of relative anonymity, but as a curiosity it remains of general interest to film enthusiasts. A later reworking of the *It's a Wonderful Life* story – which admittedly aims for a much looser reinterpretation of the Capra film's themes and events – took place in a Hallmark Christmas TV movie, *The Christmas Spirit*, which was first screened on 1 December 2013. Written and directed by Jack Angelo, this feature similarly modernised the events of the Capra film and starred Nicollette Sheridan as Charlotte Hart, a woman who finds herself in a coma but who must subconsciously communicate with the people who live in her New England town in an attempt to save the community from the machinations of an avaricious property developer. Additionally, elements of *It's a Wonderful Life*'s parallel universe storyline – comparing the world of the everyday against an altered reality where the protagonist has not had the chance to affect the community around themselves – have emerged in numerous cinema releases over the years, most recently including films such as *Mr Destiny* (James Orr, 1990), *Richie Rich's Christmas Wish* (John Murlowski, 1998), *The Family Man* (Brett Ratner, 2000) and, at the extreme end of the spectrum, Peter Capaldi's influential and supremely absurdist Academy Award-winning short film *Franz Kafka's It's a Wonderful Life* (1993).

There have been numerous stage adaptations and musical dramatisations of *It's a Wonderful Life* over the years, along with innumerable books inspired by the film. James Stewart was to reprise the role of George Bailey on 8 May

1949, for a radio adaptation of the film on NBC's *Screen Director's Playhouse*. Additionally, Stewart and Donna Reed were to be reunited in their roles as George and Mary Bailey for radio adaptations of *It's a Wonderful Life* on Lux Radio Theater (10 March 1947) and The Screen Guild Theater (29 December 1947 and 15 March 1951). Although Stewart would forever be immortalised in the modern cultural consciousness as George Bailey, he did make other interesting contributions to the world of Christmas features, first with his appearance in Richard Quine's whimsically offbeat *Bell, Book and Candle* (q.v.) and then later with his heart-rending performance as elderly widower Willy Kreuger in Kieth Merrill's short but memorable TV movie *Mr Kreuger's Christmas*, which was first broadcast on 21 December 1980. A deeply touching evocation of disheartening loneliness over the festive season, Stewart delivers an extraordinary performance throughout Merrill's feature; his portrayal of the kindly but deeply despondent caretaker Mr Kreuger culminates in an uplifting and life-affirming climax which makes this hidden gem well worth seeking out.

Perhaps most controversial, given the legendary status of *It's a Wonderful Life*, have been attempts to produce a sequel to Capra's iconic film. In 1990, Eric Till directed *Clarence*, a TV movie broadcast on The Family Channel which was written by Lorne Cameron and followed angel Clarence Odbody – now played by Robert Carradine – as he provides some heavenly guidance to the troubled Rachel Logan (Kate Trotter). While the film followed a similar storyline to *It's a Wonderful Life*, Clarence was the only character from the original movie to appear. Many years later in 2013, production companies Star Partners and Hummingbird Productions announced that they would be developing a direct sequel to

Capra's movie, which was to be entitled *It's a Wonderful Life: The Rest of the Story*. The film was to focus on Zuzu, George Bailey's youngest daughter, and it was hoped that Karolyn Grimes would reprise the role she had made famous in 1946. A 2015 release date was mooted, with a budget projected to be in the range of $25 million to $30 million. However, the rights to the intellectual property for *It's a Wonderful Life* could not be secured from their owner, Paramount Pictures (who had acquired Liberty Films in 1947), and as such the planned sequel was never to be produced.[24]

Although most cinemagoing audiences of the 1940s were unlikely to have realised it at the time, the release of *It's a Wonderful Life* had not only raised the bar for Christmas films for the rest of the decade, but it had helped to set the course of this formative genre for all time. To this day, Capra's masterpiece remains the film to beat in terms of heartwarming human drama, the encouragement of festive community spirit, and triumph over adversity. As Karen Krizanovich has noted, the film has proven to be so singularly influential that it stands head and shoulders above even the cream of the Christmas movie's 1940s golden age:

While it may not be the first Christmas movie (that honour goes to 1898's *Santa Claus*, a British short that was itself a technical landmark) *It's a Wonderful Life* is the closest thing to a postwar American Dickens. Though Capra never quite returned to the golden days of the 1930s, this is considered by many to be one of the finest films ever made. Having personally taken the film for granted for decades, seeing it on the big screen made for a transformative experience. I saw Stewart's hysteria, Reed's joy and worry, the irritation of being a parent, but also the sensuality of wholesome smalltown America. [...] There's sex and death here, elation and depression, hope and despair. Potter may win in the end but, realistically, the characters live with that because they must. It's their only choice.[25]

With its eternal charm and intertwined messages of seasonal goodwill and social responsibility, *It's a Wonderful Life* has more than earned its classic status in the world of cinema, and its reputation is unlikely to be seriously challenged either now or in the foreseeable future. As Ebert has noted: 'What is remarkable about *It's a Wonderful Life* is how well it holds up over the years; it's one of those ageless movies, like *Casablanca* or *The Third Man*, that improves with age. Some movies, even good ones, should only be seen once. When we know how they turn out, they've surrendered their mystery and appeal. Other movies can be viewed an indefinite number of times. Like great music, they improve with familiarity. *It's a Wonderful Life* falls in the second category'.[26] Similarly, the far-reaching universality of the film's themes have transcended its 1940s small town setting to ensure that *It's a Wonderful Life* continues to have resonance with audiences even when the locale and social mores of the original movie have long since passed into history. As critics such as Berardinelli have opined: 'I think *It's a Wonderful Life* has earned its legion of followers because it effectively touches upon one basic truth of life that we all would like to believe – that each of us, no matter how apparently insignificant, has the power to make a difference, and that the measure of our humanity has nothing to do with fame or money, but with how we live our life on a day-to-day basis. *It's a Wonderful Life* asks and answers a question that all of us think of at one

time or another: "What would this world be like if I had never been born?".[27] And of course, the film's persistent success
with audiences has ensured that it has become the gold standard of festive cinema, guaranteeing that innumerable later
movies and TV features would focus on comfortable small
town environments, the importance of community and the
family unit, and the ability of Christmas to profoundly transform people's characters and attitudes. Cindy Ruth Collins,
for instance, states that:

> It is no accident of Christmas programming that
> new generations give this film their unrestrained
> adulation. Capra's brilliant direction and casting,
> combined with the power of this story, have
> gained *It's a Wonderful Life*, and its beloved star, a
> multigenerational following. We, the generations
> who made this film a Christmas tradition, feel pas-
> sionately about George: about his warmth and
> kindness, his suffocating frustration and ultimate-
> ly his discovery that the same strategically bad
> luck and painful good choices which have kept
> him in Bedford Falls all these years have ironically
> worked behind the scenes to save that 'crummy
> little town' from the hellish nightmare of despair
> and hopelessness that he finds in the alternative
> universe of Pottersville.[28]

There is no question that *It's a Wonderful Life* has become the benchmark by which all other Christmas movies are
judged, and it is not surprising that Frank Capra himself
would regularly name it as the feature he considered his favourite of his entire filmography. Today, the movie remains a
landmark in American motion pictures, typifying not just the

intrinsic worth of small town life but also the merits of a Christmas shared by friends, family and the wider community. Its impact on the world of filmmaking, and popular culture in general, has been incalculable. While the world of 1940s that Capra so painstakingly recreates has long disappeared into the annals of history, audiences today still connect effortlessly with the film's key themes of altruism, social responsibility, love, mutual cooperation, selflessness, family and community. It is – and likely will forever remain – a true classic of festive cinema.

REFERENCES

1.   Frank Thompson, *American Movie Classics' Great Christ-mas Movies* (Dallas: Taylor, 1998), p.149.

2.   James Berardinelli, '*It's a Wonderful Life*', in *ReelViews*, 1 January 2000.
      <*http://www.reelviews.net/reelviews/it-s-a-wonderful-life*>

3.   Anon., '*It's a Wonderful Life*', in *Urban Cinefile*, 1 August 2002.
      <*http://www.urbancinefile.com.au/home/view.asp?a=6367 &s=DVD*>

4.   Will Chen, 'FBI Considered *It's A Wonderful Life* Com-munist Propaganda', in *WiseBread*, 24 December 2006.
      <*https://www.wisebread.com/fbi-considered-its-a-wonderful-life-communist-propaganda*>
      See also:
      John A. Noakes, 'Official Frames in Social Movement Theo-ry: The FBI, HUAC, and the Communist Threat in Holly-wood', in *Frames of Protest: Social Movements and the Framing Perspective*, ed. by Hank Johnston and John A. Noakes (Oxford: Rowman and Littlefield, 2005), pp.95-101.

5.   Kat Eschner, 'The Weird Story of the FBI and *It's a Won-derful Life*', in *Smithsonian.com*, 20 December 2017.
      <*https://www.smithsonianmag.com/smart-news/weird-story-fbi-and-its-wonderful-life-180967587/*>

6.   Patrick McGee, *Cinema, Theory, and Political Responsibility in Contemporary Culture* (Cambridge: Cambridge Universi-ty Press, 1997), p.15.

7.   Roger Ebert, '*It's a Wonderful Life*', in *The Chicago Sun-Times*, 1 January 1999.
      <*https://www.rogerebert.com/reviews/great-movie-its-a-wonderful-life-1946*>

8.   Germain Lussier, 'Is Holiday Classic *It's a Wonderful Life* Secretly (or Actually) a Sci-Fi/Fantasy Movie?', in *io9*, 9 December 2018.
      <*https://io9.gizmodo.com/is-holiday-classic-its-a-wonderful-life-secretly-or-ac-1830726913*>

9.   Jamie S. Rich, '*It's a Wonderful Life*: 60th Anniversary Edition', in *DVD Talk*, 31 October 2006.
      <*https://www.dvdtalk.com/reviews/25017/its-a-wonderful-life-60th-anniversary-edition/*>

10.   Daniel J. Sullivan, 'Sentimental Hogwash?: On Capra's *It's a Wonderful Life*', in *Humanitas*, Vol. 18, Nos. 1-2, 9 January 2012, 115-140, p.120.

11.   Raymond Carney, *American Vision: The Films of Frank Capra* (Cambridge: Cambridge University Press, 1986), p.382.

12.   Leonard Quart and Albert Auster, *American Film and Society Since 1945*, 3rd edn (Westport: Greenwood Publishing Group, 2002), pp.22-23.

13.   Chris Cabin, 'Blu-ray Review: *It's a Wonderful Life*', in *Slant Magazine*, 17 December 2011.
      <*https://www.slantmagazine.com/dvd/its-a-wonderful-life-2172/*>

14.   MaryAnn Johanson, '*It's a Wonderful Life*', in *Flick Filosopher*, 1 December 1999.

<*https://www.flickfilosopher.com/1999/12/its-a-wonderful-life-review.html*>

15. Gary Kamiya, 'All Hail Pottersville!' in *Salon*, 22 December 2001.
<*http://www.salon.com/2001/12/22/pottersville/singleton/*>

16. Anon., 'Cinema: New Picture: *It's a Wonderful Life*', in *Time*, 23 December 1946.
<*http://www.time.com/time/magazine/article/0,9171,793342,00.html*>

17. Kate Cameron, '*It's a Wonderful Life* Lifts the Spirit', in *The New York Daily News*, 21 December 1946.
<*https://www.nydailynews.com/entertainment/movies/wonderful-life-designed-lift-spirits-1946-review-article-1.2916205*>

18. Michael Willian, *The Essential It's a Wonderful Life: A Scene-by-Scene Guide to the Classic Film* (Chicago: Chicago Review Press, 2006), p.4.

19. Mark Eliot, *Jimmy Stewart: A Biography* (New York: Random House, 2006), p.206.

20. Jonathan Munby, 'A Hollywood Carol's Wonderful Life', in *Christmas at the Movies: Images of Christmas in American, British and European Cinema*, ed. by Mark Connelly (London: I.B. Tauris, 2000), 39-57, pp.39-40.

21. James Agee, '*It's a Wonderful Life*', in *The Nation*, 20 December 2000.
<*https://www.thenation.com/article/its-wonderful-life/*>

22. Martin Liebman, '*It's a Wonderful Life* Blu-ray', in *Bluray.com*, 3 November 2009.

<https://www.blu-ray.com/movies/Its-a-Wonderful-Life-Blu-ray/6097/#Review>

23. Louisa Mellor, 'The Unusual Places *It's a Wonderful Life* Has Popped Up', in *Den of Geek*, 15 December 2018. <https://www.denofgeek.com/movies/its-a-wonderful-life/33441/the-odd-places-it-s-a-wonderful-life-has-turned-up>

24. Nicholas Raymond, 'Why the *It's a Wonderful Life* Sequel Was Canceled', in *Screen Rant*, 23 December 2018. <https://screenrant.com/wonderful-life-sequel-movie-canceled/>

25. Karen Krizanovich, '*It's a Wonderful Life*: Eternally Charming and Fun', in *Little White Lies*, 14 December 2018. <https://lwlies.com/reviews/its-a-wonderful-life-1946/>

26. Ebert.

27. Berardinelli.

28. Cindy Ruth Collins, '*It's a Wonderful Life*', in *It's Christmas Time at the Movies* by Gary J. Svehla and Susan Svehla (Baltimore: Midnight Marquee Press, 1998), 146-151, p.151.

6

Miracle on 34th Street (1947)

Twentieth Century-Fox

Director: George Seaton
Producer: William Perlberg
Screenwriter: George Seaton,
from a story by Valentine Davies

WHILE *It's a Wonderful Life* (q.v.) has unquestionably earned its status as the quintessential
Christmas film of the 1940s, it was far from the
only motion picture of that decade to assume classic status
within the annals of festive cinema. For if *It's a Wonderful
Life* was to become a kind of perennial declaration of the virtues of the small town, a bygone age of the American community that has been immortalised on celluloid, then *Miracle on
34th Street* has become just as nostalgic an examination of the
spirit of Christmas – albeit one which offers a very different
kind of misty reminiscence from that which had been offered
by Frank Capra. Yet just like Capra's classic, it was – at the
original time of its release – a thoroughly contemporary take
on American lives and social conventions which would have
seemed wholly relevant to post-war audiences. *Miracle on 34th
Street* offers a surprising duality of purpose, celebrating the
commoditisation of Christmas – the energetic cultural dissem-

ination of yuletide conventions through the mass-market – at the same time as it presents apprehensions about the aggressive encroachment of commercialism into the season of giving, which saw the inclusiveness of the traditional Christmas challenged with the new demands of materialistic individualism. As Noel Murray has explained, the film's perceptive dialogue and cultural relevance have allowed it continued significance that has defied many other features of the same era: '*Miracle on 34th Street* is pure Hollywood hokum, a blatant piece of sub-Capra populism [...] but the film is pretty savvy too, getting a jump on mounting anxieties about the post-war cult of consumerism, soon to be savaged by beatniks, cartoonists, and underground stand-up comics. [...] In the battle of the classic Hollywood Christmas movies, *It's A Wonderful Life* feels charmingly ancient, fixed in an early-20th-century America that scarcely anyone today remembers first-hand. *Miracle on 34th Street* feels more modern, with slangy dialogue and naturalistic asides, and a general awareness of how Christmas has become about the intertwined stresses of shopping and selling'.[1]

Miracle on 34th Street has, of course, become especially well-known as one of the first truly prominent portrayals in film of what we now recognise as the archetypal characterisation of Santa Claus, complete with white-fur-trimmed red suit, large black belt, red hat and heart-warmingly avuncular laugh. This modern depiction of Santa, or Father Christmas, in a vibrant red outfit was popularised largely through the imagery of cartoonist Thomas Nast in the late nineteenth century, which had differed from the earlier depictions of St Nicholas clad in ecclesiastical robes (though Nast's character actually wore a tan costume in his earliest incarnations, his clothing later becoming gradually more red with the passing of the years). However, the red-suited Santa who has become so firmly embedded in today's cultural psyche owes much to Coca-Cola's widespread Christmas advertising campaigns, featuring artwork by graphic designer Haddon Sundblom, between 1931 and 1964. Sundblom's characterisation of Santa appeared considerably more jovial and buoyant than Nast's had been, and was much more recognisable as the jolly gift-bearing figure that we know today. Santa had also made prominent

Miracle on 34th Street (1947): Twentieth Century-Fox

appearances in what have come to be considered the very first Christmas motion pictures, namely the American Mutoscope Company's *Santa Claus* cycle (1897), a series of four interrelated short films which are generally believed to have been directed by American Mutoscope's famous founder, William Kennedy Dickson. Thus while Father Christmas had appeared on film before *Miracle on 34th Street* (a recognisably ebullient Santa, played by Ferdinand Munier, had appeared in Gus Meins's and Charles Rogers's 1934 comedy *Babes in Toyland* alongside Stan Laurel and Oliver Hardy, for instance), this movie has comfortably established itself as one of the earliest and most popular cinematic depictions of the character – a fact underscored by the interesting detail that it remains the only film to date which features, in the form of Edmund Gwenn, an actor who was awarded an Academy Award for his portrayal of Santa Claus.

By the 1940s, director George Seaton had earned a firm reputation as a talented screenwriter in Hollywood, having provided the scripts for films such as *A Day at the Races* (Sam Wood, 1937), *This Thing Called Love* (Alexander Hall, 1940) and *That Night in Rio* (Irving Cummings, 1941). His directorial career at the time included features such as *Diamond Horseshoe* (1945), *Junior Miss* (1945) and *The Shocking Miss Pilgrim* (1947), and he would later go on to direct such diverse films as *Williamsburg: The Story of a Patriot* (1957), *Airport* (1970) and – perhaps most prominently – *The Country Girl* (1954), for which he won an Academy Award for Best Writing (Screenplay) in 1955 and was also nominated at the same ceremony for the Best Director Oscar. Seaton had previously been Academy Award-nominated for his screenplay for *The Song of Bernadette* (1943) at the 1944 Oscar ceremony, and would later be nominated for the script he had adapted for *Airport*. But *Miracle on 34th Street* was to prove one of the crowning glories of his career, and one which would bring him no small degree of success at the Academy Awards and elsewhere. Famously, Seaton was so certain of the capacity of Valentine Davies's original story for *Miracle on 34th Street* to enrapture audiences that he was willing to go to great lengths to ensure that it would be produced. Darryl F. Zanuck, the famous studio head of Twentieth Century-Fox, was far from convinced that the film had any commercial viability and eventually agreed to a modest production budget on the condition that Seaton would agree without objection to helm three further films for the studio after *Miracle on 34th Street* was complete. Seaton assented to Zanuck's stipulation,

and the rest would become history. As Jacob Skinner has observed, '*Miracle*'s greatness can be attributed to its director,
George Seaton. His direction is solid and his script is superb,
but what really shines through is the film's sincerity, which
comes straight from him. He wanted to make it so badly that
he agreed to make three films for Fox, no questions asked, as
long as he could film this story of Kris Kringle. He believed in
the film's message, and he tells it beautifully, never allowing it
to become a sappy "message" picture, but instead a heartfelt
film about faith and the spirit of Christmas that can live within all of us'.[2]

While on a leisurely saunter through New York City in
November, a kindly old gentleman named Kris Kringle (Edmund Gwenn) wanders across the elaborate Macy's parade
for the Thanksgiving season. Kris is alarmed when he discovers that the Santa Claus hired by Macy's to head up the parade (Percy Helton) is decidedly inebriated, and chastises the
man for intending to appear drunk in front of hundreds of
adoring and impressionable children. He voices his concerns to
the parade's organiser, Doris Walker (Maureen O'Hara), who
is shocked at the intoxicated Santa's condition. However, as
Doris has severe doubts about the possibility of getting the
man sobered up in time for the parade starting, she manages
to cajole the reluctant Kris into agreeing to take his place. As
Kris's appearance fits the bill perfectly – he is pleasantly avuncular, festively plump and sports a neatly groomed white
beard – the elderly gent appears impeccably suited to the part,
and proves hugely popular with the crowd when the parade
gets underway.

Kris's appearance impresses Macy's, and the company
decide to recruit him for their annual Santa Claus display
which is situated at their flagship store on the city's 34th

Street. There he befriends a kind-hearted young cleaner named Alfred (Alvin Greenman), whom he discovers also has an annual role as Santa at his local YMCA every Christmas. Before Kris's first appearance, toy department manager Julian Shellhammer (Philip Tonge) instructs him that if he should come across any children who are undecided about what gifts they would like for Christmas, he should recommend a variety of toys that Macy's are currently overstocked with. Indignant, Kris tears up Shellhammer's list, asserting that children should always have the chance to make up their own minds about their choice of Christmas presents.

Meanwhile, Doris finds herself the target of the affections of an attorney who lives in a neighbouring apartment in the same residential block. The easy-going Fred Gailey (John Payne) has befriended Doris's young daughter Susan (Natalie Wood), but is disappointed in the little girl's lack of imagination or sense of fun. Doris explains that she has raised Susan to understand that childhood fantasies are pointless and should not be indulged, in order to avoid disappointment in later life. Fred is particularly saddened in Susan's inability to believe in Santa Claus, so when the opportunity arises he surreptitiously decides to take her along to see Kris at Macy's Christmas display. She is initially sceptical about Kris's claims that he is the real Santa Claus, but later sneaks back into the grotto to overhear him speaking to a war orphan from the Netherlands (Marlene Lyden) in fluent Dutch, much to the little girl's delight, which makes Susan begin to question her disbelief.

Kris is having an impact on more than Susan, however. When he meets a little boy who wants a toy fire engine for Christmas, which his mother assures him has proven impossible to find at any store in town, Kris is quick to recommend another shop in the area that he knows will have the item in stock. Shellhammer is thunderstruck by Kris's honesty, which he feels is certain to be losing sales for Macy's, and is particularly alarmed to discover that Kris has recommended that one parent should visit arch-rival department store Gimbel's for a better quality of ice skate. But Shellhammer's disapproval quickly turns to puzzlement when he receives a barrage of positive feedback from overjoyed shoppers, grateful for Kris's timely recommendations. Thanks to Kris, many have managed to track down gifts that they had thought impossible to obtain, leading them to hail Macy's for the company's (apparently altruistic) support for the Christmas spirit.

Doris is frustrated that Susan has become so captivated by Kris, quite in spite of her efforts to drum any vestige of the fantastic out of her youthful mind. Growing increasingly exasperated, she calls Kris into her office and beseeches him to explain to Susan that he is not the real Santa Claus, but merely playing a part for the benefit of commercial interest. However, Kris shocks her by refusing to do so – he insists that he is, in fact, the genuine article. This leads Doris to doubt his sanity, especially when she notes that his company employment record corroborates Kris's elaborate insistence that he is the true Santa. She is on the cusp of dismissing Kris from the firm's employ, coming up with an elaborate cover story that a previous employee is to be appointed in his place, when she is suddenly called to the office of company owner R.H. Macy (Harry Antrim). She and Shellhammer appear slightly in awe when Macy congratulates them for the huge success of what he believes to be a co-ordinated marketing campaign that has been generated by the toy department. Though mildly annoyed that neither he nor his advertising section had been consulted first, Macy is over the moon at the massive amount of positive publicity that has been generated by Kris's strategy of ensuring that customers get the best deal – particularly as it has meant that Macy's have pulled well ahead of the competition. Elated, Macy promises Doris and Shellhammer a sizeable Christmas bonus – much to their mild puzzlement.

As they leave Macy's office, Doris explains to Shellhammer that she is in the process of firing Kris. Stunned, Shellhammer insists that she reinstate him immediately, but Doris voices her concerns over his mental fitness for the job. Willing to compromise, and anxious not to upset Macy, Shellhammer suggests that they ask Kris to undergo psychological tests conducted by company specialist Granville Sawyer (Porter Hall). If Kris passes the assessment, Shellhammer reasons, then he must surely be of no danger to the public. Though slightly mystified at the request, Kris readily agrees to undergo the mental fitness tests when asked. He completes the assessment effortlessly, but inadvertently irritates the self-important Sawyer when he becomes concerned about the man's own mental wellbeing. Sawyer angrily dismisses Kris from his office, all the while exhibiting signs of stress and anxiety such as exaggerated nervous tics and general tetchiness.

Infuriated by Kris's questioning of his psychological health, Sawyer strongly recommends to Doris that he be dismissed from employment at Macy's with immediate effect. But as luck would have it, Doris has invited Dr Pierce (James Seay) – a resident practitioner at the nursing home where Kris lives – to her office to give his own professional opinion. Pierce insists that Kris is not dangerous to either staff members or the public, and that although he obviously harbours 'delusions' of being Santa Claus, there is no reason why he cannot be a productive and effective member of society. Shellhammer readily agrees with his assessment, being mindful of the huge commercial benefits that Kris continues to bring to the store. Sawyer is miffed, perceiving that his professional recommendation has been snubbed, but Doris remains deeply sceptical; she knows that she will be held personally responsible if Kris should commit an indiscretion during his duties. Pierce suggests that perhaps it would be beneficial if Kris was to live closer to his place of employment in the lead-up to Christmas, thus meaning that a member of the Macy's staff could accompany him to and from work. Shellhammer plots a way to convince his wife (Lela Bliss) to allow Kris to live at their home for the next few weeks, but Fred suggests that Kris can stay at his apartment instead. Delighted, Kris agrees with Fred that if he can encourage the embittered Doris to see the good in life, Kris will concentrate on helping Susan to experience the wonder of Christmas for the first time.

During a meal break, Kris is aghast when he discovers that the usually-upbeat Alfred is in a deep depression; Sawyer has convinced the teenager that he is psychologically unwell, based on the flimsy evidence that as he enjoys distributing presents in his annual role as the YMCA Santa Claus, he must be compensating for the guilt of earlier misdeeds. Assuring his young friend that his mental state is entirely unimpaired, Kris storms off to challenge Sawyer in his office. Demanding an explanation of Sawyer's blatant misdiagnosis, Kris angrily questions the validity of the man's professional qualifications. Sawyer indignantly blusters his way through Kris's accusations, but his arrogance infuriates Kris to the point where he raps Sawyer over the head with his cane. Kris leaves the office just as Shellhammer and Doris arrive. Sawyer greatly overplays the extent of his injury, and blatantly lies about the cause of Kris's attack. As Kris isn't present to give his own side of the story, they have no choice but to take Sawyer's account at face value.

No longer satisfied with simply having Kris fired from the company, Sawyer quickly hatches an elaborate scheme to have him admitted to a mental hospital. Saddened because he believes Doris to have been complicit in the scheme (even although she knows nothing about it), Kris intentionally fails the psychological examination and is confined to a secure ward. Fred is called at his office to bring in some of Kris's personal effects, and while visiting he is upset to discover that his friend has been assessed for permanent residence at the hospital.

Urging Kris to fight back against the injustice that has been perpetrated against him, Fred petitions Judge Henry X. Harper (Gene Lockhart) to hold a hearing at a court in New York over the issue of Kris's sanity. This decision is met with disdain by District Attorney Thomas Mara (Jerome Cowan), and outright alarm by Sawyer, who has been instructed by Macy in no uncertain terms to have the case dropped in order to avoid a public relations disaster for the store. However, events have already proceeded too far to derail the hearing, and when Sawyer attempts to persuade Fred to pull the plug on his case – because of the potential for bad publicity – Fred instead decides to ensure that Kris's court appearance gains the maximum possible exposure.

The hearing causes a number of problems for those involved. Harper is seeking re-election the following year, and is desperate to find a way of resolving the proceedings without damaging his prospects at the ballot box in the process. (Even his wife and grandchildren are giving him the cold shoulder at the fact that he is calling Kris's probity into question.) The judge is all too aware that any official who makes a public declaration to the effect that Santa Claus doesn't exist – particularly at a trial which is taking place at Christmas – will face certain electoral ruin. Fred, meanwhile, having accepted this most unusual of cases, finds that his position has become untenable at the law firm where he works; the partners believe the increasingly high-profile case to be fatuous and potentially damaging to their reputation. He thus resigns in order to defend Kris, which brings him into conflict with Doris who berates him for having sacrificed his long-term security in order to chase after a whimsical fantasy. Fred is maddened by her hard-headed cynicism, and fires back that she may eventually learn that the fantastic can sometimes matter more than any number of mundane certainties.

The hearing arrives, and Mara wastes no time in calling Kris to the stand and asking him – under oath – to confirm his belief that he is Santa Claus. Kris agrees wholeheartedly that he is, which leads Mara to the natural conclusion that he is insane. However, Fred shocks Harper and Mara – to say nothing of the court at large – when he asserts that while Mara cannot disprove that Kris really is Santa, he can and will establish that Kris and Santa are one in the same. Harper is alarmed, knowing that he faces a public backlash that will cripple his re-election campaign if he rules that Santa Claus is not real, and therefore agrees to let Mara and Fred present evidence to give him an opportunity to devise an impartial way out of his predicament.

R.H. Macy is called to the stand by Fred, who asks him whether he is willing to testify under oath that he believes that Kris really is Santa Claus. Macy is deeply conflicted, considering the publicity disaster – and the disappointment of so many children – which would result if he should say the wrong thing. Reluctantly, he states for the record that he does indeed believe that Kris and Santa Claus are the same person. However, once he has given his testimony he angrily dismisses Sawyer from the company's employ, blaming his inflated ego for the whole mess surrounding Kris's dismissal. Fred then surprises the court by calling Mara's own son, Thomas Mara Jr. (Robert Hyatt) as a witness. Mara Jr. asserts that he believes that Santa is real, as his father had told him so – and he believes that his father is an honest man who would not lie to him, especially about something so important. He also identifies the fact that, to his mind, Santa exists in the form of Kris. This leaves Mara with little manoeuvring room for tactics of his own, and he is grudgingly forced to admit that Santa Claus exists – but not that he necessarily exists in the form of Kris Kringle.

Fred finds himself desperately racking his brains in an attempt to prove that Kris is the genuine, original and unique Santa Claus. In the hope that she can cheer Kris up, Susan writes him a note of encouragement which (unknown to her) is countersigned by Doris. They address it to the court building and post it. At a sorting office in the city, a mail worker (Jack Albertson) discovers the letter and calls over his supervisor, Lou (Guy Thomajan), to present him with an idea. The post office are in receipt of a great many letters to Santa, most of them unaddressed or simply directed to 'The North Pole'. As the Kringle hearing is currently taking place at an actual geographical location, the sorter suggests that the vast number of letters in the dead letter office be cleared out and delivered to Kris while he is there in person.

Back at the courtroom, it is now Christmas Eve. Kris is overjoyed to receive the letter – it proves to him not only that Susan has put her faith in him, but also that Doris has some belief of her own to offer as well. Fred begins the latest round of his defence by getting the court to acknowledge that the United States Post Office is an official organ of the American Federal Government. This is accepted. He then presents Harper with three letters which have been processed by the post office, addressed simply to 'Santa Claus'. This, Fred claims, is proof that the government acknowledges the existence of Santa Claus, and that he must be present in the form of Kris as he was the person to whom the letters were delivered. Harper asks Fred if he can present further evidence to this effect and place them on his desk. Fred then calls a small army of postal delivery men into the court, who proceed to empty bag after bag of letters in front of Harper. Swamped under many thousands of letters addressed to Santa, Harper is left with no option but to rule in favour of Kris. Everyone in the court (with the possible exception of Mara) is elated with the verdict, and Kris warmly thanks Harper for having reached the right decision.

Kris reluctantly has to turn down Doris's offer of dinner – it is, after all, Christmas Eve, and he has other business to attend to. The next morning, he meets up with Fred, Doris and Susan – along with Macy and Alfred, whose temperament has returned to its cheerful norm. Susan appears downcast that she didn't receive the special gift that she had asked Kris for – a new home out in the suburbs, away from the inner-city apartment that she had grown up in. She thus resolves that Kris isn't really Santa Claus at all, but just a friendly old man. However, Susan soon changes her mind when Kris suggests a new route to Fred when driving home which will present lighter traffic; on their travels, they discover the perfect home that she has always dreamed about. The house is currently empty, a 'For Sale' notice standing outside. Susan is entranced to find that the house is exactly as she imagined it, right down to a swing in the back garden. Overjoyed at the realisation that Doris had encouraged Susan to believe in Kris, even although she appeared at first to have been disappointed, Fred suggests that he should purchase the house and move into it with Doris (his offer couching an implicit proposal of marriage). He initially appears slightly conceited, believing that he has somehow achieved an unlikely success against all the odds. However, Fred's vanity doesn't last for long: he and Doris soon discover a cane in the living room which looks identical to the one used by Kris, which leads Fred to admit that perhaps it wasn't he who had made their Christmas dreams come true after all.

At its heart, *Miracle on 34th Street* is a film about faith. Not religious faith, as in *The Bells of St Mary's* (q.v.) or the faith in a common humanity that is shown throughout *It's a Wonderful Life*, but rather a simple, robust belief in the Christmas spirit and the positive effects which can derive from it. Kris repeatedly makes the point that it is human nature to put our faith in some things which may appear indefinable or intangible, and that we should never give up hope even when the odds are stacked against us. But he also emphasises that it is important to choose carefully what it is that we put our faith in, because those beliefs will ultimately shape and define us. We see this optimistic outlook at work not just in Susan, whose natural youthful exuberance has been stymied by hard-hearted pragmatism, but also in the staid matter-of-factness evident in Doris's world view, her glacial temperament eventually thawing as a result of Kris's wistful encouragement and the idealistic Fred's steadfast and sincere romantic advances. No-one, it seems, can stand in the way of Kris's irrepressible festive spirit. Sawyer's deceit eventually leads to his own downfall, while the wily attorney Mara (very obvi-

ously visually modelled on real-life Manhattan District Attorney Thomas E. Dewey) is smart enough to know when he's
playing a game that he can't win. But Kris has no interest in
gaining the upper hand over those who oppose his message of
goodwill; his only goal appears to be propagating a universal
message of benevolence to all, typified by Christmas but relevant the whole year through. As Sanderson Beck sagely remarks: 'This fantasy promotes the Christmas spirit amid the
modern tendency to commercialize the holiday, suggesting
that intangibles such as love, kindness, imagination, and joy
are real and important'.[3]

In an America that was only just beginning to emerge
from the austerity of the war years, the film's note of caution
over the commercialisation of Christmas would doubtless
have seemed timely. Davies's original story is said to have derived from his own experiences of fighting his way through
crowds of Christmas shoppers every December in order to
buy gifts for loved ones, and asking himself what Santa Claus
would make of the commercial free-for-all that he was witnessing. Thomas S. Hischak notes that Seaton's screenplay does
diligently follow the tone and content Davies's prose original
in many respects: 'The novel is written in simple and flowing
prose with a sense of wonder, the tone of the book being that
Santa does indeed exist. Director George Seaton's screenplay
for the 1947 film adhered closely to Davies' story with minor
changes. [...] There is more humor in the film because of some
delectable character actors in minor roles. Otherwise the film
relies on the novel for plot, people, and charm'.[4] In Seaton's
script, Kris states quite emphatically his concern that the festive season is ceasing to focus on the importance of giving,
being more concerned with materialism and self-interest. His
scheme of conveying parents to stores other than Macy's, in

order to track down hard-to-find gifts or better quality presents, baffles the corporate top-brass with its simplicity and ability to generate public support for the company (even though they risk losing some Christmas revenue, many customers pledge to become loyal shoppers there throughout the rest of the year). Yet even here Kris's altruism is impeccable; presented with a sizeable bonus by R.H. Macy, Kris determines to spend it on a new X-ray machine in order to aid the diagnoses of his old friend Dr Pierce. When it becomes apparent that Macy's cheque won't quite cover the cost, Macy's arch-rival Mr Gimbel (Herbert Heyes) – present for a publicity photoshoot – not only offers to make up the difference, but to sell the machine to Kris at cost price. As has been noted by MaryAnn Johanson, the film's ability to critique the ill-effects of uncontrolled materialism while also emphasising the positive aspects of the free market at the holiday season are what make its artistic approach so effective: '*Miracle on 34th Street* isn't actually about whether Kris is the jolly old elf or just "a nice man with a white beard" – it's about whether it's insane to believe in the giving spirit of Christmas in our world today. I say "today" because even though *Miracle* is more than half a century old, the rampant commercialism that the film protests is still with us now – and it's probably even worse'.[5]

Even as early as the forties, themes deriving from commercialism at Christmas felt like a perfect fit; films such as Ernst Lubitsch's *The Shop Around the Corner* (q.v.), Don Hartman's *Holiday Affair* (q.v.) and Robert Z. Leonard's *In the Good Old Summertime* (1949) had all – in different and sometimes subtle ways – touched upon the often-problematic intersection between the festive season and the retail business. *Miracle on 34th Street* remains one of the best-known early exponents of the need to recognise the importance of unselfishness and philanthropy at Christmas, and yet rather than appearing preachy the film actually blurs the boundaries between commercial trade and individual generosity quite profoundly and with great skill. Kris seems perfectly happy to enter the employ of Macy's, and – though he is an unconventional staff member (to say the least) – he has few qualms about jumping through any and all corporate hoops that are presented to him. While he is keen to encourage parents to seek out the best bargains when purchasing gifts for their children, he has no difficulty in accepting the fact that mass-production is the most expedient way of ensuring that as many toys as possible are available to satisfy the present-buying public. And as the media storm surrounding Kris's trial provides ample testimony, effective marketing and publicity was increasingly becoming key to ensuring brisk business – a fact that is far from lost on R.H. Macy. Here, as Dave Sindelar points out, we see corporate expediency and good old-fashioned serendipity intertwined in bringing about the confluence of events that eventually saves Kris from being declared insane: 'This Christmas perennial takes aim at two targets; the increasing commercialism of the holiday (a trend which has only gotten worse as time passes) and the underlying cynicism that is the ultimate cause of it. [...] I find it quite interesting that two of the biggest factors that come into play in determining the result of the trial include the fear of public and private embarrassment on the parts of several individuals, and the passing thought of a postal employee who has hit upon a scheme to decrease his workload'.[6]

Central to the film, even though his character is technically a supporting one, is Edmund Gwenn's warm and affable interpretation of Santa Claus. Giving one of the best-known and most accomplished performances of his cinematic career,

Gwenn's portrayal owes much more to the grandfatherly jollity of the Sundblom incarnation of Santa than it does to the
comparatively schoolmasterly portrayal depicted by Nast during the American Civil War and later. Active in cinema since
appearing as Rupert K. Thunder in *The Real Thing at Last*
(L.C. MacBean, 1916), Gwenn made many appearances over
the years in features as diverse as *Condemned to Death* (Walter Forde, 1932), *The Admiral's Secret* (Guy Newall, 1934),
The Bishop Misbehaves (Ewald André Dupont, 1935), *A
Yank at Oxford* (Jack Conway, 1938) and *Lassie Come Home*
(Fred M. Wilcox, 1943). He was especially well-remembered
for his four collaborations with Alfred Hitchcock, especially as
the villainous assassin Rowley in *Foreign Correspondent*
(1940). Throughout *Miracle on 34th Street* Gwenn is excep-
tional as Kris, the compassionate old man with a not-so-secret
alter-ego, and he impresses not only as the kind-hearted figure
of legend but also (especially in the film's third act) in reflecting the deep disillusionment and occasional flicker of hopelessness that the character feels when he comes to believe that
Doris and Susan – and, by extension, the world at large –
have abandoned their trust in him. The ongoing question of
Kris's sanity, and the effectiveness of psychological assessment
in categorising him, becomes a compelling one throughout the
course of the film, and Seaton's screenplay handles this potentially sensitive topic with admirable understanding. Having
passed his employers' mental fitness tests with flying colours,
Kris angrily berates Sawyer's unrealistically high opinion of
his psychiatric talents when he is found making baseless and
sweeping analytical assumptions; as Glen O. Gabbard and
Krin Gabbard remark, this important distinction set the film
apart from many others of the time: 'In one of cinema's first
attempts to distinguish psychologists from psychiatrists, Kris

Kringle (Edmund Gwenn) scolds [a] department store psychologist (Porter Hall) for practicing psychiatry'.[7] Contrasted with the even-minded physician Pierce, who is certain that Kris poses no threat to either himself or to others – to say nothing of Shellhammer, desperately weighing the vague possibility of Kris becoming unbalanced against the vast benefits that he brings to Macy's – Sawyer becomes a memorable antagonist, petty and spiteful but riddled with insecurities and sporting an impressive anxiety complex of his own. Porter Hall plays the part to the hilt, mining the character for every smidgeon of malicious self-importance to great effect.

Of the main characters, Maureen O'Hara's performance as the strait-laced but occasionally cynical Doris stays in the memory, as does John Payne's stoic turn as the independently-minded Fred, determined to keep the Christmas spirit alive even in the cool detachment of an inner-city courthouse. O'Hara was well-known to audiences at the time for performances in *Jamaica Inn* (Alfred Hitchcock, 1939), *The Hunchback of Notre Dame* (William Dieterle, 1939) and *Buffalo Bill* (William A. Wellman, 1944), while Payne would readily have been recognised by audiences for appearances in films such as *Maryland* (Henry King, 1940), *Tin Pan Alley* (Walter Lang, 1940) and *Iceland* (H. Bruce Humberstone, 1942). Just as believable as the budding romance between Fred and Doris, and as touching as the gradual warming of Doris's affection towards the festive spirit, is Natalie Wood's portrayal of Susan's first tentative embrace of the world of her childhood imagination. Wood had previously appeared in Irving Pichel's films *Tomorrow is Forever* (1946) and *The Bride Wore Boots* (1946), but her appearance in *Miracle on 34th Street* remains easily the most prominent of her early career as a child actor. Anecdotal accounts of the time suggested that, like her character, Wood became convinced that Gwenn really was Santa Claus during the production of the film, and her tangible sense of childlike wonder is what sets apart her performance from so many others of a similar type. As J.P. Roscoe has perceived, Seaton's recognition of the magic of Christmas in the eyes of youth have helped to make *Miracle on 34th Street* a truly memorable cinematic experience: 'The movie has the classic look of Christmas including a trip to the Macy's Thanksgiving Day Parade. In the idea of a child's view of Christmas, the visuals (despite dated to the '40s) still hold true to what you imagine Christmas to be as a kid. *Miracle on 34th St.* is one of the best Christmas movies out there. It is a strong, smart movie that has held up well over the years'.[8]

There are many other memorable performances throughout the film, from Philip Tonge's dryly obsequious Julian Shellhammer to a nicely-drawn appearance by William Frawley as savvy political advisor Charlie Halloran. In particular, Gene Lockhart creates a skilfully multi-layered portrayal of Judge Harper, presenting a man who is conflicted between his approval ratings with the public and his desire to ensure that some semblance of justice is done – a tall order, under the circumstances. Both a doting grandfather and a political realist, Harper is forced to rely on his many years of legal experience to derive a satisfactory conclusion to Kris's case that won't render him permanently unelectable (and which would also guarantee that his family will never speak to him again), but still ensures that justice is done. The solution which eventually presents itself proves to be as inspired as it is strangely rational, its validity emphasising that sometimes logic can wrap itself in unusual and unexpected forms – especially where Kris Kringle is concerned. Stuart Galbraith IV has not been alone in noting that the film's contemporary edge – emphasising the modernity of New York in the forties, rather than an outright fantasy setting – has been key to its lasting appeal amongst audiences and critics alike:

Its durability is due to a combination of delightful performances, transcendentally magical moments – coupled with an all-important ambiguity – and because its biting, knowing commentary about the commercialization of Christmas sadly becomes more relevant with each passing year. [...] I'm always impressed by the film's ambiguity; Seaton and Davies are extraordinarily clever here. There's not a shred of hard evidence that Kris is anything other than an eccentric old man. Unlike most Christmas-themed movies, there are no reindeer in sight, no elves in the wings, no acts of magic. Even the famous, often misinterpreted ending leaves it up to the viewers to decide whether or not Kris Kringle and Santa Claus are one and the same.[9]

Another factor that has made the film famous is the fact that, for all its festive conventions, the studio made the unusual decision to release *Miracle on 34th Street* on 4 June 1947. Zanuck, deeply unconvinced that a Christmas film had much commercial potential, insisted that it be released in summer under the assumption that this season would be more popular with cinemagoers than the depths of winter. This left Twentieth Century-Fox with the peculiar conundrum of promoting this most festive of features while trying to conceal the fact that it was set at Christmas or contained any yuletide tropes. As Brandon A. Duhamel observes, 'the film was amazingly not even released during the holiday season in 1947, but instead saw a summer release from 20th Century-Fox who had no idea how to market a "Santa Claus" film and was looking to maximize their profits on the endeavor during the highest box office grossing period. With a stealth-marketing plan that never mentioned the film's holiday trappings, *Miracle on 34th Street* released to wide acclaim and would run for six months, right through the holiday season'.[10] Regardless of the unconventional circumstances of its release, the film performed well with audiences and also at the Academy Awards, winning Oscars for Valentine Davies's original story and George Seaton's screenplay in 1948, in addition to the Best Actor in a Supporting Role Award for Edmund Gwenn. The film was additionally nominated for Best Picture. However, the Academy Awards were not to be the only recognition that the film was to receive in 1948: it also won Seaton a Best Adapted Screenplay award at the Locarno Film Festival, as well as Golden Globe Awards for both Seaton's screenplay and Gwenn's supporting performance.

The film's success with audiences may also have stemmed from the shrewdness of its production, which has come to fascinate audiences in the years since. The opening shots at Macy's Thanksgiving Parade were filmed at the actual parade in New York City, which took place on 28 November 1946, complete with Philip Tonge introducing the appearance of Santa Claus (in character as Shellhammer) while Edmund Gwenn fulfilled the traditional role of Santa, addressing the crowd and revealing the specially-decorated shop windows of Macy's store to mark the beginning of the festive shopping season. None of this would have been obvious to the public of the time until they saw the film several months later. In order to ensure their co-operation in their respective organisations being featured in the movie, both Macy's and Gimbel's department stores were approached in advance of production, and both granted approval only on the condition that they were able to see the finished cut of the film to ensure that their companies were being represented in a fair and reputable way. Thankfully when advance screenings took place the organisations were satisfied with Seaton's fictional depiction of them, and no after-the-fact reshoots were required. The resulting verisimilitude may have greatly increased the film's sense of visual authenticity, but – as Stephen Schochet mentions – the employment of real-world locations was not without its challenges: 'The use of New York locations increased the budget of the 1947 Christmas classic *Miracle on 34th Street*. Hundreds of extras were hired to pretend they were shopping at Macy's after business hours, due to fears that actual customers might be startled by the movie maker's bright lights into tripping and falling down escalators. *Miracle*'s set builders also constructed a costly replica of Bellevue. The famed mental hospital's staff members were upset at being portrayed as cruel in earlier movies and denied the film's fictional Santa Claus the use of their psycho ward'.[11]

Critical reception of *Miracle on 34th Street* was largely favourable when it first made its appearance in cinemas, with many critics picking up on the film's originality and sense of warmth. *Variety*, for instance, declared that the 'film is an actor's holiday, providing any number of choice roles that are played to the hilt. Edmund Gwenn's Santa Claus performance proves the best in his career, one that will be thoroughly enjoyed by all filmgoers. [...] Valentine Davies' story poses question of just how valid is the belief in Santa Claus. Gwenn, old man's home inmate, becomes Santy at Macy's Department Store, events pile up that make it necessary to actually prove he is the McCoy and not a slightly touched old gent. Gwenn is a little amazed at all the excitement because he has no doubt that he's the real article'.[12] *The New York Times*'s film reviewer Bosley Crowther was similarly effusive in his praise of the movie's merits:

> Let us heartily recommend the Roxy's new picture, *Miracle on 34th Street*. As a matter of fact, let's go further: let's catch its spirit and heartily proclaim that it is the freshest little picture in a long time, and maybe even the best comedy of this year. If that sounds like wild enthusiasm for a picture devoid of mighty stars and presented without the usual red-velvet-carpet ballyhoo, let us happily note that it is largely because this job isn't loaded to the hubs with all the commercial gimmicks that it is such a delightful surprise. Indeed, it is in its open kidding of 'commercialism' and money-grubbing plugs that lies its originality and its particularly winning charm.[13]

More recent retrospectives of the film have remained positive in the main, with the endearing appeal of its main characters and central situations continuing to win fans even in today's less trustful age. Nick Davis provides a relatively rare note of scepticism, commenting that: 'I get it that none but the grinchiest could take exception to *Miracle on 34th Street*, but if you have actually seen the movie recently, and if we can set aside its ritual ensconcement as part of the yuletide avalanche of synthetic good cheer that the movie purports to lament, it's pretty astonishing how listlessly it's acted and assembled. George Seaton isn't quite Ed Wood, but there are more than enough hilariously flat or else bizarrely overdone reaction shots here to attain at least a weekend pass to

Woodville. Edmund Gwenn gives the most natural, calmly engaging performance as, strangely, the only character who isn't a completely mundane and by-the-numbers human'.[14] Others, such as Richard Scheib, have instead drawn attention to the possibility that the movie's central premise is open to more interesting lines of interpretation than those that have traditionally accompanied its analysis: 'The film's only disappointment is its fade-out at the end on the vague suggestion that Edmund Gwenn might be Santa Claus – after the time it spends arguing for his right to be such, this is surely an anticlimax. On the other hand, if one reads the ambiguity the other way, it lends to the more interestingly subversive reading, that the film is instead about the American public's own constitutionally-guaranteed right to be eccentric. Indeed, *Miracle on 34th Street* is not unlike another great classic from the era, *Harvey* (1950), which argued in favour of the joys of thorough eccentricity and the fact that people with eccentric and outrightly lunatic beliefs had a better centeredness of sanity than those who took life seriously'.[15]

However, cynicism towards the film's merits have proven to be relatively uncommon, and its supporters have continued to greatly outnumber its detractors. Laura Grieve, for instance, is largely representative of modern, nostalgic viewings of the film when she notes that 'one of my favorite things to do on Thanksgiving is watch *Miracle on 34th Street*. Since the movie begins on Thanksgiving Day and ends on Christmas, it's the perfect way to begin the holiday season. Most people are already familiar with the movie, but it must be said that it only gets better with time and repeated viewings. The film is perfection itself. [...] As with *White Christmas* and other holiday classics, memories of watching the film over past holidays add to the nostalgic glow and magic each time the movie is visited anew'.[16] Modern criticism has also taken into account the fact that the film's themes have become so indelibly entwined with the conventions of Christmas cinema, its reputation has not only grown in stature over the passing decades but has also been opened up to interesting new readings beyond the confines of the tropes of the holiday season. As Jeffrey Kauffman considers:

> The charming and still moving *Miracle on 34th Street* [is] one of those evergreen 'holiday classics' that speaks to a certain world weariness which kind of ironically makes the film's original release in the supposedly halcyon days of post World War II America kind of interesting. [...] It's interesting to note that *Miracle on 34th Street* was originally released in the summer of 1947, and that its whole emphasis on Christmas was largely ignored in its initial marketing materials. That may seem odd to longtime fans of the film who have found Edmund Gwenn's unforgettable (and Academy Award winning) turn as one Kris Kringle the centerpiece of the film, but it's perhaps indicative that George Seaton's screenplay is attempting to address issues that are more universal than any one special day.[17]

Such has been its continuing influence, *Miracle on 34th Street* has been remade several times for television over the years. These features have included Robert Stevenson's 1955 remake (also later known as *Meet Mr Kringle*), screened on CBS as part of *The 20th Century-Fox Hour* (originally broadcast on 14 December 1955), William Corrigan's 1959 version for NBC (first shown on 27 November 1959 and featuring Ed Wynn as Kris Kringle), and Fielder Cook's 1973 version for

CBS (initially broadcast on 14 December 1973). The film also inspired a Broadway musical version in 1963, *Here's Love*, which was written by Meredith Willson. Later, Davies's original novella would be adapted for theatre by Will Severin, Patricia Di Benedetto Snyder and John Vreeke in 2000. The stage play has remained faithful to the 1940s setting of the original, and has proven popular with audiences since its initial production. Also, a radio adaptation of *Miracle on 34th Street* was broadcast by Lux Radio Theater on 22 December 1947, with Maureen O'Hara, Edmund Gwenn, John Payne and Natalie Wood all reprising their roles from the Seaton movie. A second radio broadcast took place on 20 December 1948, this time without Natalie Wood's participation. The one-hour radio adaptation was later reworked into a thirty minute edition, also starring Gwenn as Kris Kringle, which would feature as part of the *Screen Director's Playhouse*. Furthermore, the events of the film have also been adapted for puppet theatre; Macy's famous department store in New York's Herald Square has showcased a special half-hour production which debuted in 2011, featuring seven original songs and vocal performances by Broadway stars including Brian Stokes Mitchell and Victoria Clark.

However, more prominent in recent years has been Les Mayfield's cinematic updating of the story in 1994, starring Richard Attenborough as Kris Kringle, which featured a screenplay by eighties film legend John Hughes (who also acted as the film's producer). Mayfield's remake updated the story in order to enhance its relevance for audiences of the mid-nineties, with Hughes deftly reworking Seaton's original screenplay to take account of the social and cultural changes which had occurred in the intervening decades. Elizabeth Perkins and Dylan McDermott make appealing leads, with Mara

Wilson's Susan appearing suitably starstruck by old Mr Kringle's effortless invocation of the wonder of Christmas. Simon Jones (instantly recognisable to a whole generation of British TV fans as the hapless Arthur Dent in the BBC's 1981 adaptation of Douglas Adams's *The Hitchhiker's Guide to the Galaxy*) also delivers a wonderfully tongue-in-cheek performance as 'Donald' Shellhammer. However, the film offers many narrative changes from Seaton's original; the psychologist Sawyer is eliminated from the plot, while Kringle's downfall is engineered instead by a rival department store. (Just as noteworthy was the fact that the real-life Macy's department store is replaced by the fictional 'Cole's' company.) However, at its core the film retains the same message of remembering the vital importance of belief, substituting the original's mailbag-festooned conclusion for a rather more low-key climax which contains an understated subtext concerning religious faith, drawing parallels between belief in the spirit of Christmas and trust in a higher power. The remake of *Miracle on 34*th *Street* split critical opinion at the time of its release, largely given the difficulty inherent in following the timelessly iconic original, and it remains to be seen how the longevity of Mayfield's film will compare to the classic which inspired it.

There is also some evidence to suggest that a sequel to *Miracle on 34*th *Street* may have once been a possibility. Star John Payne had enjoyed his part in the film so much that he is said to have become personally invested in the prospect of producing a direct follow-up which would have revisited the beloved characters of the 1947 original. He was eventually said to have written a screenplay for the sequel himself, but attempts to mount a production ultimately came to nothing. Payne died in 1989, and at time of writing no sequel to *Miracle on 34*th *Street* has ever been produced.

Even today, *Miracle on 34th Street* remains one of the best-loved of all Christmas movies. Given its enduring significance, in 2005 it was selected for preservation by the Library of Congress in the US National Film Registry, and its lasting influence continues to be felt even in the present day. As commentators such as Ace Collins have ventured, the movie's contribution to the emerging genre of Christmas cinema cannot be understated: 'One of the ironies of *Miracle on 34th Street* is that it was released in the summer and was not advertised as a Christmas film. The studio had no faith in Christmas or in the movie. But as crowds flocked to theatres to catch the film in the midst of the long, hot days of July, and as the picture was still playing in movie houses six months later during the cold holiday season's evenings, Hollywood learned its lesson. Christmas movies would work. The success of the film thus paved the way for studios to make more projects centred on holiday themes'.[18] There are very few films of any genre which encapsulate so vividly the excitement of childhood expectation at the approaching festive season, or which underscore with such panache the healthy need to retain a daily faith in the indefinable, irrespective of one's ideological, philosophical or religious background. Faced with the undeniable critical and commercial success of this archetypal Christmas film, there were few in the Hollywood studio system who were now willing to deny that this newly-emerging genre had definite artistic and economic potential.

REFERENCES

1. Noel Murray, '*Miracle on 34th Street*', in *AV Club*, 13 December 2006.
    <*https://film.avclub.com/miracle-on-34th-street-1798202201*>

2. Jacob Skinner, '*Miracle on 34th Street*', in *Film Write-Up*, 25 December 2012.
    <*https://filmwriteup.wordpress.com/2012/12/25/miracle-on-34th-street-1947-review/*>

3. Sanderson Beck, '*Miracle on 34th Street*', in *Movie Mirrors*, 2006.
    <*http://san.beck.org/MM/1947/Miracleon34thStreet.html*>

4. Thomas S. Hischak, *American Literature on Stage and Screen: 525 Works and Their Adaptations* (Jefferson: McFarland, 2012), p.146.

5. MaryAnn Johanson, '*Miracle on 34th Street*', in *Flick Filosopher*, 11 December 1999.
    <*https://www.flickfilosopher.com/1999/12/miracle-on-34th-street-review.html*>

6. Dave Sindelar, '*Miracle on 34th Street*', in *Fantastic Movie Musings and Ramblings*, 8 November 2015.
    <*https://fantasticmoviemusings.com/2015/11/08/miracle-on-34th-street-1947/*>

7. Glen O. Gabbard and Krin Gabbard, *Psychiatry and the Cinema*, 2nd edn (Washington D.C.: American Psychiatric Press, 1999), p.337.

8.   J.P. Roscoe, '*Miracle on 34th Street*', in *Basement Rejects*,
     4 December 2017.
     <*http://basementrejects.com/review/miracle-on-34th-steet-
     1947/*>

9.   Stuart Galbraith IV, '*Miracle on 34th Street*', in *DVD
     Talk*, 2 November 2009.
     <*https://www.dvdtalk.com/reviews/38505/miracle-on-
     34th-street/*>

10. Brandon A. Duhamel, '*Miracle on 34th Street*', in *Thea-
     terByte*, 22 October 2009.
     <*https://www.theaterbyte.com/bluray-uhd-
     reviews/miracle-on-34th-street-1947-blu-ray-review.html*>

11. Stephen Schochet, *Hollywood Stories: Short, Entertaining
     Anecdotes about the Stars and Legends*, 2nd edn (Los An-
     geles: Hollywood Stories Publishing, 2013), p.83.

12. Anon., '*Miracle on 34th Street*', in *Variety*, 5 June 1947.
     <*https://variety.com/1946/film/reviews/miracle-on-34th-
     street-1200415057/*>

13. Bosley Crowther, '*Miracle on 34th Street*, with Edmund
     Gwenn in the Role of Santa Claus, at Roxy – *Web* at
     Loew's Criterion', in *The New York Times*, 5 June 1947.
     <*https://www.nytimes.com/1947/06/05/archives/miracle-
     on-34th-street-with-edmund-gwenn-in-the-role-of-santa-
     claus.html*>

14. Nick Davis, '*Miracle on 34th Street*', in *Nick's Flick Picks*,
     December 2009.
     <*http://www.nicksflickpicks.com/mirc34th.html*>

15. Richard Scheib, '*Miracle on 34th Street*', in *Moria: The Science Fiction, Horror and Fantasy Film Review*, 1 March 2003.
   <*http://www.moriareviews.com/fantasy/miracle-on-34th-street-1947.htm*>

16. Laura Grieve, 'Tonight's Movie: *Miracle on 34th Street*', in *Laura's Miscellaneous Musings*, 27 November 2008.
   <*https://laurasmiscmusings.blogspot.com/2008/11/tonight s-movie-miracle-on-34th-street.html*>

17. Jeffrey Kauffman, '*Miracle on 34th Street*: 70th Anniversary Edition', in *Blu-ray.com*, 17 October 2017.
   <*https://www.blu-ray.com/movies/Miracle-on-34th-Street-Blu-ray/186945/#Review*>

18. Ace Collins, *Stories Behind the Great Traditions of Christmas* (Grand Rapids: Zondervan, 2003), p.133.

7

The Bishop's Wife (1947)

The Samuel Goldwyn Company

Director: Henry Koster
Producer: Samuel Goldwyn
Screenwriters: Robert E. Sherwood and Leonardo Bercovici,
from a novel by Robert Nathan

THOUGH not often listed alongside the titans of 1940s Christmas movie-making such as *It's a Wonderful Life* (q.v.) and *Miracle on 34th Street* (q.v.), *The Bishop's Wife* has become one of the great treasures of the post-war era of festive film-making – and yet, for some reason, its reputation has never quite rivalled those of its better-known contemporaries. Though it may seem like an often-overlooked jewel of festive movie-making, it is probably fair to say that rather than being intentionally disregarded by modern audiences *The Bishop's Wife* instead tends to be wrongly unheeded on account of its proximity to films from the same period which have acquired greater stature over the course of the passing decades.

Demonstrating an interesting distillation of themes that had manifested themselves earlier in the decade, *The Bishop's Wife* exhibits a complex melange of sentimentalism and faith-based issues blended into a gently idiosyncratic comedy-drama format. Like its aforementioned contemporaries *It's a Wonderful Life* and *Miracle on 34th Street*, it is a film where Christmas – and themes deriving from the festive season – are central to the storyline rather than merely ancillary to it. Yet it also shares *The Bells of St Mary's* (q.v.) concern with matters of religious belief (albeit that this subject matter is treated in a markedly different way) to delineate exactly why Christmas is significant not just as an annual celebration, but as an opportunity to engage with society at large and consequently to improve lives. As *The Bishop's Wife* makes clear throughout its narrative, this is not solely an opportunity presented to followers of a religion; it is accessible to everyone who seeks to make the world a better place, irrespective of whether they choose to follow a spiritual belief or not. As Sanderson Beck has astutely noted, 'this spiritual fantasy reflects how modern religion has been lost in material concerns, but joyful and loving consideration can restore people's faith in each other'.[1]

The film was a famously turbulent production, with legendary producer Samuel Goldwyn rejecting an original cut which had been directed by William A. Seiter and then contracting a new director, Henry Koster, to begin shooting from scratch. The problematic genesis of *The Bishop's Wife* was just one of the challenges faced during its production, as Michael Reuben observes:

> If the various stories about the troubled production of *The Bishop's Wife* are true, then the fact that it plays with such apparently effortless comic grace is yet another example of how little connection there is in filmmaking between the finished product and the process that created it. Legendarily autocratic producer Samuel Goldwyn fired the film's original director, William A. Seiter, when

shooting was nearly complete, and started over at an estimated cost of $1 million, a considerable sum at the time. Replacement director Henry Koster (*Harvey, The Robe*) reshot the entire picture and reportedly recast it as well, replacing original actress Teresa Wright (who was now pregnant) with [Loretta] Young in the title role, and recasting David Niven with Grant as Dudley. (There are several versions of this story.) Uncredited rewrites were performed by Billy Wilder and his partner Charles Brackett before the film reached the form in which we know it today. (The original screenplay was by Robert Sherwood and Leonardo Bercovici, adapting a novel by popular writer Robert Nathan.)[2]

Henry Koster had been active in the film industry since the early 1930s as both a director and screenwriter; the early features that he had been involved with in his native Germany were credited to his name at birth, Hermann Kösterlitz. After moving to the United States in the late thirties, Koster continued to build a solid reputation in the film world, directing features such as *The Rage of Paris* (1938), *First Love* (1939), *Spring Parade* (1940) and *Music for Millions* (1944) before starting work on *The Bishop's Wife*. Adapted by Robert E. Sherwood and Leonardo Bercovici from a novel by Robert Nathan, the film was to feature a stellar cast of youthful actors including Cary Grant, Loretta Young and David Niven. Though the product of much effort and negotiation behind the scenes, most especially including Goldwyn's eventual decision to reverse his original casting decision and switch the actors playing the angel and the bishop, the final cut of the film was to be as polished and assured as any festive fea-

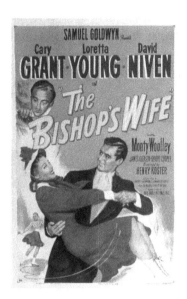

The Bishop's Wife (1947):
The Samuel Goldwyn
Company

ture of the time; as Dave Sindelar remarks, 'amazingly, the movie was originally cast with the roles of ⟦Cary⟧ Grant and David Niven reversed, which seems unthinkable watching this movie now'.[3] The end result of Goldwyn and Koster's labours was to be one of the most unconventionally offbeat – and impressive – Christmas films of the late forties.

Snow is falling and Christmas carols are being sung in an American city as a genial, well-dressed man named Dudley (Cary Grant) makes an appearance seemingly out of the blue. Dudley is entranced by the public's high spirits as they approach the festive season, and manages to narrowly avert disaster when he helps a man with impaired sight (David Leonard) to cross the road, only just saving him from being struck by a passing car. He then saves the life of a little girl in a runaway baby carriage by stepping in at the exact moment that a truck is on a collision course with her. But Dudley's timely acts of goodwill appear to be almost a secondary consideration to him; the true purpose of his presence in town seems to centre on Julia Brougham (Loretta Young), a young lady who he is revealed to be following at a distance.

Julia is on her way to buy a Christmas tree from local florist Mr Maggenti (Tito Vuolo), who she finds engaged in a lively but essentially good-natured argument with ageing intellectual Professor Wutheridge (Monty Woolley). Julia is puzzled to find that the professor is also in the process of buying a slightly dishevelled Christmas tree of his own, given that he is an outspoken atheist, but he explains that he is more interested in the nostalgia offered by the festive season than he is in its religious significance. Remembering Julia from when she lived in the area, back when her husband Henry was the minister of a local church there, Wutheridge asks how Henry's campaign to build a new cathedral is proceeding. Julia responds that the funding problems are endless, and that her husband – now a bishop – is perpetually tired and worried about the uphill struggle that he faces. A historian by discipline, the professor hands Julia a lucky Roman coin that he had bought many years ago in Brindisi, asking her to consider it a donation to Henry's fundraising drive. Julia thanks him, voicing her regret that she no longer lives in the neighbourhood with all of her old friends and parishioners.

As soon as Julia has departed, Dudley intercepts Wutheridge and pretends (much to the professor's prolonged suspicion) to have known him in Vienna when the old academic had been lecturing on Roman history there. Wutheridge eventually decides that Dudley must be a scholar himself and, with some gentle questioning, informs him that nobody in the area sees Henry Brougham now that he has been made a bishop; instead, Henry spends his time courting financial contributions from wealthy benefactors while his old church is impoverished and barely surviving.

Julia returns home to discover that she is late for a planning meeting being held between Henry (David Niven), architect Mr Perry (Ben Erway) and the formidable Mrs Hamilton (Gladys Cooper). As they study the blueprints of the new cathedral, major friction is readily apparent due to Mrs Hamilton's obvious desire to turn the building into a monument to her late husband, while Henry feels it is inappropriate to glorify any one individual in a house dedicated to the worship of God. Mrs Hamilton is infuriated by Henry's unwillingness to bend to her will, dressing him down and reminding him that it was her influence that was responsible for his promotion to bishop in the first place. She makes it clear that the building will be constructed to her own specification, and that she is completely unwilling to compromise.

Following Mrs Hamilton's departure, Henry voices his frustration at her intractability. He is keen to build a cathedral that will be for the use of everyone, not just a wealthy elite. Julia is concerned that Henry has become so worn out by the ongoing struggle to raise capital for the construction effort that he has lost sight of what is really important – his family, his friends and his wellbeing, to say nothing of his faith. But with regret, Henry tells her that he will have no choice but to continue his incessant fundraising drive over the Christmas holidays in order to tap into any potential for generosity in the season of festive goodwill. She gives Henry the professor's coin but is saddened when he casually discards it, believing it to be worthless and pouring disdain on his learned old friend. Julia is further dismayed by how short-tempered and irritable that Henry has become, remembering what a carefree and amiable man he had been prior to his promotion.

Over dinner Henry makes an attempt at rapprochement and asks Julia if she would like to spend the afternoon with him the following day, just enjoying each other's company and putting the worries of the cathedral to one side for a while. However, he soon discovers that he has other commitments and will be unable to make good on his arrangements with his wife. Irritated at the fact that he no longer seems to be in control of his own life, Henry prays desperately for divine assistance to alleviate his difficulties... only for Dudley to appear out of thin air in his study. Explaining that he has been sent in response to Henry's prayers, Dudley reveals that he is an angel. Even though he is a man of faith, this revelation stretches Henry's credulity to the limit; he begins to wonder if his exhaustion is making him hallucinate. Dudley explains that he has been assigned to lend a hand in Henry's efforts to build the cathedral, much to the bishop's obvious scepticism. However, when Julia enters the room unexpectedly, Dudley conceals his true identity and tells her that he has just been contracted as Henry's new personal assistant. When he adds that he intends to give the bishop the chance to relax a little by shouldering some of his burden, Julia is overjoyed – this is exactly what she has been praying for. Henry is now thoroughly bamboozled, but before he can question Dudley any further he discovers that the angel has vanished as quickly as he appeared.

Henry is so shocked by this turn of events that, after a sleepless night, he seems to have convinced himself that it was all simply an illusion. This is soon disproved, however, when Dudley arrives bright and early the next morning, effortlessly charming Henry's frosty but efficient secretary Mildred Cassaway (Sara Haden) and housekeeper Matilda (Elsa Lanchester). He tries in vain to convince Henry to allow him to attend the various planning and funding meetings that are scheduled for the day, thus allowing Henry the opportunity to spend time with Julia and their daughter Debby, but the bishop refuses point-blank to even consider it. Henry leaves Dudley to reorganise his study's extensive card index, but – as soon as he has departed – Dudley wastes no time in using his supernatural powers to order the various card-files in no time at all. This leaves him free to meet Julia and Debby (Karolyn Grimes) in the nearby park, where he first gives the bishop's daughter a crash-course in throwing snowballs before arranging to have lunch with Julia at her favourite restaurant, Michel's. Over some French cuisine presented enthusiastically by the owner (Eugene Borden), Julia explains that she and Henry have fond memories of the place given that they became engaged there. Dudley reassures her that she has a happy and full life ahead of her, and that she has no need to worry about the future.

On the way back home, Julia is pointing out a bonnet that she admires when she and Dudley again encounter Professor Wutheridge. By now the professor has seemingly determined that he has no recollection of Dudley from the past, but when Julia identifies him as Henry's new assistant Wutheridge invites them both back to his home for a glass of wine. They accept the kind offer, and the professor explains his regret that in years of planning to write an epic history of Rome to rival that of Edward Gibbon, he has never actually put pen to paper due to a chronic lack of inspiration. Dudley produces Wutheridge's Roman coin, retrieved from Henry's study, and explains to the professor that it is an incredibly rare piece – one of only a hundred of its kind to be minted by Julius Caesar. Enraptured by Dudley's exacting account of ancient history, Wutheridge finds that he has renewed enthusiasm for his project. Dudley assures the professor that, in spite of his advancing years, he still has time to complete it.

Back in his office, Henry grows annoyed as the hours advance with no sign of either Dudley or Julia. When they do finally arrive, he is nonplussed by Julia's sudden cheerfulness and confronts Dudley. Once Julia has gone to check on Debby, Henry challenges Dudley to prove that he is an angel once and for all by performing a miracle. Dudley gently censures the bishop, telling him that he is there to help his efforts, not perform parlour tricks. He then leaves the room through a door, which – when Henry attempts to open it – turns out to have been locked all along.

Henry begins to grow jealous of Dudley when he realises what a positive impact that he is having on Julia's disposition. The bishop's own mood is far from improved when, soon after, he discovers Dudley entertaining Debby with stories from the Bible. Henry arranges an appointment with the formidable Mrs Hamilton, but directly afterwards realises that he has double-booked himself with a recital that is being held at his old church in his honour. Although far from pleased with the arrangement, Henry allows Dudley to accompany Julia to the performance instead, while he visits Mrs Hamilton alone. The bishop meekly apologises to Mrs Hamilton for his earlier opposition to her plans for the cathedral, reasoning that it is better to bite his tongue and express contrition than to risk losing her financial support. When she accepts his apology – and promptly secures Henry's assurance that her husband's memorial notice will be on prominent display in the new cathedral (to say nothing of an appearance in one of the stained glass windows) – Henry attempts to make a speedy withdrawal in an attempt to join Julia and Dudley. However, some divine intervention leaves him trapped in one of Mrs Hamilton's chairs; nothing seems able to dislodge him from it.

At St Timothy's, Henry's old church, Dudley is introduced to the new priest Mr Miller (Regis Toomey) and his organist Mrs Duffy (Sarah Edwards). Miller is disappointed that Henry is not present, but accepts that the demands of his new role mean that his time is limited. Julia voices regret that things have changed so much since Henry's departure; the church, though homely and comfortable, is clearly very basic, while Henry has become distant from the parishioners who had held him in such high esteem. Miller seems embarrassed that only a couple of choirboys have turned up for the recital, given the diversion of the rapidly-approaching festive season, but once Dudley coaxes one of the boys into singing Miller looks on amazed as the rest of the choir begin to file into the church as if by magic. Julia is saddened that Henry is unable to join them for any of the performance, little realising that he is still trapped in a chair in Mrs Hamilton's drawing room.

After the recital is over, Dudley hails a cab while Julia – much to her dismay – notices that someone is on the verge of buying the bonnet that she has so admired from the milliner's shop. With a little fast thinking from Dudley, the potential purchaser is soon dissuaded from her new acquisition, meaning that Julia becomes the proud owner of the hat after all. They take a scenic route home, asking curmudgeonly taxi driver Sylvester (James Gleason) to drive them back via the park. On doing so, Dudley is enthused to discover that people are skating on a frozen pond. Asking Sylvester to pull over, he treats Julia to a dazzling display of ice-skating, soon encouraging her to get in on the act. Even Sylvester is persuaded to join in with the fun, the three of them eventually combining to perform an intricate synchronised routine. The whole situation has a profound effect on Sylvester, who feels so moved and energised by Dudley's involvement in his life that not only does he rediscover his faith in human nature, but – even more extraordinarily for him – he also agrees to waive his taxi fee.

Julia and Dudley arrive home later, where Henry – now released from Mrs Hamilton's troublesome chair – is infuriated by their lack of punctuality. Noticing how elated Julia seems after her wonderful evening, Henry rails against Dudley, suspecting him of being attracted to his wife. But Dudley is more concerned that Henry has ignored his principles in order to kow-tow to Mrs Hamilton and encourage her vanity. He explains to the bishop that the money required to construct the grand building in question could be used to support the poor instead. But Henry is disinterested in the noble purpose that Dudley outlines, not least because he knows that Mrs Hamilton will never accept it. He prays that Dudley be relieved of his duties in his parish and return to heaven... but Dudley appears to have other ideas. Julia is upset when Henry explains that he has dismissed Dudley from his service. However, she holds out hope of his return, assuring Debby that he will keep his promise to tell her stories of his friendship with Santa Claus.

The approach of Christmas Eve does little to improve Henry's demeanour. As he and Julia depart on a gruelling trip around the homes of affluent parishioners, the bishop asks Miss Cassaway to type up his Christmas Eve sermon. However, Dudley arrives soon after Henry leaves and offers to save Mildred the trouble: he will type the sermon for her, freeing her from a long stint of overtime. Once she has gone, Dudley burns Henry's original text and composes a new one, the typewriter mysteriously recording his every word while he dictates the sermon vocally rather than by using its keys. He also saves Matilda the bother of decorating the newly-arrived Christmas tree, using his miraculous powers to embellish it with tinsel, ornaments and fairy-lights in an instant.

But Dudley's work doesn't stop at Henry's residence. He pays an unscheduled visit to Mrs Hamilton, charming his way past her butler Stevens (Erville Alderson) into her drawing room. There, he discovers a handwritten musical composition dedicated to Mrs Hamilton and proceeds to play it on her beautiful ornamental harp. Hearing the music, Mrs Hamilton is dumbstruck and immediately tries to determine its source. On discovering Dudley, she explains that the piece was written for her by the only man that she had ever loved: a penniless young musician who had died four decades beforehand. Dudley gently coaxes her into telling him more, and she explains that although she had never truly loved her wealthy late husband, she was too terrified of poverty to marry her true soul mate. By the time that Henry and Julia arrive for their scheduled visit, Mrs Hamilton is a woman transformed; her usual cold-hearted demeanour has given way to warmth and understanding as a result of her spiritual encounter with Dudley. She tells Henry that she has seen the error of her ways, and wishes to donate all of the resources that she had intended for the cathedral fund to be distributed to the poor. The bishop is so nonplussed by this incredible turn of events that he finds himself forced to withdraw, much to the surprise of both Julia and Mrs Hamilton.

In reflective mood, Henry goes wandering past his old church, and eventually makes his way to the apartment of Professor Wutheridge. The elderly scholar is delighted to see his old friend after so long, and even Henry's relentlessly standoffish manner can't dampen the warmth of Wutheridge's welcome. He explains to the bishop that since Dudley's visit, he has inexplicably developed the power to decipher ancient Roman texts which have thus far baffled the talents of modern Latin scholars. The professor is elated that his book is finally underway after so many years of inaction, and in spite of his avowedly non-religious mindset he is forced to admit that Dudley is not a normal human being, reasoning that he must surely have been sent by a higher power. But Henry cannot share his good cheer, feeling that Dudley has poisoned Julia against him. Wutheridge scoffs at this explanation, explaining that Dudley's only action has been to make Julia happy, but Henry feels that perhaps the angel's true intention was to prove to him that his marriage has faltered. The professor assures him that the love that is shared between Henry and Julia is unlikely to be threatened by someone who is not of this earth; all that Dudley has done is to emphasise how vital it is that Henry realise the importance of the bond that he shares with Julia. Wutheridge also insists on returning the rare Roman coin to the bishop, explaining its true value to him.

Back home, Julia is admiring the newly-decorated Christmas tree when Dudley arrives. He explains that he will be leaving soon, much to his regret. With a little reluctance, he explains that he has formed an emotional attachment to her, and as such he will never see her again. Julia knows that the attraction between them can never come to fruition and, deeply upset, wishes Dudley gone from her life. She races from the room just as Henry arrives. Fuming at Dudley, who he perceives more than ever to be attempting to steal his wife from him, he demands that the angel be gone. But Dudley explains that he is already on his way, his work in the parish now done. Henry asks how this can be, given that the cathedral's construction is as remote a possibility now as it was in the beginning. Dudley replies that Henry didn't pray for a cathedral, but for guidance – and that is exactly what he has received. Telling the bishop that when he leaves, there will be no recollection of his visit by anyone who had encountered him, Dudley departs for the last time.

Just as Dudley had warned, Henry and Julia have retained no memory of the charming angel's actions over the past days... or even of his very existence. They are puzzled by the unexplained arrival of a striking angel doll in Debby's room, an enigmatic gift from an 'unknown benefactor', but have little time to ponder it before Henry is due to give his Christmas Eve sermon at St Timothy's. The little church is packed that night with a full congregation which includes Professor Wutheridge (who appears slightly bemused at his own attendance). A rather melancholic Dudley watches from a distance, though he is now invisible to the eyes of the others. Henry is puzzled when he starts to deliver his sermon and discovers that the text is very different from the one that he had written. However, the people attending worship seem enraptured by the sentiment, which is that no-one should forget the reason why Christmas has endured in the human heart for so long. Satisfied, although a little wistful, Dudley walks away from the church, his work done.

For a film which is so acutely concerned with religious faith, it is surprising to note just how inclusive *The Bishop's Wife* actually is. Although it shares a common theme with *The Bells of St Mary's* – namely that faith can achieve remarkable ends – its rather original take on the notion of divine intervention and lack of orthodox sermonising (apart from Dudley's quotation of Psalm 23, there is little direct reference to the Bible) mean that in spite of the film's concern with clerical matters, its central message of reaching out to lend a helping hand to others is actually almost as secular and all-encompassing as *It's a Wonderful Life*'s themes had proven to be. Indeed, at no point throughout the film is Henry's denomination ever mentioned, though some commentators have ventured the opinion that *The Bishop's Wife* presents, at heart, a distinctively Episcopal variation on the topics presented in *The Bells of St Mary's*. However, as John Howard Reid has commented, 'the script has a rather odd impression of Christianity (in both theory and practice) but I guess that from Hollywood such doubtful moralising is only to be expected. (The one direct biblical quote is naturally from Psalms, and the angel who romances the bishop's wife seems more directly inspired by Genesis 6:2 than anything in the New Testament)'.[4]

The Bishop's Wife marked a high water mark in the subgenre of religiously-themed Christmas films, and yet it was also to herald the beginning of a sharp decline in the production of such features; although angels and the Virgin Birth would continue to be regularly referenced in later festive film-making, movies which actively linked the historical event of Christ's birth with social issues in the everyday were to become much more sporadic in later years. That said, from George More O'Ferrall's *The Holly and the Ivy* (q.v.) all the way through to Catherine Hardwicke's *The Nativity Story* (2006), the undeniable Biblical underpinnings of the Christmas story have determined that no matter how secularised and commercialised that festive film-making has become, religion has never been entirely eliminated from the genre. As Greg Orypeck has noted: 'Today, when fewer and fewer people believe in God, the more sophisticated among us would suggest that *The Bishop's Wife* administers too generous a dose of religious hokum, without anesthesia or health warning labels. But what heart-warming sentiments after all, and what wonderful ensemble acting, brilliant photography and intelligent dialogue. It was a more innocent time then, in 1947, although World War II had replaced much of the innocence of life with its harsher realities'.[5]

Like *The Bells of St Mary's*, *The Bishop's Wife* concentrates more on the positive effects of faith in action than it does on the specifics of denominational religious practice. Samuel Goldwyn became so concerned when market research indicated that the film was being perceived by the general public as a specifically religiously-themed movie, he had publicity posters rebranded with the title '*Cary and the Bishop's Wife*' in some markets within the United States in the hope of emphasising a more secular approach to the film's subject matter. (This stratagem proved successful, with some territories demonstrating a marked increase in box-office performance as a result of the new title.) Certainly it is intriguing to consider how the irreligious Professor Wutheridge's gradual awakening to spiritual issues – moving from unyielding scepticism to grudging acceptance – is largely overshadowed by more universal themes such as the importance of family and friendship, as well as the need to stay true to a personal value system. As Richard Propes considers, 'I don't believe that faith, *per se*, is required to fully appreciate this film. Though, I can't help but believe that one's faith would be greatly enhanced by the film. The film's message is one of principle... one of love... one of family. The film is such a wondrous reminder that miracles do exist, and that we are called to be that miracle to each other'.[6]

Key to the success of *The Bishop's Wife* is its range of winning performances. The central love triangle is played with greatly nuanced subtlety by Cary Grant and Loretta Young, while a cast-against-type David Niven works hard to turn the embattled Henry Brougham from priggish killjoy into the very acme of incredulous bewilderment. Whether Niven entirely succeeds in this task is less due to any defect in his performance than the fact that the character of Henry is so difficult for the viewer to actually grow fond of. The bishop's stuffed-shirt manner and cut-glass Received Pronunciation delivery – to say nothing of his apparent single-minded obsession with cathedral-building to the detriment of his family, friends and parishioners – undeniably makes him difficult to engage with, much less warm to. As Karin J. Fowler explains, Niven's engagement with the role is all the more remarkable when his initial reluctance to being cast as Henry is considered: 'Niven loved the script for *The Bishop's Wife* [...] and thought he would be playing the role of the angel. He protested so much [at being cast as the bishop] that Goldwyn threatened to keep him out of the film'.[7] When, at the film's conclusion, we see the newly re-energised Henry – his priorities realigned by Dudley's now-forgotten spiritual influence in his life – his continued mannerly decorum makes it almost impossible to know exactly how far-reaching the change in his character and attitudes will really prove to be. Niven was already a prolific performer by the time of *The Bishop's Wife*, having made many prominent appearances in films since the early 1930s including *The Charge of the Light Brigade* (Michael Curtiz, 1936), *The Prisoner of Zenda* (John Cromwell, 1937), *Wuthering Heights* (William Wyler, 1939), *Raffles* (Sam Wood, 1939), and perhaps most famously Michael Powell and Emeric Pressburger's sublime fantasy *A Matter of Life and Death* (1946). He would, of course, continue to be active in film until his death in 1983, winning an Academy Award for his performance in *Separate Tables* (Delbert Mann, 1958). His appearance in *The Bishop's Wife* is perhaps most remarkable for his excellent comic timing and subtly ironic delivery, particularly when he becomes inexplicably trapped in Mrs Hamilton's drawing room chair (a visual gag which could have been decidedly laboured in lesser hands), and in his exquisitely fussy, hidebound way of dealing with a manifested agent of God – something that Henry has supreme difficulty dealing with, even after having spent his entire adult life preaching about such encounters.

If the film belongs to anyone, however, it is Cary Grant and Loretta Young. The suave and sophisticated Grant, an actor for whom the term 'screen legend' could have been personally designed, oozes charm from every pore, investing the dapper Dudley with warmth and charisma throughout every frame. Grant, who had already been nominated for two Academy Awards by the time that he appeared as Dudley (for performances in George Stevens's *Penny Serenade*, 1941, and *None But the Lonely Heart*, 1944), was most certainly hot property in the world of film during the late forties. Making his film debut in *This is the Night* (Frank Tuttle, 1932), he had made many appearances throughout the thirties and forties, with roles in films such as *Madame Butterfly* (Marion Gering, 1932), *Bringing Up Baby* (Howard Hawks, 1938), *The Philadelphia Story* (George Cukor, 1940), *Arsenic and Old Lace* (Frank Capra, 1944), and *Notorious* (Alfred Hitchcock, 1946), to name only a few. Grant very effectively combines his dry wit and comedic skills with his dramatic strengths to create, in Dudley, a character who is both sympathetic and appealing. From his kindly interactions with Henry's daughter Debby through to his far-reaching effects on virtually all of the supporting cast, the role seems perfectly suited to Grant's unique style of onscreen magnetism, and his beautifully understated pseudo-romance with Julia is all the more credible as a result of it. Both Dudley and Julia are fully aware that their mutual attraction can never be allowed to flourish, a fact that neither wishes to recognise but which clearly pains them grievously on an emotional level. Some critics have noted the thematic awkwardness of an implied romantic attraction be-tween a married woman and a spiritual being – who, based on his actions throughout the film, is ethically above reproach and exclusively concerned with enriching moral actions.[8] It says a great deal for the skill of Grant's performance that, when all of Dudley's miracles have been performed and his life-affirming tenets imparted, we are able to catch a tantalis-ing glimpse of the fatigued, disillusioned being behind the sharp suit and ready grin, weary of checking the excesses of humanity. As Sindelar perceives, Grant's charm, comic timing and dramatic sincerity are absolutely core to the film's success: 'If there must be movies about angels, than I couldn't ask for more than that the angel be played by Cary Grant, and that's just what this movie provides. Movies like this have the po-tential to be sickeningly sweet, but the movie accomplishes two things very well; it makes the conflicts real, resonant and touching, and it treats the magic with the lightest and deftest of touches, much of this due to Grant's performance, which is gentle, warm, effortlessly comic (he can elicit laughs with sim-ple facial expressions without once resorting to mugging) and never heavy-handed'.[9]

As Julia, Loretta Young shines as the disenchanted but loyal bishop's wife of the title, unquestioningly dedicated to her husband and faithful to her beliefs while simultaneously enraptured by the dashing, captivating newcomer who has swept into her life without warning. Young made her first cinematic appearance as a child actor in 1917, and grew in-creasingly prolific throughout the 1920s and 30s. Her abun-dant performances included roles in films as diverse as *The Devil to Pay* (George Fitzmaurice, 1930), *Ramona* (Henry King, 1936) and *A Night to Remember* (Richard Wallace,

1942), before winning an Academy Award for her performance in H.C. Potter's *The Farmer's Daughter* (1947).

The supporting cast of *The Bishop's Wife* is uniformly strong, particularly veteran actor/screenwriter James Gleason as Sylvester, the plain-speaking taxi driver who is reawakened to the joys of living by Dudley's intervention in his life, and Gladys Cooper as the excruciatingly frosty Mrs Hamilton, whose moral metamorphosis seems all the more touching when the audience become aware of the reason behind her domineering nature. Yet special mention is due to Monty Woolley's scene-stealing performance as the brilliant, eccentric and mildly cantankerous Professor Wutheridge. Woolley, who ironically enough had been a Yale University academic before becoming a highly successful actor and director on Broadway,[10] is utterly convincing as the jaded atheist scholar who is forced to confront his deeply ingrained frustration at life's disappointments. By turns comic and moving, Wutheridge is a fully rounded supporting character of the best type, and Woolley's multifaceted performance is worthy of recollection long after the film has concluded – not least given the character's pivotal importance in articulating the film's faith-oriented themes. As Orypeck observes: 'The supporting players reinforce the superb casting, typical of the time. Monty Woolley had played gruff old men with hearts of gold in at least two previous films, *Since You Went Away* and *The Man Who Came to Dinner*. Here, as retired history professor Wutheridge, whom Dudley pretends to know, he is outwardly anti-Christmas – protesting the price of a scraggly little tree, for instance – but he's one of the first to sense and appreciate Dudley's heavenly source and powers, which, strangely, Julia never does. Wutheridge, even, could be seen as the pivot of the entire film'.[11]

The Bishop's Wife had an uneven response from critics at the time of its release. While there was praise for its central and supporting performances, Hugo Friedhofer's understated musical score and the snowy location filming in chilly Minneapolis, Minnesota, there was also scepticism from some reviewers. As *Time* magazine considered at the time of the film's release, 'adapted from Robert Nathan's 1928 novel, *The Bishop's Wife* is Sam Goldwyn's and RKO's special Christmas cookie. It is a big, slick production. The only thing it lacks is taste. Some moviegoers may also be distressed by the lack of Christmas spirit in what is apparently the moral of the picture: you can't trust a soul with your wife'.[12] This mild note of critical uncertainty had waned by the eighties, when the film made its first appearance on home entertainment formats; Walter Goodman of *The New York Times*, for instance, was of the opinion that: 'This 1947 Christmas tale, written by Robert E. Sherwood and Leonard Bercovici from Robert Nathan's novel, is not for the hard-of-heart-or-head. It tells how an angel who could charm the tail off the Devil brings sweetness and light to a bishop who is in peril of being caught up in mundane pursuits; the only snag is that the angel falls for the bishop's wife. Whatever you make of the minor miracles performed along the way, there's no trouble believing that Cary would fall for Loretta or that anybody would fall for Cary'.[13]

In more recent years, *The Bishop's Wife* has grown in reputation amongst commentators, largely due to the fact it has experienced something of a renaissance in the age of streaming video and satellite TV. Eddie Harrison, for example, considered the film a minor Christmas classic: '*The Bishop's Wife* [is] a delicious slice of angelic whimsy from 1947. [...] It may not ring the Xmas bells as loudly as Capra's classic, but Henry Koster's film is a black and white delight'.[14] Others, such as J.P. Roscoe, have been considerably more guarded in their praise: 'The movie is pretty standard directing... nothing daring and very little special effects. It is kind of a joke when Grant and Young go ice skating and Grant's body double is half his size and has different hair. There are other little errors like this through the whole movie and sometimes it is a bit distracting. *The Bishop's Wife* is a nice holiday film and should not be forgotten. Compared to other films, it doesn't get as much play in during the season'.[15] Considered as a work of fantasy rather than yuletide whimsy, some critics have found the film somewhat less successful; Richard Scheib, for instance, has stated the opinion that:

> In all regards, *The Bishop's Wife* is the same familiar Hollywood light fantasy comedy that Hollywood was churning out a good deal of during the late 1930s/early 40s. [...] In its favour, *The Bishop's Wife* does offer the decidedly offbeat casting of Cary Grant as an angel. In every other respect, it comes with a singular blandness that fails to distinguish it in any way – it is not that it is a bad film, just bland. Its sentiments are overdone, its moral points obvious and the inspirational lesson to be learned a yawn. Nevertheless, it has become a Christmas perennial, along with other films from the era such as *It's a Wonderful Life* (1946) and *Miracle on 34ᵗʰ Street* (1947) and is well regarded by many. Dudley is not one of Cary Grant's better performances. As the bishop, David Niven overdoes the neurotic performance, although adds a couple of moments of droll humour the film could have done with more of.[16]

The Bishop's Wife went on to perform well at the 1948 Academy Awards, winning Gordon Sawyer the Oscar for Best Sound Recording and receiving nominations for Best Film Editing, Best Music, Best Picture, and Best Director for Henry Koster. Like so many other films of the forties, the film was later to be adapted for radio audiences. Grant, Young and Niven all reprised their original roles for a Screen Guild Theater production which was broadcast on 1 March 1948, with Niven later returning to the eponymous bishop's role for radio on 19 December 1949, acting against Tyrone Power in a Lux Radio Theater production. Grant was to join actress Phyllis Thaxter for two other radio performances, broadcast on 11 May 1953 and 1 March 1955 respectively, with both adaptations being produced by Lux Radio Theater.

The film was remade several decades later by Penny Marshall as *The Preacher's Wife* (1996), which provided a contemporary setting for the story as well as a starry cast which included Courtney B. Vance, Denzel Washington and Whitney Houston. Marshall's film exhibited less overtly festive proceedings than those of *The Bishop's Wife*, though many Christmas-related themes do remain within it – advanced by the abundant charm and aptitude of a talented cast of actors. *The Preacher's Wife* also featured an impressive number of musical numbers throughout, including many Gospel hymns, and received a well-deserved Academy Award nomination for Best Music (Original Musical or Comedy Score).

By the end of the 1940s, some of the most prominent themes in the Christmas film genre had been firmly established in the minds of critics and the general public alike. *The Bells of St Mary's* had emphasised that the Christmas spirit can – and should – be preserved all the year round, to the benefit of all. *It's a Wonderful Life* had stressed the fact that Christmas presents us with a chance to give something back to our community and value our family and friends, while *Miracle on 34th Street* underscored the point that society shouldn't allow commercialism to distract itself from the true meaning of Christmas. And finally, *The Bishop's Wife* had shown that those who celebrate Christmas should never forget the true reason which lies behind the power and influence of the festive season, irrespective of one's religious or cultural belief. Indeed, *The Bishop's Wife* in particular had demonstrated that the Christmas film had begun to take on a life of its own, the holiday's widening cultural embrace meaning that the festive season was becoming a more widely-encompassing phenomenon which was overlapping the confines of its specifically Christian heritage in order to incorporate secular society. The film also shared a common thread with the other aforementioned movies, in that it featured a genial outsider who – through spiritual or supernatural means – makes use of the Christmas spirit in order to change people for the better. Significantly, all four of these films had been nominated for the coveted Best Picture Academy Award, and collectively they have been of vital importance in cementing the key themes of Christmas cinema as well as demonstrating the cultural significance of the genre.

While *The Bishop's Wife* has grown in stature over the years after a lengthy period where it languished in the shadow of other, more prominent Christmas films of the forties, today it enjoys a reputation amongst critics as one of the finest examples of its type – even from a period which saw the release of so many classics of festive cinema. As Andy Webb has considered, 'it has to be said that *The Bishop's Wife* is both amusing and touching as you get the easy going nature of Dudley helping to sort out Bishop Henry's problems in his own special way. [...] But what is really nice is that *The Bishop's Wife* also has that magical Christmas feeling. From the opening scene with the children looking at the wonderful Christmas displays in the shop windows, through to the ice skating and the church choir recital it really does put you in that wintry, Christmassy mood. But it never feels corny, these magical scenes are so wonderfully scripted and delightfully nostalgic that they achieve their desired effect of delivering warmth but stopping before they become too schmaltzy'.[17] Just as had been the case with other Christmas films of the mid-forties, the inclusion of big name actors in these well-received and widely circulated features – to say nothing of their success at industry awards ceremonies – had led to considerable audience familiarity with the new, emerging genre of the Christmas film. Because of the critical and commercial success of festive movies in the immediate post-war period, features such as *The Bishop's Wife* helped to ensure that the genre would be destined to become a lasting fixture of the film-making world in the years to come.

REFERENCES

1. Sanderson Beck, '*The Bishop's Wife*', in *Movie Mirrors*, 2006.
    <*http://san.beck.org/MM/1947/BishopsWife.html*>

2. Michael Reuben, '*The Bishop's Wife* Blu-ray Review: Bishop Takes Queen', in *Blu-ray.com*, 31 October 2013.
    <*https://www.blu-ray.com/movies/The-Bishops-Wife-Blu-ray/77925/#Review*>

3. Dave Sindelar, '*The Bishop's Wife*', in *Fantastic Movie Musings and Ramblings*, 2 August 2015.
    <*https://fantasticmoviemusings.com/2015/08/02/the-bishops-wife-1947/*>

4. John Howard Reid, *Movies Magnificent: 150 Must-See Cinema Classics* (Morrisville: Lulu.com, 2005), p.23.

5. Greg Orypeck, 'Remembering WWII, 1947, and *The Bishop's Wife*', in *Classic Film Freak*, 21 August 2009.
    <*https://www.classicfilmfreak.com/2009/08/21/remembering-wwii-1947-and-the-bishops-wife/*>

6. Richard Propes, '*The Bishop's Wife*', in *The Independent Critic*, 22 August 2007.
    <*https://www.theindependentcritic.com/bishops_wife*>

7. Karin J. Fowler, *David Niven: A Bio-Bibliography* (Westport: Greenwood Publishing Group, 1995), p.222.

8. Greg Garrett, *The Gospel According to Hollywood* (Louisville: Westminster John Knox Press, 2007), p.6.

9.   Sindelar.

10. Ken D. Jones, Arthur F. McClure and Alfred E. Twomey, *Character People* (New York: A.S. Barnes, 1977), p.208.

11. Orypeck.

12. Anon., 'Cinema: The New Pictures', in *Time*, 8 December 1947.
     <*http://content.time.com/time/subscriber/article/0,33009,934178-2,00.html*>

13. Walter Goodman, 'Home Video: Movies', in *The New York Times*, 25 October 1987.
     <*https://www.nytimes.com/1987/10/25/arts/home-video-movies-413487.html*>

14. Eddie Harrison, '*The Bishop's Wife*', in *The Film Authority*, 8 February 2014.
     <*https://tensecondsfromnow.wordpress.com/2014/02/08/the-bishops-wife-1947/*>

15. J.P. Roscoe, '*The Bishop's Wife*', in *Basement Rejects*, 8 December 2011.
     <*http://basementrejects.com/review/the-bishops-wife-1947/*>

16. Richard Scheib, '*The Bishop's Wife*', in *Moria: The Science Fiction, Horror and Fantasy Film Review*, 12 November 2001.
     <*http://www.moriareviews.com/fantasy/bishops-wife-1947.htm*>

17.   Andy Webb, '*The Bishop's Wife*', in *The Movie Scene*, 2018.
       <https://www.themoviescene.co.uk/reviews/the-bishops-wife/the-bishops-wife.html>

8

Christmas Eve (1947)

Benedict Bogeaus Productions/Miracle Productions Inc.

Director: Edwin L. Marin
Producer: Benedict Bogeaus
Screenwriter: Laurence Stallings, adapted from original
stories by Richard H. Landau and Laurence Stallings

THE year 1947 was to prove something of an embarrassment of riches when it came to Christmas cinema. However, not all of the festive features released in that year would go on to the same level of cultural significance enjoyed by films such as *Miracle on 34th Street* (q.v.). *Christmas Eve* is one of the most unconventional slices of yuletide entertainment to appear on the big screen during the 1940s, and – while its quirky episodic structure was significantly more eccentric than the seasonal vignettes of films such as *Holiday Inn* (Mark Sandrich, 1942), *Meet Me in St Louis* (q.v.) and *The Bells of St Mary's* (q.v.) – in its sheer idiosyncrasy it would indirectly inspire many later, similarly experimental Christmas movies in the following years. However, there is no doubting that its prominence in popular culture has waned since the time of its initial release; today its reputation is not so much that of a hidden gem, but rather a lost curio of the genre.

Christmas Eve was the brainchild of producer Benedict Bogeaus, who had formerly been a property developer and, later, the one-time owner of General Service Studios. He formed Benedict Bogeaus Productions in 1944 and produced a number of films, many of which were met by widespread critical approval if not universal success at the box-office. Bogeaus was acutely aware of the ability of star power to command large audiences, even if a film's production budget was not necessarily particularly high, which led to features such as *Mr Ace* (Edwin L. Marin, 1946) – starring George Raft – and *The Macomber Affair* (Zoltan Korda, 1947), featuring Gregory Peck in the lead role. *Christmas Eve* was one of two anthology films that he was to produce; by employing different stars in a number of disparate storylines, each section could be shot at different times and then edited together into a single motion picture, allowing maximum schedule flexibility. His second attempt at this creative strategy, *On Our Merry Way* (King Vidor and Leslie Fenton, 1948), featured performances by well-known actors such as Paulette Goddard, Burgess Meredith, James Stewart, Henry Fonda and Fred MacMurray, and met with significantly greater critical appreciation, even though its commercial performance at the time was not overwhelming.

The director of *Christmas Eve*, Edwin L. Marin, was an experienced industry veteran with a prolific filmography; he directed no less than 58 feature films between 1932 and 1951, with his movies including Sherlock Holmes adaptation *A Study in Scarlet* (1933), legal drama *Man of the People* (1937), the lavishly-produced *A Christmas Carol* (1938) and wartime thriller *Paris Calling* (1941). Creatively versatile, Marin worked with many of the biggest names in showbusiness during this period, including John Wayne, Judy Garland and Peter Lorre. *Christmas Eve* would be no different in this regard, as the film's three sections featured performances by stars George Brent, George Raft and Randolph Scott respectively.

While *Christmas Eve* is unlikely to be listed amongst the most overtly festive of late 1940s Christmas films, Marin's movie nonetheless places the importance of the family unit front and centre. While this may seem less obvious in each of the individual vignettes, by the film's conclusion there is no doubting that the feature's overall message fits comfortably into the traditional convention of festive cinema that family members, working collectively, can overcome problems that would otherwise overwhelm solitary individuals.

In the heart of New York City, elderly Matilda Reed (Ann Harding) receives a visit from her smarmy, scheming nephew Phillip Hastings (Reginald Denny) at her opulent but dated mansion house. Hastings has brought with him Judge Alston (Clarence Kolb) and psychiatrist Dr Doremus (Carl Harbord), in the hope of having his eccentric aunt's mental state judged unfit so that he can assume power of attorney over her day-to-day affairs – and her considerable wealth. She unknowingly reinforces Hastings's view of her mental health when she scatters

Christmas Eve (1947): Benedict Bogeaus Productions/Miracle Productions Inc.

birdseed liberally around her drawing room and opens a window to let hungry wild birds feast before she and her guests sit down to afternoon tea.

In spite of Hastings's preconceptions, however, the unconventional Matilda remains as sharp as a tack. She sees through the 'informal meeting', and immediately recognises the flimsiness of the judge's assurances that he has no intention of ordering a court hearing to assess her mental competence (as, if this was the case, why would he be present at the meeting at all?). Hastings is concerned that Matilda is squandering her fortune; over the past year she has spent over $1.6 million, including half a million dollars on dead rats. Indignantly, Matilda corrects him and explains that she had offered impoverished children a dollar for every rat that they could catch, thus helping them earn some much-needed money while similarly preventing a public health issue. Hastings also mentions the $750,000 that she had spent on a marriage guidance project, which had only managed to save a single marriage from ending in divorce. However, she is unrepentant, pointing out that the expenditure was entirely worth the cost if it aided even one couple in staying together. Hastings is irate, claiming to have devoted a lot of effort in using his aunt's money to invest in profitable interests in other countries only to see her spending vast amounts of her savings on what he considers to be frivolous schemes.

Judge Alston tries to persuade Matilda to make Hastings the administrator of her estate, but she steadfastly refuses. While she grudgingly concedes that he has done well with the funds she had entrusted to him, she points out that she would only trust three people with her fortune – any one of a trio of orphans that she had adopted many decades beforehand. Michael, Mario and Jonathan had been raised by her as sons, but had each moved away to make their own way in the world as they refused to take advantage of her wealth for their own ends. Hastings disdainfully points out that they had simply walked out when Matilda had needed them, but she responds that she had respected their decision to make a success of their own lives independently. However, this had been many years beforehand, and she now has no idea of where they are currently located. Matilda tells the judge that if he could only meet the three men, he would understand why she is able to put her trust in them. She informs Hastings, Alston and Doremus that her adopted sons had all pledged to return to aid her in a time of need, and that she intends to have them back with her in New York on Christmas Eve – the perfect time for a family reunion. The psychiatrist and judge seem sceptical, but Hastings is positively livid with unspoken resentment.

Miles away, unbeknownst to Matilda, the dapper Michael Brooks (George Brent) is living a comfortable life as a playboy businessman. Currently staying in an upmarket apartment, he is unwillingly accompanied by his affectionate girlfriend Ann Nelson (Joan Blondell) who is deeply devoted to him. However, Michael has been rebuffing her romantic overtures, and she deduces that he has been seeing someone else. Confirming her suspicions, a gift of some jewellery is sent to him via room service with a note suggesting that his new sweetheart is on her way to see him. Ann wastes no time in throwing the package over the balcony before Michael even has the chance to open it. Then the wealthy Harriet Rhodes (Molly Lamont) arrives at the door, and Michael – thinking on his feet – introduces Ann as his sister. Ann is astonished when Harriet reveals that she is Michael's fiancée, and that they intend to be married that very afternoon.

Ann is hurt by his betrayal, but rather than depart she continues the ruse of being Michael's relative under the subterfuge that she is helping him pack up his belongings before he leaves the apartment on vacation. Harriet enthuses appreciatively about the extravagant gifts that Michael had bought her as pre-wedding presents, but he is unable to relax in her company as he suspects that Ann is up to something. He excuses himself and confronts his 'sister' when he realises that she has been unpacking his belongings rather than putting them into suitcases. Meanwhile, one of the building's bellhops arrives at the apartment door with the discarded gift – a locket containing a photo of Harriet. He complains that it had hit the doorman on the way down from the balcony, and Harriet suddenly understands what is happening.

In the next room, Michael explains to Ann that he intends to marry Harriet as it will allow for the union of two affluent families, but Ann is determined to win his heart and storms into the lounge to confront Harriet with the truth. However, they soon realise that Harriet is now all too aware that Ann is not Michael's sister, and she angrily departs. As Ann once again throws the locket over the balcony, Michael is surprised to receive a phone call from the building's reception to say that Hastings is on the way up. Michael desperately tries to get the staff to stall him, but it's too late; the unctuous businessman is already almost at the door.

As soon as Hastings arrives, it is obvious that there is tension between Michael and him. It is also clear that he has had difficulty in tracking Michael down, but has persevered as he has discovered that Matilda's seemingly-prosperous wayward son has cashed no less than $75,000 in cheques that have not cleared due to insufficient funds. Michael responds that he had intended to pay off his debts that very afternoon after he had closed a lucrative deal (not mentioning that he is actually referring to his intention of marrying Harriet). Hastings tells Michael that he is concerned that his perilous financial state will cause Matilda unwanted anxiety, and that to this end he has paid off the arrears out of his own pocket. Michael is stunned, not having considered Hastings to be the altruistic type. But as the older man leaves the apartment, Michael becomes suspicious towards his seemingly-noble actions. Ann, however, is ecstatic now that she realises that far from being a well-to-do playboy, Michael is essentially broke and no richer than she is.

Back at Matilda's mansion, the ageing matriarch has arranged a press conference to attract the attention of journalists to her search for her three adopted sons. The hope is that by appearing in newspapers, the public may be able to help her track them down. One of the journalists (Marie Blake) cottons on to the fact that Hastings is trying to have her declared mentally unfit to manage her own finances, leading to a deluge of press coverage highlighting the fact that her rationality is in question.

At an upscale restaurant in the city, Michael meets Ann but is shaken when he spots one of the newspaper headlines reporting that Matilda's control of her fortune is in jeopardy. Michael realises that Hastings's scheming has left him with little room to manoeuvre; he has been told in no uncertain terms not to go to the mansion, yet has no money to pay back the $75,000 that Hastings had used to clear Michael's debts. Ann is tetchy, believing that Michael is simply unwilling to come to Matilda's aid. She instinctively distrusts Hastings, and it is clear that Michael's own suspicions are growing.

Michael and Ann pay Hastings a visit at his well-appointed offices. Hastings angrily denies any wrongdoing, claiming (not entirely convincingly) that he already has too much responsibility with the section of Matilda's estate that he currently manages, and is seeking no further accountability. He emphasises that he had only paid off Michael's liabilities because he wanted to spare Matilda any embarrassment or shock. Michael is canny enough to realise that this payment was intended as a hint for him to get out of town – preferably as far away from Matilda as possible, so that he doesn't jeopardise the forthcoming mental competency hearing. Realising that Michael is insolvent, Hastings gives him $10,000 in cash from his safe to help him on his way. Ann is appalled that Michael has put his own financial health ahead of his support for Matilda, and promptly walks out in disgust.

Meanwhile, Judge Alston is heatedly confronting Matilda about all the recent press coverage, which has put significant pressure on him due to the assumption that he is trying to compel her into court. It is also doing little good to his public reputation. Hastings, however, is delighted – the way that events have played out, the judge will be more or less forced to push the matter into a legal hearing, making it all the more likely that the court will rule in his favour. But Matilda is unapologetic, pointing out that the press interest was essential if she is to track down all three adopted sons in time for their Christmas Eve reunion.

Neither man realises that Matilda has enlisted the services of Private Detective Gimlet (Joe Sawyer), who has been working behind the scenes to find any trace of the three missing wards. She is delighted when Gimlet reports that Michael has been traced to New York, but is soon disappointed to discover that he has departed the city in a hurry due to his debts.

She is even less impressed to learn of his intention to marry Harriet Rhodes, considering her to be an unsuitable partner. Gimlet also relates that he is confident of tracking down Mario, but has so far been unable to find enough evidence of his current whereabouts.

Deep in South America, the aforementioned Mario Torio (George Raft) is a fugitive from the US Justice Department. He meets his beautiful girlfriend Claire (Virginia Field) on a train platform as she returns to the town where he lives. Mario owns the glamorous Yank's Club, but on arriving there he makes an unwelcome discovery – an FBI agent, Joe Bland (John Litel), is waiting in his office. Mario is alarmed, as he has committed a crime in the United States which is so serious, he is guaranteed a prison sentence of twenty years if he ever returns home. Bland assures Mario that he hasn't flown south to make an arrest, but rather that he hopes to enlist his help in apprehending another fugitive. The agent hints heavily that Mario's assistance could see his wanted status reduced or even discarded, but Mario distrusts his motives and refuses to cooperate with the authorities. As Bland is leaving the office, he mentions the name of the outlaw he is attempting to track down – Gustav Reichman – which causes Claire to react in shock.

Bland reveals to Mario that Reichman is a former member of Hitler's Nazi regime who has managed to escape to South America after the Axis Powers lost the war. He is now wanted for war crimes at the Nuremberg Trials, and Bland believes that he may try to contact Mario on account of his underground connections – if he hasn't done so already. The agent assures him that his compliance will be regarded favourably back in the United States, and that this would be an especially timely development given Matilda's current dilemma.

Mario refuses to believe Bland's story that Matilda's mental competency is being questioned and has him thrown out of the building. However, he later discovers that Claire has also left the premises and is confused by her sudden absence.

Having mulled over the possibilities, Mario realises that he can't risk the possibility that Bland's account of events back home is accurate and decides to book a flight to the United States the next morning. His aide (Walter Sande) is aghast and tries to convince him that he already has everything he needs in South America; the authorities can't be trusted, he claims, and Mario is sure to be incarcerated the moment his plane sets down on an American runway. But Mario is determined, and also instructs his adviser to check out Claire's story; was she really out of town over the weekend as she claimed?

Back in New York, Gimlet reports to Matilda that Mario was involved in a crime in New Orleans under the name of 'Mario Volpe', and subsequently managed to escape from federal agents in order to leave the country. Gimlet explains that Mario has been responsible for some serious unlawful activity and is now resident somewhere in South America. Matilda is upset to think that her adoptive son is potentially in danger, and instructs Gimlet to step up his search for the last remaining ward, Jonathan.

Mario's aide tells him that according to his investigations, Claire did not stay at the hotel she had claimed to while she was away from the town. This inflames his suspicions still further. Upon leaving his house, Mario is abducted by a group of thugs and bundled into a car, where he is taken to a private yacht berthed nearby. There, tied and bound, he meets Reichman (Konstantin Shayne) who subjects him to violent questioning. Reichman reveals that Claire is in possession of cash and jewellery belonging to him – valuables that have a collective worth in excess of $10 million – but refuses to believe that Mario has no knowledge of this fact. The one-time Nazi clearly suspects that the two are working together. However, Mario insistently tells him that he has no idea of Claire's alleged theft. Realising that Mario intends to leave for New York the next day, Reichman believes that he plans to abscond with the stolen loot and that Claire will join him later.

Reichman discloses the fact that he also has Claire in custody; she corroborates Mario's story that he has no idea about the location of the money. Claire attempts to strike a bargain with Reichman; she will reveal the whereabouts of his funds if he will set Mario free. He readily agrees, but once she tells him she has deposited the money in a hidden bank account he immediately reneges on his promise and tells her that he will require further proof. Mario knows that the Nazi has no intention of letting him go, and Claire recognises that this is also true for herself. However, she has the last laugh: the reason why she didn't go on vacation over the weekend as planned was because she was making arrangements to transfer all of Reichman's funds to the American occupational forces in Berlin. Knowing that this would put her life in danger, she had sought to deliberately alienate Mario – whom she deeply loves – to throw him off the trail for his own safety.

Outraged, Reichman has Mario taken away to be locked up, planning to throw him overboard when the yacht leaves the coast so that his body is never found. However, Mario escapes his captor's grasp and races into the ship's engine room, where he enters into a gunfight with one of the crew. Reichman hears gunshots and realises that the ship's engines are coming to a standstill. He concocts a strategy to shoot Mario as soon as he attempts to rescue Claire, little realising that he has been out-thought; as soon as the resourceful nightclub owner has overcome the engineer, he goes to the deck of the ship and takes advantage of the higher vantage point to shoot Reichman from a vent above his position. The dying fascist, in a final act of spite, shoots Claire as he falls to the ground. Mario is heartbroken as he races to her side and, begging his forgiveness for what has happened, she dies in his arms.

Back at the mansion, Gimlet is screening film footage of rodeo riders holding onto bucking broncos for dear life. He believes that one of the riders may be the remaining adoptive son, but Matilda doesn't recognise any of them. Then, out of the blue, she sees Jonathan (Randolph Scott) as he gets onto a horse... only to be thrown into the air moments afterwards. Elated, she orders Gimlet to track him down and bring him to New York as quickly as he can.

Later, Williams (Dennis Hoey) – Matilda's butler – is preparing Christmas punch while she instructs her chauffeur to pick up Jonathan from Grand Central Station. Hastings arrives with Judge Alston and demands to know what is going on; Christmas Eve is here at last, and there is still no sign of any of the three missing men. However, Matilda remains confident that the reunion will soon be taking place and proposes a toast to her sons' safe arrival.

At Grand Central Station, Jonathan – a.k.a. The Pendleton Kid – is met by Williams, who warmly greets him. However, rather than allowing himself to be ushered to Matilda's car, Jonathan insists on taking his old friend the butler for a drink at a bar in the station. This exchange frustrates a mysterious woman, Jean Bradford (Dolores Moran), who had attempted to intercept Jonathan before Williams arrived. The butler and the rodeo rider have a whisky together, but Williams is anxious to return to Matilda's mansion as soon as possible. He doesn't realise that the attractive Jean has caught Jonathan's eye. As they leave the bar, a charity auction is taking place, and Jonathan playfully outbids Jean for a baby basket, which he then gifts to her. Unexpectedly, Jean claims that she is expecting a baby (in spite of showing no physical sign of being pregnant) and asks Jonathan to accompany her to 128 West Meredith Street. Williams is alarmed, knowing too well the urgency of returning Jonathan to Matilda, but the younger man is determined to help the enigmatic stranger and tells the butler that there is to be a detour.

Jonathan and Jean arrive at a nondescript house and are met by the owner Mrs Bunyan (Claire Whitney), who demands to know the purpose of their visit. Jean nonchalantly tells her that she is there for a baby and strides into the hallway, leaving Jonathan deeply confused. Jean confidentially tells Jonathan that she is there to adopt a child, and that she needs him to masquerade as her husband. Obviously attracted to her, Jonathan agrees to go along with the ruse, but Jean makes it plain that it is simply a business arrangement; she doesn't immediately return his affections.

Dr Bunyan (Douglass Dumbrille) arrives in the drawing room and is immediately suspicious of the two visitors. When they tell him that they have come to adopt a child, he smells a rat and demands that they leave. However, when Jonathan pulls his gun on the doctor – and, after Jean talks him down, offers a generous bribe instead – Bunyan eventually agrees to let them see the three baby girls currently living on the premises in secret. Jean and Jonathan both seem charmed by the tiny infants, but Bunyan insists that the children cannot leave the premises – for any price – without all of the necessary adoption papers. Furthermore, he deduces that Jean is working surreptitiously for a humane society and has somehow convinced Jonathan to aid in her subterfuge. He thus orders them both to leave the premises before he calls in the police. However, what he doesn't realise is that Jean is actually working undercover for the Welfare Association in alliance with the authorities, and is investigating suspected illegal activity at the orphanage.

Realising that the orphanage is a criminal operation, Jonathan demands to see the doctor's credentials. Bunyan ushers him further into the house, claiming to have all the necessary papers stored in another room. But Jonathan is knocked unconscious by a concealed Mrs Bunyan, who warns her husband that Matilda's car is still parked outside. Jean witnesses the doctor promptly sending the car away, and is then attacked by Bunyan and his wife before she has the opportunity to call the police for backup. Jonathan regains consciousness and, hearing the children crying, races to their aid. He realises that the doctor and his wife have fled the property and left him there to face the consequences of their wrongdoing. Sure enough, police cars can be heard approaching soon after. Jonathan recognises the fact that he, Mario and Michael were rescued from a similar situation in their infancy, and thus he locks the house's front door and races to save the children. Leaving from the rear of the property just as the police break through at the front, Jonathan meets Williams (who had not been convinced by Bunyan's attempts to get rid of the car) and speed off before they can be apprehended. Meanwhile, the police officers searching the house discover Jean bound and gagged in a closet, freeing her just as their colleagues arrive with Dr and Mrs Bunyan who have been caught trying to flee the scene. Jean is appalled that Jonathan appears to have stolen the three babies, but is able to remember the distinctive registration plate of Matilda's car.

Over at the mansion, Matilda is disconsolate. It is now late on Christmas Eve, and there is still no sign of any of her three wards. The judge is about to leave when Jonathan suddenly arrives – along with the three babies from the orphanage. The elderly woman is overjoyed to see her long-lost son after so many years, but Hastings is quietly livid. Moments later, Jean appears with a police escort (having tracked the car to Matilda's address) and angrily accuses Jonathan of having abducted the infants. However, when she realises that he has only acted in their best interests her attitude softens.

The surprises continue when Michael then turns up, along with an indignant Ann who feels certain that he is only there to swindle Matilda out of her money. But he has exactly the opposite in mind. He introduces Ann as his fiancée, and is promptly repudiated by Hastings who pompously tells the assembled party that Michael had swindled vast sums from him. Not to be outdone, Michael explains that he had used the money given to him by Hastings to investigate his overseas manufacturing investments (supposedly set up using Matilda's money) and has found nothing. Hastings's claims of administering his aunt's funds responsibly had all been an elaborate deception; he had simply been pocketing her cash for his own ends. Matilda surprises everyone by revealing that she knew of his dishonesty all along, but came to the conclusion that he lacked the courage and the conviction to build a life for himself the way that her three wards had done. This is the reason why she was so resolved that he would not be allowed to take control of her estate.

Matilda hears carollers singing 'O Come All Ye Faithful' and, knowing that it is his favourite Christmas song, is reminded of Mario. Desperate to save face, Hastings suggests that she is merely hearing things, but – sure enough – the last of the three wards is arriving at the front door. Just as Mario greets Williams, however, Agent Bland arrives to take him into custody; assuming that the mansion was the first place he would head on his return to America, the FBI agent has been lying in wait. But on seeing Matilda's joy at Mario's return, Bland reluctantly offers to wait until after Christmas dinner before arresting him. Hastings is now aghast; all three men have reunited against all the odds, just as Matilda said they would.

The three brothers warmly greet each other, but Judge Alston is less enthused by Mario's arrival; he points out his knowledge of crimes that he has committed in New Orleans. Mario takes Hastings to one side, and reveals the true story: ten years ago, Hastings had set up a dirty deal in New Orleans and had then fled, leaving an unsuspecting Mario to take the blame for it. Keen to keep Matilda's good name safe, Mario tells Hastings that he will not report the truth to the authorities, but the price of his silence is that Hastings will leave the city that very night – just as Mario is being forced to do.

With Hastings choosing to 'suddenly depart' from the premises, the judge voices his appreciation at having met all three of Matilda's estranged wards; it is clear that the attempt to rule her mentally incapacitated will no longer be made. Matilda finds the moment highly emotional. She knows full well that Jonathan is a penniless rodeo rider, that Michael is a persuasive lothario, and that Mario was forced into a life in the criminal underworld due to Hastings's scheming. Yet she is still jubilant that all three of her beloved sons have managed to gather together around the dining table once again, after so many years have passed. As they all sit down to dinner, Matilda proposes a toast: not just to her sons, but to her new daughters and granddaughters as well.

Christmas Eve is one of the most unusual festive movies of the 1940s. While the wildly different styles of its three vignettes may have been intended to provide creative variety, in the final analysis their inclusion leads to a deeply uneven tone which never quite matches up with the framing story set in Matilda's New York mansion. The film certainly features a suitably festive opening sequence, with illustrations of a snowy Central Park and New York brownstones accompanied by a cheerful medley of Christmas carols courtesy of composer Heinz Roemheld, but following this there is precious little in the way of yuletide trappings on display until the film's conclusion has arrived. Eccentricities such as Aunt Matilda's elaborate dining room table train set (which delivers food and drink) seem like an awkward fit with Mario's shady goings-on in South America, or Jonathan's rodeo-riding shenanigans. The screenplay by Laurence Stallings, adapted from original stories written by Stallings and Richard H. Landau, labours hard to paper over the cracks which lie between these markedly dissimilar narratives, but in the final analysis the film all too often feels like an cumbersome mishmash of qualities where the end result is something less than the sum of its parts. As John Grant has suggested, the film features numerous interesting performances, but the conspicuously lopsided tonal attributes continually undermine director Marin's creative intentions:

This is not a movie that's susceptible to sober analysis. Two of the three episodic strands are comedies, the one involving Michael being a rather slight sitcom (although a very funny blonde-bombshell turn from Blondell makes it work) and

the one involving Jonathan being quite a lot clev-
erer, scripter Stallings clearly having a lot of fun
filling Jonathan's dialogue with as much cheesy
cowpoke imagery as possible. The central episode,
the one involving Mario, is more weighty: the scene in which Reichman beats up a pinioned Mario
is certainly not played for laughs, and the subsequent tragedy is as certainly poignant. Raft's at the
top of his game here; it's hard not to feel a pang of
regret that he couldn't have tried equally hard in
some of his more prominent roles. [...] Pleasingly
amiable and with a topnotch performance from
Harding, *Christmas Eve* has become surprisingly
obscure when you bear in mind the caliber of its
cast.[1]

Grant's observation about the cast is certainly germane;
the stars of the film were unquestionably prominent in their
day, with George Raft famed for his appearances in crime
thrillers – often in gangster roles, as in films including *Scarface*
(Howard Hawks, 1932) and *Each Dawn I Die* (William Keighley, 1939). (Raft's assured performance in *Christmas Eve* is all
the more remarkable considering that he endured first-degree
burns on his right leg when an engine caught fire on the set,
consequently setting his costume ablaze.) Randolph Scott was
closely identified with Western movies, including *Sunset Pass*
(Henry Hathaway, 1933), *Man of the Forest* (Henry Hathaway, 1933) and *Wagon Wheels* (Charles Barton, 1934), though
he had an extremely prolific acting career which showcased
his considerable versatility in numerous other genres. George
Brent was a similarly resourceful actor, often cast in support
of female stars such as Barbara Stanwyck in *Baby Face* (Alfred E. Green, 1933), Greta Garbo in *The Painted Veil* (Rich-

ard Boleslawski, 1934), and Bette Davis in *Dark Victory* (Edmund Goulding, 1939). He made many other appearances in popular movies of the time including *42*nd *Street* (Lloyd Bacon, 1933), *Submarine D-1* (Lloyd Bacon, 1937), and *The Fighting 69*th (William Keighley, 1940). Sherlock Holmes aficionados are also likely to welcome the droll performance of Dennis Hoey as Williams, Matilda's butler; throughout the 1940s he played Inspector Lestrade against Basil Rathbone's famed portrayal of the legendary detective. Ann Harding, well-known for her appearances in films such as *The Animal Kingdom* (Edward H. Griffith, 1932) and *Eyes in the Night* (Fred Zinnemann, 1942), was only in her mid-forties when she portrayed Matilda, leading to considerable make-up being applied in order to make her look suitably aged for the part. As Harding was a celebrated actress of the time, however, the casting choice seemed unusual to many critics given that many in the audience would have been well aware of her true age and thus may have found the conceit distracting. As Laura Grieve astutely discerns: 'Though she has convincing old-age makeup, Ann Harding (born 1901) was younger than Randolph Scott (born 1898), a month older than George Raft, and a little over two years older than George Brent (born 1904)! One wonders why an older actress along the lines of, say, Ethel Barrymore wasn't cast in the part'.[2]

Perhaps because of its clumsy juxtaposition of styles, *Christmas Eve* is a difficult film to categorise within the canon of the Christmas movie genre. Some, such as Gary J. Svehla, have noted that in spite of its noticeable lack of obvious festive trimmings, the movie's overarching theme does at least fit comfortably into the wider pantheon of the genre's conventions: '*Christmas Eve* is a most positive and forceful proponent of the Yuletide essence and its story detailing how the unity of the family can heal all wounds is most specifically indicative of the holiday spirit'.[3] Yet while Matilda's search runs through the movie as its central thread, the conclusion – when it comes – seems rushed and overly expedient in its numerous convergent incidents, leaving the result somewhat less convincing or satisfying than it might otherwise have been (though admittedly, exposing the common link of Hastings's duplicity is quite effective). The film was, however, prescient in its presentation of a non-traditional family unit, emphasising that such an extended family has the same capacity for loving provision and mutual support as the customary nuclear model. This would become a dominant theme in later films such as *White Christmas* (q.v.) and *We're No Angels* (q.v.), amongst many others. Some commentators, such as Grieve, have lamented the fact that the film's explicit engagement with Christmas tropes is ultimately so trifling: '*Christmas Eve*, originally released on Halloween 1947, is quite an odd film. [...] They all sit down to Christmas dinner in the final moments, which despite the movie's title is about as Christmasy as the movie gets, other than the preparation of some special Christmas punch'.[4] While the film admittedly does lack much of the visual association with the festive period that had come to be expected of a Christmas movie, the problematic nature of its composite narrative may perhaps have made this deficiency inevitable; it would be much easier to mentally situate the screwball comedy of Michael and Ann's constant romantic squabbling with the holiday season than would ever have been the case with the dark, *Casablanca*-esque criminal underworld inhabited by Mario and Claire. As Andy Webb has commented:

> The thing about this 1947 version of *Christmas Eve* is that whilst not dark it has at times a much dark-

er tone, you could almost say that rather than being a Christmas movie with touches of other genres it is in fact other genres with a touch of
Christmas. As such when the detective whom Matilda hires tracks down Mario in South America it
has more of a 'you dirty rat' feel to it with Mario
played by George Raft giving it the full criminal
beans. It then becomes more of a camp western
when we catch up with Jonathon [sic] played by
Randolph Scott with this being Scott's last non-
western movie as the next 14 years of his career,
up to when he retired, were dominated purely by
westerns. But this tone and the mix up of them
doesn't sit comfortably with me especially when it
can go from the darkness of Mario being worked
over to something more comedic. What this all
boils down to is that *Christmas Eve* is still an entertaining movie, if you enjoy older movies. But it
lacks the Christmassy feel which I certainly like
and ends up too much of a mixed bag.[5]

Christmas Eve met with considerable scepticism at the
time of the film's release, with critical responses ranging from
the lukewarm to the outright hostile. *The New York Times*,
for instance, remarked that: 'For this episodic potpourri about
a rich, aged eccentric maiden lady about to be declared mentally unfit, and her three errant wards, tries hard to emulate the
pattern of such successful episodic yarns as [Julian Duvivier's
1942 anthology film] *Tales of Manhattan* and only succeeds in
being transparent, plodding and occasionally confusing. [...]
Told in flashback their activities are unfolded in a rather abrupt and sometimes implausible fashion. Of the headliners in
the cast none is precisely convincing'.[6] *Time* magazine was, if

anything, even more damning in its summation: '*Christmas Eve* [[...]], a less appetizing holiday confection, concerns an eccentric old gotrocks (Ann Harding) and her far-flung adopted sons (George Raft, George Brent, Randolph Scott). They surmount the world, the flesh and the devil to reach her side on Christmas Eve – just in time to save her from the booby hatch for spending $500,000 on 500,000 dead rats. Producer Benedict Bogeaus spent considerably more on this dead rat'.[7]

The film does admittedly have its entertaining qualities, not least Reginald Denny's commendable turn as the hiss-worthy Phillip Hastings – milking every drop of slippery obsequiousness from this odiously deceptive character – and Joe Sawyer is clearly having fun as the hardboiled Private Detective Gimlet (gleefully mining the part for every possible clichéd truism as he does so). Similarly, Joan Blondell provides an engagingly comic performance as the jilted Ann Nelson, while Konstantin Shayne is supremely entertaining as Gustav Reichman, the most stereotypically sadistic former Nazi character imaginable (at a point when this kind of role was a rather well-populated field, given its proximity to the end of the war).

However, perhaps in part due to the film's relative obscurity in the present day, *Christmas Eve* has not been witness to a revival in its critical fortunes in more recent times, with reviewers continuing to be unconvinced of its merits. Dennis Schwartz's view is representative of many modern appraisals when he considers that 'all three episodes were weakly conceived, plodding, slow-moving, far-fetched, uninteresting and unconvincingly acted. The final Christmas Eve gathering, where everything gets neatly wrapped-up like a Christmas gift, makes for a lousy present when opened. [[...]] The feel-good story tries too hard to be a cheery Christmas story, but its dry mixture of lame comedy and limp drama comes off as ridiculous melodrama'.[8] Jeffrey M. Anderson has echoed these views, drawing attention to the film's inelegant mélange of styles when he observes that '*Christmas Eve* is not the holiday classic I was hoping for. It's awkward and convoluted, and it's difficult to imagine what anyone was actually thinking when they went to work on it'.[9] However, not all evaluations have been uniformly adverse in their judgement. *Vienna's Classic Hollywood*, for instance, has proposed a divergent view, claiming that the film's greatest disadvantage is that its duration does not allow sufficient time for any of the individual segments to be fully developed, meaning that the final product seems rushed and its narrative inadequately elaborated upon: '*Christmas Eve* was entertaining, with a few reservations. The three stars only share a couple of scenes. [...] The problem with the script is the mix of comedy and drama. The Brent and Scott episodes are pure comedy, while the Raft story is straight drama. In fact, each story was strong enough to be a full length feature'.[10]

Christmas Eve was later rereleased under the considerably less festive title of *Sinner's Holiday*, and many years later would be remade for television. Stuart Cooper's *Christmas Eve* was broadcast on NBC on 22 December 1986, and featured a slightly altered storyline. In this version of the tale, wealthy matriarch Amanda Kingsley (Loretta Young) – who is a philanthropist with a special interest in helping impoverished youngsters – is diagnosed with a terminal illness and discovers that she has little time left. As a final act, she resolves as a matter of urgency to reunite her three long-lost grandchildren Harley (Wayne Best), Melissa (Season Hubley) and Josh (Patrick Cassidy) – each of whom are living in different locations across the United States – with her son Andrew (Arthur Hill), their estranged father, before time runs out. She hires private detective Morris Huffner (Ron Leibman) with the aim of bringing together the misplaced trio on Christmas Eve. The remake has enjoyed considerably greater critical approval than the original film, with Young winning a Golden Globe Award for her performance. However, like its predecessor the TV movie has become a rather obscure feature in more recent times. Neither the 1947 or 1986 versions of *Christmas Eve* would have any connection with Mitch Davis's ensemble comedy-drama *Christmas Eve* (2015), which was released many years later.

Christmas Eve was a brave experiment in festive filmmaking which never quite succeeds in its admirable creative intentions. There are few Christmas movies remotely courageous enough to pull off an attempt at a narrative which features mendacious philanderers, charismatic rodeo riders and deadly former Nazis (especially only a few years after the Second World War had ended), but Marin and Stallings certainly give it their best shot. That they should fall short in their efforts is hardly the worst of failings, and while the film is flawed there is no denying its occasional charms and appealing eccentricity. Its three parts may well be deeply incongruent, but they are also highly distinctive with each of their respective stars giving creditable performances; Ann Harding's steely determination as the unshakeable materfamilias Matilda ties all of the sections together like a Christmas ribbon to produce an interesting, if decidedly rickety, festive gift. While *Christmas Eve* will never rival the classics of the golden age of festive filmmaking, it nonetheless provided an admirable attempt to try something different with a format that was then only in the nascent stages of development, laying the groundwork for other such attempts in later decades.

REFERENCES

1. John Grant, '*Christmas Eve*', in *Noirish*, 25 December 2013. <*https://noirencyclopedia.wordpress.com/2013/12/25/chri stmas-eve-1947/*>

2. Laura Grieve, 'Tonight's Movie: *Christmas Eve*', in *Laura's Miscellaneous Musings*, 29 January 2016. <*http://laurasmiscmusings.blogspot.com/2016/01/tonights-movie-christmas-eve-1947-olive.html*>

3. Gary J. Svehla, '*Christmas Eve*', in *It's Christmas Time at the Movies* by Gary J. Svehla and Susan Svehla (Baltimore: Midnight Marquee Press, 1998), 18-22, p.22.

4. Grieve.

5. Andy Webb, '*Christmas Eve*', in *The Movie Scene*, 2016. <*https://www.themoviescene.co.uk/reviews/christmas-eve-1947/christmas-eve-1947.html*>

6. A.W., 'At the Broadway', in *The New York Times*, 28 November 1947. <*https://www.nytimes.com/1947/11/28/archives/at-the-broadway.html*>

7. Anon., 'Cinema: The New Pictures', in *Time*, 8 December 1947. <*http://content.time.com/time/subscriber/article/0,33009,934178-2,00.html*>

8. Dennis Schwartz, '*Christmas Eve*', in *Ozus' World Movie Reviews*, 25 December 2012. <*http://homepages.sover.net/~ozus/christmaseve.htm*>

9. Jeffrey M. Anderson, 'Christmas Peeve', in *Combustible Celluloid*, 19 January 2016.
    <*http://www.combustiblecelluloid.com/dvds/christmas_eve.shtml*>

10. Vienna, '*Christmas Eve*', in *Vienna's Classic Hollywood*, 4 November 2015.
    <*https://viennasclassichollywood.com/2015/11/04/christmas-eve-1947/*>

It Happened on Fifth Avenue (1947)

Roy Del Ruth Productions

Director: Roy Del Ruth
Producer: Roy Del Ruth
Screenwriter: Everett Freeman, with additional dialogue by
Vick Knight, from an original story by Herbert Clyde Lewis
and Frederick Stephani

WHILE *Christmas Eve* (q.v.) can be considered a
lost curiosity of festive cinema, it was far from
being the only yuletide feature of 1947 to have
since drifted into relative obscurity. *It Happened on Fifth
Avenue* has similarly earned the status of a cult rarity, and yet
it was also to bear a surprising number of parallels with *Miracle on 34th Street* (q.v.), which premiered in the same year.
Aside from sharing a frosty New York City setting, both
films premiered much earlier in the year than the now-
traditional Christmas release window – *It Happened on Fifth
Avenue* was to premiere on 19 April 1947, with *Miracle on
34th Street* emerging a few months later on 4 June 1947. Further underscoring these intriguing similarities, Herbert Clyde
Lewis and Frederick Stephani's original story for *It Happened
on Fifth Avenue* was nominated for an Academy Award,
going head-to-head with Valentine Davies's story for *Miracle*

on 34th Street. It was Davies who would eventually emerge triumphant, but little could anyone at the time have anticipated the way in which *Miracle on 34th Street* would so prominently take its place within the annals of early Christmas cinema while *It Happened on Fifth Avenue* would eventually disappear into the mists of memory – at least, until recently.

Today, perhaps the most noteworthy fact about the film's production is that its story had originally been optioned by none other than Liberty Films in 1945; Frank Capra was intended to direct. However, as cinema history tells us all too clearly, Capra had very different ideas. As J.P. Roscoe notes, *It Happened on Fifth Avenue* 'has a bit of an odd history. The picture was originally optioned for Frank Capra but Capra chose to take *It's a Wonderful Life* instead. The movie then remained in obscurity for years and finally became back in print on 2008 and has had a bit of a resurgence'.[1] Roscoe is correct that the film has experienced a long and circuitous route back to recognition amongst cineastes, which is especially regrettable given the general critical approval that it met at the time of its original release. Making the deterioration of its profile in later years all the more peculiar, *It Happened on Fifth Avenue* was also the subject of an ambitious publicity campaign in 1947 which featured a number of celebrity endorsements on its advertising, and the commendation of leading figures such as Orson Welles, Frank Capra and even Al Jolson certainly caught the public eye – even if it also drew criticism from some quarters, such as *The Washington Post*, for being too ostentatious a sales pitch for what was, at heart, an unpretentious screen comedy.[2]

It Happened on Fifth Avenue was the first film to be produced under the banner of Allied Artists Pictures, an offshoot of Monogram Pictures. Monogram was considered at the time to be a studio which specialised in low-budget films, so the establishment of Allied Artists was intended to mark a move into higher-budget territory and certainly helps to explain the enthusiastic and elaborate marketing which accompanied the release of the new division's flagship movie. As David C. Tucker has observed, 'today *It Happened on Fifth Avenue* is a favorite with many viewers as a Christmastime treat, and remains one of Gale [Storm]'s best-known films. However, its original release was in springtime. The picture's originally announced budget was $1,000,000, an immense sum by Monogram standards. [...] The film was Roy Del Ruth's first venture as an independent producer, with release to be arranged through Monogram. Monogram formed a division called Allied Artists Pictures, aimed at producing and distributing higher-budget films than what they normally made, with *It Happened on [Fifth] Avenue* to be the first project'.[3] Even with the greater production budget, the film still ended up costing 30% more than its intended financial resources. Unlike the similarly festively-themed *Miracle on 34th Street*, whose summertime release was explained by Twentieth Century-Fox's lack of confidence in a film based on Christmas themes to achieve box-office success, *It Happened on Fifth Avenue* was thought to have been aimed for a release during the Christmas 1946 period and subsequently delayed until spring the following year.

Helming *It Happened on Fifth Avenue* was Roy Del Ruth, a screenwriter and later director who had established a solid reputation for films such as *The Desert Song* (1929), the first feature to be released by Warner Bros. in full colour, as well as commercially successful movies including *Gold Diggers of Broadway* (1929), *Bulldog Drummond Strikes Back* (1934) and *Born to Dance* (1936) – a rare musical outing for James

Stewart. Del Ruth also directed Ricardo Cortez as Sam Spade in *The Maltese Falcon* (1931), the first cinematic adaptation of Dashiell Hammett's detective mystery which is now largely forgotten due to the meteoric success of John Huston's famous 1941 version of the tale which starred Humphrey Bogart and Mary Astor. Between 1932 and 1941, Del Ruth was recognised as the second highest-paid director in Hollywood, and was chosen to be one of seven directors to take part in the production of *Ziegfeld Follies* (1946), an all-star musical comedy involving many of MGM Studios' top talents including Judy Garland, Fred Astaire, Gene Kelly and Lucille Ball. Thus Del Ruth was at the height of his creative powers when he took to the director's chair for *It Happened on Fifth Avenue*

It Happened on Fifth Avenue (1947): Roy Del Ruth Productions

– a film that would be an unusual diversion even for a professional who had been responsible for such an artistically varied filmography.

On New York's famously upmarket Fifth Avenue, a guide on a tour bus is pointing out the grand homes of the rich and famous to an enraptured audience of passengers. One of the high-class dwellings he indicates is the palatial mansion belonging to industrialist Michael

J. O'Connor, the second-richest man in the world. It is winter, however, and the building is currently boarded up; O'Connor is wintering in Virginia during the cold weather. Nobody suspects that crafty vagrant Aloysius T. McKeever (Victor Moore) has discovered a loose panel in the property's perimeter fence, and has surreptitiously gained entrance to the mansion via a nearby underground access-way.

McKeever (and his inseparable companion, Sammy the dog) wastes no time in making himself at home, rewiring the house's circuit breaker to evade suspicion – if anyone enters the house, opening the door will cut the power to the lights, helping to maintain the illusion that no-one is living there. McKeever reveals that he has used this same strategy many times over the years; whenever the O'Connors leave New York on vacation, he moves into their house so that he can live in comfort during the cold of winter. After a bath, he changes into one of O'Connor's expensive suits, getting ready to wait out the big chill.

Elsewhere in the city, a block of residential apartments is being emptied in preparation for demolition; O'Connor's company intends to build an 80-storey skyscraper on the site to house new offices. However, the tenant in apartment 4G steadfastly refuses to be evicted. Former G.I. Jim Bullock (Don DeFore), who has had enormous difficulty finding a home due to the post-war housing crisis, claims that he would rather the building be torn down around him than vacate the premises. After officials have no success in talking him down, Bullock shackles himself to his bed with a pair of handcuffs he had stolen from a Japanese military policeman during the Pacific campaign, but even this tactic is unsuccessful – a group of removal men simply remove Bullock, complete with the bed, from the apartment. Bullock is furious, and swears that he will somehow have retaliation on O'Connor.

Now homeless, Bullock is reduced to sleeping on a bench in a freezing cold Central Park. McKeever passes by, dressed in O'Connor's smartly-tailored clothing (complete with top hat), and his dog Sam pulls a grass sprinkler under the bench, causing Bullock to become soaking wet. McKeever apologises and soon realises that Bullock is a kindred spirit, being destitute in the winter. Feeling responsible for Bullock becoming drenched in such cold weather, McKeever invites him back to stay at the mansion, but he doesn't reveal that he is a trespasser on O'Connor's property.

As his clothing dries out, Bullock looks around the mansion's drawing room and quickly deduces that the property belongs to O'Connor and his family. He immediately rails against McKeever, believing him to be the man responsible for demolishing his apartment building after it had taken him three months to find somewhere to stay. McKeever reluctantly reveals that he is just a house guest, and that he is only taking up residence at O'Connor's property while the businessman is out of town. He is thus unable to do anything about Bullock's long-term housing problems, but does invite the younger man to join him during the winter.

Meanwhile, in Bubbling Springs, Virginia, the real Michael J. O'Connor (Charles Ruggles) is fuming at a newspaper report focusing on Bullock's promise of revenge as he is ejected from his apartment. However, it is obvious that his only real worry is the bad publicity surrounding his new skyscraper; he has no real concern for Bullock's plight at all. O'Connor has called a conference of company executives at his extravagant winter home to discuss his post-war construction plans. He reveals that the new skyscraper is only the first part of a much more ambitious scheme that will eventually culminate in a vast air cargo network – one which will bring a whole new node of global trade to New York. The executives are sceptical, knowing that it is inconceivable that O'Connor will be able to acquire enough property in the city to make it possible to construct such a sprawling complex, but his assistant Farrow (Grant Mitchell) points out that the US Government will provide the key. A former Army camp near the city, covering 300 acres, is to be sold off in December. Officials from the Federal Government have made it clear that they will accept a reasonable offer, and O'Connor believes that if he can provide the necessary capital, the site will be perfect for situating his new trade complex.

The meeting is interrupted when the headteacher at the school attended by O'Connor's daughter calls to request an urgent conversation. It transpires that Trudy, his teenage daughter, has gone missing from school, and the staff members have no idea as to her whereabouts. O'Connor is concerned that Trudy may have absconded to be with her mother – his estranged wife, Mary, who is living in Florida. He orders Farrow to engage the services of a private investigator in New York, with the plan of tracking down Trudy as quickly as possible.

Back at the O'Connor mansion in New York, McKeever and Bullock are startled when the lights suddenly go out – someone has entered the property through the front door. They watch quietly as Trudy (Gale Storm) heads to her room and starts to sift through her belongings, obviously intending to run away from home. Not realising her identity, Bullock assumes that she is a burglar and wrestles Trudy's mink coat from her, believing that she intends to steal it. Trudy is nonplussed, having never seen either of the two men before, and attempts to phone the police. McKeever stops her in the nick of time, and asks Bullock to speak with him privately. With some reluctance, McKeever reveals that he is not really a house guest – or, at least, that O'Connor has no idea that he is staying at his property. Realising that they are both itinerants, they have no right to dictate what Trudy can or can't do; with no idea of her identity, they reason that she has just as much entitlement to be there as they do. Neither man realises that Trudy has been listening to the entire conversation from the doorway of her room, and finds it amusing that McKeever has managed to stay at the property between November and March every year without even coming close to being detected by its owner.

Keen to play along with the two good-natured interlopers, Trudy takes on the assumed surname Smith and pretends that she had broken into the property in order to 'borrow' some suitable clothes for a job interview at a music shop the next day. Bullock isn't convinced by her explanation and McKeever keeps up the pretence of being the householder, so Trudy pretends to faint, alarming both men. Later, they prepare some food and drink to help revive her health, but the lights again go out unexpectedly – two police patrolmen check on the property at ten o'clock every night. The three 'intruders' decamp from the kitchen into the house's ice box, and McKeever is forced to reveal that both he and Bullock are homeless, living at the mansion without O'Connor's permission. As the patrolmen leave the building after their inspection, satisfied that it is safely unoccupied, they meet a private detective who is searching for the missing Trudy. However, as far as they are concerned there has been no sign of her.

Back in the kitchen, Bullock voices concern over Trudy's wellbeing; as she has spun a tall tale about coming from a big family in a small town, he worries that she will be unsafe in the big city as she lacks experience of the dangers that may befall her. McKeever tries to convince her to return to her own home (little realising that the mansion *is*, in fact, her home), but she convinces them both that her father is a violent drunkard and that she would be unsafe if she returned to him. Thus they decide to invite her to stay, at least as long as it takes to complete her job interview the next day.

In the morning, Trudy goes to the Melody Shop in Times Square as planned and impresses the manager with her musical skills. Though the job involves selling sheet music, a high level of competency in singing and playing the piano is also required, but Trudy gives a performance that instantly gets her the job; she is told that she is to start work the next day. Bullock, who obviously feels a growing attraction to the mysterious young woman, is waiting outside the music shop and joins in the celebration over the news that she has been hired. On the way back to the mansion, they stumble across two families who are living in a car, and Bullock recognises the wives of two of his old wartime Army comrades, Margie (Dorothea Kent) and Alice (Cathy Carter). They, like Bullock, are unable to find accommodation for themselves and their children, but are hopeful that they will be able to rent an apartment in a nearby building. However, little do they realise that the landlord has asked Whitey (Alan Hale Jr.) and Hank (Edward Ryan) for three months' rent in advance, making it too expensive a proposition for them – even if they pool their resources. Worse still, the landlord refuses to accommodate children or pets. Realising that the two families desperately need somewhere to stay until they can find a more permanent home, Bullock invites them all back to the mansion.

McKeever is concerned by the number of people who are now living in O'Connor's home. After all, when he broke in it was with the understanding that he would treat the property with respect; now that it is unknowingly being shared by such a large group, he feels that the situation is being taken advantage of. However, Trudy manages to convince him that there will be ample space in the immense mansion for everyone; as long as they can continue to evade detection, all will be well.

Margie immediately picks up on the attraction between Trudy and Bullock, though Trudy feels (wrongly) that Bullock doesn't share her affections. Meanwhile, over a game of pool (where McKeever reveals himself to be an ace player), Bullock, Whitey and Hank are lamenting the lack of employment opportunities in town. McKeever reveals that as he could never earn enough money to fund the lavish lifestyle that he aspired to, he is now content to let other people work for a living while he attends to his own way of doing things. When the others indicate that they would prefer to earn their living by more conventional means, McKeever hatches a plan; with a large number of abandoned Army camps lying derelict around the country following the conclusion of the Second World War, there is huge potential to redevelop them for new business opportunities. Bullock is enthused by the idea, believing that a co-operative of former G.I.s could be assembled to purchase and renovate old barracks for new purposes. McKeever suggests that they look at Camp Kilson, just outside New York City, little realising that O'Connor already has his eye on it for his new trading development. Hank and Alice (who had held an administrative post during the war, and thus has first-hand experience of federal bureaucracy) agree to drive to Washington D.C. and find out how much it will cost to purchase the land from the government.

Trudy and Bullock continue to grow closer. She wears a fashionable designer dress to play pool with him, and after their usual verbal sparring they share a kiss. The next day, Trudy takes up her new $30-a-week post at the music store. As she leaves work, she is intercepted by her father, who is waiting outside in an expensive chauffeur-driven car. O'Connor is annoyed at having to cut short his time in Virginia to chase after his daughter, but Trudy makes clear that she won't be encouraged back to finishing school. Furthermore, she reveals that she has fallen in love, and explains the situation with Bullock and McKeever staying at the mansion. O'Connor is stunned to hear that squatters have taken up residence in his home and resolves to call the police, but Trudy – furious at his controlling attitude – angrily berates him before giving him the slip.

Some time later, O'Connor and Trudy are reunited at Central Park, and Trudy explains that in spite of her luxurious lifestyle she is deeply unhappy. Her parents' separation has badly affected her, and she has become profoundly lonely since being sent to boarding school. O'Connor tells Trudy that if it will make her happy, he will gladly meet Bullock, for whom she has professed her love. However, she has one condition – that he should hide his true identity and take on a fake persona, to ensure that Bullock's feelings for her are genuine. If he should realise that Trudy's father is a multimillionaire, she will always wonder if his interest was motivated by money rather than his heart. Grudgingly, O'Connor visits a second-hand clothing emporium and purchases a new wardrobe to replace his costly, tailor-made wool suit.

Later that day, Trudy is passing through the park with McKeever and Bullock when she 'discovers' O'Connor sitting on one of the benches. Trudy concocts a falsehood that O'Connor must be a starving vagrant and stops to talk to him. Clearly not relishing the deceit, O'Connor introduces himself as 'Mike' – simply a homeless man down on his luck. He vaguely recognises Bullock, having seen him in the newspaper coverage of the apartment eviction, but can't quite place his face. Trudy's deception is aided when a policeman arrives and tries to get rid of O'Connor, believing him to be a hobo loitering on the park grounds. McKeever is highly reluctant to introduce yet another guest to the increasingly well-populated mansion, but feels that he has little choice when the policeman is on the cusp of ejecting him from the park.

Back at the mansion, O'Connor is aghast to see his hallway full of clothes-lines airing damp laundry, and is similarly horrified to encounter McKeever wearing one of his smoking jackets and puffing on a costly cigar. McKeever is full of his usual hospitality, offering O'Connor the chance to scrub up and have some food – little realising that the other man is seething at his private property being occupied by strangers. Bullock arrives with a scale model of one of the Army barracks he intends to convert into accommodation for couples and young families, but O'Connor pours cold water on the idea, pronouncing it unworkable and unprofitable – much to Bullock's chagrin.

O'Connor is alarmed when he realises that a baby is staying at the mansion, believing that it is Trudy's. Considering the infant must have been born after an elopement between Bullock and Trudy, he solemnly assures his daughter that he will support the marriage and will continue to stand by her. Little does he realise that the infant is actually the

258

child of Hank and Alice, being looked after by Margie and Whitey while the other couple are in Washington. He is dumbfounded when he realises that Trudy and Bullock are not in fact married, believing that the child must have been born out of wedlock, but is interrupted in his indignation when Alice and Hank suddenly arrive back with mixed news. It transpires that Camp Kilson is still on sale to the highest bidder, but an offer of $150,000 has already been made. There are only ten days left to exceed this proposal. McKeever immediately suggests that they advance a higher offer, and worry afterwards about how they intend to actually raise enough capital to make good on the agreement.

McKeever has put O'Connor to work in the kitchen; he is only allowing him to stay at the mansion on the condition that he earns his keep, as he is apprehensive about his frequent bursts of temper (not realising even remotely the cause which lies behind them). McKeever explains that if O'Connor wants to stay, it will need to be in the servants' quarters so that he doesn't disturb the young families living upstairs. Indignant, O'Connor retreats into the ice box with a telephone and rings one of his executives, giving out precise instructions about various business dealings – some of them running into millions of dollars. He doesn't realise that McKeever and Bullock are listening in, and when he discovers their presence he fears that his cover has been blown. However, they instead consider that O'Connor must be a fantasist who has become overwhelmed with the experience of living in a mansion and has started to believe that he really is a millionaire businessman.

Relegated to the servants' quarters, O'Connor struggles to make his bed, never having had to perform basic housework tasks in many years. Trudy sneaks in once everyone else is asleep and tries to maintain her father's co-operation, but O'Connor has had enough. He tells her that he will no longer tolerate the presence of McKeever and the other 'house guests', and that if she can't persuade them to leave willingly within the next day, he intends to call the police and have them charged with vagrancy and trespassing.

Afraid that her romance with Bullock is now in jeopardy, Trudy contacts her mother in Florida and urges her to return to New York as quickly as possible. Mary (Ann Harding) meets her daughter at the Waldorf Towers as requested, and hears the whole, intricate story. Eager to help her daughter keep her new romance on track, Mary offers to assist by coming to stay at the mansion under an assumed identity. Though she hasn't seen O'Connor in the four years since they separated, Mary feels that she knows his character well enough to ensure that she can aid Trudy in getting her way driven.

Back at the mansion, O'Connor is being berated by McKeever for raising suspicion by using the front door (all access to the house is strictly by clandestine means only) when he suddenly smells Irish stew being made and is reminded of the time he first met his wife. Sure enough, on a visit to the kitchen to ascertain the source he runs straight into Mary... and the pair almost immediately begin bickering. Mary approves of the match between Trudy and Bullock, while O'Connor is dead against it. While Mary points out that they had also been very young when they got together, O'Connor responds that the failure of their marriage should be ample warning of the dangers of impulsive romance. Knowing her ex-husband's pride and arrogance, Mary taunts him by saying that she knew he wouldn't have the stamina to keep up the pretence of pretending to be a vagrant. In response, O'Connor asserts that he can maintain the deception for as long as is necessary, thus being manipulated into doing exactly what Trudy had wanted from the start.

Bullock is elated; a couple of hundred of his fellow ex-soldiers have managed to put together an average of $500 each, meaning that his barracks renovation project is now a more realistic prospect. He has even managed to get a construction company involved, in the hope that they will pitch in the rest of the necessary investment to make the ambitious scheme come about. O'Connor listens with growing concern, and surreptitiously phones Farrow. It is revealed that O'Connor's corporation owns an interest in the very construction company that Bullock intends to do business with. Quickly improvising, O'Connor tells Farrow to instruct the company to disregard Bullock's renovation idea and instead to offer him a well-paid job... in Bolivia. The only stipulation must be that Bullock has to remain a single man in order to be considered for the post.

Over dinner, McKeever celebrates the harmony of the unconventional cooperative currently living in the mansion, and points out that they must be considerably happier there than the O'Connors ever were. Irritated, but still concealing his true identity, a disgruntled O'Connor asks him what he knows about the rich family who owns the property. McKeever replies that Michael O'Connor had been a poor boy who rose up the ranks of business to become the second-wealthiest man on the planet, but in spite of his vast wealth he is reputed to be ill-tempered and obsessed with the acquisition of even greater riches. His wife, on the other hand, is said to be just as cantankerous and in denial about being in middle-age, living the life of a socialite in Palm Beach without any real satisfaction or contentment. Mary and O'Connor are both rattled by his uncomfortably accurate appraisal.

Later, McKeever tells O'Connor that he is anxious about the lack of food in the ice box. When he lived at the mansion alone in previous years, he never ate enough to noticeably deplete the larder, but with eleven people staying at the property there is now little left to eat. As everyone else is out working (McKeever considers himself the house supervisor), he suggests that O'Connor find work to help contribute to the food budget. The business mogul bristles at the very idea of manual labour, but – sure enough – McKeever manages to win the argument, and the covert millionaire is soon shovelling snow from the sidewalks of New York so that he can chip in to the running of the house. Farrow arrives in an expensive car, and is aghast to see his illustrious boss clearing snow. O'Connor is anxious to know how plans are proceeding for the air cargo hub, but Farrow is dismayed to report that they have again been outbid for the Army camp; their unknown rivals have now bid $195,000. O'Connor authorises an increase in their own bid to $200,000, in the hope that they will still be able to purchase the land by the closing date.

After returning to the mansion with some much-needed groceries, O'Connor asks Bullock how the meeting with the construction company had gone. Bullock tells him that although they had turned down his barracks regeneration proposal, they had offered him a $12,000 a year job in Bolivia... which he had turned down. To O'Connor's dismay, Bullock confides that as a patriotic American he would have no intention of leaving the country that he loves – and furthermore, too many of his fellow ex-soldiers are counting on him to see through the project to turn former barracks buildings into affordable housing. The penny finally drops, and

O'Connor realises that Bullock is the mystery would-be purchaser who has been constantly outbidding him for the rights to Camp Kilson.

While the others decorate the Christmas tree, Mary tends to O'Connor's ailing back – considerably worse for wear after his constant shovelling throughout the day. They reminisce about their lives as newlyweds, and O'Connor realises that although they were constantly strapped for cash, they had good friends and simpler pleasures all those years ago. Their meeting is interrupted by McKeever – who, suspecting that the pair are sharing a romantic encounter, demands that O'Connor return to his room in the servants' quarters immediately. Meanwhile, Trudy is becoming wary of what Bullock might think if he knew of her true identity and furtively asks him if he cares what her name is. Unaware of the intent of her question, he replies that her name is immaterial; once they have the opportunity to get married, she will be free to change it to Bullock anyway.

The next morning, McKeever apologises to O'Connor for his earlier prudishness, but explains that it is important to set a good example for the young people staying at the mansion. O'Connor emphasises that nothing untoward had happened, but McKeever tells him that it is obvious that Mary is in love with him – he simply doesn't see it. Though McKeever still has no idea of who they really are, O'Connor starts to wonder if Mary really does still harbour feelings for him after so many years apart. He visits her in her room, and they again recall the happier days of their youth. McKeever passes the doorway and tells them that they should consider marriage before it's too late; they obviously have great affection for each other, and he feels that sharing the responsibilities of life will do them both good. He adds that they should take care not to end up old and alone, as he has done. Once McKeever has gone, O'Connor tells Mary that he has never stopped loving her, and that the divorce was a mistake that he had never truly wanted. Mary feels exactly the same way, and they embrace – their love rekindled thanks to the change that has come about through their strange new circumstances.

Christmas Eve arrives, and McKeever takes on the role of Santa Claus as he distributes gifts under the Christmas tree (with his dog Sammy acting as his own personal elf). The guests join in a festive singalong, but forget about the ten o'clock arrival of the police patrolmen who check the property daily. The two officers are flabbergasted when they discover the collected 'house guests', but the smooth-talking McKeever is not only able to dissuade them from making an arrest – he also invites them to the party, along with their wives. Though the policemen are unable to attend, they leave in good spirits and promise not to evict the group – at least, not until the new year has arrived.

Trudy notices that Bullock appears downcast; he reveals that he was outbid for the Army camp, and that it has been sold to Michael O'Connor. They lament the fact that O'Connor seems determined to buy every property in New York City. Somewhat shamefaced, O'Connor slips away from the party, but Mary follows him and voices her disappointment in his conduct. He replies that he hadn't realised that Bullock was his opponent until recently, but at any rate there is no room for sentiment in business. Mary is crestfallen, realising that O'Connor hasn't changed nearly as much as she had hoped. Trudy is also disconsolate; while elated by Bullock's gift of a winter coat, she knows that his dream of providing affordable housing to hundreds of ex-servicemen is now dead.

On Christmas morning, Bullock goes to Camp Kilson to tell his fellow former soldiers that there will be no barracks renovation project. The gathered assembly has barely enough time to process the news before O'Connor's corporate executives arrive and demand that the camp be completely cleared so that demolition work can begin. None of them realise that O'Connor has tagged along with Bullock and is watching events unfold from a distance. Believing that Farrow is actually O'Connor, the amassed ex-soldiers start pelting him with rotten fruit – much to the real O'Connor's unspoken amusement.

Bullock takes Trudy to an Italian restaurant for dinner, and reveals that as he is still broke and has nowhere to stay, he has little choice but to consider the offer of the job in Bolivia more seriously. Trudy is hurt and resentful that he is willing to put his material needs before their relationship, but he can see no alternative. She tells her parents of her dismay when she returns to the mansion. Mary immediately puts two and two together, remembering that O'Connor owns the construction company that has offered Bullock the job, and Trudy angrily confronts her father. Realising the error of his actions, O'Connor tells her that he will withdraw the Bolivian offer and will instead give Bullock a position in the USA. But Trudy is incensed that her father can't see that Bullock is a self-made man who simply wants to make his own way in the world – much the same as O'Connor himself once did. Mary's suspicions of her ex-husband's nature now further confirmed, she tells O'Connor that she will be leaving for Florida the next day – and that Trudy will be welcome to come with her. He will once again be alone in his mansion.

O'Connor seeks McKeever's counsel, but the usually ebullient man is disheartened. He points out that after Bullock's collective lost the bidding war for the Army camp, the good humour has been sucked out of the mansion. Though he has spent many happy winters there, he feels disinclined to return the following year. This gives O'Connor pause for thought. Bullock arrives, similarly depressed at the prospect of leaving for South America, and is suspicious when O'Connor suddenly tries to talk him out of the move. Instead, the enigmatic industrialist tells him that he is friendly with one of the janitors working at the O'Connor Building, and that the caretaker has managed to arrange an appointment between Bullock and O'Connor within the next hour. Bullock is hugely sceptical, but reluctantly agrees to go along with the plan.

As promised, Bullock, Whitey and Hank all arrive at O'Connor's skyscraper and are immediately ushered into an opulent private office. There, they meet face-to-face with 'Mike'... but, unable to believe that he is O'Connor, they force him into a nearby closet and lock him in before 'the real O'Connor' appears. Only after Farrow arrives and vouches for the corporation's owner do they finally realise that 'Mike' really is Michael J. O'Connor. Now appreciating the depth of his mistake in outbidding Bullock for the Army camp, he agrees to transfer the deeds to the former G.I.s so that they can redevelop the barracks buildings as planned. However, he stipulates one condition – under no circumstances can they reveal to McKeever that he is the genuine O'Connor.

On New Year's Eve, the 'guests' at the mansion celebrate with a special dinner. McKeever raises a toast to 'Mike' for having provided the food for their festivities, pointing out that as the patrolmen will be expecting the house to be vacated by the following day, they will all need to leave the premises early this winter. Emotionally, he points out that although their paths may never cross again, he is glad that they have all become friends, as to be without friends is the most critical form of poverty. On that note, they applaud the New Year chimes together.

The next day, the mansion's interior has been returned to its original state, and the guests congregate in the O'Connors' backyard to say their goodbyes. Trudy and Bullock offer to let McKeever stay with them after they get married, as do O'Connor and Mary, but the wily old vagabond turns down both proposals. Instead, he reveals that he always makes his way down to O'Connor's winter residence in Virginia, essentially swapping venues; every year, as soon as O'Connor heads back to New York City, McKeever leaves for Bubbling Springs. Before O'Connor has the chance to fully process this information, McKeever gifts him with the key to the Guggenhoff mansion; as the family are vacationing in Europe, it will be empty and thus the perfect place for Mary and O'Connor's honeymoon. McKeever adds that while he hopes the couple's relationship will be a long and happy one, he will be back the following November to find out how things have gone. They all leave via the loose panel in the perimeter fence that McKeever had used when he first arrived and, as the old tramp wanders off with Sammy in his arms, O'Connor reflects that while McKeever is perpetually penniless, he is a far richer man than a millionaire like him will ever be. He adds that it is time to have the unfastened panel repaired in the fence; next year, McKeever will be welcome to enter through the front door.

It Happened on Fifth Avenue is a restrained but heartwarming comedy with few affectations beyond telling an entertaining (and occasionally moving) story well. Like so many other Christmas films of the period, the importance of friendship and family is placed at the forefront of the film, and yet audiences are presented with a very different kind of family unit – one based upon friendship and collaborative support, which eventually proves able to rejuvenate each of the lives within a more traditional nuclear family. (Indeed, Trudy initially eschews her conventional family altogether because she considers the prospect of friendship with the kindly but eccentric intruders to be preferable to her stuffy existence at finishing school, or her strained relationship with her parents.) While the basic premise that money isn't the answer to everything – and, indeed, that wealth can bring its own problems – had been well explored on screen by the 1940s, Everett Freeman's screenplay is able to balance the familiarity of the subject with some genuinely unexpected moments of emotional revelation and personal epiphany. As Robert Wilfred Franson has remarked, '*It Happened on Fifth Avenue* is a light romantic comedy, rather more good-natured comedy than romance. It takes place from the beginning of November through New Year's Day, and is considered a peripherally Christmastime movie. [...] *It Happened on Fifth Avenue* is a pleasant film, its real story being the growth of fellow-feeling among good people learning about each other and helping each other, a miniature Brotherhood of Man. The mansion's temporary cabal of residents become a kind of elective family, and all are the better for it'.[4] Making the sometimes convoluted situations of the plot seem slightly more plausible is the historical context which underpins the events of the film. Following the Second World War, many regions of America – particularly large, urban areas such as New York – struggled to offer sufficient accommodation for men and women returning from wartime occupations, meaning that the film would have had undeniable topicality for the audiences of the time. Certainly the themes of mutual cooperation and the importance of altruism, by no means unusual for a Christmas film of the period, are given an unusually concentrated focus due to the notion of former G.I.s pooling resources to overcome a common difficulty: the basic right to a home for them and their families. Alonso Duralde has perceptively stated: 'When Senator Joseph McCarthy and his goons set out to look for Communist influence in Hollywood, they no doubt went nuts over *It Happened on Fifth Avenue*, a movie that champions the poor, challenges the rich to rediscover their humanity and generosity, and even celebrates the joy of communal living and the power of collective bargaining. [...] From the sparkling performances to some hilarious bits involving an uneven restaurant table and a moth-obsessed tailor, this is a quirky and sweet holiday movie that deserves discovery'.[5]

As Duralde suggests, the film includes many appealing performances and inspired situations, ranging from the charming antics of McKeever's mischievous dog Sammy to the second-hand clothing dealer's entertainingly theatrical monologue about the dangers of wool suits. The scene in the Italian restaurant, where Bullock and Trudy's budding relationship is at threat, beautifully offsets its dramatic content with some virtuosic antics as the waiter drolly attempts (and fails) to rectify the problem of a wobbly table, while an over-enthusiastic house band will not be deterred from playing on – no matter the circumstances. The film does, of course, contain a fair amount of implausible situations – not least the sheer improbability of the second-richest man in the world not being recognised by anyone while he is living under an assumed name (even if the industrialist is reclusive to the point that he hasn't been photographed by the press, as is claimed during the film). Similarly, while the audience eventually comes to expect some rather contrived plot convolutions, there are also a few puzzling anomalies regarding characterisation; as Laura Grieve has pointed out: 'It's a well-written film with everyone in the large cast having a moment to shine in the 116-minute running time. There's just one thing I wondered – the film completely skips over Jim learning that Trudy (Storm) is the daughter of the fabulously wealthy Michael O'Connor. It's just inferred at the end that now he knows! I wonder if the scene was left on the cutting-room floor? [...] *It Happened on Fifth Avenue* is recommended as a quite enjoyable change of pace from the usual Christmas classics'.[6]

It Happened on Fifth Avenue contained four original songs, one of which – 'That's What Christmas Means to Me' – has a festive theme (as its title suggests). Written by Harry Revel, it has no relation to the many other extant, identically-titled songs such as either the Eddie Fisher or Stevie Wonder singles. One of the most curious aspects of the film is the fact that, while singer and actress Gale Storm was cast as Trudy and much is made of the character's musical talents, Storm's voice was re-dubbed in all of the scenes where Trudy can be heard singing. As Terence Towles Canote explains, 'Roy Del Ruth apparently believed that actors should act, dancers should dance, and singers should sing, and there should never be any overlap among them. Ultimately, Gale Storm's voice was dubbed by someone else, a fact obvious to anyone who has seen her musicals'.[7] Storm would become a popular figure on American television during the 1950s due to her appearances on the CBS/NBC sitcom *My Little Margie* (1952-55) and CBS/ABC's *The Gale Storm Show* (1956-60). In 1955, her cover version of Smiley Lewis's 'I Hear You Knockin'' reached number two on the *Billboard* Hot 100 Chart.

While *It Happened on Fifth Avenue* has become one of the lesser-known Christmas films of the 1940s, its unconventional approach and emphasis on effective characterisation as much as festive incident has meant that its lengthy withdrawal from cultural significance seems all the more unjust. As commentators such as David Cornelius have taken note, the film was released at a significant point in the directorial career of Roy Del Ruth:

> Pleasantly sweet in its lightweight charms, *It Happened on 5th Avenue* features an almost Capra-esque story – no surprise, then, that the film was originally considered for Capra's Liberty Films. It eventually found its way instead into the hands of director Roy Del Ruth, who had recently left MGM and was about to enter the downward spiral of his career, with such misfires as *The Babe Ruth Story*, *Phantom of the Rue Morgue*, and *The Alligator People* soon to come his way. *5th Avenue*, which would be the first release from new B-grade studio Allied Artists, is something of a middle ground between those flops and his earlier MGM musical successes.[8]

Because of its relatively high profile in comparison to films released under the Monogram banner, *It Happened on Fifth Avenue* marked a confident start for Allied Artists Pictures, even if its domestic box-office receipts struggled to claw back its budget. In spite of its relative lack of major star power, all of the actors concerned give engaging and amiable performances. Ann Harding, who would appear as Aunt Matilda Reed in *Christmas Eve* the same year, had been a leading star for RKO Pictures throughout the 1930s and was frequently 'on loan' by the studio to companies such as Paramount Pictures and Metro-Goldwyn-Mayer. Victor Moore had been a huge star on Broadway throughout the 1920s and 1930s, and was also active as a director, writer and comedian. Charles Ruggles enjoyed a career that spanned six decades, often in comedic roles, and was to appear in almost a hundred motion pictures including *Ruggles of Red Gap* (Leo McCarey, 1935) and *Bringing Up Baby* (Howard Hawks, 1938). He was also active on stage and television, including the ABC/NBC situation comedy *The Ruggles* (1949-52). Don DeFore was a well-known name on Broadway and in cinema during the 1930s and 40s, but was arguably best known for his television work which included ABC's long-running situation comedy *The Adventures of Ozzie and Harriet* (1952-66) – his recurring role in the series earned him a nomination for a Prime-time Emmy Award for Best Supporting Actor in a Regular Series in 1955. Between 1954 and 1955, he was President of the National Academy of Television Arts and Sciences.

The film met with a generally positive reception from the critics of the time. Bosley Crowther of *The New York Times* recognised both the film's cordiality and the familiarity of its core themes, pronouncing that 'Roy Del Ruth and the others who helped him in making this film apparently went about it as though they were on a new tack. They took that dog-eared story of the hard-hearted millionaire given a lesson in human relations by a kindly disposed vagabond and they dressed it up in such trimmings as to make it look almost fresh'.[9] *Time* magazine's critic was considerably more restrained in their appraisal, similarly noting the derivative approach to the film's central premise by opining that the 'most plausible explanations for the picture's success are: 1) the presence of Victor Moore, past master of creaky charm and pathos; 2) a show as generally old fashioned, in a harmless way, as a 1910 mail-order play for amateurs; 3) the fact that now, as in 1910, a producer cannot go wrong with a mass audience if he serves up a whiff of comedy and a whirlwind of hokum'.[10]

Modern reviews of the movie have centred more close-ly on the place that it has taken within the broader pantheon of Christmas cinema – not least in relation to the other, more prominent features which were to emerge during the same era. Morgan R. Lewis, for instance, notes that the film exhib-its many of the tropes which were becoming established with-in the genre during its golden age: 'Though it doesn't feature any element of the supernatural, the way *It's a Wonderful Life* does, *It Happened on Fifth Avenue* does feature a Scrooge-like character, good honest people who can't catch a break, a Christmas miracle, and a schlubby "angel" of sorts who brings it all together. [...] The story works well because of those characters. It has a nice warm Christmas-centered heart to it, with an uplifting character arc and even a decent musical number with an original Christmas song. And it's a funny film, with both physical and situational humor'.[11] Simi-larly, as Jessica Pickens observes, the film's appealing, larger-than-life figures and the experienced cast of character actors combine to make it the equal of any number of festive Holly-wood star vehicles:

It's easy for this Christmas film to slip through the cracks. It isn't as well-known as other Christmas classics such as *Miracle on 34ᵗʰ Street* or *White Christmas*. And many of the leads are character actors rather than superstars who star in other Christmas films. [...] It isn't surprising that Capra considered this film. The theme of the poor creat-ing life lessons for the rich is similar to many of his other films. *It Happened on Fifth Avenue* is fun-ny, far-fetched and charming. It's a comedy that makes fun of the rich, like the O'Connors, and makes the poor the heroes. The O'Connors have an opportunity to look at their lives with the help of McKeever: Michael has disregarded everything for money, Mary lives in Palm Springs and denies she's middle-aged, and Trudy is unhappy.[12]

Not all commentators have been equally convinced of the film's merits. Roscoe, for example, comments that 'it is generally classified as a Christmas movie since one of the pivotal scenes takes place at Christmas time (the conclusion features New Year's Eve). [...] I wish that the movie had really utilized New York City [and] taken advantage of the location... much like its Oscar competitor *Miracle on 34th Street* which looked better'.[13] As Roscoe suggests, there is little comparison between the outstanding location filming of George Seaton's celebrated film and the rather obvious back-projection that is often employed by Roy Del Ruth to simulate the urban locations of New York. However, the films take a very different approach to their subject matter – *It Happened on Fifth Avenue* assuming a rather more intimate scale than that of the celebrated *Miracle on 34th Street* – and in spite of the occasional similarities between them in terms of period and location, there are also many divergences in methodology. Others have commented on the fact that Del Ruth's film, for all the general admiration of its critical reception at the time of it release, has perhaps become best-known in modern years for its nearly complete disappearance from public view. As *Vitaphone Dreamer*'s reviewer 'Meredith' has remarked: '*It Happened on Fifth Avenue* is so funny. It's got a touch of screwball in it. It's silly, but it tugs at the heartstrings. It was nominated for the Best Writing, Original Story Academy Award and lost to another holiday classic, *Miracle* *on 34th Street*. After going into almost total obscurity for nearly twenty years, it was released on DVD for the first time in 2008'.[14]

As the above assessment suggests, *It Happened on Fifth Avenue* has often been unfairly overlooked within the genre of Christmas films – and popular culture generally – on account of its reduced profile. It was broadcast on television during the 1950s as part of a larger package of motion pictures from Allied Artists Pictures and Monogram Pictures which were licenced for TV airings, but its profile dwindled in successive decades and, by the early 1990s, the film was essentially unobtainable both in terms of TV broadcast and availability on home entertainment formats. It took until 2008 before *It Happened on Fifth Avenue* was released on DVD by Warner Home Video, and the following year it was to be broadcast by Turner Classic Movies, gradually acquiring a cult following amongst a whole new audience. The film has also been screened by the Hallmark Movie Channel from 2014 onwards.

Lux Radio Theater was to broadcast an hour-long radio adaptation of *It Happened on Fifth Avenue* on 19 May 1947, with many of the film's cast reprising their original roles from the movie – including Charles Ruggles, Victor Moore, Don DeFore and Gale Storm. A television remake of the story was also broadcast as the eighteenth episode of Lux Video Theater's seventh season, on 3 January 1957, with Gene Lockhart in the role of Michael O'Connor, William Reynolds as Jim Bullock and Diane Jergens as Trudy O'Connor. Additionally, the film has been remade twice as Hindi-language productions for the Indian market, as *Pugree* (Anant Thakur, 1948) and *Dil Daulat Duniya* (Prem Narayan Arora, 1972). Moving the action to India, both films share roughly the same central premise of *It Happened on Fifth Avenue* but otherwise dispense with its Christmas-themed trappings.

It Happened on Fifth Avenue is one of the best-kept secrets of 1940s Christmas cinema, and it has only been in the past decade that it has started to gain the recognition that it deserves. With its likeable characters, universal themes of co-operation and goodwill and an enjoyably fanciful premise, it has long deserved greater acknowledgement than it has been afforded. The central supposition that it is impossible to be truly happy if we are separated from our fellow human beings is filtered through the prism that the O'Connors, whose vast wealth has made them unapproachable and/or detached from the mainstream of society, cannot be entirely satisfied until they recognise that they must reconnect with their more humble roots. The more sympathetic characters, such as Bullock and his fellow ex-G.I.s, seek only to have a fair chance at accessing life's essentials, such as somewhere to live and an honest day's pay. By the film's conclusion, everyone finds themselves satisfied one way or another, but we are left in little doubt that the most content of all is the optimistic McKeever who – in spite of the precariousness of his penniless state – remains acutely aware of life's simple pleasures and the need to live each day to the fullest. Thus while *It Happened on Fifth Avenue* contains ample evidence of one of Christmas cinema's fundamental thematic conventions – namely, the ability of the festive season to transform and reconfigure personal attitudes – there is also much to be learnt from McKeever's cheerfully free-wheeling approach to life, where every obstacle can be overcome by constructive, collaborative action and an optimistic deportment that encourages us to think outside the confines of stubborn social conformity.

REFERENCES

1.   J.P. Roscoe, '*It Happened on Fifth Avenue*', in *Basement Rejects*, 16 December 2013.
     <*http://basementrejects.com/review/it-happened-on-fifth-avenue-1947/*>

2.   Richard Coe, '*Fifth Avenue* a Nice Little Film That's Been Gushed About Too Much', in *The Washington Post*, 8 May 1947, p.2.

3.   David C. Tucker, *Gale Storm: A Biography and Career Record* (Jefferson: McFarland and Company, 2018), p.89.

4.   Robert Wilfred Franson, '*It Happened on Fifth Avenue*', in Troy Novant, January 2013.
     <*http://www.troynovant.com/Franson-3/Del-Ruth/It-Happened-on-Fifth-Avenue.html*>

5.   Alonso Duralde, *Have Yourself a Movie Little Christmas* (Milwaukee: Limelight Editions, 2010), pp.66-67.

6.   Laura Grieve, 'Tonight's Movie: *It Happened on Fifth Avenue*', in *Laura's Miscellaneous Musings*, 25 December 2011.
     <*https://laurasmiscmusings.blogspot.com/2011/12/tonights-movie-it-happened-on-fifth.html*>

7.   Terence Towles Canote, '70 Years of It Happened on Fifth Avenue', in *A Shroud of Thoughts*, 18 December 2017.
     <*http://mercurie.blogspot.com/2017/12/70-years-of-it-happened-on-fifth-avenue.htm*>

8.   David Cornelius, '*Warner Brothers Classic Holiday Collection*, Vol. 2', in *DVD Talk*, 11 November 2008.

<https://www.dvdtalk.com/reviews/35677/warner-brothers-classic-holiday-collection-vol-2/>

9.   Bosley Crowther, 'The Screen in Review: *It Happened on Fifth Avenue*, With Victor Moore in Bright, Gay Mood, Opens at Rivoli', in *The New York Times*, 11 June 1947. *<https://www.nytimes.com/1947/06/11/archives/the-screen-in-review-it-happened-on-fifth-avenue-with-victor-moore.html>*

10.   Anon., 'Cinema: The New Pictures', in *Time*, 16 June 1947. *<http://content.time.com/time/subscriber/article/0,33009,855765-2,00.html>*

11.   Morgan R. Lewis, 'It Happened on Fifth Avenue', in *Morgan on Media*, 18 December 2013. *<https://morganrlewis.wordpress.com/2013/12/18/it-happened-on-fifth-avenue/>*

12.   Jessica Pickens, 'Christmas at Comet's: *It Happened on Fifth Avenue*', in *Comet Over Hollywood*, 22 December 2013. *<https://cometoverhollywood.com/2013/12/22/christmas-at-comets-it-happened-on-fifth-avenue-1947/>*

13.   Roscoe.

14.   Meredith, 'A Christmas Discovery: *It Happened on Fifth Avenue*', in *Vitaphone Dreamer*, 14 December 2016. *<https://vitaphonedreamer.wordpress.com/2016/12/14/a-christmas-discovery-it-happened-on-fifth-avenue/>*

10

Three Godfathers (1948)

Argosy Pictures Corporation

Director: John Ford
Producers: John Ford and Merian C. Cooper
Screenwriter: Laurence Stallings and Frank S. Nugent,
from an original story by Peter B. Kyne

ALTHOUGH it is a fact often forgotten, in the late 1940s the tale of the *Three Godfathers* was the most remade Christmas-themed movie after *A Christmas Carol*. As has been mentioned earlier in this book, big screen adaptations of Peter B. Kyne's 1913 Western novella *The Three Godfathers* were a popular fixture of early festive cinema – even prior to the birth of the 'talkies'. First to appear on the silver screen was Edward LeSaint's *The Three Godfathers* (1916), which was to be remade a few years later by John Ford as *Marked Men* (1919). Ford's silent movie is now sadly thought to be lost. Several years later, William Wyler remade the movie as *Hell's Heroes* (1930), and Kyne's story would be adapted again by Richard Boleslawski in 1936 (this time with the original title, *The Three Godfathers*). However, John Ford was to return to the story in 1948 to create a full-length colour version, and this is now widely considered to be the definitive adaptation of Kyne's yuletide tale.

As Ron Scheer has noted, 'the way this film was transformed in its journey from the printed page to the screen has director John Ford written all over it. Peter B. Kyne's novel [...] was published in 1913. Ford directed [his] first film adaptation of the novel [in 1919], with Harry Carey. When Carey died in 1947, Ford decided to remake the story in Technicolor and dedicate the film to his memory'.[1] Emphasising the personal nature of the project, the movie is dedicated to Carey in the opening credits, and his son – Harry Carey Jr. – was cast in one of the 1948 film's main roles by Ford.

Three Godfathers' Old West setting made it a rather alternative Christmas movie. The eponymous trio of outlaws eventually come to take on a role analogous to that of the Three Wise Men of the Nativity story – though of course, while it is clear that the infant in their charge has no special supernatural power in and of himself, their desire to take care of the child and return him to the safety of civilisation displays the kind of altruism and selflessness that is key to many cinematic Christmas narratives. Religious symbolism relating to the Nativity is scattered judiciously throughout the film, but central to the narrative is the theme of redemption and transformation – surely one of the most common tropes in all of festive cinema. As Sanderson Beck observes: 'In this version of Peter Kyne's story, filmed before in 1919, 1930, and 1936, three bank robbers adopt an orphaned baby in the desert while running from the marshal. [...] Even violent criminals can be turned into caring people by circumstances that appeal to their love'.[2]

Director John Ford was already a *bona fide* legend of Hollywood by the late 1940s, having won the coveted Academy Award for Best Director for *The Informer* (1935), *The Grapes of Wrath* (1940) and *How Green Was My Valley*

(1941). He would also later be conferred a Best Director Academy Award for *The Quiet Man* (1952), making him the current record-holder for this category of Oscar. He received a further five Academy Award nominations in categories such as Outstanding Production and Best Motion Picture, and a number of his films are now preserved in the Academy Film Archive including *Four Sons* (1928) and *The Battle of Midway* (1942). He directed in excess of 140 films in his long career,

Three Godfathers (1948): Argosy Pictures Corporation

and he has come to be regarded as one of the single most significant and influential film-makers of the twentieth century. Hugely intelligent, very widely read and reputedly somewhat eccentric, Ford's varied career included movies which spanned historical dramas to wartime documentaries, though – with his famous penchant for painstakingly-judged location shooting and inspired long shots – it is for his prolific work in the Western genre that he will likely be especially well remembered, not least those which he made in collaboration with his friend and frequent professional associate John Wayne. His many films, such as *Stagecoach* (1939), *The Searchers* (1956), *The Man Who Shot Liberty Valance* (1962) and *Cheyenne Autumn* (1964), would have vast impact on the way that the West was depicted on screen and in popular culture. In addition to his abundant work in the cinema industry, Ford was also a decorated veteran of the US Navy, holding the rank of Commander during active service in 1942-45, and then as Rear Admiral in the reserve forces during 1946-62. He was the recipient of no less than twelve medals during his distinguished Naval service.

It is December in the parched, arid desert of Arizona in the nineteenth century. Outlaw Robert 'Bob' Hightower (John Wayne) arrives in the frontier town of Welcome, along with his associates Pedro 'Pete' Rocafuerte (Pedro Armendáriz) and young William Kearney, also known as 'The Abilene Kid' (Harry Carey Jr.). Hightower plans to rob the town bank, as Welcome is close to the Mexican border which will make it relatively easy to escape justice once the townsfolks' cash has been stolen. The trio are more used to cattle rustling than robbery, and Hightower worries that the inexperienced Kid will be unable to handle the pressure of a heist. He instructs him to wait nearby with the horses to ensure their getaway, while he and Pete handle the bank raid.

Upon entering the town, the three bandits meet the town's genial sheriff, Buck Sweet (Ward Bond), and his wife Kerry-Lou (Mae Marsh). Mrs Sweet offers them coffee and enquires if the trio had encountered their niece and her husband, who are travelling to the town by wagon via the nearby settlement of New Jerusalem. The Sweets hope for a Christmas family get-together, but worry that their niece's husband – who is notoriously feckless – may have taken the wrong turning at some point during the journey. However, Hightower is more concerned with finding the location of the town's bank, where he plans to conduct 'some business'. Sweet sends the men in the right direction, but is clearly suspicious of their motives.

On the way to the bank, Hightower and his comrades encounter the winsome Ruby Latham (Dorothy Ford), the daughter of the local bank president Oliver Latham (Charles Halton), whose return after a long absence makes her the recipient of a euphoric welcome from the townsfolk – including a number of would-be suitors. While the people of Welcome are distracted, Hightower and Pete hold up the bank; Pete fires off his gun as a distraction, startling the townspeople's horses, as the trio make good their escape. Meanwhile, Sheriff Sweet is in the process of identifying the outlaws from wanted posters when he hears Pete's gunshots. The US Marshals give chase, and the Kid is wounded by a gunshot as the trio flee from justice. Injured, the Kid loses his horse but is rescued by Hightower before he can be arrested. Sweet commandeers a horse-drawn wagon and pursues the three bandits, following them into the desert beyond the boundaries of the town.

Eventually Hightower and his companions manage to elude Sweet, though not before the sheriff fires a bullet through their water bag. He and his deputy, Curley (Hank Worden), head to the nearby railroad depot, while Hightower seeks sanctuary in a rocky area deeper into the desert. Hightower despairs when he realises that their water supply has been depleted, realising that Sweet had fired at it intentionally to force the outlaws to seek another source of water nearby (thus making them easier to capture).

At Welcome's freight depot, Sweet immediately sets about deputising a number of the townsfolk to aid in tracking down the fugitives. The bank's president, Mr Latham, is concerned that the sheriff has underestimated the importance of taking the bandits into custody, so (much to his horror) Sweet deliberately misinterprets him and loudly announces that a $100 reward has now been posted by the bank for every one of the three outlaws if they are arrested. The sheriff and his new deputies head off on the train, hoping to apprehend Hightower and his accomplices further along the track.

Meanwhile, conditions are grim for the three felons. With only Hightower's small canteen of water left to sustain the three of them – and the Kid still bleeding profusely from his wound – their chances seem slim. The trio head for a water tank near a railway track, which holds a thousand gallons of water. This will not only allow them to replenish their supplies, but should also give them the chance to clean out the Kid's gunshot wound. Before they can reach the tank, however, the train carrying Sweet and his deputies arrives, and several armed men are dropped off to guard the area. The sheriff's plan is obviously to cut off any attempt by the outlaws to gain access to drinking water. The dehydrated Hightower is frustrated, knowing that he and Pete have no way of rushing or circumventing the guards – especially with the Kid still wounded.

Refusing to be beaten, Hightower considers the sheriff's next move and realises that he is likely to follow the rest of the railroad track, meaning that the logical response is to head for a water tank in the opposite direction. If they can reach that tank, and assuming it is unguarded, the best option will be to head east and cross the border there. Pete is sceptical, realising that they will never be able to reach the tank without needing to find water in the interim, but Hightower assures him that they will be able to extract moisture from cactuses they find along the way.

The three men make their way across the scorching desert, heading for a natural water hole that Hightower knows about thanks to his detailed knowledge of the terrain. A sandstorm strikes up, making transit difficult and uncomfortable, but they persevere. Eventually they are forced to take shelter in some brushy undergrowth, but once the storm has passed they realise that their remaining horses have bolted. Now forced to travel the rest of the way on foot, the outlaws know all too well that their situation has become even more desperate.

Sweet has reached the water tank at Apache Wells to the south. He meets Miss Florie (Jane Darwell), custodian of the train station, who tells him that she has seen nothing unusual in the area. The deputies debark from the train, as do a number of pack mules. None of them realise that the outlaws are some distance away, and are now approaching the location of the water hole. Upon arriving, however, Hightower discovers that there is no water to be found – only an apparently-abandoned wagon with its horses nowhere to be seen. He investigates further, and discovers that the water hole has been accidentally destroyed by the owner of the wagon, who had been inexperienced in the ways of the wilderness. Not realising that the natural water hole needed time to refill, the man had used dynamite in an attempt to gain easy access to the liquid within, thus rendering it unusable. The stranger had then lost control of his horses and had taken off after them on foot; having never been seen again since, he is presumed dead. His wife had remained in the wagon with a small amount of water, but four days after her husband's disappearance her supply is now at an end. Worse still, the woman is heavily pregnant and is now ready to give birth. Hightower despairs of the hopelessness of their condition, to say nothing of his increasingly acute appreciation of their lack of water.

None of the three men have any experience of midwifery, but eventually Pete is nominated to help deliver the baby as he is a father (thus making him the most practiced of the three by default). While a nervous Pete makes his way to the wagon, Hightower and the Kid extract what little water they can from some nearby cactuses, storing it in their canteens. However, much of it is needed for the baby's mother (Mildred Natwick), meaning that their own situation seems no less precarious than before. It takes until twilight before the baby is delivered, and his mother – now clearly ailing – asks the three outlaws to join her in the wagon. Knowing that she has little time to live, she names the child Robert William Pedro after her three unexpected benefactors, and implores the trio to take care of her baby. The three men readily agree to do their best, even given the overwhelming battle for survival they currently face. The woman names them all her baby's godfathers and, kissing her infant son goodbye, she dies. The outlaws give the child's mother a respectful burial near the water hole just as night falls.

Back at Apache Wells, Sheriff Sweet voices grudging respect for Hightower's tenacity and reflects that with his gift for tactics and outthinking his opponents, he must be one talented chess player. In spite of the lawman's strategy, reasoning that the bandits would take the most direct route to the Mexican border, there has been no sighting of the three men. Trying to second-guess the fugitives, Sweet deduces that they must have headed towards the water hole to the north of their current position in order to evade detection. The sheriff thus decides that he and his deputies should head off in pursuit.

Little does Sweet realise that Hightower and his associates are currently getting to grips with the challenges of caring for a newly-born baby. Lacking any experience of looking after an infant, they are soon squabbling over how best to ensure his wellbeing – though they are at least in agreement that food and water are the first priority. Pedro and the Kid find a chest of baby accessories in the wagon – including an instructional book on effective infant care. However, this actually manages to provide them with more questions than answers – and a good deal of confusion. Thankfully six tins of condensed milk are packed amongst the supplies, meaning that they are able to provide the baby with some much-needed sustenance. It becomes increasingly clear that the Kid is suffering badly from the infected gunshot wound in his shoulder.

The Kid has become convinced that he, Hightower and Pete have all been guided to their current situation by God in order to ensure that their innocent godson will survive his current predicament. He reads from a copy of the Bible that is packed with the baby supplies and sees parallels between their situation and that of the Three Magi who travelled from the east to encounter the infant Jesus in a Bethlehem manger. Considering the Biblical theme, he comes to the conclusion that they must head for the town of New Jerusalem in the hope that the baby will be safe there. However, this will involve a long journey across an expanse of stifling desert, and Hightower realises that even with the water that has been harvested from the nearby cactuses, they will have scant supplies for the baby – much less for themselves.

While Hightower and his associates depart, Sweet and his deputies are riding across the desert to the water hole. The outlaws disagree on the way to New Jerusalem until the Kid points out that there is a bright star hanging over the town to light the way. Hightower and Pete are dumbfounded at the Biblical parallels as they head off into the arid wasteland on foot, taking turns to carry the baby. Eventually they reach a sprawling salt flat which lies between them and the town, and the increasingly feverish Kid realises that he will be unable to cross it alive.

Sweet has arrived at the wagon with his deputies, and is appalled by the scene he discovers. Finding the wagon empty of inhabitants, he nonetheless unearths some clothing and recognises it as belonging to his niece, who he knew to be heading from New Jerusalem to Welcome. Naturally he suspects foul play. When the deputies take their horses to the water hole for a drink, they discover that it has been destroyed with explosives and wrongly (if understandably) deduce that the outlaws have replenished their water supplies and then obliterated the source in order to deter any pursuers. Knowing that this will potentially be fatal for any oblivious travellers who are passing through the area and discover that they are unable to refill their supplies of water, Sweet is quietly enraged. He tells his deputies that the bank president's reward of $100 to capture the bandits dead or alive has now been superseded – he will add $50 of his own money, but only if they are brought in dead.

Far away, Hightower and his companions still face an exhausting hike over the unforgiving salt flats. They are eventually forced to leave their remaining supplies behind as their strength is slowly but steadily sapped by the blazing sun. Soon their canteen is depleted, and eventually discarded too. The Kid's earlier macabre predictions soon prove tragically correct when he collapses, the baby still in his arms. Hightower and Pete regretfully realise that their friend is now beyond their ability to help. With his last breaths, the Kid asks Pete to read Psalm 137 from the Bible they found at the wagon. His final request is carried out, and he slips away into death.

Lacking the strength to bury their fallen comrade, Hightower and Pete stagger onwards. However, they are now so severely dehydrated that they can barely stand upright. As they pass over a rocky outcropping, Pete trips and suffers a nasty fall, breaking his leg in the process. Realising that he now has no chance of reaching New Jerusalem, Pete persuades Hightower to put the child's safety first and keep going. The town, he assures his friend, is closer than he thinks. Before Hightower can resume his trek, Pete asks him if he will leave his pistol – just to ward off coyotes if he is attacked and unable to defend himself. Hightower agrees, and Pete – remembering that Christmas will be on the following day – wishes his friend the compliments of the season as he heads off into the distance. As Hightower heads onward with the baby in his arms, a single gunshot can be heard ringing out.

Unaware that Sweet and his deputies are in close pursuit, Hightower continues to stumble over mountainous terrain in the hope that he will reach the town before the last of his stamina fails him. The sole surviving outlaw almost loses consciousness as he staggers along a windy mountain pass, but is mindful of his responsibilities to his little godson and somehow finds the strength to continue. Rifling through what little possessions he has left, he discovers the Bible belonging to the child's mother and disdainfully tosses it aside. However, something compels him to retrieve it, and he reads a passage from Matthew's Gospel where Jesus Christ foretells the location of a donkey and a colt. Unable to hide his contempt, he again throws the Bible off into the distance and resumes his agonising march to New Jerusalem.

Finally at the end of his strength, Hightower collapses and anticipates his death. But whether through hallucination or supernatural means, he hears the ghostly voices of Pete and the Kid urging him to force himself onward for the sake of the baby. His deceased companions offer him some much-needed encouragement, and Hightower is confused when he can't find the source of their voices. Calling back to them, his delirious shouting can be heard by Sweet and his men, who have now entered the mountain pass in their hunt for the outlaws. Suddenly, as Hightower emerges from the pass he is amazed to discover – as the Bible had predicted – a colt and a donkey, wandering freely in the desert. Now desperately fighting unconsciousness, he gently places the baby onto the horse's saddle and staggers the rest of the way to his destination.

Hightower finally arrives in New Jerusalem, and heads straight for the heart of town – the saloon. The bar is ornamented with Christmas decorations, and the patrons are singing carols as they celebrate Christmas Eve. The townsfolk fall into shocked silence as the dishevelled Hightower stumbles through the doorway, gently places his godson onto the bar, and promptly asks the bartender for a cool beer and some milk for the baby. Sweet arrives moments later and furiously demands that Hightower draw his pistol for a duel. However, the fugitive is now completely exhausted and collapses to the ground before he can comply.

Some time later, Hightower has recovered from his arduous journey and is being held in custody at the Welcome sheriff's office. Sweet is able to test his prowess with a chessboard at last, as they play a game through the bars of Hightower's cell. Now that the full story of what happened at the water hole has been explained, the sheriff and the outlaw have become the best of friends – to the point that Hightower is let out of his cell to share dinner with Sweet and his wife. The Sweets have been looking after baby Robert during Hightower's imprisonment and, though they are fully aware of his side of the story, they are keen to be granted full custody of the child. However, Hightower takes his responsibility to the infant's mother seriously and refuses to sign adoption papers to transfer guardianship.

The argument is interrupted when the time comes for Hightower to stand trial for the bank robbery. He is anxious for his godson's safety, knowing that he faces up to twenty years' imprisonment for his actions. However, now that the townsfolk know of his bravery they are inclined to put his criminal behaviour into a wider context of events. The trial takes place in the saloon, and the presiding judge (Guy Kibbee) hears the jury declare Hightower guilty – but only under extenuating circumstances. The judge points out that he has the authority to order Hightower's incarceration for up to two decades, in addition to the caveat that he will never again be allowed to set foot in Welcome. However, the former outlaw has become a popular figure around town, and his care of the baby – even at risk to his own life – has made him a hero to the people of the town. Hightower states that he will be willing to grant temporary custody of the child to his uncle and aunt, the Sweets, but that he will never grant a permanent adoption as he will always uphold his promise to the baby's mother. Impressed by his integrity, the judge hands down the minimum sentence of a year and a day. The townspeople assemble to see Hightower's departure, giving him a true hero's farewell – including a choir solemnly singing the old hymn 'Bringing in the Sheaves'. Kerry-Lou Sweet solemnly promises Hightower that she will take the very best care of his godson, and as he boards a train to Yuma he receives a warm send-off from Ruby Latham (who had baked him a cake containing a hacksaw), and she promises to write to him in prison. It is obvious that the townsfolk are anxious to see him back once he has completed his sentence, as he has promised to return to Welcome – as a truly reformed character.

Even in this formative period of the Christmas movie genre, *Three Godfathers* felt like a breath of fresh air in its blend of Western tropes and the newly-emerging conventions of Christmas cinema. With its inspired teaming of the square-jawed, practical Hightower, the droll and occasionally hot-headed Mexican *bandito* Pete and the guilelessly charming Abilene Kid, the film takes its audience on an intriguing journey as these characters make a moral transition from self-interested criminals to selfless heroes – all on account of their unexpected custodianship of an innocent orphan. The screenplay by Laurence Stallings and Frank S. Nugent leans heavily on religious symbolism, though – in spite of accusations of ham-fistedness from some critical quarters – it actually follows the action of Peter B. Kyne's prose narrative fairly closely. As Scheer explains, '*The Three Godfathers* was already a kind of Christmas story in Kyne's hands. Not exactly the three wise men, the central characters are on the run following a failed bank job. But crossing the desert, they come upon a pregnant woman in the final hours before giving birth. The new mother dies, after leaving her infant son to the care of the three men, who promise to be his godfathers and to bring him up right. With a dwindling supply of water, they start on a trek to a mining camp called New Jerusalem (New Bethlehem being maybe too obvious). Only one of them eventually arrives with the baby. It is Christmas, and so ends Kyne's novel'.[3]

Interestingly, while tales of redemption and individual transformation have become central to many Christmas movie narratives over the years, the Western setting of *Three Godfathers* has allowed the film to transcend this singular thematic interpretation due to the multiplicity of possible readings. It is, as Ace Black argues, ultimately a film which labours hard to emphasise the fact that transfiguration of character can be brought about by many factors, ranging from the spiritual (the Biblical references and miraculous occurrences) to the domestic (the responsibility of caring for the innocent and defenceless): 'Towards the end, *3 Godfathers* does start to layer on the religious symbolism in gooey dollops. Mysterious mules, the Bible, a shining star, and the town of New Jerusa- lem all enter the fray as the young baby treks across the desert in the arms of three not so wise but quite determined men. The screenplay by Laurence Stallings and Frank S. Nugent veers towards a mishmash of Christmas metaphors, and loses a bit of its grittiness. [...] Big things sometimes come in small packages, and in *3 Godfathers* a tiny baby becomes the im- mense addition to the lives of three hardened men suddenly exposed to what really matters'.[4] Not all commentators have been entirely convinced by the film's approach, however, with some criticising it for a lack of subtlety and over-reliance on convenient but implausible resolutions. As Dennis Schwartz has contended, for instance: 'Ford relates this tale to the bibli- cal parable of the Magi. [...] Its most endearing scene has John Wayne arrive in New Jerusalem to lay the baby on the saloon bar on Christmas Day. Wayne responds with "Set 'em up, mister, milk for the infant and a cold beer for me". The reli- gious symbols were too heavy-handed to have much affect, except to mar the film into a dull mawkish stupor. Wayne as the Prodigal Son delivering the Christ child seemed a bit of a stretch. At best, it's one of Ford's lesser films where the scen- ery is more spectacular than the over sentimental story'.[5]

As Schwartz and many others have suggested, the film does indeed contain some spectacular scenery, with Ford's famous wide-angle shots being used to highly successful effect in capturing the austere beauty of Californian vistas in loca- tions such as Death Valley National Park, Alabama Hills and the Mojave Desert (though the film itself is actually set in southern Arizona). Winton Hoch's cinematography is top-notch throughout, as is Richard Hageman's stirring music score which perfectly accompanies it. (Hageman also played the saloon pianist, displaying some excellent comic timing, in the New Jerusalem scenes at the end of the film.) For all its technical excellence, however, the film's success lies primarily in the winning performances of its cast, headlined by none other than 'The Duke', John Wayne, as the arch-pragmatist Robert Marmaduke Hightower. First appearing in *Brown of Harvard* (Jack Conway, 1926) as a Yale University football player, Wayne continued in mainly supporting parts before making a famous appearance as the lead in *The Big Trail* (Raoul Walsh, 1930). He became a household name after starring in *Stagecoach* (John Ford, 1939), and further fame beckoned thanks to appearances in films such as *Tall in the Saddle* (Edwin L. Marin, 1944), *Back to Bataan* (Edward Dymytryk, 1945) and *Red River* (Howard Hawks, 1948). He was to win the Academy Award for Best Actor in a Leading Role for his portrayal of Rooster Cogburn in *True Grit* (Henry Hathaway, 1969), and was also nominated in the same category for his role in *Sands of Iwo Jima* (Allan Dwan, 1949) and for Best Picture for his film *The Alamo* (John Wayne, 1960), in which he also starred as Davy Crockett. Wayne was awarded the Congressional Gold Medal in 1979 and the Presidential Medal of Freedom in 1980, and his many other accolades have included an airport, marina and elementary school being named in his honour. Now considered one of Hollywood's most recognisable stars of all time, and immediately synonymous with the American Western movie, Wayne made an appearance in more than 170 features during his long career, and his contribution to popular culture (and indeed the box-office) is incalculable. Though *Three Godfathers* is generally considered to be one of his lesser roles, this cinematic icon puts real heart into the role of Robert Hightower, emphasising not only the character's hard-headed credentials as an unsentimental outlaw but also his unflappable sense of honour as he risks his liberty and even his life to keep a promise to a dying mother that he will keep her child safe at all costs.

The supporting cast of the film is uniformly excellent, from Ward Bond's gregarious but dryly calculating Sheriff Buck 'Purly' Sweet through to Charles Halton's prissy bank president Oliver Latham, Jane Darwell's uproarious Miss Florie, and of course Dorothy Ford's appealing, astute Ruby Latham (who makes the most of her brief screen time). Yet the pairing of Pedro Armendáriz and Harry Carey Jr. comes close to stealing the show; the rambunctious hot-head Pete and the quietly spiritual Bill Kearney, otherwise known as the Abilene Kid, make for a truly memorable pairing. With Pete's jovial temperament and occasionally quick temper juxtaposed with the Kid's courteous disposition (he has surprisingly impeccable manners for a cattle-rustling outlaw) and later delirium, the duo are believable both as friends and fellow lawbreakers. Armendáriz was one of the most popular Latin American movie stars of the period, hailing from Mexico City and famous in his native country as well as amongst international audiences. His appearance in *Maria Candelaria* (Emilio Fernández, 1943) brought him prominence when the film was bestowed the Palm d'Or Award at the Cannes Film Festival, and fame also followed his performances in John Ford's *The Fugitive* (1947) and *Fort Apache* (1948). He is also warmly remembered for his final cinematic role as Kerim Bey in the second film in the *James Bond* series, *From Russia with Love* (Terence Young, 1963). Harry Carey Jr. had served in the US

Navy during World War II, moving into acting after the conclusion of the conflict. Some of his most prominent roles came in John Ford movies including *She Wore a Yellow Ribbon* (1949), *The Searchers* (1956) and *Cheyenne Autumn* (1964), though he would appear in a wide variety of films over the years such as *Gentlemen Prefer Blondes* (Howard Hawks, 1953), *Shenandoah* (Andrew V. McLaglen, 1965) and *Cahill: US Marshal* (Andrew V. McLaglen, 1973). His many television roles included appearances in well-known series such as *The Lone Ranger* (1955), *Gunsmoke* (1959), *Bonanza* (1959), *Wagon Train* (1959) and *Rawhide* (1959).

The production of *Three Godfathers* contained numerous clever touches that were synonymous with John Ford's meticulous attention to detail, such as a gardener being employed to keep a cactus watered overnight so that water could be extracted from it during the day in one of the scenes near the wagon where the child is born, while the 'stubborn' mules which seemingly refuse to board the cattle train were actually fitted with special reins that impeded their motion, dragging them backwards whenever they were pulled in a forward motion. Yet unusually for a Ford film, there are also a number of slightly questionable creative choices on display. For instance, Hightower speculates that the unnamed mother of Robert William Pedro is aged between 28 and 30, when in actual fact actress Mildred Natwick was 43 when she played the 'young mother' during the time of the film's production. When Dorothy Ford's Ruby Latham is first introduced upon her return from Colorado, anachronistic power lines are clearly visible behind her head as she talks to Hightower from atop her stagecoach. The Bible which is referred to throughout the film seems to change randomly between a version with cross-references in the margin and another with a more conventional layout. And there is also quite possibly the film's most fa-mous production error: the fact that the infant boy Robert William Pedro is actually played by a baby girl – a fact that is quite obvious in the scenes where the child is greased and put into a diaper for the first time.

While *Three Godfathers* was popular both with critics and at the box-office at the time of its initial release, it has faced a more nuanced analytical reaction in more recent years as reviewers have reassessed its merits and significance both within the canon of Christmas movie-making as well as amongst Western films of the time. While the strength of Stallings and Nugent's characterisation has long been consid-ered one of the most robust aspects of *Three Godfathers*' pro-duction, Ford's skill in visually articulating the moral redemp-tion of these unexpectedly complex figures has also been high-lighted by some reviewers. As Mitch Lovell has remarked: 'Even though Ford is a rough-and-tumble manly man's direc-tor, he still has a knack for pulling at your heartstrings. He does so in such a subtle manner that the emotional core of the story slowly sneaks up on you. By the end of the movie, you'll be simultaneously holding back the tears while grinning from ear to ear. [...] He's less concerned with mapping the charac-ters' progress across the desert and more with mapping the expressions on the characters' faces as they transform from wanted outlaws to protective guardians'.[6] Here, of course, we see Ford's widely-recognised talent of emphasising scale and natural landscapes turned on its head, his eye for detail in-stead being focused on accentuating the tiniest yet most signif-icant of gestures and facial expressions. As the reviewer for the *Let's Not Talk About Movies* blog has so eruditely ob-served about Hightower's ethical epiphany: 'It looks phony (it is phony for this rough man of the West), but it turns into genuine acts of kindness and civility – the man grows into the gesture and becomes him, a signature of the man he has become through the trials and tribulations that have become the period to a life of bad manners, bad habits and bad choices. And the film ends with that same gesture, sending the man off to his fate, but promising the return of a better man and a better future. This is all done with pictures, part of the skein of direction that Ford imposes on the film that, combined with the exquisite cinematography of Winton Hoch, makes this odd, anti-Christmas Christmas film something of a precious gem for the Holidays'.[7] Certainly it is true that for a film which pivots upon the notion of individual enlightenment and personal principle, the harshness and struggle for survival conveyed by the wilderness of the Old West setting ensure that the philanthropy and self-sacrifice that are depicted never come across as either mawkish or overly emotional. Here, as Ed Howard has suggested, Ford alternates between grand scale and intimately detailed, keenly-observed characterisation to great effect:

> As with [Mark] Rothko, one gets the sense that for Ford, size itself is a signifier of spiritual feeling and philosophical inquiry: the pale expanse of the sky and the salty white ground envelop these men, inescapably confronting them with their own mortality. [...] That the film's denouement takes place on Christmas is only the most obvious of the parallels between the stories, though this heavy-handed symbolism merely makes explicit the themes and ideas already apparent in the film's more subtle moments. At the same time, Ford's treatment of these symbolic religious elements gives the film's final act a kind of sentimental poetic spirit, em-

bodied in the broad emotional strokes of the climax, which subverts traditional Western ideals and denies the lawman his cathartic showdown with the last outlaw standing. Instead, the ending is a moving affirmation of family bonds and community.[8]

While not every recent critical appraisal of *Three God-fathers* has been unerringly positive in nature, analysis has generally tended towards the sceptically subdued rather than the outright hostile. Some, such as Adam Kuhn, have negatively critiqued the casting of Wayne as the film's lead, opining that 'there is simply something "off" with *3 Godfathers*, and I think, believe it or not, it has a lot to do with John Wayne, who I feel is severely miscast in this role. It is a lighter, sweeter, funnier role, and while I don't want to say he doesn't have that in him (just look at [William A. Seiter's 1943 film] *A Lady Takes a Chance*), I will say that he sticks out like a sore thumb in this film, unable to hang with the type or brand of comedy that Ford is going for in this "fish-out-of-water" story'.[9] Others, including Derek Winnert, were to claim that the film fails only in comparison to the soaring heights of Ford's other, more critically-acclaimed cinema: '*Three Godfathers* [...] is a pleasant success thanks to Laurence Stallings and Frank S. Nugent's good-hearted screenplay, the warm performances and Winton Hoch's beautiful photography in Technicolor. However, it lacks the rigour, bite and achievement of, for example, Ford's *Stagecoach*, *The Searchers* or *The Man Who Shot Liberty Valance*, and the cynically minded will probably need a strong stomach for the sentimentally inclined story'.[10] Similarly, Gregory Meshman has related the film unfavourably to Ford's wider filmography, noting the gulf which exists between the appealing big screen fantasy of the Old West that is depicted and the starker, deadlier reality of the historical era in question: 'Of all Ford's westerns, this is the one that best shows his unblinking attachment to a sentimental, mythical view of the West – one governed by codes of decency and chivalry that only existed in his head. This is the film against which the revisionist westerns of the 1960s and 1970s were aligned: mounted gunmen sweetened into cuddly uncles, for the benefit of the American public. It's phoney, it's bunk – and it might just persuade you of a beautiful lie'.[11] However, perhaps the most pointed criticism of all has been Laura Grieve's perceptive observation that for a film which places such importance on symbolism and visual grandeur, *Three Godfathers* makes some curious lapses into extended periods of exposition:

> The movie has much going for it: Classic scenes of Fordian beauty, shot in gorgeous Technicolor by Winton C. Hoch (*She Wore a Yellow Ribbon*); some of Ford's typical humor and sentiment, to leaven the stressful drama; and excellent performances by many beloved faces from Ford's 'Stock Company'. That said, some of the editing (by Jack Murray) and storytelling choices are strange or confusing. [...] I also didn't care for the script when Bob tells the expectant mother's story to the other men, in a scene that goes on and on as he sits there talking. While Ford films often had classic dialogue, it seemed unusual for so much narrative to be verbally described rather than seen.[12]

Ultimately, as a Christmas film the success of *Three Godfathers* rests on the emphasis Ford places on contrasting the rugged harshness of the Old West setting with the uplifting and transformative nature of the festive season. Every-thing from the colourful decorations bedecking the New Jeru-salem saloon to Sheriff Sweet's attempt at a shootout inter-rupting the townsfolk's Christmas carols works to challenge our assumptions about cinematic depictions of the holiday season; while earlier movies such as *Meet Me in St Louis* (q.v.) had placed yuletide settings within historical narratives, the sun-baked deserts of the South-West seemed the least like-ly location for the quasi-Biblical events which eventually play out – from the star hanging above New Jerusalem through to the mystifying appearance of the donkey and colt. Tag Gal-lagher astutely notes that 'everything in *3 Godfathers* looks forward to Christmas, as to a moment of universal renewal. [...] *3 Godfathers* tends to be a minor movie, its long stretches of desert monotony redeemed by magic moments, of which by far the best is the finale'.[13] For all the grand revelations that Christmas has the power to profoundly reshape expectations of life and our understanding of our own personal capabilities, *Three Godfathers* is at its most effective when it lingers on the small but beautiful observations of life's pleasures – High-tower's game of chess with the sharp-witted Sweet, enjoying the sumptuous delights of Kerry-Lou's dinner table, or flirting with the beautiful (and shrewd) Ruby. It is, as Keith Phipps proposes, within the incongruous venue of this vast rustic canvas that intimate truths of unexpected significance are found: 'The fairy-tale-like *3 Godfathers* casts Wayne as one of a trio of outlaws charged with caring for a baby, and discover-ing responsibility and perhaps his soul (the two go hand-in-hand for Ford) in the process. [...] In Ford's vision, we're all little guys, even larger-than-life types like Wayne. It's there in his signature shot – men and women dwarfed by his Monu-ment Valley's timeless, towering peaks, living in the shadow of eternity, knowing it, but carrying on and finding meaning anyway'.[14] With *Three Godfathers*, Ford makes the point that enlightenment – whether moral or spiritual – can take place in even the least expected of places, and under the most unlikely of circumstances. This theme of personal redemption and character reformation would, of course, be revisited by later Christmas films such as *The Lemon Drop Kid* (q.v.) and *We're No Angels* (q.v.), while *Three Godfathers'* central theme of unexpected surrogate guardianship of an infant child would be influential to many later movies such as popular French comedy *Trois Hommes et un Couffin* (Coline Serreau, 1985), remade for American audiences as the hugely successful *Three Men and a Baby* (Leonard Nimoy, 1987). Ford's cast of engaging anti-heroes find new purpose in their unexpected roles as guardians, abandoning a self-serving life of criminal activity in order to take up a more fulfilling function as protector and surrogate parent. That they do so within a Christmas setting – albeit a deeply uncommon one – further accentuates the film's wider theme of celebrating community over self-centred individualism, contrasting the idyllic neighbourhoods of Welcome and New Jerusalem with the bleak, potentially lethal terrain which surrounds them (typified by a prolonged battle in order to simply survive – a conflict which both Pete and the Kid eventually lose, in spite of their best attempts). Thus *Three Godfathers* is essentially a tale of hope – of the power of Christmas to reshape attitudes, and the ability of domesticity to tame even the most determined of maverick loners. While the Western setting may have made these themes seem all the more conspicuous, they were nonetheless tropes which would be revisited time and again over the years that were to follow.

REFERENCES

1.   Ron Scheer, '*3 Godfathers*', in *Buddies in the Saddle*, 19 July 2011.
      <*http://buddiesinthesaddle.blogspot.com/2011/07/3-godfathers-1948.html*>

2.   Sanderson Beck, '*3 Godfathers*', in *Movie Mirrors*, 2006.
      <*http://san.beck.org/MM/1948/ThreeGodfathers.html*>

3.   Scheer.

4.   Ace Black, 'Movie Review: *3 Godfathers*', in *The Ace Black Blog*, 6 February 2014.
      <*https://www.theaceblackblog.com/2014/02/movie-review-3-godfathers-1948.html*>

5.   Dennis Schwartz, '*3 Godfathers*', in *Dennis Schwartz Reviews*, 27 June 2004.
      <*https://dennisschwartzreviews.com/3godfathers/*>

6.   Mitch Lovell, '*3 Godfathers*', in *Video Vacuum*, 20 August 2018.
      <*https://thevideovacuum.blogspot.com/2018/08/3-godfathers-1948.html*>

7.   Anon., '*3 Godfathers*', in *Let's Not Talk About Movies*, 25 December 2012.
      <*http://letsnottalkaboutmovies.blogspot.com/2012/12/3-godfathers-1948.html*>

8.   Ed Howard, '*3 Godfathers*', in *Only the Cinema*, 14 April 2009.

<*http://seul-le-cinema.blogspot.com/2009/04/3-godfathers.html*>

9. Adam Kuhn, '*3 Godfathers*', in *Corndog Chats*, 14 March 2018.
<*https://corndogchats.com/2018/03/14/3-godfathers-1948/*>

10. Derek Winnert, '*Three Godfathers*', in *Derek Winnert.com*, 17 August 2018.
<*http://www.derekwinnert.com/three-godfathers-3-godfathers-1948-john-wayne-pedro-armendariz-harry-carey-jr-classic-movie-review-7458/*>

11. Gregory Meshman, '*3 Godfathers*', in *DVD Beaver*, 20 December 2005.
<*http://www.dvdbeaver.com/film/DVDReviews19/3_godfathers_dvd_review.htm*>

12. Laura Grieve, 'Tonight's Movie: *3 Godfathers* (1948) at the Lone Pine Film Festival', in *Laura's Miscellaneous Musings*, 15 October 2016.
<*http://laurasmiscmusings.blogspot.com/2016/10/tonights-movie-3-godfathers-1948-at.html*>

13. Tag Gallagher, *John Ford: The Man and His Films* (Berkeley & Los Angeles: University of California Press, 1986), p.261.

14. Keith Phipps, '*John Wayne/John Ford Film Collection*', in *The Onion A.V. Club*, 20 June 2006.
<*https://film.avclub.com/john-wayne-john-ford-film-collection-1798201750*>

11

Holiday Affair (1949)

RKO Radio Pictures Inc.

Director: Don Hartman
Producer: Don Hartman
Screenwriter: Isobel Lennart, from a story by John D. Weaver

ONE of the last high-profile Christmas movies of the 1940s, *Holiday Affair* was one of the most mature and thoughtful romantic narratives to emerge in the genre at the time of its release. While there had been numerous other Christmas-themed romances throughout the decade, such as *Remember the Night* (Mitchell Leisen, 1940) and *The Shop Around the Corner* (q.v.), *Holiday Affair* was to be a rather more adult-oriented take on the issue of emotional entanglement, focusing less on festive whimsy than it did on the serious challenges of dealing with widowhood and raising a child as a single parent.

In its willingness to deal head-on with sobering social topics deriving from the end of World War II, it shared some degree of commonality with *It Happened on Fifth Avenue* (q.v.), though given its New York City setting and central love affair it is actually most often compared with *Miracle on 34th Street* (q.v.). As Brian Camp has explained the comparison: '*Miracle on 34th Street Lite*. That may be a convenient way to sum up *Holiday Affair* (1949) with Robert Mitchum and Janet Leigh, a Christmas-themed Hollywood movie that was obviously inspired by the success of the earlier film. It has a New York department store setting (at least part of the time) and a lawyer in love with a beautiful widow with a precocious young child. There's even a kindly old man (the department store head in an unlikely turn of behavior) who functions as a Santa Claus figure and a scowling floorwalker at the store who functions as a villain in the way some of the department store personnel in the earlier film did'.[1] Yet moving beyond these similarities, the dynamic of the core romance in *Holiday Affair* is quite different from that of *Miracle on 34th Street* in the sense that it takes the form of a love triangle; whereas Fred Gailey's main stumbling block to winning the heart of the independently-minded Doris Walker in the earlier film had been her reluctance to settle down or ingenuously accept the wonder of the festive season, the two male protagonists of *Holiday Affair* instead found themselves emotionally competing for the affections of the female lead. As Artemisia d'Ecca observes, the film remains 'fascinating for the time, the place, the setting, and the casting – Robert Mitchum in a Christmas movie? One of the surprisingly few movies of the period about a woman widowed by World War II (Connie, played by Janet Leigh) and how she manages (with difficulty)'.[2]

As d'Ecca suggests, today *Holiday Affair*'s greatest claim to fame in the wider canon of Christmas cinema is the unconventional selection of actor Robert Mitchum for the starring role. Very much cast against type, Mitchum was primarily known for 'tough guy' roles including no-nonsense US Army officers, shady underworld antiheroes and hard-hitting roles in Westerns. For all his established *film noir* credentials, however, *Holiday Affair* marked a sudden shift in tone for this iconic screen legend, who temporarily switched the hard-edged exterior for which he had become known in exchange for a much more thoughtful, measured approach as a kind-hearted, reflective bachelor who has become a drifter following his tour of duty in the Second World War. The abrupt gear-change may have seemed jarring but, as *The Blonde at the Film*'s critic 'Cameron' clarifies, there was more to the situation than necessarily seemed obvious at the time:

You might be surprised to see Robert Mitchum in this light comedy-romance; after all, he'd found great success in westerns, war films, and then *film noir* in the mid-to-late 1940s with classics such as [Vincente Minnelli's] *Undercurrent* (1946), [Edward Dymytryk's] *Crossfire* (1947), and [Jacques Tourneur's] *Out of the Past* (1947). But on August 31, 1948, he was arrested with some friends for marijuana possession, and he was convicted in January 1949 of 'criminal conspiracy' to possess the drug. He was sentenced to 50 days at a prison farm in Castaic, CA in 1949, but after two years probation, the conviction was wiped from his record. As you can imagine, Mitchum's arrest and conviction were big news, and 1948-1949 was an interesting time in his career. The scandal made him a bigger name (no publicity is bad publicity!) but also threatened his popularity in some quarters. (Some claim that he was assigned the role in *Holiday Affair* to help clean up his image.)[3]

Based on John D. Weaver's short story *Christmas Gift*, the director of *Holiday Affair* was Don Hartman, who was

Holiday Affair (1949): RKO
Radio Pictures Inc.

better known in Hollywood for his work as a screenwriter. He was twice nominated for an Academy Award, in 1936 for the original story for *The Gay Deception* (William Wyler, 1935) with Stephen Morehouse Avery, and then in 1943 for the original screenplay of *Road to Morocco* (David Butler, 1942) with Frank Butler. Though he penned numerous screenplays for prominent films including *Waikiki Wedding* (Frank Tuttle, 1937), *Road to Singapore* (Victor Schertzinger, 1940) and *The Kid from Brooklyn* (Norman Z. McLeod), as a director Hartman worked with some of the biggest names in American cinema such as Ginger Rogers in *It Had to Be You* (1947), Cary Grant in *Every Girl Should be Married* (1948) and Lana Turner in *You Belong to My Heart* (1951). From an early career as a playwright, stage manager and actor for the Dallas Little Theatre, his time in Hollywood also included employment as a producer and popular song lyricist.

It's Christmas in New York City, and Steve Mason (Robert Mitchum) is working as a sales clerk at the upmarket Crowley's department store. As he demonstrates an expensive electric train set to a crowd of enraptured children – complete with seasonal falling snow – a customer named Connie Ennis (Janet Leigh) arrives and asks for his assistance. Steve grows suspicious when she unquestioningly produces $79.50 cash (plus the exact tax costs) to pay for the expensive train set without even waiting to hear his sales pitch, deducing that she must be working undercover for a rival company as a comparative shopper. His reservations are further developed when she insists on taking the heavy package away with her rather than having it delivered to her home, suggesting that she wants to keep her identity concealed from the store. Sure enough, Connie retreats to a public payphone and calls her employer, reporting back on a variety of items that she had been pricing at a number of different stores in the city. She arranges to bring in the train set the following day.

Connie returns home to her apartment to be greeted by her young son Timmy (Gordon Gebert), who – knowing that the holidays are close at hand – is delighted by the sight of the large package in her arms. While freshening up for dinner, he can't resist a peek inside the decorative box and is overjoyed when he catches sight of the elaborate train set. However, his elation is short-lived when Connie notices his fascination with the parcel and emphasises that it isn't a gift – it's just something she has to take into work the next day. Poor Timmy is disconsolate, but Connie assures him that it's important to keep realistic expectations in life; if we hope for things that we are never likely to get, all we can really anticipate is continual disappointment.

Later, Connie's good-natured, long-term boyfriend Carl Davis (Wendell Corey) arrives at the apartment. The smooth-talking lawyer helps with the washing-up, and during their flirtatious banter he raises the prospect of marriage... only for Connie to emphasise that she needs more time to grieve after the loss of her husband in the war. Carl is concerned at her apparent inability to move on with her life, having courted her for two years, but she assures him that she will let him know when the time is right for their romance to move on to the next level. Once Carl has returned home, Connie visits Timmy in his bedroom and tries to gauge his feelings about the marriage proposal. However, Timmy is resistant to the idea; he believes that a union between Carl and his mother contains too much risk of change to his everyday routine, and desperately wants everything to stay the same as it has been since his father died.

The next day, Connie returns the train set to Crowley's but discovers that Steve has realised that she works for a competing store. He explains that he should report her to the store detective, who will circulate her photograph around every department and ensure that she is unable to operate anywhere in the store in the future, but – knowing that this will lead to her dismissal from the company that employs her – she tells him that she is the sole wage earner in her household and has been supporting her six-year-old son alone since her husband was killed in the war. As a veteran himself, Steve decides to save her job and takes down her details in order to issue a refund, but entreats her never to return to the toy department. Seconds after she has gone, however, one of the store's officious floorwalkers ominously asks Steve for a word.

Shortly after, Connie is buying an outsize shirt in the menswear department when Steve unexpectedly joins her. Asking why he is away from the store's toy section, he explains that his manager had determined Connie's true purpose and had fired him for not having turned her over to security. She feels guilty about being responsible for his dismissal, and agrees to join him for lunch at his 'favourite restaurant'...

which turns out to be tasty fast food from a vendor at Central Park. They enjoy each other's company, and Connie discovers that Steve's dream is to build boats for a living. However, due to his long tour of duty in the war he was convinced to go for a responsible job in the finance industry, but soon found it dull and badly-paid. Desperate for some variety in his life, he took up a job working on a ship operating between the USA and South America. This derailed his corporate career but instilled in him his desire to construct boats of his own. Now he is taking any casual post he can get, no matter how short-term, as he is buying into a shipyard operated by a friend who lives in California. It might never make him rich, but it's a dream worth striving for. Connie seems impressed by his freewheeling, nonconformist attitude to life.

With some alarm, Connie realises that they've been talking for two hours and that she is running late if she is to fulfil her professional responsibilities for the rest of the day. Now with no job to go to, Steve offers to accompany her and help make her cover story more believable by posing as her boyfriend. Amused by his appealingly alternative way of looking at the world, she agrees to let him join her for the afternoon. Steve's ruse appears to work, and soon he is burdened by all sorts of household items as they struggle along a crowded shopping precinct. However, the pair are unexpectedly separated when Connie jumps onto a passing bus while (though she does not realise it at first) Steve is swept away by a passing multitude of Christmas shoppers.

Back at her apartment, Timmy and Carl are busy decorating the Christmas tree. Connie arrives back early, much to their disappointment as they had hoped to surprise her by presenting her with a fully-ornamented tree for the holidays. She is perturbed, pointing out that she has 'misplaced' some of the goods that she had bought for her employer – in other words, the items that Steve was holding when she lost track of him – but Carl offers to take her and Timmy to dinner in the hope of cheering her up. Timmy seems anxious, clearly troubled at the prospect of the deepening romantic ties between Carl and Connie as he fears that it will turn his world upside down. Carl is sympathetic of the little boy's reservations, but seems confident that he can make a new family unit work – provided that Connie is willing to give him a chance. Their conversation is interrupted when Steve arrives at the door, still carrying all of the household items from earlier. He explains that he had difficulty finding her home, but persevered until he was able to track her down (with a little help from her employer's payroll department). Steve and Carl are surprised – and more than a little suspicious – to encounter each other, neither knowing of the other's existence until now. Connie awkwardly introduces the two men, trying to explain her new acquaintance with Steve, and then exits to make everyone a drink – leaving Steve and Carl to a supremely stilted discussion about the weather. Steve notices a photo of Connie with her late husband, and Carl points out that Connie does a great job of keeping his memory alive for Timmy, who was too young to remember his father. However, Steve is unconvinced, reflecting that it is unhealthy to dwell on the past at the expense of the here and now.

Connie arrives back with the drinks, and Timmy appears as they share a toast. Knowing that Carl made a point of emphasising how much Timmy looks like his father, Steve instead mentions that the boy is the spitting image of Connie, which immediately focuses his attention. Steve strikes up a conversation with Timmy, finding him responsive to his friendly chinwag, and innocently asks what he wants for

Christmas. Still stinging from the realisation that he isn't receiving the much-sought-after train set, Timmy laments that he always receives clothes as Christmas gifts, then lets slip the fact he has worked out that Carl has bought him a camera. Far from being grateful for the prospect of a thoughtful gift, however, Timmy grows resentful and begins physically attacking Carl, obviously aggrieved at the man's growing closeness to Connie. Carl defends himself and drags Timmy to his room, causing Connie to accuse him of roughly mishandling her son. Indignant at her attitude, Carl leaves the apartment in exasperation.

Now alone with Connie, Steve is curious about why she didn't explain to Carl about their earlier encounter at Crowley's. She replies that she didn't think it was significant enough to mention, though Steve believes that her omission may have made their acquaintance seem more important to Carl than it actually was. Steve also ventures the belief that in Carl trying to assert himself as the surrogate man of the house, he had inadvertently provoked Timmy's emotional outburst. Connie refutes his interpretation of events and points out that her life would be so much easier if she didn't have suitors to worry about, intimating things were considerably more straightforward when it was just her and Timmy. Steve decides to take his leave, fathoming that – whether she realises it or not – Connie is obsessed with trying to hold on to a bygone past, and is unfairly forcing her son to be a carbon copy of his late father rather than letting him just be a little boy. Realising that he has struck a nerve, Connie denies his analysis and asserts that she plans to marry Carl, thus changing the status quo irrevocably. Steve tells her that she will be making a mistake, and also ensuring further issues with Timmy who is sure to end up constantly competing with Carl. His apparent certainty infuriates Connie, who insists that she knows what is best for her and her son.

Before he departs, Steve decides to say goodbye to Timmy. The young boy feels guilty about having treated Carl badly; he is confused at having behaved so poorly, as he likes the approachable lawyer and is generally happy to have him around. Steve convinces him to apologise and keep the peace. Revealing that he has been eavesdropping on Connie's conversations, Timmy asks Steve what had happened to get him fired from Crowley's, and when Steve gives him a sanitised version of events Timmy reveals his overwhelming disappointment at not having been the recipient of the deluxe train set he had momentarily spied in the decorative box. In spite of Connie's appeal to Timmy not to aim for unattainable goals, Steve tells him that he needs to have high ambitions if he wants to achieve anything really good in life. He then wishes the boy a merry Christmas, before leaving the room and repeating the same greeting to Connie – only, in her case, there is an unexpected and passionate kiss to accompany the sentiment. Connie is stunned by his boldness as he finally exits the apartment.

Some time later, on Christmas Eve, Connie joins Carl for dinner at a high-class restaurant where he apologises for his earlier abrupt departure. Connie is also sorry that she had failed to mention having met Steve before he arrived at the apartment, but Carl assures her that this wasn't what had concerned him. Rather, he was upset at her reaction when he tried to restrain Timmy while he was out of control. If they are to get married, he wonders, how does she expect him to react to Timmy – as her son alone, or as their shared responsibility? Connie reassures him that she is confident that once they are married, Timmy will be a son to both of them – a fact which reassures Carl no end. She then surprises him by not only agreeing to his earlier marriage proposal, but suggesting that they tie the knot on New Year's Day. Carl is stunned by the suddenness of her change in attitude, but is delighted to accept.

The next morning is Christmas Day, and Connie is awakened from her sleep by a euphoric Timmy. Her son is absolutely overjoyed by the arrival of a mystery package that he had discovered outside the apartment door, and – curious as to the source of his exultation – she is dumbfounded to discover the costly electric train set from Crowley's, which Timmy has already unpacked in the living room. The gift came with an enigmatic note, explaining that it has been sent to Timmy 'from Santa', though Connie is unable to identify the handwriting. Believing that Connie was responsible for buying him this much-desired present, Timmy voices his amazement that she had worked out that he wanted the train set so badly – the only person he had ever mentioned it to was Steve.

When Carl telephones to wish Connie a happy Christmas, she voices her concern at the prospect of Steve having bought Timmy such an expensive gift ($80 in 1949 being equivalent to roughly $834 in 2019 when adjusted for inflation). Carl believes that Steve is trying to make a move on Connie by paying for such an extravagant gift, thus winning over Timmy's heart. She points out that Timmy would be distressed to lose his dream Christmas present, and Carl offers to pay Steve back rather than return the train set. However, Connie is unhappy at the prospect of Carl having to part with such a large amount of his own money – not least as he has already bought a considerate gift of his own for Timmy – and resolves to work the issue out herself.

Connie explains to Timmy that it was Steve, not her, who had bought him the train set. Her son is amazed, having only met Steve on the one occasion, and Connie says that he must have made a big impression on the former store clerk. She tells Timmy that she intends to visit Steve at the hotel where he is staying, so that she can thank him for his generosity and have a discussion about other issues. Timmy wants to join her, but she explains that he will have to stay at home in order to greet his grandparents (her late husband's mother and father) when they arrive to exchange gifts. Carl will also be coming to join them for dinner later, though this prospect excites Timmy less than the prospect of Steve paying a visit. Connie considers an appearance from Steve to be unlikely, but Timmy suggests that she take him a necktie (initially meant as a gift for Carl) as a Christmas present.

Connie visits the hotel where Steve is renting a room, only to discover that he had checked out earlier on Christmas morning. She is crestfallen that he hasn't left a forwarding address, but the hotel receptionist inadvertently gives her a clue of his whereabouts – Central Park, the location of their recent lunch. Sure enough, she soon finds the near-penniless Steve on a park bench feeding a squirrel, and enquires why he would buy Timmy such a lavish gift. Steve replies that he did it simply because he wanted to, and steadfastly refuses any attempt Connie makes to repay him. He assures her that he was determined to buy Timmy an unexpected gift because, as the boy has been bought up not to expect surprises, Steve felt certain that receiving the train set would emphasise the fact that sometimes it is a good thing to really wish for something he wants in life and know that – even just occasionally – he will have the chance to actually get it.

Connie gives Steve the necktie, explaining that it is a gift from Timmy. He is so pleased to receive it, he puts it on in place of his existing tie, giving the old one to a passing homeless man (who is similarly grateful for the gesture). Connie tells Steve that Carl is upset at what he perceives to be an attempt to win her affections, and explains that she and Carl are to be married on New Year's Day. Steve congratulates her, but again voices his belief that she is making a mistake. He feels that she is marrying Carl not because she is in love with him, but rather due to the fact that he seems like a safe choice who won't excessively disturb her unexciting but essentially safe existence. In Steve's opinion, Connie is trying to stifle any potential for surprise in her life... but as he points out, not all surprises are necessarily bad ones. Connie is indignant about his far-reaching pronouncements concerning her life choices, but her response is interrupted when a little girl approaches Steve with an unexpected gift. The tramp who received the necktie was so touched by Steve's generosity, he wanted to give him something in return – a sterling silver cruet set – which he has given to the girl to pass on. Steve is moved, if not a little puzzled, by the impoverished man's thoughtfulness. Connie asks Steve why he has left the room he was renting at the hotel, and he replies that he has moved to cheaper accommodation as he soon intends to relocate to California in order to work on the boatyard that he has been investing in. As soon as he can afford the train fare, he will be leaving New York. This, he reasons, will not only remove any romantic competition from Carl's life, but will also help to make Connie's existence even quieter and less stimulating – surely what she has been aiming for, in his opinion. Annoyed by the glibness of his constant witticisms and the perceived arrogance of his observations, she walks off.

Arriving back at her apartment, Connie is pleased to discover that her in-laws (Griff Barnett and Esther Dale) have arrived to share Christmas with her and Timmy. Connie is exasperated when she learns that Timmy has spent all day enthusing about Steve, emphasising that it is Carl that she is actually due to marry – not the unfathomable Mr Mason. Mr and Mrs Ennis are confused, given that Timmy had led them to believe the exact opposite, and it is obvious that they have misgivings about a union with the pleasant but essentially insipid Carl. Moments later, Carl arrives and barely has time to exchange pleasantries before asking what had happened during her meeting with Steve. When Connie explains that Steve had refused to accept payment for the train set, both Carl and her parents-in-law make the point that it seems unusual that a near-stranger would spend so much on a gift without some kind of motive. Tired of insinuations, Connie tells them that Steve intends to leave the city in the near future and will be heading for the other side of the country, making it unlikely that they will ever see him again.

Her account of events is interrupted when the doorbell rings, and she opens the apartment door to reveal a police detective named Johnson (Larry J. Blake). He explains that Steve is currently being held in custody, and asks if she will accompany him to the precinct's police station in an attempt to ascertain his involvement in a crime. Connie, Carl and Timmy all head for the station, where a police lieutenant (Henry Morgan) explains that a man had been mugged near Central Park that morning – struck on the head and tied up with Steve's necktie – and his wallet stolen along with a set of silver salt and pepper shakers (a Christmas present intended for his aunt). Shortly after, Steve had been found 'loitering' in the park, and when questioned had identified the tie as having previously belonged to him. The silver cruet set was also on his person at the time, leading the police to arrest him on suspicion of theft and assault. However, as the victim was unable to identify his assailant, Steve must prove his innocence. Carl steps in to defend Steve, and asks if the wallet had been found on him when he was searched. The lieutenant replies that it hadn't been, but that this proves nothing as the money could easily have been hidden elsewhere in the park. Connie tries to explain everything that happened during her meeting at the park, including the reason for her being there, but the account is so helplessly convoluted that the lieutenant finds it all impossibly far-fetched. In particular, he is very doubtful that a nearly-broke drifter would buy an expensive train set for someone who is more or less a stranger, or – when he appeared to be hiding when the police arrived – that he happened to be feeding a wild squirrel at the time. However, in spite of all the convolutions Connie's story matches Steve's perfectly, and given that the evidence is almost completely circumstantial the lieutenant decides to let him go free. Carl, whose lofty attitude had needled the lieutenant to the point that he had potentially endangered Steve's freedom, offers to loan him the money for his train fare so that he can leave New York as soon as possible. Far from oblivious to Carl's real intentions, which are not necessarily as altruistic as they appear, Steve thanks him but insists that he will leave under his own steam as soon as he can find work to pay for his departure.

Much to Carl's discomfiture, Timmy insists point-blank that Steve join the family for Christmas dinner. While Steve is the life and soul of the party, effortlessly charming Mr and Mrs Ennis, his presence makes the meal somewhat uncomfortable as he and Carl seem to be continually – if politely –

competing for Connie's affections. Mrs Ennis unknowingly manages to make a *faux pas* by commenting that the necktie Steve is wearing looks exactly like the kind that Connie always bought her late husband... not realising that it was, in fact, a gift Steve had received from Connie. The remark makes Carl silently flinch. Mr Ennis then gives a heartfelt after-dinner speech extolling the virtues of a long and happy marriage, which prompts Carl to launch into a Christmas address of his own. He points out that having never had a family, this has been his first Christmas surrounded by kith and kin – though he hopes that when he and Connie are married, the annual dinner will become a family tradition. Meaningfully, he excludes Steve from his ideal line-up of guests but does nobly add that he wishes the man well in his forthcoming move to California. Timmy seems somewhat unaffected by Carl's heartfelt oration and prompts Steve to give a speech of his own. Though initially reluctant, Steve begins by thanking everyone for their hospitality, then shocks all present by telling Connie that although Carl is a pleasant and dependable person that she is making a grave error of judgement in accepting his marriage proposal. Instead, he suggests that she marry him instead. Steve reasons that every time he tries to leave Connie's life, some chance influence ends up bringing him back to her. He knows that if he doesn't speak up now, he will most likely lose her forever. Connie is incredulous at his sheer directness, but rebuffs his engagement request. Accepting her response at face value, he wishes everyone a merry Christmas and departs, leaving all present in stunned silence.

The following day, Timmy fights through the New York crowds to take his train set back to Crowley's, believing that if he can get a refund he will be able to give the funds to Steve (realising that his friend is now virtually insolvent).

essentially lacklustre potential husband and a more
less predictable love-match – the plot of *Holiday*
mes considerably less conventional due to the fact
f Connie's suitors seem equally appropriate part-
erent ways. While Carl may seem unexciting in
to the bohemian drifter Steve, we are left in no
he is a decent and patient man who has obvious
both Connie and Timmy, and it is not too diffi-
ine the pair in a durable but somewhat humdrum
gether. Steve, on the other hand, lacks Carl's
me and sense of social respectability, but his droll
entric outlook on life make him seem the more ap-
he two simply because he is happy to flaunt con-
rder to lead the kind of life that suits him. (It is
dividual viewer to decide whether Steve's desire
ense of optimism and self-reliance in Timmy is ei-
rate or cynically opportunistic, given his feelings
mother.) As Camp observes: 'It's an "adult film"
ense of the word. I don't mean that it's made for
certainly suitable for all ages – but that it's about
behave like real adults and aren't infantilized by
dustry's compulsion to manipulate audience emo-
ve the designated hero an obvious edge. So many
medies from the classics to the run-of-the-box-
ms that seem to dominate the multiplexes at holi-
el the need to demonize one side of a romantic
make the end coupling so inevitable that it's a
clusion'.[4]
l the refinement of its central romance and the
stry of its three leads, *Holiday Affair* takes a simi-
approach to the festive season itself; for all its at-
enes of bustling department stores and frosty

However, one of the carriages is crushed when he steps into a packed elevator, meaning that it the set is ineligible for return. Upset by the decision, Timmy decides to take his complaint right to the top (literally) and rides the elevator to the eighth floor to visit Mr Crowley, the store's owner. Crowley's secretary, Emily (Helen Brown), is somewhat taken aback with the young man's request, but agrees to let him meet the owner in person. Thankfully Crowley (Henry O'Neill) is a rather avuncular gentleman and, upon hearing of Timmy's request, agrees to meet with him. Detecting that the boy is distressed, Crowley reassures him that he will look into the problem and – when he learns of Steve and his cash-flow problems – politely asks Timmy to tell him the whole story.

Unbeknownst to the well-meaning youngster, Carl and Connie are worried sick at Timmy's absence. Neither had realised that he had managed to sneak out of the apartment, and they are concerned that he has somehow become lost in the city. They have searched the entire neighbourhood, and Carl is on the phone to the police to report Timmy as a missing person. However, Connie then spots a chauffeur-driven car parking up outside the apartment building, and the well-meaning Crowley dropping Timmy off on the sidewalk. She and Carl are hugely relieved to see him back safely, but are astonished when he relates his tale of having walked all the way downtown on his own – not least when he tells them of his meeting with Crowley. The kindly store owner has indeed paid the full $80 refund for the train set, and Timmy pleads for Connie to make sure that Steve gets the cash as soon as possible. Carl points out that they have no idea of Steve's whereabouts, but Connie remembers the address that he had given the police the day beforehand while he was in custody.

Once they have tracked down Steve's location, Connie is reluctant to leave the car and asks Carl to hand over the money from the refund on her behalf instead. Realising the extent of her feelings for the inscrutable Steve, Carl finally reaches his limit and tells her that he is aware of the emotional conflict she is experiencing. He understands the fact that although a marriage between them would be agreeable and stable, it is Steve that she truly loves. Now unavoidably faced with the truth of her inner turmoil, Connie finds that she can't deny his version of events, and they part on amicable terms.

Connie meets Steve in his hotel room and hands back his money, explaining Timmy's decision to seek a refund for his train set. Steve is genuinely moved by the young boy's thoughtfulness, and – impressed by Timmy's sense of maturity in the matter – points out that he can now get on the first cross-country train headed for California. Connie is fascinated by the blueprints and models that he has designed for ships, which are on display in the room – his obvious talent makes it clear that his aspirations of building seagoing vessels aren't simply a pipe dream. She tells him that she will no longer be marrying Carl on New Year's Day, but Steve decides not to propose again. He explains that he has realised that he, Carl and Connie were not in the love triangle he had first supposed. Rather, it is Connie's dead husband who is the real stumbling block to a relationship between the two of them. Until she can find it in herself to move on with her life, Steve points out, any attempt at a lasting relationship will be a futile waste of time. Connie is upset, feeling that Steve wants to take away the happy memories she has of her husband and their time together, but he assures her that he simply wants her to live in the present. He has no intention of competing

with a ghost for her affecti[...]
but Steve remarks that she [...]
for in life because she seems[...]

A few days later, Ste[...]
her that he will be toasting[...]
train to California. Connie[...]
party with some friends, b[...]
that she will be going alon[...]
time comes for him to lea[...]
will be left lonely and isola[...]
dening. Connie finally adn[...]
love with Steve, and has de[...]
ising that there is no time[...]
the railway station and j[...]
before it departs. As ever[...]
chimes of midnight, usher[...]
Steve embrace at last – t[...]
earnest.

In spite of surface[...]
more than simply anothe[...]
the 1940s had been the la[...]
of this subgenre, Don Ha[...]
greater maturity than m[...]
fantasy scenarios that s[...]
Christmas in Connecticu[...]
plotlines involving a love[...]
nist and two competing[...]
with fanciful circumstanc[...]
more contemplative emot[...]
sicality considerably. Wh[...]
dicament to the strong, i[...]
in that earlier film – tha[...]

mitted but[...]
exciting bu[...]
Affair bec[...]
that both[...]
ners in dif[...]
comparison[...]
doubt that[...]
affection fc[...]
cult to ima[...]
marriage t[...]
steady inco[...]
wit and ecc[...]
pealing of t[...]
vention in[...]
left to the[...]
to foster a[...]
ther consid[...]
for the boy[...]
in the best[...]
adults – it's[...]
people who[...]
the movie i[...]
tions and g[...]
romantic cc[...]
office romco[...]
day times f[...]
triangle an[...]
foregone cor[...]

For a[...]
subtle chem[...]
larly muted[...]
mospheric s[...]

Central Park venues, the real Christmas content of the movie lies in its presentation of holiday traditions and the way that it weaves them seamlessly into its narrative. Trimming the tree, exchanging gifts and sharing a family Christmas dinner are all co-opted by Steve in his pursuit of Connie, leaving Carl on the defensive – a fact that he is far from unaware of. As Andy Webb perceptively remarks, 'if *Holiday Affair* had been a movie set at any other time of the year it would mean it would be quite forgettable but thankfully with it being set at Christmas it adds to the charm. The fun opening scene with a toy train which we watch in the toy store makes you smile as does watching how Steve is with the young children in the toy department. That cuteness continues when we have Steve and Timmy together and throw in a Christmas tree and snow in Central Park and the various issues begin to melt away. It doesn't stop it from feeling only average but it does mean it is a nice nostalgic Christmas movie'.[5] As Webb suggests, the film's festive setting is never overplayed, and – for all its essential function as a narrative device – the holiday season is never allowed to overpower the key theme of choosing a heartfelt romantic love over an expedient partnership. As commentators such as Jessica Pickens have noted, the film's combination of a post-World War II setting (the social issues that are highlighted, along with Connie's widowhood) and a festive milieu may heighten the stakes of the film (given Connie's desire to marry on New Year's Day, and Steve's determination to leave New York around the same time), but *Holiday Affair* is always driven by the understated conflict of the love triangle situated at the heart of its action:

Robert Mitchum's character forces Janet Leigh to face a truth she has been hiding from. Leigh's character is flustered both by her feelings and by the harsh reality quoted to her by Mitchum. In most films that feature a love triangle, one of the characters is majorly flawed: they're sloppy, rude or not very smart. This allows the audience to know exactly who which hero they should be cheering for. What's interesting about *Holiday Affair* is that this isn't the case. While Robert Mitchum is the hero of the story, Wendell Corey isn't made out to be a buffoon. Corey's character, Carl, is really an all-around good guy. He's patient about Leigh's marriage decision, knowing she experienced tragedy with the death of her husband. In the end, he realizes they both have to do what is best for themselves and that he should be with someone who loves him back.[6]

The reason that *Holiday Affair* has become something of a minor classic of 1940s Christmas romances is not simply due to the appealing interplay between its main characters, but also on account of the longevity and continued relevance of many of the issues that the film addresses. While many serious subjects are addressed at various points, their treatment is all the more effective for being filtered through a very human lens. We witness Connie's heartfelt trauma and sense of loss at her husband's death, but also the impact on Timmy from him being unconsciously shaped into a miniature version of his father. (The one issue that Steve and Carl agree upon is the need for Connie to move on with her life, given her self-imposed determination to stymy any potential change to her domestic environment.) In this sense, as Sanderson Beck discerns, the way in which Connie and Timmy respectively process their grief has a powerful cumulative bearing on both of them: 'A young widow with a son causes a man to lose his job at Christmas time and is wooed by him while her steady friend asks her to marry. [...] This romantic comedy portrays nice people who manage to work out a triangle without any malice or violence. The feelings of the child represent those of the mother she eventually comes to recognize'.[7] The resolution of this long-running trauma is all the more effective for the subtlety of how it gradually plays out, and certainly transcends the often insubstantial contingent subplots which surround it. That the film dealt quite so directly with the serious issue of grief is laudable in and of itself, but Isobel Lennart's screenplay similarly does not shy away from other difficult topics – while concurrently ensuring that their gravity is never allowed to overwhelm the film's otherwise cosy, homely Christmas setting. As Cameron states: 'Like *It's a Wonderful Life*, *Holiday Affair* was not a hit when it first came out, and actually lost money, but thanks to TV broadcasts over the years, it's become a holiday standard. [...] Although this movie is mostly a light comedy, it does deal with some complicated, sophisticated issues: we've got grief, a blended family, the difficulty of keeping the memory of a loved one alive without letting it overwhelm or stifle you, and the effect of WWII on society'.[8]

Key to the success of *Holiday Affair* is its winning central performances, chief among them being a charmingly compelling turn from Robert Mitchum in a rare comedic role. While seeing Mitchum out of his usual *film noir* territory may initially seem jarring, he forges the somewhat offbeat character of Steve Mason into a highly watchable figure. With his endless mellow pronouncements and sphinx-like eccentricities, Steve seems like a somewhat atypical romantic lead for the period – and Mitchum ensures that it is never less than fun to spend some time with this engagingly oddball drifter. His take on the character is all the more compelling given his famous reputation for portraying 'hard men' figures at the time. Mitchum is now widely considered to be one of the most distinctive actors of Hollywood's golden age; his many performances included roles in *Thirty Seconds Over Tokyo* (Mervyn LeRoy, 1944), *Nevada* (Edward Killy, 1944), *Out of the Past* (Jacques Tourneur, 1947) and *The Big Steal* (Don Siegel, 1949), and he was nominated for the Best Supporting Actor Academy Award for his portrayal of Lieutenant Bill Walker in *The Story of G.I. Joe* (William Wellman, 1945). His many later appearances included roles in prominent movies such as *The Night of the Hunter* (Charles Laughton, 1955), *Cape Fear* (J. Lee Thompson, 1962) and *Farewell, My Lovely* (Dick Richards, 1975). He would eventually appear in more than 110 films during his long career, and also worked at various times as a director, author, composer, singer and poet. Many years later, Robert Mitchum would make another contribution to Christmas cinema when he played the powerful but somewhat addlebrained network president Preston Rhinelander in *Scrooged* (Richard Donner, 1988). His comic performance as the perplexing executive, again somewhat against type, won Mitchum much critical praise at the time.

Of *Holiday Affair*'s other key players, Janet Leigh had made a prolific number of acting appearances in spite of her relatively young age at the time of production (at 22, she was only 14 years older than her on-screen son Gordon Gebert), with roles in films including drama *If Winter Comes* (Victor Saville, 1947), biographical musical *Words and Music* (Norman Taurog, 1948) and as Meg March in the Louisa May Alcott adaptation *Little Women* (Mervyn LeRoy, 1949). Perhaps most famously, she would go on to play Marion Crane in Alfred Hitchcock's *Psycho* (1960), a role which would win her the Golden Globe Award for Best Supporting Actress and a nomination for an Academy Award in the same category. Wendell Corey was a popular fixture on stage and screen as well as, in later years, television and radio. His cinematic roles included parts in crime movie *Desert Fury* (Lewis Allen, 1947), harrowing World War II drama *The Search* (Fred Zinnemann, 1948) and film noir drama *The Accused* (William Dieterle, 1949). Corey was a versatile performer, with roles spanning many genres including science fiction, Westerns and crime dramas, though arguably his most memorable appearance was as Detective Lieutenant Thomas J. Doyle in the classic mystery thriller *Rear Window* (Alfred Hitchcock, 1954). Between 1961 and 1963 he was the President of the Academy of Motion Picture Arts and Sciences, and also served on the Board of Directors of the Screen Actors Guild.

All three of the main stars of *Holiday Affair* were respected acting luminaries who would later be honoured with stars on the Hollywood Walk of Fame, and they received solid assistance from the film's numerous supporting actors – among them Gordon Gebert's exuberant performance as the incorrigible Timmy Ennis and Henry O'Neill's brief but memorable turn as the genially benevolent department store owner Mr Crowley. (Crowley's was actually a real department store at the time, though not in New York City. Instead, it was the name of a famous chain of department stores which were established in downtown Detroit in 1909, and which eventually expanded to that city's suburbs. They were famous for their Thanksgiving and Christmas parades in Michigan, though eventually the company was sold in the mid-1980s.) The film also benefits from a droll extended cameo from Harry Morgan (appearing here as 'Henry Morgan') in an early role as the precinct's solemn-faced police lieutenant. Morgan would later become instantly recognisable to generations of Americans as police officer Bill Gannon on Universal Television's *Dragnet* (1967-70) revival series, and as firm-but-fair commanding officer Colonel Sherman T. Potter in CBS's Korean War comedy-drama *M*A*S*H* (1972-83) between 1975 and 1983. Director-producer Don Hartman also appears in a brief uncredited cameo as a man leaving the phone booth at Crowley's department store near the beginning of the film.

Holiday Affair did not fare well at the box-office at the time of its first appearance in cinemas; even with a national release date of Christmas Eve 1949, its commercial performance was weak and the film met with a sceptical critical reception. Following its New York premiere screening in the November of that year, Bosley Crowther of *The New York Times* described the film as 'an amiable little romance in which a boy meets a girl at Christmas-time, and the sentiments are quite as artificial and conveniently sprinkled as the snow is provided – for those who like such things – in RKO's *Holiday Affair*, a strictly holiday item which came to Loew's State yesterday. Light-weight in story and treatment, it is one of those tinsel-trimmed affairs which will likely depend for popularity upon the glamour potential of its stars. [...] No doubt, a great many people will find this sugar to their taste. This corner finds it much too saccharine for either credibility or delight'.[9] Hartman's movie subsequently disappeared from view for many years until, in the manner of many other Christmas features of the 1940s, it was rediscovered by more recent audiences thanks to annual TV screenings on Turner Classic Movies. It has since developed a low-key cult following amongst fans of the Christmas movie genre.

Even in the present day, commentators are divided as to the film's merits. Some, such as Kristen Lopez, have praised the appealing central performances, opining that 'the movie's plot is corny and goes where expected, but the acting makes up for the frivolous plot. Mitchum and Leigh have strong chemistry even if the film becomes sillier and fluffier with time. I've definitely seen worse Christmas films, and I recommend checking this out for a pleasant holiday evening. [...] *Holiday Affair* lacks the power of an *It's a Wonderful Life*. It's a light romantic distraction to slow you down from the hustle and bustle of the holiday. The acting is great and the love story is sweet. Just don't get wrapped up too much in the plot outside of the romance'.[10] Other reviewers, including Iain Stott, have instead remarked that *Holiday Affair*'s success is largely attributable to its comforting informality: 'Populated only by nice people doing nice things – although admittedly against a backdrop of loss and heartbreak – and featuring four tremendously charismatic performances, this gently entertaining and oft delightful seasonal romantic comedy proves decidedly amiable throughout'.[11]

Not all appraisals have been quite so affirmative, however. Gary Loggins points out that for all the film's charms, he is able to identify definite limitations: 'It's all pretty harmless, and you know from the get-go Janet's going to wind up choosing Mitchum over boring Wendell Corey, who's got all the charisma of a doormat. *Holiday Affair* will make you smile, but it's not laugh-out-loud funny. There's some good moments, and it's a rare chance to see Mitchum do romantic comedy, but this isn't a can't-miss film. In fact, it didn't do well at the box office, and RKO put Bob back in *noir* territory with his next film, *Where Danger Lives*. It's only when *Holiday Affair* began showing on television that it developed a devoted following'.[12] Andy Kaiser was, if anything, even more damning of the film's perceived drawbacks, finding fault with everything from the central premise and thematic influences to the performances and characterisation: '*Holiday Affair* is a bizarre and almost frighteningly misguided yuletide knockoff of *Miracle on 34th Street*. [...] Mitchum was assigned to the film (quite humorously I might add) in an attempt by the studios to repair his tarnished image following his notorious arrest and jailing for marijuana possession. His no nonsense presence adds gravitas somewhat, but his character is so creepy, and what's even more disturbing is the way the film views him in a positive manner. Add to that an agonizing and insufferable child actor and a syrupy screenplay and this becomes a holiday affair to forget'.[13] On the whole, however, the film has managed to remain an annual staple of Christmas viewing on account of its pleasingly irregular quirks, which still manage to make it feel agreeably fresh amongst the many other festive romances of the same period. David Cornelius, for example, has related the film's inter-character dynamics favourably in comparison to later, far more commercially successful movies such as *Joe Versus the Volcano* (John Patrick Shanley, 1990), *Sleepless in Seattle* (Nora Ephron, 1993) and *You've Got Mail* (Nora Ephron, 1998), reflecting that:

> *Holiday Affair* sticks rather closely to the formula that would still work for Tom Hanks and Meg Ryan decades later, and for all its occasional surprises (both men are blunt about their rivalry in delightfully unexpected ways), you'll never [be] less than two steps ahead of the plot. No matter. Isobel Lennart's screenplay (working from a story by John D. Weaver) knows full well that we know full well how things will end, so it spends its time

instead playing with the lightness of character interaction. Mitchum makes a terrific romantic lead precisely because of his Mitchum-ness – his Steve never falls for sappy actions or cheap sentiment; instead, he offers his feelings straight up. His interplay with Leigh's Connie is a sweet treat, carrying the movie through its more routine segments.[14]

Holiday Affair was to be adapted for radio by Lux Radio Theater, broadcast on 18 December 1950, with Robert Mitchum and Gordon Gebert both reprising their roles as Steve Mason and Timmy Ennis respectively. Decades later, the story was to be remade as a TV movie in collaboration between USA Network, RKO Pictures and Jones Programming Partners. Premiering on 16 December 1996, the remake – also entitled *Holiday Affair* – was directed by Alan Myerson and again drew on John D. Weaver's short story for its inspiration. The cast included Cynthia Gibb as Jodie Ennis, David James Elliott as Steve Mason, Tom Irwin as Paul Davis, and Curtis Blanck as Timmy Ennis.

Holiday Affair may not necessarily be remembered as a top-tier feature of 1940s festive cinema, but it demonstrated an interesting level of maturity in the genre as the world moved into a new decade. In particular, there is a noticeable lack of whimsical fantasy in the film; it is everyday people, rather than fanciful phenomena, which are responsible for the remarkable acts that are on display. An extraordinary romance is kindled through fair-minded adults working out their feelings in a reasonable way, while the day is saved not by an eleventh-hour intervention from Santa Claus but rather a well-meaning business mogul with a heart of gold. With the inescapable appeal of its lead characters, a surprising degree of emotional contemplation and the underlying sense of warmth that is lent to proceedings, *Holiday Affair* helped to lay the groundwork for other, even more sophisticated Christmas romances that would appear on the big screen in later years.

REFERENCES

1. Brian Camp, 'Merry Christmas: *Holiday Affair* (1949) with Robert Mitchum and Janet Leigh', in *Brian Camp's Film and Anime Blog*, 22 December 2012. <*https://briandanacamp.wordpress.com/2012/12/22/merry-christmas-holiday-affair-1949-with-robert-mitchum-and-janet-leigh/*>

2. Artemisia d'Ecca, *Keeping Christmas Well* (Dublin: Phaeton Publishing, 2012), pp.295-96.

3. Cameron, '*Holiday Affair*', at *The Blonde at the Film*, 6 December 2017. <*https://theblondeatthefilm.com/2017/12/06/holiday-affair/*>

4. Camp.

5. Andy Webb, '*Holiday Affair*', in *The Movie Scene*, 2012. <*https://www.themoviescene.co.uk/reviews/holiday-affair/holiday-affair.html*>

6. Jessica Pickens, '*Holiday Affair* (1949) and interview with Gordon Gebert', in *Comet Over Hollywood*, 30 November 2018. <*https://cometoverhollywood.com/2018/11/30/holiday-affair-1949-and-interview-with-gordon-gebert/*>

7. Sanderson Beck, '*Holiday Affair*', in *Movie Mirrors*, 2006. <*http://san.beck.org/MM/1949/HolidayAffair.html*>

8. Cameron.

9.   Bosley Crowther, '*Holiday Affair*, Tinsel-Trimmed Trifle
      With Mitchum and Janet Leigh, at State', in *The New
      York Times*, 24 November 1949.
      <*https://www.nytimes.com/1949/11/24/archives/holiday-
      affair-tinseltrimmed-trifle-with-mitchum-and-janet-leigh-
      at.html*>

10.   Kristen Lopez, '25 Days of Christmas: *Holiday Affair*', in
      Journeys in Classic Film, 11 December 2008.
      <*https://journeysinclassicfilm.com/2018/12/11/25-days-of-
      christmas-holiday-affair-1949/*>

11.   Iain Stott, '*Holiday Affair*', in *An Evening Illuminated*, 12
      December 2012.
      <*http://artemisnt.blogspot.com/2012/12/holiday-affair-
      1949.html*>

12.   Gary Loggins, 'Christmas Confection: *Holiday Affair*', in
      Cracked Rear Viewer, 23 December 2015.
      <*https://crackedrearviewer.wordpress.com/2015/12/23/ch
      ristmas-confection-holiday-affair-rko-1949/*>

13.   Andy Kaiser, '*Holiday Affair*', in *Andy's Film Blog*, 21
      December 2012.
      <*http://filmreviewsnsuch.blogspot.com/2012/12/holiday-
      affair.html*>

14.   David Cornelius, 'Warner Brothers Classic Holiday Collec-
      tion, Vol. 2', in *DVD Talk*, 11 November 2008.
      <*https://www.dvdtalk.com/reviews/35677/warner-
      brothers-classic-holiday-collection-vol-2/*>

12

The Lemon Drop Kid (1951)

Paramount Pictures / Hope Enterprises

Director: Sidney Lanfield
Producer: Robert L. Welch
Screenwriters: Edmund L. Hartmann, Robert O'Brien and
Frank Tashlin, with additional dialogue by Irving Elinson,
from a story by Edmund Beloin based on Damon Runyon's
original short fiction

THE New York underworld and Christmas movies may seem like an unusual amalgamation, but *The Lemon Drop Kid* proved that the festive season and organised crime in the big city could be a winning (if somewhat unlikely) combination nonetheless. While it is undeniably true that *The Lemon Drop Kid* hardly depicts gangland culture in the same way as Francis Ford Coppola's *The Godfather* (1972) – and, in spite of that latter film's own prominent Christmas-themed scenes, Bob Hope was certainly not Al Pacino – there was still a certain subversiveness in taking the season of goodwill and intermingling its upbeat tropes with that of the shady criminal world. The result would be one of the most humorous highlights of 1950s festive cinema.

The Lemon Drop Kid was based upon the work of journalist and prolific short story writer Damon Runyon, whose many colourful tales of gangsters, hustlers and gamblers – along with his idiosyncratic style of prose vernacular – made him one of the most distinctive figures in American literature during the early twentieth century. Though respected for his journalistic writing, working for various newspapers owned by the famous publishing mogul William Randolph Hearst, it is for his vivid, lively short fiction that Runyon has been best remembered, and he has become especially well-known for the stage musical *Guys and Dolls* (1950) which premiered four years after his death and was based on a number of his stories – most especially 'The Idyll of Miss Sarah Brown' and 'Blood Pressure'. The musical won the Tony Award for Best Musical, and has been revived many times over the years. Due to its success, it would later be adapted for the big screen as *Guys and Dolls* (Joseph L. Mankiewicz, 1955), a starry production featuring leading actors such as Frank Sinatra, Jean Simmons and Marlon Brando. While this film may well be the most recognisable adaptation of Runyon's work in popular culture, *The Lemon Drop Kid* was also successful enough with audiences to merit not one but two cinematic outings. The first, *The Lemon Drop Kid* (Marshall Neilan, 1934), featured a screenplay by Howard J. Green, J.P. McAvoy and Damon Runyon himself, and is reasonably faithful to the original source material. Starring Lee Tracy as Wally Brooks, the eponymous 'Lemon Drop Kid', along with Helen Mack, William Frawley and Minna Gombell, the film met with general critical approval but could not be considered a Christmas feature given its close fidelity to Runyon's prose tale. William Frawley was to be the only member of the original film's cast to appear in the later film, albeit in a different role.

The production of the 1951 version of *The Lemon Drop Kid* would experience some degree of behind-the-scenes turbulence before it appeared in cinemas. Produced by Bob Hope's own production company, Hope Enterprises, the film was envisaged as a star vehicle for the hugely popular comedy actor and entertainer. Sidney Lanfield was hired as director, having previously helmed films starring Hope such as *My Favorite Blonde* (1942), *Let's Face It* (1943) and *Where There's Life* (1947). Lanfield is, however, equally well-known for being the director of the famous Sir Arthur Conan Doyle adaptation *The Hound of the Baskervilles* (1939), which was to be the first onscreen pairing of Basil Rathbone's Sherlock Holmes and Nigel Bruce's Dr John Watson. He would later be nominated for a Primetime Emmy Award in 1964 for his well-received work on ABC's World War II comedy series *McHale's Navy* (1962-66). Lanfield left the production of *The Lemon Drop Kid* with only around two-thirds of the movie having been filmed, and directorial duties were then assigned to an uncredited Frank Tashlin – also one of the film's screenwriters – who set to work completing the movie with his customary creative drive. Tashlin was famous as an inventive animator and illustrator, having directed many Warner Bros. *Looney Tunes* cartoons and other short features, some of which involved

The Lemon Drop Kid (1951): Paramount Pictures/Hope Enterprises

live action puppetry. He would later go on to become a creatively industrious director of numerous motion pictures, with
his features including *Son of Paleface* (1952), *Susan Slept Here*
(1954), *Hollywood or Bust* (1956), *Bachelor Flat* (1961) and
The Alphabet Murders (1965). He was also a highly productive screenwriter, penning scripts for numerous films between
the 1940s and 1960s (sometimes uncredited). His screenwrit-
ing efforts saw him nominated three times for a Writers Guild
of America Award between 1949 and 1958, whereas his film
directing was twice nominated for the Top 10 Film Award by
Cahiers du Cinéma.

It's the second of December in sunny Florida, and at a
busy racetrack the infamous racing tout and general swindler
The Lemon Drop Kid (so called for his fondness for citrus-
flavoured hard candy treats) is trying with difficulty to keep
his fraudulent activities off the radar of vigilant patrolling
policemen. The sharp-suited, smooth-talking Kid (Bob Hope)
works his way around the spectators, acting as a tipster of
sorts as he poses in a variety of guises to make naïve onlookers
believe that he has valuable information about the horses'
chances. The credulous visitors offer to share their winnings
with him if the racing bet he advises is successful, little realising that he has done exactly the same thing for every horse in
the race (thus supposedly guaranteeing himself income for
nothing).

The Kid meets a woman who intends to enter a wager
in the race and convinces her to place her bet on the one remaining horse in his list. Unfortunately for him, she turns out
to be the girlfriend of infamous gangster Moose Moran (Fred
Clark), who knows the Kid's reputation as a swindler only
too well. Moran had asked his girlfriend to bet $2,000 on
what would have been the winning horse, and is livid that the

Kid had persuaded her at the last minute to gamble instead on the horse that would end up in last place. Realising his error too late, the Kid tries desperately to leave but discovers that he can't check out of the hotel he is staying in because the credit manager wants to have a few words with him. Before the Kid has any chance to talk his way out of his predicament, a couple of Moran's men arrive in the hotel lobby and tell him in no uncertain terms that their boss wants to see him immediately.

More than a little nervous, the Kid is brought to Moran's palatial residence and is perturbed by how well the gang leader has taken his losses – not just the $2,000 he lost on the horse bet, but the $10,000 in winnings that he would have gained if the Kid hadn't interfered. However, it is all an elaborate act; after the Kid is shown another of Moran's enemies being beaten up on the premises, he realises that he is in very deep trouble – not least when 'Sam the Surgeon' (Harry Bellaver) pretends to have extracted a diamond from the victim's innards, when in actual fact it had been hidden in the heel of the man's shoe. Moran warns the Kid that he wants his $10,000 back in full, or else he will make him pay for the consequences of his actions. Naturally the Kid doesn't have that kind of cash, or else he wouldn't be running small-time scams to make ends meet – but knowing that his life is in danger if he doesn't comply, he offers to raise the money in full by Christmas, now just a few weeks away. Moran realises that if he has the Kid murdered as an example to his adversaries, he will have to write off the entire $10,000 as a loss, but if he lets the Kid go then there is still a chance he can recoup his deficit. Reluctantly, Moran agrees to let the Kid head to New York City in the hope that he will be able to somehow devise a plan to gather all of the necessary funds. However, the gang boss warns him that there is no sense in trying to run – there is nowhere he can possibly go that he won't eventually be found. Moran intends to be in New York by Christmas, and tells the Kid plainly that he expects to be repaid no later than Christmas Eve. Any hint of failure will mean that the charismatic swindler won't live to see Christmas Day.

The Kid arrives in New York in the middle of a raging blizzard, and – still dressed for the warm weather of Florida – is forced to steal the coat of a passing Dachshund to stave off the freezing temperatures. He meets old acquaintance Nellie Thursday (Jane Darwell), an elderly newspaper-seller who is having difficulty with her landlord over substantial unpaid rent. Nellie is delighted to see the Kid, not least as he owes her money. Unfortunately for her, he not only lacks the funds to repay her but was actually hoping to borrow even more money so that he can retrieve his winter clothing from a pawn shop. Nellie's husband Henry, a highly proficient safe-cracker, is set to be released from prison on Christmas Eve after a long stretch of incarceration, and she is desperate to raise the funds necessary to get the landlord off her back. She had planned to move to a residential home once Henry leaves prison, but her application was disregarded due to her husband's criminal record and thus she needs to hold on to her existing apartment at all costs.

Eventually the Kid looks up 'Brainey' Baxter (Marilyn Maxwell), an old flame who still lives in the neighbourhood. Brainey's affections for him remain undimmed, even though he had abruptly disappeared six months earlier when he was on the trail of a choice scam opportunity in Florida. While Brainey is under no illusions about the Kid's tendency towards tall tales and fast-talking, he tries to convince her that he is a reformed character and even offers to marry her – emphasising that all he needs is $10 for a marriage licence. She readily comes up with the cash, and he races off back into the snow... so that he can use the money to buy back his winter wardrobe.

Next, the Kid pays a visit to Oxford Charlie (Lloyd Nolan), a local crime boss who owns a nightclub nearby. Charlie is having major problems with unpaid taxes, however, and his accountant is struggling to come up with solutions. Thus when the Kid turns up with talk of a new hustle he has devised, which he invites Charlie to buy into (for the conveniently round figure of $10,000), his old contact has no hesitation in having him ejected from the building. As he is leaving, the Kid passes a volunteer who is dressed as Santa Claus, raising money for charity with a metal pot on a street corner. This sight immediately gives the Kid an idea.

Some time later, the Kid has somehow managed to acquire a rather sorry-looking Santa suit (complete with straggly false beard) and is merrily soliciting funds from the public for an undisclosed cause – i.e. to finance his own needs. However, he is recognised by a passing beat cop (Harry Shannon) and promptly arrested for panhandling. Taken to court, the Kid is unable to afford the $50 fine (the public donations he wrongfully collected are to be given to a real charity) and thus is sentenced to ten days' imprisonment. Knowing how little time he has left to repay Moran, the thought of being out of operation for so long leaves him in a state of mild panic. As he leaves the courtroom, he meets Nellie who is being ushered into the next hearing – she has been apprehended by her landlord after sneaking back into her apartment after eviction to reclaim some of her belongings. The Kid sympathises with her plight, but is already in enough trouble of his own.

Allowed one phone call, the Kid gets in touch with Brainey to let her know of his predicament. As she works as a singer and dancer at Oxford Charlie's nightclub and is in the midst of a rehearsal, she is unable to come straight to his aid, and mocks the Kid's usual dishonesty (given that as far as she was aware, he was supposed to be obtaining a marriage licence rather than impersonating a charity volunteer). However, she secures a $50 advance on her wages from Charlie and comes to the Kid's aid; after he has had the chance to believe that he has finally had his comeuppance, she bails him out.

Before the Kid can be released from his cell in the police station, he is visited by Sam the Surgeon who warns him that he only has fifteen days left before Moran expects him to pay up in full – and there is no point trying to hide in prison, as Moran has plenty of associates on the inside. Thinking on his feet, the Kid explains that he has had a new plan. Moran owns a casino in the city which is currently abandoned. The Kid suggests that it be converted into a home for elderly residents such as Nellie, and he will then apply for a licence from the city to collect donations in order to fund the project. Naturally, of course, he will then use these public contributions to pay off Moran, meaning that all of the residents will be ejected from their home before Christmas. Even the hard-nosed Sam thinks this is a heartless scheme, but – given that it allows the Kid to enter the New Year alive rather than dead – the con man seems at peace with the idea.

Continuing to stall Brainey's desire for a marriage, the Kid immediately sets about enlisting new recruits to aid in his plan. He visits musclebound wrestler The Super Swedish Angel (Tor Johnson), gambler Straight Flush Tony (Jay C. Flippen) and mobster Gloomy Willie (William Frawley), amongst others, and manages to talk them all into helping him. The

Kid arrives at the police station in a limousine and picks up Nellie just as she is discharged from custody. He takes her to Moran's swanky casino, which she discovers – to her considerable surprise – has been converted into the 'Nellie Thursday Home for Old Dolls'. The Kid's associates have wasted no time in purloining items from around the city to convert the former gambling den into a comfortable residential home, and Nellie is touched by their apparent philanthropy. She is also surprised to learn that other occupants have already moved in – little realising that the Kid's contacts are actively rounding up elderly people to populate the new home (and thus making his 'cover story' seem all the more believable). Gambling tables are converted into comfortable beds for the residents using stolen wrestling mats and linen purloined from a hotel. While the new inhabitants are delighted with the comfortable surroundings, Nellie grows suspicious about the fact that the notoriously ruthless Moran would donate such an opulent building for the care of the elderly. However, before the issue can be discussed the residents are alarmed when the Kid – attempting to turn off the lights – accidentally hits the wrong switch and sends all of the beds/gambling tables (along with their occupants) careening into hidden compartments behind false walls. It turns out that a special mechanism has been fitted to the casino by Moran in order to hide all of the gambling apparatus from raids by the authorities. Brainey attempts to release the alarmed senior citizens but the bank of electric switches blows a fuse, meaning that the Kid's associates are forced to manually rescue them instead.

The next day, the Kid meets his partners-in-crime at Houlihan's Bar and discovers that the line-up of crooks and mobsters make the most belligerent and unlikely team of Santas imaginable. After a quick (and almost sincere) pep-talk, the Kid impresses on his cohorts the need to raise $10,000 before Christmas Eve – after all, the safety of the elderly residents depends on the generosity of the public. None of them suspect the Kid's true motive, which is simply to save his own neck. This time, however, there will be no risk of being apprehended by the law as the Kid has obtained all the necessary paperwork from the authorities; the Nellie Thursday Home is now a legitimate charitable organisation. While these dubious characters make a deeply unconventional gang of Jolly Old Saint Nicks as they spread across the city, they all get into the spirit of things and are soon racking up donations in their respective pots.

Brainey decides to take a short sabbatical from her job at the nightclub in order to watch over the Nellie Thursday Home until Christmas. Oxford Charlie agrees to her request, but is stunned when she tells him that the Kid and his cohorts have managed to raise $2,000 in just a couple of days. Desperate for money to pay off his own tax bills, Charlie decides to cut himself in to the Kid's scheme. Unknown to anyone, back at the casino/home the Kid is storing the donation money inside a hollow statue in the grounds to keep it away from prying eyes.

The following morning, Charlie and his men arrive at the casino in a pair of florists' vans. Reasoning that the Kid's charity is entitled the 'Nellie Thursday Home for Old Dolls', Charlie believes that the 'home' is technically anywhere that Nellie Thursday is resident. (In other words, if he relocates her to another dwelling, that then becomes the legitimate beneficiary of the donation money.) The Kid returns to the casino later to discover that it is deserted and the statue has been completely emptied of cash – much to his astonishment, given that he had revealed its location to no-one. However, when he spots oversized footprints in the snow he immediately suspects Oxford Charlie's involvement (as he knows nobody else in town with size 14 feet).

Knowing that his survival depends upon the retrieval of the donation money, the Kid and his associates drive out to Charlie's opulent mansion in Nyack to confront him. The Kid challenges Charlie to explain himself, little realising that the gangster has been speaking with Moran on a long-distance line to Florida. While the Kid demands the return of the donations and the residents (none of whom are happy with their sudden change of address), Charlie reveals that he knows the truth behind the Kid's ruse and explains the full scheme to all present. Nellie and the other residents are disappointed to hear of his duplicity, but the various allies who had volunteered to help him are all furious at having been taken for fools. Fully aware that Moran intends to deal with the Kid soon, Charlie makes an offer to the men – if they continue to operate as Santas and raise money for the bogus charity, he promises to deal them in on the proceeds.

The Kid manages to slip away from Charlie's property before the others can take their revenge, but Brainey catches up with him and expresses her revulsion at his treachery. The Kid tries to justify his actions, explaining that his head will be on the line if he doesn't devise some way of regaining his lost income. However, he acknowledges that he has no way of stealing the funds back from Charlie given the considerable resources that are available to him as an organised crime kingpin. Brainey is disgusted by his self-serving attitude, not least that he seems to care little for the fates of the elderly people he had gathered together to populate Nellie's home. She resolves to turn her back on him, claiming that he has played one con trick too many. With just over a week left until Mo-

347

ran will expect to be paid back, the Kid finds himself with neither allies nor any remaining semblance of a plan.

Christmas Eve arrives, and the Kid – now frantic as the hour of reckoning nears – visits a pawn shop in the hope of trading in some goods. He is amazed to meet Nellie there, who has managed to escape from Oxford Charlie's clutches and is trying to pawn her wedding ring in the hope of raising some much-needed cash before her husband is released from prison. Having a sudden attack of conscience, the Kid drags her away before she can part with her ring and tells her that he intends to steal back the donation cash from Charlie by any means possible. After all, with Moran breathing down his neck he now has nothing left to lose. Nellie is loath to trust him after his earlier dishonesty, but she cautions against an attempt to infiltrate the mansion; Charlie has many gangsters at his disposal, and they are all well-armed. Not to be out-done, however, the Kid suddenly hatches a plan and asks Nellie if she will help him to implement it.

Stealing clothing and a wig from a department store display window, the Kid arrives at Charlie's mansion under the pretence of being an elderly and destitute woman named Mrs Beazley who is in search of shelter. The Kid enters Charlie's inner sanctum just as the mobster is storing all of the donation money in a bag for transit; he intends to move all of the residents to a more secure location, and offers to take 'Mrs Beazley' with them (in order to avoid her reporting their location to the police). The Kid very nearly blows his cover, first by dropping a trademark box of lemon drops and then when he deliberately tries to exchange his handbag for Charlie's case of loot. His authenticity fares little better with the elderly residents when they discover that not only does he have a bag of wool and no understanding of how to knit, but also that he has a revolver stashed away in the same container.

As Charlie's men start to move the elderly women into vans for transit, the Kid slips away and confronts Charlie in his office. He tries to pull a gun on the double-dealing crime boss, but discovers to his horror that he has lifted the wrong bag and is thus unarmed. A fight ensues, and eventually the Kid overwhelms Charlie and makes off with the bag of cash. More by luck than design, he manages to evade Charlie's thugs and commandeers a bicycle so that he can get back to the city.

As night falls, the Kid meets Moran at his casino and hands over the $10,000 in full – much to the gangster's considerable surprise. Just as he has paid up, however, Charlie arrives and demands the full amount that was stolen from his mansion... which came to $16,000. Knowing that he can't repay both of them, the Kid discovers that he has fallen out of the frying pan and into the fire. Out of the blue, he hits a switch on the wall and suddenly gambling tables emerge from all of the room's hidden compartments. No longer beds intended for elderly residents, the tables are now fully set up for games of chance such as roulette and blackjack... and appear from the walls complete with croupiers and gamblers (including the women from Nellie's home, who have managed to escape Charlie's grasp in the chaos caused by the Kid). Moran is aghast, knowing that he is in danger of being charged with operating an illegal casino operation if the authorities become aware of what is happening. Sure enough, the Kid has arranged a police raid at exactly that moment, and Moran is taken into custody. Charlie fares no better, as a judge takes guardianship of the donation money and determines that it really will be contributed in full to the Nellie Thursday Home. He too is arrested.

Elated at having been spared a grisly fate, the Kid thanks the assembled 'gamblers' just as Nellie's husband Henry (Francis Pierlot) arrives – having finally been released from prison. The Thursdays are overjoyed at the reunion, not least as they know that they will have a secure home – against all odds. As it happens, Henry has returned at just the right time; the Kid wants to serve ice cream for the guests, and all of the silverware is stored in Moran's safe. After some persuasion, Henry agrees to put his legendary skills to the test... with explosive results. The Kid and Brainey are reconciled and, after his endless postponements and obfuscation, they finally agrees to marry. Brainey is suddenly dejected, realising that they don't have enough money to carry out the ceremony, but the Kid – always ready with an answer – assures her that he will pawn Moran's silverware as soon as everyone has finished their dessert.

One of the most immediately obvious aspects of *The Lemon Drop Kid* is its sharp deviation from the Runyon source material. The screenplay, by Edmund L. Hartmann, Robert O'Brien and Frank Tashlin, bears little in common with any aspect of the original story of the same name, save for the protagonist's name (plus his titular penchant for lemon drops) and his activities as a racetrack scam artist. As Thomas S. Hischak has explained: 'While still very funny, Damon Runyon's short story *The Lemon Drop Kid* has a very somber subtext and is one of the author's handful of touching tales. [...] The 1951 Paramount remake is a comic vehicle for Bob Hope and as such is very enjoyable but little of Runyon survived the transition'.[1] While the film is arguably a Bob Hope star vehicle first, a Christmas movie second and a Damon

Runyon adaptation in distant third place, this improbable fusion nonetheless proves to be a winning formula. Between the film's commendably daffy setups through to the unconventional characterisation (hard-hearted mobsters becoming oddly sentimental for the duration of the holiday season – though of course, only up to a point), *The Lemon Drop Kid* was suitably distinctive to stand out from the pack at the time of release. Yet for all the outlandish situations and flawless comic timing, the film also succeeds on account of its judicious restraint. James Plath notes that 'directors Sidney Lanfield and Frank Tashlin don't give Hope the same long leash to improvise and mug for the cameras as he normally has, but that's in keeping with the spirit and tone of the Damon Runyon tales. [...] Most of the humor is situational – a clever line here, or a wry remark there. But there's something in *The Lemon Drop Kid* that's endearing enough to make it a nice alternative to the usual Christmas movies that families watch together every holiday season'.[2]

The Lemon Drop Kid takes place over a lengthy period of the festive season (the story begins in early December and concludes on Christmas Eve), and it immediately establishes its tone with the Kid's wonderfully daft schemes for conning people who are placing bets at the racetrack in Florida; Hope's ability to instantly change tack, attitude and even accent is comedy gold. When the action moves to the sub-zero streets of New York, the Christmas ambiance really kicks in with abundant blizzards, cheerily-decorated shop windows and street corner Santa Clauses as far as the eye can see. The film has been noted for its inspired opening credits sequence, where props relevant to the film are featured as decorations on a Christmas tree – a clever motif that has been reprised in many later festive movies. And while, at its heart, *The Lemon*

Drop Kid is essentially a tale of personal redemption at Christmas, there is so much more to recommend it than this timeworn convention of the genre would suggest. While it is a Bob Hope movie first and foremost, the festive heart of the narrative is never forgotten or underplayed. As Jessica Pickens has observed: '*The Lemon Drop Kid* is your Bob Hope film with his usual and humorous jokes. One of my favorite "Bob Hope" jokes is when he steals a sweater from a dachshund to stay warm in the New York snow. But *The Lemon Drop Kid* stands a little apart from the rest of Hope's films. It's particularly heartwarming. For example, when Bob Hope sets up the old woman's home, he and Marilyn Maxwell tuck [in] all the old women and sing them a lullaby and it's adorable. [...] *The Lemon Drop Kid* isn't a mainstream Christmas film, but it's filled with the warmth and spirit of the holidays'.[3] Ultimately, the film provides convincing triumph over adversity, not just from the more nefarious criminal figures (who seek to use the apparent altruism of the Kid's schemes to further their own ends), but also from the trying social conditions of the time. The Kid may well be the most self-centred of con men, but even he gets caught up in the common humanity of the festive season; the Nellie Thursday Home is saved, ensuring that its elderly residents will have a secure home at a time when many were struggling with housing shortages and soaring rental fees, and the more malign gangsters are removed from the equation – thus ensuring that they will not be able to further jeopardise the safety of the vulnerable seniors. As Sanderson Beck remarks, 'this comedy satirizes the New York underworld by having them play opposite roles of charity workers. The Kid perpetually plays his cons, but somehow the final result is that the biggest gangsters are caught while the old ladies get the help they need'.[4]

The Lemon Drop Kid is especially well-known for introducing the song 'Silver Bells' to the world – even now a popular track during the holiday season. Composed by Jay Livingston and Ray Evans, the song was first recorded by Bing Crosby and Carol Richards in September 1950 with accompaniment by John Scott Trotter and his Orchestra, and the Lee Gordon Singers. However, it was for its cinematic debut in *The Lemon Drop Kid* that the song became famous, with Hope and Maxwell's rendition being recorded between July and August 1950 – just before the Crosby/Richards version was released by Decca Records. Livingston stated in a number of interviews that the song's lyrics were inspired by the sound of street corner Santa Clauses ringing their bells to encourage donations over the holiday period, thus fitting the film's action perfectly. When *The Lemon Drop Kid* premiered in March of the following year, it was to feature a more elaborate showcase for 'Silver Bells' than the original director, Sidney Lanfield, had intended. As Laura Grieve explains: 'Hope was dissatisfied with director Sidney Lanfield's static original staging of "Silver Bells". Frank Tashlin rethought the scene as a stroll through the city streets and directed what appears in the final film. The evocative, nostalgic sequence is beautifully done'.[5] In later years, Hope would adopt the track as his own personal Christmas song and performed it many times, not least as an annual tradition on his Christmas TV special (where it was usually performed as a duet with a guest star). As Robert Hornak expounds, the song's prominence and popularity was not without its humorous side too:

The movie's claim to fame, outside of being one of Hope's more start-to-finish solid outings, is having gifted the world with the now-traditional Christmas song 'Silver Bells'. It's always hard to imagine a song so ubiquitous ever having a start-dot on any timeline anywhere, much less that it would've sprung from an otherwise remote Bob Hope comedy. Asterisk: Hope, *et al,* intended a Christmas '50 release, but things went sideways and it was delayed till spring of '51. Meanwhile, Paramount smelled cash all over the song and gave it to Hope's *Road to* cohort, Bing Crosby, whose recording of it was an instant hit. Reshoots of the musical scene were ordered, with the longer version of the song – but to unknowing audiences, it must've appeared that Hope was hanging on Crosby's coattails. Who knows Hope's reaction to all this, but there must've been some glee in the fact that the first time we hear 'Bing's' warm-hearted holiday song, it's over a montage of crooks in fake Santa costumes bilking ill-gotten loot as a payout to a mobster.[6]

Vital to the success of *The Lemon Drop Kid* is, of course, the presence and performance of Bob Hope himself. Hope milks every scintilla of comic potential from the wily, silver-tongued Kid, brilliantly capturing the character's blind panic at the prospect of Moose Moran's revenge while capitalising on every scheme possible – no matter how bizarre – to make money as the Kid goes into swindle overdrive in an attempt to save his own neck. Hope's performance is full of many enjoyable moments, not least when emphasising the Kid's phobia of commitment and responsibility (his reluctance to get a nine-to-five job is so great, he has developed a kind of nervous tic at the very thought of it). From catching fleas from a stolen dog coat he purloined to stay warm in a glacial New York snowstorm to the out-and-out trickery during his street corner stint as Santa Claus, Hope clearly seems to relish the comic potential of the role and never ceases to make the most of it. In particular, his talent for physical comedy comes to the fore when desperately trying to realign the askew head of a statue (where the Kid has stashed his ill-gotten gains) without Brainey noticing – a masterpiece of silent dexterity – and his performance has such charm that it is easy to overlook occasions where credulity is stretched beyond breaking point (such as the stolen 'Mrs Beazley' costume, which just so happens to fit perfectly when it is pilfered from a shop window). There are also a number of inspired Bob Hope in-jokes throughout; one of the street corner Santas asks the Kid to 'put something in the pot', which riffed on a long-running gag from his hugely popular radio shows *The Pepsodent Show Starring Bob Hope* (1938-48) and *The Bob Hope Show* (1948-55), while the Kid – encountering a dairy cow that has been brought to the Nellie Thursday Home to provide cream for the residents' coffee – decides to call the wayward bovine 'Crosby', after Hope's friend and regular co-star Bing Crosby.

Hope was one of the most popular American comedians and comic actors of the twentieth century, starring in 54 feature films and appearing in many other short films and motion pictures. With a career that ran for almost eighty years, he became especially well-known in popular culture for the wildly popular *Road to* series of satirical comedy films which co-starred Bing Crosby and ran from 1940 to 1962. Also a talented singer, dancer and author, Hope was a consummate performer who never forgot his roots in vaudeville and stand-up comedy. He hosted the Academy Awards on nineteen separate occasions (still a record) and was recognised by the Academy with five honorary awards between 1940 and 1965. Hope was immortalised as a pop culture figure for his abiding love of golf and his many appearances in television specials (some 272 specials starring Hope were produced by NBC between 1950 and 1996). His many film performances included roles in *Thanks for the Memory* (George Archainbaud, 1938) (which introduced his perennial signature song of the same name), *The Ghost Breakers* (George Marshall, 1940), *My Favorite Blonde* (Sidney Lanfield, 1942), *The Paleface* (Norman Z. McLeod, 1948), *Fancy Pants* (George Marshall, 1950), *Paris Holiday* (Gerd Oswald, 1958) and *Bachelor in Paradise* (Jack Arnold, 1961), amongst a great many others.

The Lemon Drop Kid also featured many inspired supporting performances from actors such as Marilyn Maxwell – perhaps best-known at the time for films such as *Lost in a Harem* (Charles Reisner, 1944) and *Champion* (Mark Robson, 1949) – and Jane Darwell, whose touching performance seemed impossibly distant from the rambunctious Miss Florie in *Three Godfathers* (q.v.). With over a hundred film appearances in her long career, Darwell was particularly renowned for her Academy Award-winning performance in the famous John Steinbeck adaptation *The Grapes of Wrath* (John Ford, 1940), and as the gentle Bird Woman in *Mary Poppins* (Robert Stevenson, 1964). Strong support is also provided by Lloyd Nolan with his tongue-in-cheek turn as the scheming Oxford Charlie, and Fred Clark as the quietly menacing Moose Moran (a performance that oozes drolly-delivered intimidation). There is also a brief role for a legend of cult sci-fi, as Steve Sunday has indicated: 'You might have recognised one of the Santas – Tor Johnson (the huge bald one) went on to star in the 1959 Ed Wood movie *Plan 9 From Outer Space*, which is often called the worst movie ever made, and is so terrible it has become a cult classic'.[7]

Contemporary critics were divided over the effective-ness of *The Lemon Drop Kid* at the time of its release. *The New York Times*, for instance, was broadly convinced of the film's virtues, observing that 'Damon Runyon's old story, *The Lemon Drop Kid*, which was about a race track tipster who leaped from the frying-pan into the fire, has been given a pret-ty thorough shakedown under the capable hands of Bob Hope in the slapstick farce of the same title that came to the Para-mount yesterday. The consequent entertainment, populated throughout by Mr Hope, may be a far cry from Mr Runyon's story, but it's a close howl to good, fast, gag-packed fun'.[8] By contrast, the review in *Variety* was less persuaded by the movie's merits, opining that '*The Lemon Drop Kid* is neither true Damon Runyon, from whose short story of the same title it was adapted (story by Edmund Beloin), nor is it very funny Bob Hope. Although Hope is the principal interest and gets most of the laughs, his comedy style, and particularly his wise-cracking lines, are at the root of the picture's failure. It not only destroys the Runyonesque sentimental flavor but actual-ly pulls the props from under the inherent humor of the sto-ry'.[9] It should be said that in spite of this marked critical divi-sion, the film was a commercial success and performed very compellingly in cinemas.

The reputation of *The Lemon Drop Kid* has continued to grow in the decades since its release, with many critics in recent years approving of its offbeat charms. While the film has arguably become one of the lesser-seen festive features of the 1950s, Bob Hope's star billing and modern releases on home entertainment formats have nonetheless brought it to the attention of a whole new generation of viewers. Commen-tators such as Paul Mavis, for instance, have noted that the movie's fine balance of creative qualities have been key to its success: '*The Lemon Drop Kid* is [[a]] superior Hope vehicle, achieving a nice balance between a solid plot (based on a Damon Runyon short story), some funny set-pieces (many courtesy of co-director Frank Tashlin), a classic Christmas tune (the lovely 'Silver Bells'), and Hope's effortlessly amusing delivery of hilarious one-liners. Hope is a good fit here within the Runyon milieu, critically because he doesn't play up any of the material's inherent sentimentality. He's outwardly cynical and hard, even when he's putting up a genial front in order to con someone, and he correctly lets the audience pick out the humor and sweetness in the material, instead of delivering it to them on a plate with tears and meaningful looks'.[10] The finesse of Hope's comic portrayal of the Kid has been a common thread in much recent analysis of the film. Brian Orndorf is among the reviewers who have rated the film favourably within the context of Hope's wider filmography: '*The Lemon Drop Kid* is hardly an acting challenge for Hope, with the material playing to his strengths of sarcasm and light panic, mixing it up with co-stars and the elements, including one impressive physical gag that catches the Kid in heavy NYC winter winds, sliding backwards on the sidewalk. In fact, there are more than a few stunt-heavy gags in the effort, making *The Lemon Drop Kid* more active than the average Hope endeavor, offering a pronounced sense of screen energy'.[11]

Notes of scepticism regarding *The Lemon Drop Kid*'s effectiveness have tended to focus on areas of characterisation, such as – in Sunday's review of the film – the fact that the Brainey Baxter character's overwhelming attraction to the Kid causes her to be blind to his faults in ways which stretch credulity to breaking point: 'Brainy could have any man she wanted but she chooses a heartless and penniless con-man. Even after he steals her money (and her coat), and abandons

358

her, she still wants to marry him. They say love is blind, but in this case I think it was blind, deaf, and suffering from a concussion. It is only when ⟦the Kid⟧ is finally revealed as being behind the lowest and dirtiest tricks in the history of Christmas movies that she finally starts to question whether he is the man for her. Unethical scams aside, Bob Hope is really good in this'.[12] Overall, however, the film's good-natured tone and infectious sense of exuberant amusement have been the aspects that have attracted the appreciation of critics, including Derek Winnert: 'Hope is perfectly cast as Damon Runyon's cowardly, boastful, fast-talking hero in this very funny Paramount Pictures remake of a 1934 film of the same title. ⟦...⟧ A great gallery of support actors backs the star to satisfying effect and a handful of songs for Hope to sing rounds out the vintage fun'.[13] And interestingly, for all the film's well-regarded if relatively low-key reputation today, *The Lemon Drop Kid* was representative of a sea-change in cinematic comedy taking place in Hollywood at the time, meaning that its significance as a Christmas comedy film in particular may have been somewhat underemphasised in modern times. As Glenn Heath Jr. has explained:

Released at the tail-end of the screwball comedy era, *The Lemon Drop Kid* represents the genre at its most friendly and benign. The biting social critique of Preston Sturges and the elaborate verbal battles of Leo McCarey are noticeably absent in Sidney Lanfield's breezy tale. [...] Musical numbers, fast-motion chase scenes, characters in drag, and a final double-cross make *The Lemon Drop Kid* a constantly evolving series of genre conventions. The film can never seem to slow down and address anything close to serious, and Hope laps it up the entire time, tiptoeing around danger, avoiding long-term relationships, and finally poking fun at the absent Bing Crosby. Of course, in the end, the women of *The Lemon Drop Kid* regain order, tying the Kid down to a normal existence. Still, one can't help but get caught up in the juvenile insanity, and *The Lemon Drop Kid* reminds of a cinematic time where even the most heinous criminal acts had a sugary coating.[14]

During the Christmas of the film's year of release, Bob Hope would reprise his role as the Lemon Drop Kid in an hour-long Lux Radio Theater adaptation which was broadcast on 10 December 1951. This audio feature played perfectly to Hope's strengths as a performer of the spoken word, complementing his deserved reputation as one of America's biggest radio stars at the time, and helped to further accentuate the film's profile amongst the general public.

While *The Lemon Drop Kid* has not enjoyed the wide exposure and critical acclaim of many other Christmas films of the 1950s, its relative lack of conspicuousness is thankfully now being challenged thanks to greater awareness of its charms. Favourable reappraisals of the film in recent years have helped to reinvigorate its profile amongst aficionados of festive cinema, ensuring that its madcap energy is finding new fans almost seventy years after its initial release. With its captivating combination of fast-talking but genial hoodlums, kind-hearted showgirls, farcical situations and atmospherically chilly urban environments – to say nothing of a Christmas Eve conclusion that manages to provide a happy ending for just about everyone (bullying gang leaders notwithstanding), *The Lemon Drop Kid* is a treat for any cineaste nostalgic for a slice of silver screen comedy at its nuttiest and most appealing.

REFERENCES

1.   Thomas S. Hischak, *American Literature on Stage and Screen: 525 Works and Their Adaptations* (Jefferson: McFarland, 2012), p.119.

2.   James Plath, '*The Lemon Drop Kid*', in *Family Home Theater*, 13 July 2017.
    <*https://familyhometheater.com/2017/07/13/review-of-the-lemon-drop-kid-blu-ray/*>

3.   Jessica Pickens, 'Musical Monday: *Lemon Drop Kid*', in *Comet Over Hollywood*, 21 December 2015.
    <*https://cometoverhollywood.com/2015/12/21/musical-monday-lemon-drop-kid-1951/*>

4.   Sanderson Beck, '*The Lemon Drop Kid*', in *Movie Mirrors*, 2007.
    <*http://san.beck.org/MM/1951/LemonDropKid.html*>

5.   Laura Grieve, 'Tonight's Movie: *The Lemon Drop Kid*', in *Laura's Miscellaneous Musings*, 26 December 2011.
    <*https://laurasmiscmusings.blogspot.com/2011/12/tonights-movie-lemon-drop-kid-1951.html*>

6.   Robert Hornak, 'Blu-Ray Review: *The Lemon Drop Kid*', in *ZekeFilm*, 6 July 2017.
    <*http://www.zekefilm.org/2017/07/06/blu-ray-review-the-lemon-drop-kid-1951/*>

7.   Steve Sunday, '*The Lemon Drop Kid*', in *Black and White Movies*, 1 January 2017.
    <*https://black-and-white-movies.com/the-lemon-drop-kid/*>

8. Bosley Crowther, 'The Screen in Review: Bob Hope a Hapless Race-Track Tout in *The Lemon Drop Kid* Opening at Paramount', in *The New York Times*, 22 March 1951.
    <*https://www.nytimes.com/1951/03/22/archives/the-screen-in-review-bob-hope-a-hapless-racetrack-tout-in-the-lemon.html*>

9. Anon., '*The Lemon Drop Kid*', in *Variety*, 31 December 1950.
    <*https://variety.com/1950/film/reviews/the-lemon-drop-kid-1200416853/*>

10. Paul Mavis, '*The Bob Hope Collection*', in *DVD Talk*, 7 December 2010.
    <*https://www.dvdtalk.com/reviews/45799/bob-hope-collection-the/*>

11. Brian Orndorf, '*The Lemon Drop Kid*', in *Blu-Ray.com*, 4 July 2017.
    <*https://www.blu-ray.com/movies/The-Lemon-Drop-Kid-Blu-ray/173529/#Review*>

12. Sunday.

13. Derek Winnert, '*The Lemon Drop Kid*', at *Derek Winnert.com*, 14 July 2019.
    <*http://www.derekwinnert.com/the-lemon-drop-kid-1951-bob-hope-marilyn-maxwell-lloyd-nolan-jane-darwell-william-frawley-classic-movie-review-8705/*>

14. Glenn Heath Jr., 'DVD Review: *The Lemon Drop Kid*', in *Slant*, 18 October 2010.
    <*https://www.slantmagazine.com/dvd/the-lemon-drop-kid/*>

Scrooge (1951)

George Minter Productions

Director: Brian Desmond Hurst
Producer: Brian Desmond Hurst
Screenwriter: Noel Langley

S CROOGE remains among the most famous of all British-produced Christmas movies. With its unparalleled central performance, it would not only prove to be the apex of the United Kingdom's contribution to the genre in the 1950s but remains even today one of its best-loved and most enduring festive features. If the late forties had introduced films with a common theme of the power of Christmas to transform attitudes and lives, the early fifties would present audiences with a number of films which typified the ability of the holiday season to improve individual viewpoints for the better, and in lasting ways. *Scrooge* was to be the first of many adaptations of Charles Dickens's *A Christmas Carol* to grace cinema screens in the post-war period, and arguably one of the most effective ever produced. It has become, for many people, one of the very finest versions of the story ever to be committed to celluloid, in no small part due to the bravura performance of Alastair Sim who, in one of his best-known roles, came to set the benchmark by which all future evocations of the Ebenezer Scrooge character would be held up. As Kate Carnell Watt and Kathleen C. Lonsdale have rightly asserted, 'Sim's performance as Scrooge remains the standard by which all others are judged'.[1]

Although Brian Desmond Hurst's *Scrooge* has now come to be considered one of the most successful of all adaptations of Dickens's festive tale, it was by no means the first to appear in cinemas. Earlier decades had seen the release of numerous film versions of *A Christmas Carol* – both silent and with audio tracks – which had included Harold M. Shaw's *A Christmas Carol* (1914), Rupert Julian's *The Right to Be Happy* (1916), Henry Edwards's *Scrooge* (1935), and – perhaps most notably – Edwin L. Marin's *A Christmas Carol* (1938), which featured a memorable turn from Reginald Owen as Dickens's famously short-tempered miser. Yet Hurst's rendering of *Scrooge* was a very far-reaching and detailed adaptation with great attention to period detail, and one which added layers of dimension to the character of Dickens's legendary skinflint in a way that so few other variations on the tale have managed to equal either before or since. Also active as a producer, Brian Desmond Hurst began his directorial career in 1934 with *The Tell-Tale Heart* and was a prolific filmmaker throughout the thirties and forties, helming popular features including *Riders to the Sea* (1935), *Prison Without Bars* (1938), *The Lion Has Wings* (1939), *Dangerous Moonlight* (1941) and *Theirs is the Glory* (1946). He remained involved in the world of film until the early sixties, but in the view of many commentators *Scrooge* would always remain his greatest creative accomplishment. Such has been the interest in his directorial career, including significant scholarly accounts of his work, Hurst is now regarded as one of Northern Ireland's finest film directors.

The story of *A Christmas Carol* has become arguably the most instantly recognisable of all festive tales not related to the actual Nativity, and has become so immediately familiar through its many appearances in film and on television (to say nothing of radio, audiobooks and even computer games) that to attempt any but the most brief of synopses seems like a rather redundant endeavour. There can be only a few who are unaware of the details of Dickens's account – first published by Chapman and Hall in 1843 – of the covetous, tight-fisted businessman Ebenezer Scrooge. As Chale Nafus explains:

> Like so many of [Dickens's] works, *A Christmas Carol* was written from the heart and personal experiences or observations. [...] His prior novel *Martin Chuzzlewit* was not selling well, and Dickens wanted to earn enough money to take his family to Italy. A charming Christmas tale might just be the answer to his needs. Inspired to pen 'a cheerful, glowing, heart-moving story in which he would appeal to all of people's warmest feelings', he threw himself into his writing. Beginning in mid-October, he emerged six weeks later with *A Christmas Carol in Prose, Being a Ghost Story of Christmas*, a 69-page manuscript. The 6000 copies of the first edition sold out the very first day of distribution.[2]

While *A Christmas Carol* has become famous for many reasons – as a Victorian ghost story, a fantasy of the festive season, a proto-science fiction (or even early time travel) tale, and as perhaps the most famous of all Dickens's short works – it arguably remains best-known in popular culture for his evocation of the complex, penny-pinching character at the heart

of the narrative, Mr Ebenezer Scrooge. As Carlo DeVito has
elucidated, Dickens brought the character so vividly to life
partly because of real-life influences, and also on account of his
own personal reaction to the many disagreeable attitudes that
Scrooge holds: 'Who would give Scrooge his voice? Dickens
turned to men he loathed. He turned to men with whom he
violently disagreed. There were several men whom Dickens
used to put words into Scrooge's mouth. He based the miserly
part of Scrooge's character on a noted British eccentric and
miser named John Elwes [...] and it is popularly thought that
Scrooge's opinions and comments on the poor of London were
based on those of demographer and political economist Thomas Malthus'.[3] Single-mindedly obsessed with the pursuit of
wealth while simultaneously contemptuous of the poor and
needy, Scrooge's fixation on commerce at the expense of human concerns makes him cold-hearted and disdainful towards

Scrooge (1951): George Minter Productions

even the faintest notion of joy and charity. Yet it is the celebrated and all-encompassing transformation of his character
that has made the tale so memorable that it has endured over
the centuries since its inception.

Ebenezer Scrooge (Alastair Sim) is a money-lender in
Victorian London with a heart of ice and a reputation for
ruthlessness. Leaving the London Exchange on a snowy
Christmas Eve, he encounters some other businessmen (Peter
Bull and Douglas Muir) and makes known his utter contempt
for the festive season, reinforcing their view of him as a hu-
mourless pinchpenny. Scrooge's offices still bear the signage of
'Scrooge and Marley', though his erstwhile business partner
died on Christmas Eve some years prior. As the day's events
unfold, Scrooge coldly refuses all forbearance to a debtor who
owes him money (Clifford Mollison), refusing to take into
account the severity of the man's personal circumstances, and
similarly declines to make a charitable donation when volunteers (Noel Howlett and Fred Johnson) come calling in support of the needy at Christmas, instead asserting that the poor
already have a clear choice: prison, a workhouse, or death.
Watching all of this frosty indifference with horror is
Scrooge's diffident but good-natured clerk, Bob Cratchit
(Mervyn Johns). Later, Scrooge is visited by his ebullient
nephew Fred (Brian Worth), who invites him – as he does
every year – to join him and his wife for dinner on Christmas
Day. However, Scrooge aloofly turns down the offer (as he
always does), pouring scorn not only on the holiday season
but also on his nephew's choice of marital partner.

With supreme reluctance, Scrooge grudgingly accepts
Cratchit's reasoning that if he opens his offices on Christmas
Day there will be no-one to conduct business with, and thus
the hapless clerk is allowed one day's leave with pay – albeit

that Scrooge expects him back earlier than usual on Boxing Day. The offices are closed at end of business, and Scrooge retires to a cheap restaurant before heading back to his austere home. As he gains entry, however, he is shocked when he sees his door-knocker transform into the ghostly visage of Marley (Michael Hordern), even though his old partner has been dead for seven years. He tries to pass off the experience as a mere hallucination, but later that evening – as he eats a meagre supper – Marley appears as an apparition and beseeches Scrooge to change his ways. In life, Marley had been as covetous and cruel as his business partner, but now in the afterlife he is cursed to walk the earth for eternity, confined by unbreakable chains that were forged by his greed and mercilessness in life. Now all he can do is try to convince Scrooge to reform his behaviour before he joins him in the same fate. In an attempt to bring about this transformation of character, he warns that three ghosts will visit Scrooge that night – the first to arrive at one o'clock.

Sure enough, when the clock chimes the allotted hour Scrooge is faced with the arrival of the Spirit of Christmas Past (Michael Dolan), who explains to Scrooge that they will be visiting his past in an attempt to pinpoint the root cause of his present attitudes. They pass through the years to Scrooge's boarding school days, where a young Ebenezer (George Cole) is neglected by his father, who indirectly blames the boy for the death of his wife (Scrooge's mother having died in childbirth) and deliberately keeps him at a distance. The boy Scrooge therefore feels unwanted and becomes remote but invested in his studies. His beloved sister Fan (Carol Marsh) unexpectedly visits him at school and explains that he can now return home, claiming that their father's attitude has now changed for the better.

Years later, Scrooge is working for the jovial merchant Mr Fezziwig (Roddy Hughes), his first employer whom he warmly remembers. Fezziwig is organising a Christmas party for his staff, and Scrooge – though he did not realise it at the time – now reflects with amazement that the jolly man was able to bring about a great deal of happiness at next to no expense. Visiting another occasion from his early life, Scrooge witnesses his engagement to his beautiful, kind-hearted fiancée Alice (Rona Anderson). She is able to accept him for who he is, thus setting right the emotional sense of rejection that derives from his isolation in early life.

However, Scrooge's character takes a turn for the worse when he is encouraged to leave Fezziwig's employ and join the business of the sinister Mr Jorkin (Jack Warner), who lures him into his service with the promise of greater wealth and new opportunities. Jorkin is the diametric opposite of Fezziwig, with no regard for individual lives – he sees the world as an essentially heartless and uncaring place, and financial gain as the only reasonable aim in life. Some time later, Fan lies on her deathbed, but Scrooge – now under the spell of monetary acquisition at all costs – refuses to play any part of the upbringing of her infant son Fred. The older Scrooge is dumbfounded at his younger self's callousness and implores the dying Fan to forgive him. But the scene is merely a memory, and she can hear none of his pleas – no matter how heartfelt they may be.

While working in a clerical post for Jorkin's business, Scrooge meets a young Jacob Marley (Patrick Macnee), and the pair realise that their respective worldviews have much in common. They become fast friends, and over time they eventually pool their resources and business acumen to buy Fezziwig's business, replacing his company sign with their own.

Scrooge feels that his career is advancing, but Alice is heart-broken at his increasing avarice and emotional insensitivity. She ends their engagement, realising that he can never love her nearly as much as he does the pursuit of money. The younger Scrooge seems dispassionate about the situation, sensing an opportunity to rid himself of another distraction from his acquisitive aims, but his older self feels the loss of Alice's affections anew – and ever more acutely.

Over the years, Scrooge and Marley's wealth – and greed – continue to increase sharply. They become members of the Board of Directors at the Amalgamated Mercantile Society, and – with some shrewd financial judgement – save the company from closure after Jorkin's long-term misappropriation of funds have left it on the verge of collapse. They thus not only rescue it from insolvency, but also take a controlling interest as a result. Years later, Marley is on the point of death, but Scrooge refuses to be with him for his final hours as he will not allow any diversions from his business activities. When he finally comes to Marley's bedside after working hours, he finds that his only friend has died before he could reach him. Rather than lament his old partner's passing, however, the unsentimental Scrooge wastes no time in securing Marley's capital and property for himself.

Witnessing his own deterioration from an optimistic young man into a cold-hearted, grasping skinflint – many years passing by in a matter of minutes – Scrooge finds himself with regrets and far-reaching questions about his choices in life. He barely has time to register his return home before he encounters the Spirit of Christmas Present (Francis de Wolff). This spectral entity intends to show Scrooge how Christmas should be celebrated – not alone in a cold, empty house, but in the company of friends and family. Though unseen, they visit the

Cratchit family on Christmas Day and discover a loving, caring household full of fun and happiness, even though their income is meagre. Having regarded Cratchit as little more than a mechanism rather than a human being, Scrooge is taken aback to discover what a devoted father and husband the man is. Cratchit and his wife (Hermione Baddeley) have a large family for which they have provided admirably given their poverty, and their sense of cheerful contentment that Christmas Day is infectious. Scrooge is chastened when the family refuse to toast his health, as they know too well how badly the miser treats his employees. He also grows concerned about the Cratchits' youngest child, Tiny Tim (Glyn Dearman), who has mobility problems and has fallen ill with severe pulmonary issues (possibly consumption, now known as tuberculosis). Scrooge asks the Spirit if Tim is likely to survive his affliction, and it is implied that – unless things change – this will not be the case.

Next, the Spirit takes Scrooge to visit Fred and his wife (Olga Edwardes), who are enjoying the festivities with friends. They are hosting a lively dinner party, and Scrooge discovers that while the Cratchits were resentful of his dictatorial behaviour, here he is being treated as a figure of ridicule in his absence. To Scrooge's surprise, Fred continually defends his uncle from the jibes that are being directed at him. Given Scrooge's constant denigration of Fred, he is touched and somewhat humbled by the younger man's sense of decency and fair-play. After this, Scrooge is taken to see the much-older Alice – his one-time fiancée, with whom he has had no contact since the failure of their relationship. She is now helping the sick and destitute at a workhouse, essentially fulfilling the reverse role of Scrooge in society (given that his business interests rely upon preying on the vulnerable).

The Spirit next shows Scrooge two emaciated, ailing children – Ignorance and Want – and warns that they should be avoided at all costs. Scrooge is puzzled by the apparently metaphorical beings, asking why they have no sanctuary, but the Spirit turns his earlier words against him – his haughty dismissal of the poor and needy as being fit only for incarceration, seclusion or death. Scrooge is now fully aware of the malice of his words and runs from the scene, partly in fear but mostly in shame. Soon enough, he encounters the final ghost – the Spirit of Christmas Yet to Come (Czeslaw Konarski).

This third Spirit does not speak, but rather silently indicates events that have yet to transpire. Scrooge is shown a future Christmas at the Cratchit family where everyone is in mourning at the death of Tiny Tim; they are all clearly broken-hearted at the young boy's demise, but nonetheless are bravely trying to retain some aspect of the festive spirit in spite of their obvious sense of loss. Scrooge is appalled to see what has happened. Next, he sees a recently-deceased person's paltry belongings being pawned at a pawnbroker's shop for a derisory amount of money and slowly realises that they are his own possessions. Businessmen from the London Exchange debate over whether they should attend Scrooge's funeral, but reflect that it is unlikely that anyone else will be there. One of them sardonically comments that they would only be attending if a lunch was being provided afterwards, knowing all too well Scrooge's reputation for penny-pinching in life. Finally, Scrooge is shown his own grave, which is ignored and abandoned, and realises that he will die unloved and unworthy of remembrance – thus following in the footsteps of Marley. Overcome with grief, not just for himself but for the wasted potential of his life, he desperately pleads for the opportunity to change his attitudes and behaviour forever.

To his amazement, Scrooge awakens in his own bed on Christmas morning, realising that his supernatural experiences had all taken place on the one single night. Realising that he has no time to spare, he encounters his housekeeper Mrs Dilber (Kathleen Harrison) and gives her a Christmas gift of a guinea – as well as a promise to raise her salary by 500%. After years of his morose, self-centred behaviour, she is terrified by his abrupt change in attitude, fearing that he has taken leave of his senses. Scrooge then arranges to have a large turkey delivered to the Cratchits' house in time for Christmas dinner. The family are amazed by this anonymous present; only Tiny Tim suspects its true source, but the family can't accept that Scrooge would be capable of an act of kindness – especially such an extravagant one.

Scrooge arrives unannounced at Fred's dinner party, which plays out very differently from the version shown to him by the Spirit earlier. The former misanthrope now becomes the life and soul of the party, joining in with the evening's entertainment, and his nephew is stunned and elated at the total alteration of his manner. Now Scrooge is no longer the butt of the other guests' jokes, but a welcome presence among their number. The next morning, he arrives very early at Bob Cratchit's front door and petrifies the clerk by threatening to fire him for being slightly late for work. However, it soon becomes clear that he is only joking, and the reformed miser offers his amiable employee a long-overdue raise in his salary – as well as a promise that he will help to support his family. As the film ends, we discover that Tiny Tim not only recovered from his illness but also regained his mobility as well – and all of this on account of the benevolence of Scrooge, who eventually became like a second father to the young boy.

There are two main factors which set Hurst's *Scrooge* apart from previous adaptations of *A Christmas Carol*: the immense quality of Alastair Sim's lead performance, and the way in which Dickens's famous story is further developed by screenwriter Noel Langley in order to deepen the viewer's understanding of Scrooge's motivations. As Fred Guida noted in his landmark study of the many adaptations of *A Christmas Carol*, Hurst's *Scrooge* is particularly noteworthy in the fact that it goes to great lengths to examine the seminal influences which came to define Scrooge's character and, while the screenplay observes the way in which the character's driving force in life is shaped by this formative stimulus, it never dominates proceedings to the expense of all else: 'Scrooge's life is not the sole dimension of the film. It may indeed be the screen's first psychological *Carol*, but director Brian Desmond-Hurst and screenwriter Noel Langley (who was one of the screenwriters of *The Wizard of Oz*) have skillfully integrated both Scrooge and his past into a beautifully balanced effort'.[4] Much of this is detailed in subtle deviations from, and embellishments to, the original source material. Langley's screenplay provides an explanation of Scrooge's departure from his employment with the jovial Mr Fezziwig, introducing a new scenario which describes his corruption by another businessman – Jack Warner's Mr Jorkin – who, in concert with Marley, Scrooge eventually proceeds to usurp. (Jorkin's professional attitudes seem foregrounded in those of the hard-nosed, utilitarian school board superintendent Thomas Gradgrind from Dickens's 1854 novel *Hard Times*, as he has more in common with this character than the similarly-named but comparatively timid 'Mr Jorkins' of the celebrated 1850 book *David Copperfield*.) The details of Scrooge's birth are also changed, with his sister Fan – originally his younger sibling in the novella –

now becoming older than Ebenezer, while it is explained that Scrooge's mother had died during his birth, providing some explanation for the otherwise-ambiguous antipathy between Scrooge and his resentful father. As Fan is depicted in the film as dying as a result of Fred's birth, this same irrational antagonism is eventually passed on to uncle and nephew. Also, the breakdown of Scrooge's romance with his fiancée Alice (named Belle in Dickens's book) is made all the more poignant by revealing that, after she ends their engagement due to Scrooge's increasingly unmanageable greed, she devotes her life to caring for the destitute – a goal that would have been anathema to the unreformed Ebenezer. Intriguingly, Alice's late-in-the-day appearance at the workhouse suggests the subtlest hint of a possible reconciliation between her and Scrooge – a prospect rarely mentioned in other versions of the tale.

In the hands of a less able screenwriter, any changes to Dickens's eminently well-known story may have led to disaster, but taken collectively the embellishments added by Langley enhance the already compelling nature of a narrative which is so intimately concerned with redemption and transformation. As Andy Webb has observed:

What in a way makes [*Scrooge*] so good is that it makes Ebenezer's journey so interesting and unlike other versions really explains not only his transition from miser to Christmas joy giver but his initial transition into becoming a miser. As such almost half the movie is given over to Ebenezer being taken to his past and we not only see the usual elements of him falling in love and becoming obsessed with money making but we also see the death of his sister, learn of his issues with his father and see him joining forces with

Marley. And all of this combines to allow us to understand that following the death of his sister Fan he became hard and cold to protect himself from more heartbreak. He threw himself into work and saw making money as a way of protecting himself from the world, becoming emotionless out of self preservation rather than just being mean. But we also see how that self preservation transforms into an almost sadistic nastiness giving him pleasure from being curmudgeonly.[5]

Few other adaptations of A Christmas Carol have gone to such lengths to present Jacob Marley as a living, breathing human being – complete with dimensions of character and malign, avaricious purpose – as well as in his more familiar guise as a wailing, chain-rattling spectre. Indeed, while Scrooge has naturally always been the central figure of any adaptation of Dickens's tale, Hurst's film is at pains to develop supporting characters such as Fred, Fan and even Fezziwig with greater clarity than has been offered by many later variations on the story. The result is that Scrooge's character is fleshed out in a much more persuasive way, making his eventual conversion to morally responsible behaviour all the more convincing. As Sanderson Beck has remarked, 'this famous parable of Christmas challenges the tendency to get up caught up in materialistic efforts while losing contact with feelings that guide us to help people other than ourselves',[6] and certainly Hurst's adaptation is never less than diligent in its efforts to articulate Scrooge's ethical transformation in a more thoughtful and believable way than many other cinematic variations on the traditional Dickensian tale.

It is all too easy today to overlook the sharp contemporaneity of A Christmas Carol at the time of publication; while it may seem permanently preserved in a very specific historical context for modern readers, Dickens's moral concerns were very immediate when the novella first made its way into the hands of bibliophiles in 1843. As Michael Zupan has noted, the ethical core of the story which Dickens articulates with such heartfelt panache has retained its universal relevance not only on account of the tale's immortalisation within popular culture, but also because its warnings about elevating materialism over social responsibility have never lost their central significance: 'For me, the greatest achievement of *A Christmas Carol*, is that for a story that so blatantly takes the moral high ground on greed, corruption, and just simply being kind to your fellow man in general, it doesn't come off as being overly preachy. I instantly disconnect with any film that makes me feel like there's an enormous imaginary finger being maliciously pointed at me, but that never happens with Dickens' classic tale. Sure, the message is there so all of us can benefit from it, but the audience doesn't have to internalize that message as guilt, because they're simply observing the message as it's being conveyed to Scrooge by the spirits of Christmas past, present, and future'.[7] As Zupan suggests, the immediacy of Dickens's moral apprehensions are such that they have never worn thin for all their heightened familiarity; his earnest entreaty to live a principled and humane life continues to ring out even in the modern day. The profound realisation on Scrooge's part – that the very materialism which has consumed him cannot offer him the defence he seeks from what he perceives to be a hostile and essentially deceitful society – is expressed particularly well by Langley's screenplay, allowing not only for the intense emotional insight of Scrooge's enlightenment but also amplifying his euphoria when he realises that he has been offered one last, unexpected chance to set things right. Phyllis Strupp observes that 'the ghosts showed Scrooge that his wealth would not protect him from the world's sordid reproach after all – others would use his death as an opportunity to carry off his beloved possessions. He would be mourned by no one. [...] Galvanised by this grim portrait, Scrooge finally accepted that he had a choice in the matter. He experienced a profound *metanoia* and decided to change his life's course. He awakened on Christmas morning a new man, joyfully determined to use his wealth to help other people'.[8] Few other adaptations of *A Christmas Carol* have quite so successfully articulated Scrooge's dismissive yet strangely plaintive exclamation of 'humbug' as expressing his derision towards festive good cheer, which he regards as little more than a superficial attempt to deceive. He has little concern as to whether festive well-wishers are lying to themselves or attempting to lie to others; all that matters to him is that he will not allow himself to be likewise hoodwinked. Because Scrooge perceives the world solely in terms of practical industry and acquisition of wealth (though not material wellbeing – witness his austere lifestyle and ascetic, unadorned home), he has come to regard any kind of jollity or altruism as essentially bogus, and has nothing more than contempt for anyone who appears to take a contrary view. Unable to place his trust in other people, he has discovered that he can have reliable confidence in his ledger book alone – he finds a kind of honesty in hard figures that he believes is singularly missing from society at large. Hurst's version of the story brings this fact to life even more vividly than other variations had done, due to its closer observation of Scrooge's developmental process – both in professional and psychological terms. As Jeffrey M. Anderson has astutely reflected:

Of all the direct adaptations of Charles Dickens' slim 1843 novel, this one has earned the near unanimous distinction of being the best. Part of the reason is the perfect pacing from director Brian Desmond Hurst. Many versions of *A Christmas Carol* are too truncated while others drag on far too long. This one moves through a brisk 86 minutes with just enough time to linger on poignant moments. Another factor is the superb performance by Alastair Sim [...] whose Ebenezer Scrooge never shows a hint of villainy. His miserliness comes from anger, loss, hatred and sadness, but never evil. When he heads home for Christmas Eve, he stops for dinner at a pub. He orders more bread, but upon learning that it will cost him extra, he cancels the order. He looks annoyed, but also unbearably sad, as if that bread could somehow have brought him great happiness.[9]

The success of any adaptation of *A Christmas Carol* rests almost entirely upon the strength of its lead actor, and in the opinion of a vast majority of critics – both now and at the time of release – Alastair Sim was to establish quite simply the most convincing evocation of Ebenezer Scrooge ever to be committed to film. As Nafus has commented: 'Adhering to a faithful adaptation, [Hurst] was able to create the classic version of *A Christmas Carol* (retitled for the American market). He was aided by a cast of priceless character actors. The often expressionistic, *noir*-ish cinematography of C.M. Pennington-Richards provided the chills of a horror film. But it was Alastair Sim's note-perfect performance as the avaricious businessman Ebenezer Scrooge that ensured the film's perfection'.[10] From his short-tempered, cantankerous first appearance all the way through to Scrooge's joyous realisation that he has achieved a redemption he would never have believed possible (and, indeed, would never before have even considered seeking), Sim throws himself completely into the performance of a lifetime, and it is no surprise that – in the eyes of commentators such as Zupan – his presentation of the character has become the benchmark by which all subsequent performances have been judged: 'Alastair Sim is the best Scrooge I've ever had the pleasure of seeing. Most other actors who have played the bah-humbugger merely appeared to be grumpy old men, but Sim? I could feel the ice emanating from his skin, and I was chilled even further by the emptiness in his soulless eyes. For the first time in a very long time, I didn't feel as if I was watching a mediocre stage version of *A Christmas Carol* shot on film. I bought Sim's portrayal as Scrooge like no other, and this justified the rest of the story in its entirety in far more engrossing ways than I've ever bared witness to'.[11] Sim had been known to British cinemagoing audiences since the mid-1930s, having worked previously as a lecturer in elocution at the University of Edinburgh and then as a stage actor, being particularly well-known for his time performing at London's Old Vic. He became a much-loved performer throughout the United Kingdom, being cast in a wide variety of comedic and dramatic roles throughout the thirties and forties, with appearances in films including *The Private Secretary* (Henry Edwards, 1935), *Waterloo Road* (Sidney Gilliat, 1945), *Green for Danger* (Sidney Gilliat, 1946) and, appearing with Gordon Harker, the *Inspector Hornleigh* series (starting with Eugene Forde's *Inspector Hornleigh* in 1939). Sim would, of course, go on to further success with films such as *The Happiest Days of Your Life* (Frank Launder, 1950), *An Inspector Calls* (Guy Hamilton, 1954) and *The*

Belles of St Trinian's (Frank Launder, 1954), and was nominated for a BAFTA Award for his appearance as army chaplain Captain William Paris in Frank Launder's *Folly to Be Wise* (1953). He also reprised the role of Ebenezer Scrooge some two decades later in Richard Williams's well-regarded animated adaptation of *A Christmas Carol* (1971), which was transmitted by the American Broadcasting Company. Reuniting Sim with his *Scrooge* cast-mate Michael Hordern as Jacob Marley and featuring sterling narration from Michael Redgrave, the film won Richard Williams the Academy Award in the Best Short Subject: Animated Films category at the 1973 Oscar ceremony. Sim was appointed Commander of the Most Excellent Order of the British Empire (CBE) in 1953, and continued to perform to great acclaim until the time of his death in the 1970s.

It was not only Sim's acting prowess which elevated his performance as Scrooge above those of his predecessors. His outward appearance, gestures and distinctive delivery all combined to create a kind of definitive depiction of the character; Dickens's bewildered miser, misplaced within the experiences of his own life as his bitterness and cynicism gradually begin to erode, has rarely seemed like such a tangibly human character than when entrusted into the hands of Hurst and Sim. As Thomas M. Leitch has noted: 'What Sim was doing was simply giving expression to Scrooge's joy by inventing new external behavior and [...] his interpretation of the character, which is of course written into Langley's screenplay as well, is Dickensian in its illumination of the continuity between Scrooge's zestful selfishness and his equally zestful incredulity at his miraculous conversion and escape from death (a particular theme of Desmond-Hurst's adaptation that is by no means universally observed in other adaptations)'.[12] After such a strong run throughout the 1940s of American films which had dealt with the ability of Christmas to reshape attitudes and alter lives for the better, a return to Dickens's story – arguably among the most prominent exponents of this theme in Western film and literature – needed to be robust in its presentation of the potential transformative power residing within the festive season. Fortunately Hurst was able to meet this challenge with such success that it has not only become one of the best-known Christmas films of the 1950s, but is also among the most-watched of all British motion pictures originating from that decade. As Donald Clarke has remarked, 'this *Scrooge* was made as Britain was recovering from the Second World War and a fetid atmosphere of making-do hangs over the depictions of urban poverty. Hurst (a Belfast man, honoured by a plaque in Queen's Film Theatre) was able to employ whole divisions of unequalled character actors to flesh out the dark corners with an energy that George Cruikshank would have admired. [...] The film is, of course, all about Scrooge. The fact that Alastair Sim was always some version of the same character – a befuddled Scot who fails to hide inner warmth – does nothing to undermine his claim to be Britain's greatest comic actor. He here achieves something that few Scrooges have managed before or since'.[13]

The supporting cast of *Scrooge* is also consistently solid. Mervyn Johns's cinematic career started in 1934, following which he quickly built a prolific body of work as a character actor in a wide variety of films such as *Jamaica Inn* (Alfred Hitchcock, 1939), *Saloon Bar* (Walter Forde, 1940), *The Halfway House* (Basil Dearden, 1944), *Counterblast* (Paul L. Stein, 1948), and *Edward, My Son* (George Cukor, 1949). As a memorable Bob Cratchit, meek but earnestly honourable, he enjoys good on-screen chemistry with Hermione Baddeley,

Hurst's excellent casting choice for Mrs Cratchit. Baddeley, who had been appearing on cinema screens since the late 1920s, had built a successful career with performances in films which included *Brighton Rock* (John Boulting, 1947), *No Room at the Inn* (Daniel Birt, 1948) and *Passport to Pimlico* (Henry Cornelius, 1949). She would later go on to widespread critical acclaim for her appearance as Elspeth in *Room at the Top* (Jack Clayton, 1959), which earned her nominations at both the Academy Awards and the BAFTA Awards. Yet perhaps most prominent of all the supporting players is Michael Hordern's impressive Jacob Marley, a character who proves to be merciless in life but tortured in death. His performance is all the more remarkable given that many of his scenes with Alastair Sim did not take place on the same set; to enable a spectral effect, Hordern's performance was edited into sequences with Sim in post-production with the use of an optical printer. An esteemed stage actor, Hordern's cinematic career – which began with Carol Reed's *A Girl Must Live* (1939) – had appeared in films as diverse as *School for Secrets* (Peter Ustinov, 1946), *The Small Voice* (Fergus McDonell, 1948), *Portrait from Life* (Terence Fisher, 1948), *The Astonished Heart* (Antony Darnborough and Terence Fisher, 1950) and *Flesh & Blood* (Anthony Kimmins, 1951) before his performance in *Scrooge*. His later appearance as the King in Bryan Forbes's *The Slipper and the Rose* (1976) was to earn him a nomination for Best Supporting Actor at the 1977 BAFTA Awards. Appearing in nearly 140 cinematic roles in his career, Hordern was later celebrated for his television performances and as a radio personality. He was appointed a CBE in 1972, and was knighted in 1983.

The film's incidental cast is every bit as remarkable, and features a veritable roll-call of British character actors of the time including George Cole – arguably best-known as the comically unscrupulous entrepreneur Arthur Daley in Thames Television's *Minder* (1979-94) – and Hattie Jacques, immediately recognisable to generations of Britons for her many roles in the long-running *Carry On* series of film comedies (1958-78) between 1958 and 1974. The film also included performances by Patrick Macnee, later to play John Steed in Thames Television/ABC Weekend TV cult espionage series *The Avengers* (1961-69), and Jack Warner, who would be immortalised as the iconic police constable George Dixon in the BBC's crime drama *Dixon of Dock Green* (1955-76). Yet particular praise must go to Kathleen Harrison for her impeccably well-judged comic performance as Mrs Dilber, Scrooge's charlady. (The character is actually a composite of the laundress in Dickens's novella and the hitherto-unnamed house cleaner mentioned in the original text.) Her humorous interactions with Sim's Scrooge, particularly her shock at his unexpected levity on Christmas Day, still raise a smile even after the many decades since the film's initial release.

The film also benefits greatly from Richard Addinsell's dynamic musical score, which is restrained when necessary but always able to convey the emotional resonance of Scrooge's journey of personal self-discovery with finely-honed precision. The soundtrack contains many traditional Christmas carols of the period, beautifully woven into Addinsell's themes, which add estimably to the film's chilly December atmosphere. Worthy of note too is the sumptuous set design by an uncredited Freda Pearson, which perfectly captures the finer points of life in the mid-nineteenth century. This is especially true of Scrooge's joyless offices and stark living quarters, but also in the many rewarding little details which present themselves in the Cratchits' modest home and in Fred's warmly welcoming abode. While the special effects may seem rather implausible and unpersuasive by today's standards, they were creditable enough at the time of production and – at least in the appearance of the various ghostly apparitions in the film's shadowy monochrome – certainly help to add to the Gothic ambiance of proceedings.

Scrooge performed very well at the British box-office at the time of its release, and also received a generally favourable response from reviewers. However, its American release was less approvingly regarded, with a decidedly lukewarm critical reception and far less convincing rate of commercial success. *The New York Times*'s Bosley Crowther was largely complimentary of the film, commenting that: 'Brian Desmond Hurst, who produced [the film], has not only hewed to the line of Dickens' classic fable of a spiritual regeneration on Christmas Eve, but he has got some arresting recreations of the story's familiar characters. [...] What we have in this rendition of Dickens' sometimes misunderstood *Carol* is an accurate comprehension of the agony of a shabby soul. And this is presented not only in the tortured aspects of Mr Sim but in the phantasmagoric creation of a somber and chilly atmosphere. These, set against the exhibition of conventional manifests of love and cheer, do right by the moral of Dickens and round a trenchant and inspiring Christmas show'.[14] Other publications, such as *Time* magazine, were considerably less effusive, comparing Hurst's *Scrooge* unfavourably with the earlier Dickens adaptations of David Lean which had met with near-universal critical acclaim: '*A Christmas Carol* [...] is a serviceable new edition of Charles Dickens' evergreen story, arriving from Britain in time for the holiday trade. Several cuts below the best British film versions of Dickens (*Great Expectations*, *Oliver Twist*), the picture at times may tax a moviegoer's seasonal good will. Though Dickens' frank sentimentality calls for broad treatment, Brian Desmond Hurst's direction is too often heavy as well. Able Character Actor Alastair Sim is the dependable old brandy that gives this plum pudding a lift'.[15] *Variety*, on the other hand, gave the film a negative appraisal, disparaging what their reviewer considered to be a dark and cheerless tone which permeated proceedings: '[*Scrooge* is] a grim thing that will give tender-aged kiddies viewing it the screaming-meemies, and adults will find it long, dull and greatly overdone'.[16]

While *Scrooge* faced initial scepticism from critics and the moviegoing public in America when first released, this was not always to be the case. J.P. Roscoe notes that: 'Released as *A Christmas Carol* in the US, the film was released as *Scrooge* in the United Kingdom and has since often just fallen under that title (probably to avoid being confused with all the other versions of *A Christmas Carol*). The movie is often considered the landmark version of the film that other versions are compared to, and it is shown regularly around the holidays'.[17] As Roscoe suggests, within a few years of the film's cinematic release it eventually began to appear on television in the United States, especially between the late 1950s and mid-1960s, and it gradually developed a growing and affectionate reputation amongst the viewing public. This has been further enhanced by *Scrooge*'s subsequent release on home entertainment formats (a number of them colourised from the original monochrome presentation of the film). Today, it is commonly regarded amongst many reviewers as one of the finest Christmas films ever made, and its influence extends far beyond other adaptations of *A Christmas Carol*, succeeding as a fine Victorian costume drama just as much as a sentimental fable of the festive season. The views of modern critics have been overwhelmingly positive, with David Parkinson of the *Radio Times* offering the opinion that 'this is easily the best screen version of the much loved yuletide tale. The ever-versatile Alastair Sim is impeccable as the miser who comes to see the error of his ways through the promptings of the spirits of Christmas Past, Present and Future. Michael Hordern makes a splendid Jacob Marley and Mervyn Johns a humble Bob Cratchit, while George Cole does well as the younger, carefree Scrooge. Beautifully designed by Ralph Brinton and directed with unexpected finesse by Brian Desmond Hurst, this is not to be missed'.[18] Others, such as Richard Scheib, have singled out Langley's screenplay for particular praise: 'This version is one of the best written of the adaptations, spending more time exploring Scrooge's past than any other screen adaptation to date. This does have a tendency to slow the film down at some points – and there are some scenes, like a long one with several Cockney char ladies sitting around debating over who gets Scrooge's belongings, that could have been cut altogether. However, Charles Dickens's dialogue remains largely intact and comes with an often incisive bite on screen'.[19] Among the few contrary voices are *Time Out*'s Tom Charity, who has criticised Hurst's direction, the film's pace and its sometimes melancholic atmosphere: 'A jobbing director who knew how to point a camera, Hurst never betrayed much facility for cutting or movement. He stages the action competently, but the transitions between scenes are so choppy you wonder where the ads are. Add to this a prosaic adaptation by Noel Langley which gets bogged down in the backstory (the relatively dull visitation from the ghost of Christmas Past which explains how nice Ebenezer – a bashful Cole – fell from the path of righteousness), some rather depressed-looking spirits, and the cringeworthy sentimentality of the Tiny Tim scenes, and you have what Scrooge himself might call "Ho-hum-bug'".[20] In general, however, recent reviews of *Scrooge* have been almost entirely affirmative of the film's merits, with commentators such as James Berardinelli being representative of the majority by praising not just the performances, but also the excellence of the production:

> Take away the lead actor, and this version of *Scrooge* would still have been a credible reworking, with capable performances, a strong atmosphere, and superior costume and set design. The movie was made on an English soundstage in the early 1950s, but the look is of London a century earlier. Today, with modern special effects, this would not be as great an achievement as it was more than forty years ago. The black-and-white cinematography, brilliantly achieved by C. Pennington-Richards, is as crucial to the film's success as any other individual element. Rather than making *Scrooge* seem quaint and outdated, the black-and-white approach lends it a sense of eerieness and mystery that no color version has managed to recapture.[21]

In many ways, *Scrooge* was a mélange of the traditional and the modern, mixing the perennial key themes of Dickens's classic story with the more progressive, contemporary viewpoints that had been advanced by American Christmas films of the mid-to-late forties. Whereas films like *The Bells of St Mary's* (q.v.), *Miracle on 34*[th] *Street* (q.v.) and *The Bishop's Wife* (q.v.) had embedded a long-established assemblage of long-held cultural attitudes towards the Christmas spirit and the holiday season into a modern-day framework, *Scrooge* instead emphasised the enduring universality of Dickens's subject matter – benevolence, social concern and compassion furthered by the irresistible nature of festive goodwill – as being as relevant to a modern cultural setting as it had been to a bygone one. This *modus operandi* is advanced by an always-perceptive screenplay which is acutely concerned with fleshing out Scrooge's personal motivations, elevating him from a mere cipher for greed and self-interest (as has so often been the case in lesser adaptations) into a tragic, misguided everyman and emphasising that by selecting the wrong life choices, his unfortunate fate could so easily by repeated by anyone.

Scrooge was emblematic of a gear change in Christmas films, continuing the theme of the festive season's power to reform and improve both outlooks and individual lives while paving the way for new approaches later in the decade. While the angels popular in the Christmas movies of the mid-forties may have behaved quite differently to the ghosts encountered by Scrooge, their purpose was more or less the same: to encourage their earthly charges to recognise the error of their ways and alter their conduct, for the betterment of both themselves and those around them. Yet as the austerity of the immediate post-war era was beginning to give way to a new age of optimism and confidence, so too would Christmas films begin to change as the decade continued. *Scrooge*, with its timeless appeal and engaging performances, had typified all that was attractive about the most traditional of Christmas tales, related in a way that was relevant and pleasing to contemporary viewers. But as audiences advanced further into the 1950s, there was a new appetite for fresh and exciting approaches to festive film-making – one which would see the balance of the traditional and the innovative shift in the most creative and compelling of ways.

REFERENCES

1. Kate Carnell Watt and Kathleen C. Lonsdale, 'Dickens Composed: Film and Television Adaptations 1897-2001', in *Dickens on Screen*, ed. by John Glavin (Cambridge: Cambridge University Press, 2003), 201-16, p.206.

2. Chale Nafus, 'Holiday Favorites 2012: Chale and the Noir Side of *Scrooge*', in *Slackerwood*, 10 December 2012. <*http://www.slackerwood.com/node/3345*>

3. Carlo DeVito, *Inventing Scrooge: The Incredible True Story Behind Dickens' Legendary* A Christmas Carol (Kennebunkport: Cider Mill Press, 2017), pp.44-45.

4. Fred Guida, *A Christmas Carol and its Adaptations: A Critical Examination of Dickens' Story and Its Productions on Stage, Screen and Television* (Jefferson: McFarland, 2000), p.107.

5. Andy Webb, '*A Christmas Carol* (a.k.a. *Scrooge*)', in *The Movie Scene*, 14 February 2018. <*https://www.themoviescene.co.uk/reviews/a-christmas-carol-1951/a-christmas-carol-1951.html*>

6. Sanderson Beck, '*Scrooge (A Christmas Carol)*', in *Movie Mirrors*, 2007. <*http://san.beck.org/MM/1951/Scrooge.html*>

7. Michael Zupan, '*A Christmas Carol*', in *DVD Talk*, 6 November 2012. <*https://www.dvdtalk.com/reviews/57588/christmas-carol-2012-a/*>

8.   Phyllis Strupp, *The Richest of Fare: Seeking Spiritual Securi-
        ty in the Sonoran Desert* (Scottsdale: Sonoran Cross Press,
        2004), p.179.

9.   Jeffrey M. Anderson, 'The Turn of the *Scrooge*', in *Combus-
        tible Celluloid*, 14 December 2007.
        <*http://www.combustiblecelluloid.com/classic/christmascar
        ol.shtml*>

10.   Nafus.

11.   Zupan.

12.   Thomas M. Leitch, *Film Adaptation and its Discontents:
        From* Gone with the Wind *to* The Passion of the Christ
        (Baltimore: Johns Hopkins University Press, 2007), pp.74-75.

13.   Donald Clarke, '*Scrooge* Review: A *Carol* that Hits All the
        Top Notes', in *The Irish Times*, 15 December 2016.
        <*https://www.irishtimes.com/culture/film/scrooge-review-
        a-carol-that-hits-all-the-top-notes-1.2904075*>

14.   Bosley Crowther, 'The Screen in Review: Dickens' *A
        Christmas Carol*, With Alastair Sim Playing Scrooge, Un-
        veiled Here', in *The New York Times*, 29 November 1951.
        <*https://www.nytimes.com/1951/11/29/archives/the-screen-
        in-review-dickens-a-christmas-carol-with-alastair-sim.html*>

15.   Anon., 'Cinema: Import', in *Time*, 3 December 1951.
        <*http://content.time.com/time/magazine/article/0,9171,889
        415,00.html*>

16.   Anon., '*A Christmas Carol*', in *Variety*, 14 November 1951.

17.   J.P. Roscoe, '*A Christmas Carol* (*Scrooge*)', in *Basement
        Rejects*, 30 November 2011.

<*http://basementrejects.com/review/a-christmas-carol-scrooge-1951/*>

18.   David Parkinson, '*Scrooge: A Christmas Carol*', in *Radio Times*, 26 November 1999.
        <*https://www.radiotimes.com/film/jh5yg/scrooge/*>

19.   Richard Scheib, '*Scrooge*', in *Moria: The Science Fiction, Horror and Fantasy Film Review*, 5 December 2018.
        <*http://www.moriareviews.com/fantasy/scrooge-1951.htm*>

20.   Tom Charity, '*Scrooge*', in *Time Out*, 24 June 2006.
        <*https://www.timeout.com/london/film/scrooge*>

21.   James Berardinelli, '*Scrooge*' in *ReelViews*, 1 January 2000.
        <*http://www.reelviews.net/reelviews/scrooge*>

14

The Holly and the Ivy (1952)

London Film Productions / De Grunwald Productions

Director: George More O'Ferrall
Producer: Anatole De Grunwald
Screenwriter: Anatole De Grunwald, from the play by
Wynyard Browne

IF *Scrooge* (q.v.) can be considered the jewel in the crown of Britain's contribution to the golden age of Christmas cinema, *The Holly and the Ivy* must be considered one of its best-kept and most appealing secrets. Though today it has become an exponent of 1950s festive film-making that is rarely discussed, this relatively little-known movie is nonetheless a genuinely intriguing curio – a record of post-war Britain which vividly depicts a world of very particular social attitudes and cultural mores that were being briskly swept away by the winds of change. Strangely, many aspects of the society it depicts almost feel more alien and archaic than the Victorian slums and dingy counting houses of Brian Desmond Hurst's *Scrooge*, released the previous year. Yet *The Holly and the Ivy* preserves all of the era's defining socio-cultural anxieties in a kind of cinematic aspic for future generations to observe; while we as modern day observers know that the Britain we are watching was at the point of a rapid transformation that would change it forever, this fact was not lost on the film's characters either.

The basis for *The Holly and the Ivy* was a stage drama written by Wynyard Browne, an English dramatist and novelist. Known for plays such as *Dark Summer* (1947), *A Question of Fact* (1953) and *The Ring of Truth* (1959), his traditionalism was to make his work rapidly seem less relevant with the dawn of 'kitchen sink realism' in the late 1950s and early 1960s, which completely transformed British stage drama. Also remembered for his novels *Sheldon's Way* (1935) and *The Fire and the Fiddle* (1937), Browne famously adapted Harold Brighouse's 1916 stage drama *Hobson's Choice* into a screenplay for David Lean's 1954 film adaptation. Browne is today arguably best-remembered for *The Holly and the Ivy*, perhaps on account of the play's later adaptation for the big screen by Anatole de Grunwald. As Jessica Pickens observes: '*The Holly and the Ivy* originated as a play by Wynyard Browne, which premiered on London's West End at the Duchess Theater in 1950. Browne based the play on his own family members. Maureen Delaney [sic] and Margaret Halsan [sic] are the only actors who were in both the play and the film. Without knowing this was a play, you can tell this film was adapted from the stage by the extent of dialogue, long scenes and drama. [...] Though *The Holly and the Ivy* isn't your standard, bright Christmas film, it is still lovely and hopeful despite the problems of its characters. It's a good, under seen film that moves quickly'.[1]

The director of the cinematic version of *The Holly and the Ivy* was George More O'Ferrall, a decorated British director and producer (as well as appearing occasionally an actor) whose films included *Wuthering Heights* (1948), *Angels One Five* (1952) and *The Heart of the Matter* (1953). O'Ferrall was also well-known for producing stage plays, though he is almost certainly best recognised for his pioneering work on television, for which he was awarded the prestigious Royal Television Society Medal in 1948 for his two-part production of William Shakespeare's *Hamlet*. He would later be awarded the RTS Baird Medal for outstanding contribution in television, and the celebrated RTS Gold Medal in 1973. Additionally, two of his films (*Angels One Five* and *The Heart of the Matter*) were nominated for BAFTA Awards in the Best Film and Best British Film categories. O'Ferrall was appointed Head of Drama for Anglia Television between 1959 and 1964. While *The Holly and the Ivy* was one of only a small number of films that O'Ferrall would direct in his lengthy and versatile career in the entertainment industry, it has only been in recent years that the feature has come to receive greater critical recognition – not least on account of the significance of its period of production, as P. Peters has noted: 'The performances and clipped enunciation may seem antiquated to those reared on the kitchen sink realism that was about to transform British film-making. [...] While *The Holly and The Ivy* now radiates a nostalgic glow, it is actually a revealing record of a country on the cusp of the dramatic social, economic

The Holly and the Ivy (1952):
London Film Productions/De Grunwald Productions

and cultural change that has, sadly, made faith, fidelity and family feel like relics of a distant past'.[2]

In late 1940s London, widow Lydia Moncrieff (Margaret Halstan) laments that she looks likely to be spending Christmas with strangers at a hotel when she receives a letter from Wyndenham, a village in Norfolk. Opening it, she discovers to her delight that she has been invited to spend the holiday season with her niece Jenny and her family, sparing her from a lonely holiday season. Elsewhere in the capital, at a classy gentleman's club Colonel Richard Wyndham (Hugh Williams) reveals to friends that he too will be joining his cousin, the Reverend Martin Gregory, at his home in Norfolk for the festivities. They joke that he is an unlikely character to be spending Christmas at a vicarage, and he tells them that he was almost enrolled as a parson himself – before eventually deciding on an Army officer's life instead. Richard also reveals that Martin's daughter Margaret – a fashion journalist in the city – will be joining him on the journey. He phones her at the office of the magazine where she works, but she is nowhere to be found... and in spite of his best efforts, he is unable to reach her at home either.

Another relative, the prickly Aunt Bridget (Maureen Delany), has received a Christmas invitation to the Wyndenham vicarage, but is reluctant to leave her cat Blossom behind while she is away. A considerate neighbour agrees to look after the feline houseguest in her absence, freeing Bridget to go on holiday without concern. She mentions that she will look forward to seeing her nephew Michael again. However, at a British Army training camp, the aforementioned Michael (Denholm Elliott) is currently enlisted to National Service and finds that his leave has been cancelled after he is discovered having a romantic tryst with a local woman. Michael tells the Company Sergeant Major (William Hartnell) that his presence at Christmas is important to his family, but when the NCO disagrees Michael then requests that the matter be brought to the attention of the camp's commanding officer. The sergeant promptly puts Michael on a charge for insubordination, and the next morning he is brought before the Company's Major (Robert Flemyng). Michael explains that his mother has died the previous spring, and that as this will be the first Christmas that his father will be a widower he had promised to get home if at all possible. The Major appears unmoved by the young man's appeal, but once he has been marched away the officer makes clear to the sergeant that he intends to be lenient given that it is the festive season.

On Christmas Eve, Lydia and Bridget meet on a train leaving London and are delighted to see each other – clearly relishing the opportunity to spend Christmas away from the bustling city. Little do they realise that Michael is making the journey home via the rather less glamorous means of hitching a lift in a van. Meanwhile, Richard is heading to Wydenham in his car, though his passenger seat remains conspicuously empty – clearly he has been unable to convince the elusive Margaret to join him on the trip to Norfolk.

That night, Jenny (Celia Johnson) – the parson's daughter – is busy setting up a model Nativity scene in the village church while the choir rehearse Christmas carols. Her boyfriend, Scottish engineer David Paterson (John Gregson) comes to see her, eager to have a discussion before her relatives arrive. It seems that they have had a minor disagreement, and Jenny feels that there is nothing more that needs to be said. However, they are still obviously on good terms, and they head back to the vicarage where Jenny is halfway through putting up the Christmas decorations. Unwilling to be further deflected, David tells her that he has received a firm offer of a job constructing aerodromes in South America, and that he would like her to come with him – as his wife. However, Jenny is conflicted. While she is obviously in love with David, she feels a sense of duty to her father and is unwilling to abandon him only a few months after the death of her mother. He assures her that Martin, the parson, will be able to cope perfectly well on his own, and worries that by the time he returns to England in five years' time (by which point he will be 39 and she will be 36) that they will have wasted so much time that they could otherwise have spent together. But Jenny feels that with all the duties involved in running a church, Martin will still need someone to look after him and his home. She is horrified when David offers to have a word with Martin, and forbids him even to mention the fact that they are in a relationship together.

Martin (Ralph Richardson), an Irish vicar in late middle age, arrives from his study in a flustered state – having unintentionally fallen asleep at his desk. He worries that he will have missed presiding over the parish infants' Christmas treat at the church, but Jenny assures him that there is still time for him to get there. Martin asks if David has heard anything about his new job and is pleased to hear that the engineer will be setting sail in January, knowing that he has worked hard for the post. It transpires that Martin had always wanted to visit South America himself, having once been keen to work as a Christian missionary there. Clearly knowledgeable about the region and its flora and fauna, Martin voices subtle disappointment at the fact that his duties have never taken him away from his humdrum life in Britain. However, he seems so absent-minded and disorganised that it is a wonder he can make it out of his front door without Jenny there to make sure that he has everything he needs for the youth service. Martin voices regret that while David has devoted himself to a job that produces practical outcomes, nobody seems to want a parson around anymore – if he keeps his distance they complain that he isn't sufficiently engaged, but if he becomes too involved they protest that he is an interfering busybody.

Once Martin has left the vicarage to lead the service, David asks Jenny why they never see Margaret, Martin's younger daughter. Jenny replies that her sister is heavily involved with her job in the world of fashion and takes her writing career very seriously. Margaret seems to have no time to spend with her family these days. David enquires if either of Jenny's aunts might consider staying with Martin in the long term, but she replies that neither would consider the possibility. Determined to find a workable solution, he then suggests that Martin should consider employing a housekeeper to look after his home while he concentrates on his church responsibilities. But Jenny remains reluctant, feeling that although this would take care of the practicalities of the situation, it would still mean that Martin would be living alone – and as a parson, it is difficult for him to find company as people are hesitant to be themselves around a church leader. While David is not unsympathetic to her dilemma, he feels that it is unfair that Jenny's life opportunities are being stymied by Margaret's success in London. If they could only persuade her younger sister to return to Wyndenham, things would be much simpler – and as David points out, he would rather turn down his lucrative chance of professional advancement if the alternative is having to leave his true love behind. Jenny points out that the great irony of the situation is that in earlier years, she was always the sister with the greatest *wanderlust* while Margaret preferred to stay at home.

Michael returns after his long journey from the Army training camp. He is elated to see Jenny and David again, and points out that he only narrowly managed to arrange a 48-hour compassionate leave pass to get home for Christmas. Jenny disapproves of the fact that he'd emphasised the supposed importance he places on hearth and home to his commanding officer, feeling that he was being self-serving and deceitful. Sure enough, once she has left the room Michael admits that while he loved Christmas as a child, as an adult he always finds it strangely depressing. As he and David continue to decorate the room, Michael reflects that Martin might well consider retiring but for the fact that the parson is determined that his son should have the opportunity to attend Cambridge University – and as he still has another year of National Service to serve, that will mean that Martin will need to spend the next four years at least in his post if he hopes to finance Michael's undergraduate studies. Michael feels guilty about this fact, and is unsure about whether he really wants or needs a university degree in any respect. Though David points out that it would hold many professional advantages, Michael feels happier taking a more freewheeling approach to life than years of structured learning would afford him. He bemoans the fact that being a parson's son carries certain social expectations, and reflects that Margaret may well have chosen to move so far away in order to escape these suffocating obligations.

Next, Aunts Lydia and Bridget arrive – the snow now piling down outside. There is immediate tension caused by the overbearing Bridget, who distrusts David's presence and is sceptical of Michael's temporary return from the Army. Jenny tries to make her aunts feel welcome, and Lydia immediately deduces that her niece and David are in love. David implores her not to reveal the fact that he and Jenny are secretly engaged, pointing out that it hasn't yet been publicly announced. As Bridget frets over the prospect of ducks' eggs being prepared for a meal, believing them to be poisonous, Richard's car arrives at the house. There is surprise that he has come alone, and Richard explains that when he had finally managed to contact Margaret she had decided not to join the family for Christmas, telling him that she was suffering from flu. Jenny is saddened, knowing that her father will be disappointed when he hears the news.

The family now assembled, David leaves in order to return to his own parents' farm nearby. Lydia congratulates Jenny on her relationship with David, horrifying her as – with Richard and Bridget both present and overhearing the revelation – she has no hope of maintaining the secret of her engagement. When she explains that she wants to keep the situation hidden from Martin, Bridget is appalled – blaming her own lifelong spinster status on having cared for her own mother, she believes that Jenny needs to take the chance on a loving romance without delay... even if it means leaving Martin and the vicarage behind.

Martin returns from the church service, pleased to see his family gathered at his home. He is especially surprised to see Michael, believing that his son would be unable to leave barracks in time for Christmas, but is puzzled by Margaret's absence. Richard explains that when he had seen her earlier that day, she had not felt well enough to travel. Martin tries to call her on the telephone to check on her wellbeing, but Richard stops him with the excuse that she may well be sleeping due to her illness. None of them are aware that the solitary Margaret (Margaret Leighton) is presently heading to Norfolk by train.

The family sit down to dinner, and – as an aside – Martin points out that while clearing out his desk recently he uncovered over a thousand sermons: around ten years' worth of them. He feels saddened by the fact that since being ordained he must have written approximately 150 books' worth of sermons, but feels that nobody has taken any notice of their content. Lydia assures him that his words have been of great comfort over the years to many people, including herself. As the conversation continues, Margaret arrives at the vicarage and feels emotional at her return home after such a long time. She pours a drink to settle her nerves, but before she can collect herself Richard emerges from the dining room and is shocked to see her. He explains that he has told everyone that she has the flu as a cover story, suggesting that he actually knows the truth to be quite different – that she simply didn't want to come in the first place. Margaret replies that she felt unable to spend Christmas alone in her flat, but now that she has reached the vicarage she isn't sure she can stand the thought of the festive season with her relatives either.

Before she can slip upstairs to her old room, Jenny discovers that her sister has returned and whisks her into the dining room to see the family. Everyone is thrilled – if surprised – when they realise that she has made the journey. Martin is concerned for her wellbeing and pours her a glass of whisky, but is taken aback when she refuses it with an emotional outburst. To clear the air, Lydia mentions that she loves Christmas and that it is her favourite of all the Christian festivals. Surprising everybody, Martin says that he can't stand Christmas himself, believing that the holiday has become contaminated by commercialism and stripped of its religious significance. He can't even take any pleasure in his Christmas Day sermon, knowing that his congregation would rather be at home opening presents instead of listening to a spiritual discourse. Michael chips in the fact that there is rarely a sense of a 'normal' Christmas when you live in a vicarage, as the church services start early and nullify any chance of exchanging gifts in the morning like most families. In spite of his distaste for the season, Martin withdraws to his study – he still has this year's sermon to write, and Christmas Day is fast approaching.

When Jenny goes to wash the dishes, Bridget chides Margaret for not having provided enough help for her sister. However, Margaret is unrepentant, pointing out that she considers Jenny to be domestically-oriented while believing herself instead to be a professionally-motivated individual, uninterested in such matters. The sisters meet in the kitchen, and Jenny explains her predicament in more detail. Margaret is pleased to hear that Jenny has found happiness, but refuses point-blank to consider returning to Wyndenham even on a temporary basis. Jenny finds her sister cold and hard-hearted, believing that she has changed for the worse over the years. For her part, Margaret feels that her cynicism is merely a by-product of being realistic about an essentially cruel world, and believes that she no longer belongs in Norfolk – or at her old home, the vicarage.

When Jenny prompts her sister for further details of her circumstances, Margaret relents and explains that some years ago she had fallen in love with an American serviceman who had been killed in action during the Second World War. Unbeknownst to her family, Margaret had fallen pregnant by him and carried the baby to term, but felt unable to tell any of her family that she was with child as it coincided with her mother's ultimately-terminal illness. Jenny is disappointed that Margaret hadn't shared the news with her, especially given the difficulties of raising a child alone, but looks forward to meeting her nephew now that she knows of her existence. Tearfully, Margaret explains that this will not be possible as her son, Simon, had died the previous year as a result of meningitis. He had only been four years old, and Margaret is obviously still heartbroken over the loss of her young child.

Now that Margaret's secret has been revealed, Jenny asks her – given that she no longer has any familial reason to stay in London – if she won't reconsider returning to the village, and the support of her family. But Margaret has made her mind up; if she came home, she would need to constantly keep up the façade of normality by pretending that her son had never existed, but if she revealed to their father that she had given birth to a child out of wedlock she feels that he would subject her to moral judgement, even though she feels that her marital status is an irrelevant matter.

The rather intense discussion is interrupted when a group of carollers arrives at the front door of the vicarage. While the others are distracted, Richard speaks with Margaret and reveals that he had known everything about Simon but had never shared the matter with the rest of the family. Furthermore, he is aware that Margaret has developed an alcohol-dependency problem and warns her that if she is unable to keep it under control, she should never have come from London – eventually her alcoholism will become clear to everyone there. Margaret reveals that she has lost her faith in God, and asks Richard if he has retained his own. When no response is forthcoming, she notes that she might just have found the ability to believe again if he, her pragmatic godfather, had done so too.

Feeling hemmed in, Margaret detects that Michael is similarly bored and feeling suffocated by the edgy domestic situation. She suggests that they go to the local cinema to see a film. As they depart, Martin emerges triumphantly from his study with his completed sermon. He has chosen as his central theme the old Christmas carol 'The Holly and the Ivy', which he explains has very ancient origins. To enliven an otherwise-dull conversation around the fireplace, Martin explains that there are many traditions which have come to underpin the festive season over the centuries. Lydia ventures wistfully that Christmas never quite feels the same in adulthood; it's as though the magic of the festive season slowly drains away after youth has passed. When Jenny and Richard leave to make a pot of tea, Lydia and Bridget try to persuade Martin that the time has come for him to retire. However, the parson won't hear a word of it, believing that he still has years of service to give to the church and his community. Lydia suggests that he deserves some time to himself after so many decades of unstinting support to his congregation, but Martin interprets this as meaning that she feels that his work has no merit. He points out that too many of the villagers believe him to have a role akin to a civil servant – there to marry them and bury them but never inclined to listen to the spiritual guidance that he provides. It is clear that he has become disillusioned by his vocation, and Bridget says that she believes the clergy have started to lack relevance only because they have become complacent. Lydia again tries to persuade him to retire while he still has his health, in the hope that he can enjoy life after his long career. Bridget interjects that he must think of Jenny's needs too. But Martin is confused by her statement – isn't his daughter perfectly free to leave home at any time of her own choosing?

When Jenny returns with the tea, she is appalled that her aunts have raised the prospect of her leaving. However, before the matter can be discussed in any detail Margaret arrives – clearly drunk. After a rather baffling diatribe which seems to be aimed at no one person in particular, she faints. Martin naïvely believes this to be the result of her flu, but Bridget can recognise drunkenness when she sees it. As though to prove her point, Michael appears moments later and is also heavily inebriated. He spins a yarn about having been at the cinema, but it is obvious that he and Margaret have actually visited a pub instead. Lydia and Bridget excuse themselves, and Martin asks Michael to tell the truth about what has been going on. But that, Michael shouts back, is the whole problem – neither he nor his siblings ever feel able to tell their father the truth about anything. The melancholic young man heads off to bed, and Martin voices his gratitude that Jenny is always there to keep things running smoothly. She reaffirms her sense of duty to her father, which – in light of recent events – seems to give him pause for thought.

The next morning is Christmas Day. Richard descends the stairs with gifts to put under the Christmas tree, and Jenny is already making preparations for the family meal. Richard reveals that Margaret has decided to take the next train back to London, much to Jenny's disappointment. Jenny has noticed her sister's drink problem, and Richard regrets that her staying alone in London is exacerbating the issue. The atmosphere in the house is far from festive, with Margaret emotional and upset about the previous evening while Michael is hung over and feeling miserable. Michael reveals to Richard that he too has lost his faith in religious matters, and yet he still dreads his father's moral disapproval at his conduct the night before.

Bridget decides that she too wants to leave and return to London as soon as possible, but Lydia persuades her to stay – especially as roast goose (one of her favourite dishes) is set to be served for the family dinner. Martin returns after conducting the morning church service, and immediately encounters Michael who apologises for his drunkenness the previous evening. Martin appears to brush it off, but is concerned that his son has become too fond of the bottle. He points out that it is not the degree of inebriation that matters, but rather the fact that he chooses to get drunk at all. Furthermore, he accuses Michael of having been responsible for Margaret having been drinking, and is angered when his son suggests that she is – and always was – responsible for her own choices. Finally, his frustration having reached boiling point, Michael blurts out how he really feels. He is exasperated by the fact that everyone has constantly been tiptoeing around Martin, incessantly lying to him and desperately attempting to conceal the truth at every turn in case they upset his moral sensibilities. He points out that Margaret didn't need any help in getting drunk, as she has alcohol addiction issues. Furthermore, Jenny wants to get married to David but is afraid to say anything in case it should upset her father. Martin is amazed, explaining that he had been actively trying to encourage a relationship between the pair but was concerned that his efforts had been in vain. He wants all of his children to be happy, and is stunned that they ever would have thought otherwise.

Michael then drops the ultimate bombshell and tells Martin about Margaret's pregnancy – something that neither he nor Jenny had known about until the previous night. He blusters that none of them had felt even remotely able to tell Martin about these issues because, as a parson, he would inevitably have looked upon them in shock and disapproval.

What's more, he would surely expect everyone else to feel the same way. But in reality, the only thing shocking Martin is that any of his children would have believed that he was distant and unapproachable. As he points out, the whole reason he became a parson was so that he could help people with their problems – not judge them. Over the years he has given assistance and brought comfort to many people who have suffered similar problems, and feels deeply disconsolate that his own offspring had felt unable to bring their difficulties to him directly.

In the kitchen, Jenny confides in Lydia that she intends to break off her engagement with David and stay at the vicarage indefinitely. Lydia believes that this is a huge mistake and that Jenny should pursue the prospect of marriage, not evade it. She points out that Bridget has become so cantankerous and argumentative on account of the bitterness that has come from many years of loneliness, and beseeches her niece not to make the same error in life.

Martin intercepts Margaret as she tries to slip out of the house and tells her that he knows everything. He is genuinely saddened by the fact that she had to endure such incredible emotional trauma alone, just because she felt unable to tell her family about what she was going through. Margaret tells him that she always felt that religion got in the way of her being honest with him, and – deeply wounded – he explains that the whole purpose of his Christian faith has been to support and empathise with people, not offer them platitudes and hypocrisy. Martin makes clear that as far as he is concerned, his faith is not a collection of reassuring homilies, but a cohesive and meaningful way of better understanding the world and caring for others. He tells her that he understands her need to get back to her little son, and is aghast when he learns that the child has died. Furthermore, Margaret confesses that she hates her life in London now; she has no real friends, can't bear to be alone in her luxurious flat, and feels that her writing career has deteriorated into producing an endless stream of purple prose about banal subjects in order to meet tight deadlines. Martin genuinely regrets the amount of emotional pain she must have suffered in losing not only her lover but also her child. However, Margaret assures him that the grief has made her see her life with far greater clarity than before, and she has come to believe that nothing has any lasting significance; everything is essentially meaningless, she considers... but as he is a parson, she doesn't expect him to grasp the enormity of her new-found nihilism. However, Martin understands only too well, having faced a similar existential crisis in his own youth. He points out that whereas she considers religion nothing more than an assortment of fairy-tales, he knows it to be a means of providing meaning and understanding that rationalism and materialism cannot provide. Just as there are many different types of questions in life, so too are there different means of seeking answers. Margaret seems silently humbled by Martin's quiet understanding of her situation, and his steadfast refusal to impose moral judgement on her life.

Bridget confronts Martin and chastens him for having been oblivious to Jenny's love for David. She emphasises that she feels Margaret has been selfish in refusing to return to Wyndenham to look after the vicarage, but Martin is irritated by her hectoring tone. As the church bells ring out for Christmas, Martin realises that he too has learnt a lesson about the season and its importance – one that he has overlooked for too long. In spite of his earlier misgivings, Christmas really does give him an opportunity to reach out to people

– and after all, if it has provided the chance for his family to open up to him at last, there is no reason why he can't similarly have an impact on his parishioners too. Pausing only to grab his coat and galoshes, he dashes off into the snow to deliver his sermon.

David arrives just as Martin departs, and is baffled by the copious warnings from Bridget, Lydia and then Michael that the family's pent-up secrets have finally exploded like an overtaxed pressure cooker. He meets Margaret for the first time and confronts her about her apparent refusal to return home, but is baffled when she tells him that the exact opposite is true – after her heart-to-heart with her father, she now intends to move back to Norfolk. When Jenny hears the news, she is overjoyed; having been close to ending her relationship with David, she now realises that recent developments have meant that she can start a new life with him – and with her father's blessing. The whole family come together at the Christmas church service, a new chapter beckoning for them all.

While the theme of familial discord at Christmas and the need to keep up the pretence of the perfect family unit during the festive season was certainly not a new one, having been explored at length (albeit often in a comedic context) in films such as *Christmas in Connecticut* (q.v.), *The Holly and the Ivy* was to examine these complex issues with far greater seriousness. While the film was not without its humorous moments (not least in the entertaining interplay between the irritable, irascible Bridget and the genteel, sanguine Lydia), it discusses emotional issues in far greater depth than many other Christmas movies of the time. In part this contrast seems even more marked in the sense that the crushing weight of stifling post-war British cultural attitudes seemed a world away from the more inclusive features being produced in America, such as those in progressive metropolitan settings – *Miracle on 34th Street* (q.v.), *It Happened on Fifth Avenue* (q.v.), *Holiday Affair* (q.v.) – and others which were instead inclined towards more traditional and/or small-town environments, including *Meet Me in St Louis* (q.v.) and *It's a Wonderful Life* (q.v.). Yet while the social topics that are raised by the film – alcoholism, an extramarital birth, and infant mortality – are all treated contemplatively by the screenplay, their gravity seems heightened by the fact that these matters were all still highly taboo in the strait-laced British society of the time and thus were rarely discussed. The famous British 'stiff upper-lip' (perhaps best epitomised in the no-nonsense character of Richard, a former Army officer) naturally meant that difficult issues were often underplayed or deliberately obscured in the society of this period in order to avoid scandal, indicating that the film's candid consideration of them was actually quite a bold move for the era of production. For all the subtle comic relief of Michael's breezily flippant witticisms and the obstreperous Bridget's constant complaining (she is always either too hot or too cold – sometimes both), the tone is overwhelmingly one of an ominous build-up of emotion that the audience can tell is gradually accumulating to the point of an inevitable eruption. Yet being predominantly set between Christmas Eve and Christmas Day, there is also little doubting the film's unmistakeable festive ambience, harking back to a kind of yuletide celebration that seems much more restrained and significantly less commercial than those of the modern day. As Gary J. Svehla remarks: 'Bittersweet, dysfunctional, and melodramatic, *The Holly and the Ivy* is not great cinema, but it does remind us of both the pain and the passion evoked by the wondrous season of Christmas. Bringing members of the family together, each of whom has some type of burden to bear, the strength of the family and the breaking down of barriers leads to not exactly Christmas bliss but rather to the healing warmth and potential for hope that crackles with every log placed on the Christmas fire'.[3]

The Holly and the Ivy is a powerful meditation on loneliness; people seeking to avoid a solitary existence, others who are coming to terms with the impact of solitude on their lives, and some who feel alone even when amongst others. Lydia struggles with the seclusion of being a widow, her life having been altered by her bereavement, whereas Bridget feels that she has no choice but to embrace the single life due to her personal circumstances (having looked after her parents until they were in old age). Jenny craves an escape from her repressive existence at the vicarage, but her love for her father and sense of personal responsibility precludes her from making a clean break. Michael believes himself to be labouring under a huge burden of expectation, but worries that Martin may disapprove if he decides to take a different professional route from the one that is expected of him. And Margaret is forced to deal with incredible heartbreak as her partner dies in action and then, having had to raise her infant alone, finds herself powerless as she is tragically unable to prevent his own death from illness. While Richard has been made aware of her situation, he too finds it impossible to tell Martin about the tragedy that has befallen Margaret as he is unwilling to betray his niece's confidence. All are stunned to realise that Martin, far from being the fanatical religious zealot that they suppose, is actually deeply pained by their suffering because he knows that he would have been able to support each of them if they had only revealed their problems to him sooner. Yes, he is a parson, but he is also a loving father who wants the best for his children – even if their lives haven't proceeded quite as he had expected. As Laura Grieve discerns: 'Over the course of Christmas Eve and Christmas, the parson and his children learn to reveal their true selves and reach new understandings. This is an interesting and absorbing film. It's somewhat somber in tone, as difficult problems must be faced, but it ends on an optimistic note, with truth telling, reconciliation, and hope for the future. [...] The script was adapted from a play by Wynyard Browne, and at times it definitely feels like a filmed play, with a talky script and most of the film, after the opening, set in the family home. For the most part, however, it's so well acted that the viewer becomes caught up in the drama and forgets the staginess'.[4]

While it is true that with almost all of the film's action taking place in a few rooms of a village vicarage, its stage-based origins are very obvious, by that same token the sense of claustrophobia perfectly matches the bubbling emotional turmoil that eventually leads to the film's affecting climax. *The Holly and the Ivy* presents us with a collection of distinctive characters who range from hesitant to domineering, but who all seem well-rounded and relatable. As D.J.M. Saunders has commented, '*The Holly and the Ivy* is not mistakable for a lost gem from [Jean] Renoir or [Kenji] Mizoguchi. Yet it does make the most of a story told "in real time" – a lifelike dramatic structure which would have certainly got the nod from Aristotle. So, in an admittedly subtle rather than overtly pulsating British film, there's a real sense of repressed social realities belatedly [acknowledged] and – all the more urgently – being addressed. [...] What remains in the mind, in fact, are the many stunningly well-acted scenes from a brilliantly well-cast ensemble. Among them, I've been singling out Margaret Leighton's glamourous but fragile victim of rigid morality. But structurally at least, it's Ralph Richardson around whose character everything revolves'.[5] With little in the way of what might be termed conventional action, the film revolves almost entirely around the interplay between this group of characters, and – because they are all complex, very human, and often quite likeable – the audience is encouraged to emotionally invest in the difficulty of their situation and their need for reconciliation. It is, as Andy Webb has suggested, a highly effective dramatic approach: 'There is such a beauty about *The Holly and the Ivy* with this glimpse not only at the past but also of these various characters. Take Martin who despite not liking delivering Christmas day sermons is focused solely on his life as a pastor and is oblivious to the feelings of his family and how Jenny is going to end up an old maid because she feels obliged to care for him. Ralph Richardson plays him perfectly so that he is naïve to the world and set in his ways'.[6] Because Martin is such a multifaceted character, a sense of mystery is woven around him. Jenny feels such familial duty towards her father, she is willing to put her life on hold to maintain his domestic status quo. Michael dreads his moral judgement. Margaret cannot bear the prospect of his disappointment. Yet it is left to the audience to decide whether he is the pious martinet they believe him to be, or perhaps someone deeper and more complicated than his children have ever given him credit for. As Peters notes, an undeniably Chekhovian influence hangs over proceedings, with familial discord being used as a means of investigating considerably more wide-ranging themes: 'Russian screen writer Anatole de Grunwald imbues this poignant adaptation of Wynyard Browne's West End stage hit with [Anton] Chekhov's spirit and relocates the Russian's genius for deftly drawn characters to a rambling Norfolk parsonage on Christmas Eve. Apart from a few introductory scenes in the capital, director George More O'Ferrall does little to hide the story's stage origins. But the family's confinement in a remote, snowy village reinforces the sense of detachment that Richardson's offspring have mistakenly imposed upon him and allows the screenplay to focus on such Chekhovian themes as the vagaries of emotion, the agony of disillusion, the breakdown of communication and the desecration of authority'.[7]

One of the major themes of the film, which parallels the family members' drift away from each other and their later mutual understanding, is their rediscovery of the magic of Christmas. Michael feels that the festive season has lost its indefinable charm, which he has never truly experienced since childhood. For Margaret, Christmas is simply a painful reminder of her lost child and the reluctance she feels at reconnecting with a family she has held at arm's length for too long. Only Jenny seems to retain an appreciation for the season and its customs, as even Martin has come to feel disenchanted by the way that commercial concerns have essentially side-lined the true meaning of Christmas. As Pickens elucidates: 'Set on the snowy English countryside, *The Holly and the Ivy* (1952) has a cozy, warm feel to it. But this isn't a happy or magical Christmas film. [...] While the holiday surroundings are inviting and happy, no one seems to like Christmas much. Jenny decorates the house "because it's what we always do". David says decorating is a waste of time. Michael and David agree that Christmas is depressing. Margaret wonders why she even returned home. Even the Reverend says he hates Christmas, because it focuses more on drinking and commercialism and "No one remembers the birth of Christ". He also hates giving his Christmas sermon, because he knows everyone is fidgeting and "wanting to get home to baste their tur-

keys"'.[8] It is only at the conclusion of the film that the characters begin to re-engage with the conventions of the festive
season; though some have developed scepticism or even outright hostility towards their previously-held religious beliefs,
they are still able to join Martin at the Christmas church service as one cohesive family unit because they realise that celebrating the spirit of the season can mean different things to
different people. Though the capacity for Christmas to bring
families together was far from a revolutionary concept even at
this early stage in the genre's development, *The Holly and the
Ivy* was also congruent with other Christmas films from the
mid-1940s – such as *It's a Wonderful Life* and *The Bishop's
Wife* (q.v.) – which used the festive season as a means for
celebrating the family unit and being reminded of why the
people who choose to be close to us matter so dearly. While
the film fits comfortably into pre-existing conventions of
Christmas cinema, as Webb notes, it also offers a highly distinctive viewing experience:

> Over the years I have watched a number of
> Christmas reunion movies, you know the sort
> where the children and other relatives return to
> their parent's home for Christmas and we get a se-
> ries of confrontations, secrets as well as issues
> worked through. Well that is essentially what you
> get in *The Holly and the Ivy*, but an awfully Brit-
> ish take on it with a drama which takes place in a
> rural community with characters who have some
> old fashioned/traditional values. As such what you
> don't get in *The Holly and the Ivy* is the raucous
> nature of modern dysfunctional family dramas. [...]
> What this all boils down to is that *The Holly and
> the Ivy* is a really beautiful Christmas movie with

a rich tapestry of characters and drama which makes it fantastic to watch. Plus this delivers a bygone British Christmas not yet destroyed by commercialism.[9]

Absolutely core to the success of *The Holly and the Ivy* is a superlative performance by Ralph Richardson as the patriarchal parson Martin Gregory. With Martin's soft Irish lilt, endearing absent-mindedness and kindly demeanour, it is easy to forget that Richardson was actually only 50 years old when he portrayed the compassionate country vicar; his appearance and mannerisms make him eminently believable as a character many years older than his actual age. A towering figure of the British stage on par with his contemporaries John Gielgud and Laurence Olivier, Richardson was also a prolific film performer with roles in many prominent features including *Things to Come* (William Cameron Menzies, 1936), *The Day Will Dawn* (Harold French, 1942), *School for Secrets* (Peter Ustinov, 1946), *The Fallen Idol* (Graham Greene, 1948), *Richard III* (Laurence Olivier, 1955) and *Doctor Zhivago* (David Lean, 1965). He was nominated for the Academy Award for Best Actor in a Supporting Role on two occasions – for performances in *The Heiress* (William Wyler, 1949) and *Greystoke: The Legend of Tarzan, Lord of the Apes* (Hugh Hudson, 1985) – and won the BAFTA Film Award for Best British Actor for his role in *The Sound Barrier* (David Lean, 1952), being nominated a further three times between 1967 and 1985. Richardson was knighted in 1947, and would make a further contribution to Christmas features with an appearance as Ebenezer Scrooge in an adaptation of Charles Dickens's *A Christmas Carol* for NBC's *Fireside Theatre* (1949-58) anthology series in 1951.

The film is also well-served by its many supporting performances, not least from Margaret Leighton in the role of Martin's troubled daughter Margaret. Arguably best-known for her appearance in *The Go-Between* (Joseph Losey, 1971) – for which she was awarded the BAFTA Film Award for Best Actress in a Supporting Role and received a nomination for the Academy Award for Best Supporting Actress – Leighton's numerous well-regarded performances included roles in films such as *The Winslow Boy* (Anthony Asquith, 1948), *Calling Bulldog Drummond* (Victor Saville, 1951) and *Carrington V.C.* (Anthony Asquith, 1955). She was appointed a Commander of the Most Excellent Order of the British Empire (CBE) in 1974. Celia Johnson, who played Jenny Gregory, was instantly recognisable to audiences of the time as Laura Jesson in David Lean's *Brief Encounter* (1945), and enjoyed a long career with well-regarded appearances in *In Which We Serve* (Noel Coward and David Lean, 1942), *This Happy Breed* (David Lean, 1944) and *The Captain's Paradise* (Anthony Kimmins, 1953). Johnson received nominations for BAFTA Film Awards on no less than six occasions, winning the Best Actress in a Supporting Role Award for her performance as Miss Mackay in *The Prime of Miss Jean Brodie* (Ronald Neame, 1969). She was made a CBE in 1958, and then a Dame Commander of the Most Excellent order of the British Empire (DBE) in 1981.

Of the other actors in the cast, a youthful Denholm Elliott particularly impresses as the disaffected but generally good-natured Michael Gregory. A prolific performer with over 120 appearances on film and television, Elliott became the only actor to date who has won a BAFTA Film Award for Best Actor in a Supporting Role over three consecutive years for his roles in *Trading Places* (John Landis, 1983), *A Private*

Function (Malcolm Mowbray, 1984) and *Defence of the Realm* (David Drury, 1985). He was especially well-known in popular culture for playing historian, museum curator and dean of students Dr Marcus Brody in *Raiders of the Lost Ark* (Steven Spielberg, 1981) and *Indiana Jones and the Last Crusade* (Steven Spielberg, 1989). Elliott was awarded a CBE in 1988. Veteran character actresses Margaret Halstan and Maureen Delany both stand out as highly skilled comic performances in the roles of Lydia and Bridget respectively; the two actresses would be the only performers to appear in both the stage version and film adaptation of *The Holly and the Ivy*. Additionally, cult sci-fi fans will also no doubt spot a brief appearance by William Hartnell, the first incarnation of the BBC's time-travelling *Doctor Who* (1963-), as the Company Sergeant Major at the Army training camp where Michael is undergoing his National Service duties.

In spite of the obviousness of its stage-based origins, *The Holly and the Ivy* proved to be popular with British critics at the time of the film's release. *The Times* of London, for instance, even noted its genesis as a stage drama as being a positive factor: 'So often the best British films turn out to be photographed stage plays. Indeed it is paradoxically true that their virtues tend to increase the more they depend upon a faithful transcription of the play and upon actors who belong first and foremost to the theatre. Such a film is *The Holly and the Ivy* and an admirable and satisfying film it is'.[10] American reviewers were rather more tempered in their appraisal of the film's merits, however. When it arrived in US cinemas in 1954, some fourteen months after its British debut, *The New York Times*'s Bosley Crowther considered *The Holly and the Ivy* to be only a qualified success: 'Although it is wrapped in Christmas trimmings and has a light sort of English Yuletide air, it is not a straight comedy, however. It is more a drama of the searching of souls around a family hearthside at Christmas. ⟦...⟧ Let us not malign this little picture. It is literate and deftly played by the above-mentioned cast of fine performers, under the direction of Anatole de Grunewald ⟦sic⟧ from his own script. But it is a drama of minor complication. The country parson is a good sort, after all'.[11]

The film's reputation has remained mixed in more recent years, and indeed it has only been since its re-emergence on home entertainment formats that it has been rediscovered by commentators. Some, such as Derek Winnert, have bemoaned the staginess of the production, remarking that only the performances truly merit critical attention: '*The Holly and the Ivy* is a rather tepid film of Wynyard Browne's stage hit that gains nothing on the big screen, except as a useful record of Richardson and Johnson's screen performances. This faded film seems dated and sentimental, and has stagey and cramped handling, but the stalwart, ideal Fifties British cast helps a lot'.[12] Others, such as Tom Hutchinson of the *Radio Times*, regretted the film's lack of conventional Christmas cheer: 'The stage origins of this well-played family drama (by Wynyard Browne) are all too obvious, as widowed vicar Ralph Richardson gathers his children around him at Christmas in his Norfolk rectory only for the festive spirit to be dampened by a startling revelation. Almost inevitably, Celia Johnson is on hand like a thick cardigan to provide comfort, and despite the clunky direction by George More O'Ferrall the final outcome is bleaker than you expect'.[13] By way of balance, other reviewers such as *The Observer*'s Philip French have been voiced general approval of *The Holly and the Ivy*, noting that although it may not be a conventional Christmas film it nonetheless explores the enigmatic significance of the festive season:

'Closely adapted from a well-made West End play by the largely forgotten playwright and novelist Wynyard Browne, this is a lovable, life-enhancing seasonal movie. Set at Christmas and about the meaning of Christmas, it preserves in amber the austere atmosphere of postwar Britain'.[14] Perhaps most meaningfully of all, Jeffrey Richards has praised O'Ferrall's film for the way in which it so vividly preserves a very particular evocation of a Britain that was right on the brink of vast social and cultural change:

Although it is opened out here and there, the bulk of the action takes place during Christmas Eve and Christmas Day, 1948, in the vicarage at Wyndenham, Norfolk. This Christmas becomes a time for revelation and soul-baring, as the play explores the secrets and evasions within the family, all of which come tumbling out, as they assemble for their annual Yuletide reunion. [...] The film preserves a whole vanished era of British acting, a well-spoken, upper-middle-class school of restraint. It is fashionable to mock the well-bred gentility and well-modulated voices of the early 1950s. But they preserve exactly a particular strand of British life and a well-defined value system which centred on restraint and self-sacrifice, not making a fuss, not hurting people, and doing the right thing.[15]

Although today *The Holly and the Ivy* is arguably as well-known for its rousing Malcolm Arnold overture as it is for its cinematic significance, the film has been unfairly neglected as one of British cinema's most nostalgic depictions of a family Christmas experience in a long-gone period of recent history. It may never be considered as the most action-packed or broadly comedic portrayal of British family life, but there is no denying the genuine sense of warmth and mutual concern that fortifies the multifarious interplay between these discontented, apprehensive and – above all – memorable characters. *The Holly and the Ivy* may not have received as many airings as other films of Christmas cinema's golden age, but those who make the effort to track it down will be rewarded with an experience that is often profound, sometimes haunting, and reflective of the very best qualities of the festive spirit.

REFERENCES

1. Jessica Pickens, 'Christmas on Film: *The Holly and the Ivy*', in *Comet Over Hollywood*, 13 December 2017. <*https://cometoverhollywood.com/2017/12/13/christmas-on-film-holly-and-the-ivy-1952/*>

2. P. Peters, '*The Holly and the Ivy*', in *Moviemail Film Catalogue*, November 2009, p.13.

3. Gary J. Svehla, '*The Holly and the Ivy*', in *It's Christmas Time at the Movies* by Gary J. Svehla and Susan Svehla (Baltimore: Midnight Marquee Press, 1998), 24-28, p.28.

4. Laura Grieve, 'Tonight's Movie: *The Holly and the Ivy*', in *Laura's Miscellaneous Musings*, 7 December 2011. <*http://laurasmiscmusings.blogspot.com/2011/12/tonights-movie-holly-and-ivy-1952.html*>

5. D.J.M. Saunders, 'Home Is Not Just for Christmas... or Thanksgiving... or Middle-Class Chaps, However Decent', in *Bright Lights Film Journal*, 25 December 2014. <*https://brightlightsfilm.com/holly-and-the-ivy-christmas-wynyard-browne-play/*>

6. Andy Webb, '*The Holly and the Ivy*', in *The Movie Scene*, 2018. <*https://www.themoviescene.co.uk/reviews/the-holly-and-the-ivy-1952/the-holly-and-the-ivy-1952.html*>

7. Peters.

8. Pickens.

9. Webb.

10. Anon., '*The Holly and the Ivy*', in *The Times*, 27 October 1952, p.10.

11. Bosley Crowther, 'Literate British Drama Opens', in *The New York Times*, 5 February 1954.
<https://www.nytimes.com/1954/02/05/archives/literate-british-drama-opens.html>

12. Derek Winnert, '*The Holly and the Ivy*', in *DerekWinnert.com*, 12 February 2019.
<http://www.derekwinnert.com/the-holly-and-the-ivy-1952-ralph-richardson-celia-johnson-margaret-leighton-denholm-elliott-john-gregson-hugh-williams-maureen-delaney-margaret-halstan-classic-movie-review-8120/>

13. Tom Hutchinson, '*The Holly and the Ivy*', in *Radio Times*, 26 October 2009.
<https://www.radiotimes.com/film/cfb8n/the-holly-and-the-ivy/>

14. Philip French, '*The Holly and the Ivy*: Review', in *The Observer*, 1 November 2009.
<https://www.theguardian.com/film/2009/nov/01/holly-and-ivy-philip-french>

15. Jeffrey Richards, 'Crisis at Christmas: *Turkey Time*, *The Holly and the Ivy*, *The Cheaters*', in *Christmas at the Movies: Images of Christmas in American, British and European Cinema*, ed. by Mark Connelly (London: I.B. Tauris, 2000), 97-113, pp.107-08.

15

White Christmas (1954)

Paramount Pictures

Director: Michael Curtiz
Producer: Robert Emmett Dolan
Screenwriters: Norman Krasna, Melvin Frank
and Norman Panama

W*HITE Christmas* is almost certainly the best-known of all American festive films produced in the 1950s. It also proved to be one of that decade's most successful screen musicals. With its lavish song-and-dance numbers, extravagant sets and winning charm, the film marked a significant break from the other, comparatively low-key Christmas films which had immediately preceded it earlier in the decade. *White Christmas* was already guaranteed some degree of cinematic significance due to the fact that it was filmed in Technicolor with the VistaVision process – the first film to use the then-pioneering technique. As Peter Lev has observed: 'The first VistaVision film was *White Christmas* (1954), a musical starring Bing Crosby and Danny Kaye, which showed off the process's visual quality, depth of field, and image height. The film often creates depth by presenting a narrow stage viewed from the audience area – such compositions would have been hard to fit into CinemaScope's elongated image'.[1] However, *White Christmas* was also to be noteworthy for other reasons. The film largely eschewed the character-changing profundities which had been common to many of the festive movies of the mid-to-late forties, instead focusing on the holiday season as a time of exuberant joy and celebration. The result is a film with an infectious sense of fun and goodwill; a Christmas movie that it is almost impossible to dislike. As Luke Bonanno suggests, 'many holiday movies are successful upon release, but few have demonstrated the lasting value of *White Christmas*. This 1954 musical represents the height of entertainment from its time. [...] Though it may be stagey, frothy, and perhaps a bit prolonged at exactly two hours, those qualities all distinguish the picture and add to its appeal. In truth, it's tough to imagine this film ever being truly out of style. As long as music, romance, mankind and Christmas continue to exist, there will be an audience for this charming diversion'.[2]

It is fair to say that with *White Christmas*, films of the festive season underwent a dramatic shift in momentum when compared to what had come before. The vibrant colour, and also the fine detail of the VistaVision process, saw the Christmas movie edging away from the austerity of the post-war years – a fact made all the more explicit due to *White Christmas*'s unabashed patriotism. It is a film which celebrates America and the innate power of show-business as much as it does the holiday season, bringing together the finest elements of the United States' famous 'can do' attitude to emphasise exactly what it is about Christmas that has the ability to fire the imagination. This evocation of a uniquely American take on the festive season is one of the many reasons why the film has become so distinctive, as Eric Michael Mazur remarks: 'This film, created to exploit the formula developed in *Holi-*

day Inn, reinforces the American nature of these holidays, particularly Christmas. The central events occur at the patriotically-named Columbia Inn (the figure represented across American history), and both times the song "White Christmas" is sung, the audience is filled with American servicemen – the first time at a USA-type event for combat soldiers in Europe and the second time at a military reunion at the inn. In each of these scenes, there is a strong connection made among the Christmas holiday, this particularly non-theological song, and American patriotism'.[3]

Although popular legend has come to regard the film as an ostensible remake of Mark Sandrich's well-regarded *Holiday Inn* (1942), which had also starred Bing Crosby and featured many popular Irving Berlin songs, in truth the plot of *White Christmas* bears little more than a superficial similarity to the earlier film, which had featured a rural inn that opened for business exclusively on public holidays (of which Christmas was but one). Also starring Fred Astaire and Marjorie Reynolds, *Holiday Inn* has become famous as the first film to feature Berlin's song 'White Christmas' and, though it is a fact that is often overlooked in recent years, Crosby also performed the song to great acclaim in Stuart Heisler's *Blue Skies* (1946) some years later. As Stanley Green has commented, the track's remarkable longevity meant that '"*White Christmas*" was not only the most popular song in [*Holiday Inn*], it would go on to become far and away the most popular secular Christmas song of all time'.[4]

Given the overwhelming popularity of Berlin's 'White Christmas' song, it seemed logical that a film would be developed to further showcase its now-widespread fame. Indeed, as Jay Nash suggests, *White Christmas* would at one point have borne far greater similarity to its illustrious predecessor: 'This film was originally designed to reunite Crosby and Fred Astaire, who had appeared together in two Irving Berlin musicals, the memorable *Holiday Inn*, 1942, which introduced the great standard "White Christmas", and *Blue Skies*, 1946. ⟦...⟧ Crosby had introduced the song 'White Christmas' in *Holiday Inn*, 1942 (singing it with the beautiful Marjorie Reynolds), and he sang it again in *Blue Skies*, 1946, and yet again in this outstanding production, furthering its enormous popularity and where it again went to the top of the charts. The perennial song remains a standard at Christmas time'.[5] However, *White Christmas* was to go through a number of production changes during its lengthy gestation period, and over the years there has been some divergence in accounts of how the now-legendary pairing of Bing Crosby and Danny Kaye eventually came about. For instance, Martin Chilton notes that 'the film was first mooted in 1949 but Fred Astaire disliked the script and pulled out, as did Donald O'Connor. Danny Kaye accepted, and shrewdly negotiated 10 per cent of the take, which was not bad for a movie that became the highest-grossing

***White Christmas* (1954):**
Paramount Pictures

428

film of 1954, bringing in $12 million'.[6] On the other hand, other commentators such as Jessica Pickens have cited ill-health rather than creative disagreements as the reason for Donald O'Connor's departure from the production: 'Fred Astaire was originally slated to play Danny Kaye's role. The plan was to reunite Crosby and Astaire after their initial holiday hit *Holiday Inn* (1942). Astaire felt he was too old for this type of role and dropped out. Donald O'Connor then was set to replace Astaire, but O'Connor fell very ill. Danny Kaye was then cast along side Bing Crosby'.[7] Whatever the reason for the eventual casting of Kaye alongside Crosby, the end result would be one of the most memorable on-screen collaborations in 1950s popular culture.

Helming *White Christmas* was celebrated Hungarian director Michael Curtiz, who was well-known to the film-going public by the mid-fifties for his prolific and high-profile output, most famously including the renowned wartime drama *Casablanca* (1942) for which he was to win an Academy Award. Highly active in European filmmaking (as Mihály Kertész) prior to a move to America in the 1920s, he was responsible for many successful films from the late twenties onwards and was primarily known at the time for his work with Warner Bros.; his features included *The Mystery of the Wax Museum* (1933), *British Agent* (1934), *Captain Blood* (1935), *The Charge of the Light Brigade* (1936), *Four Daughters* (1938), *Angels with Dirty Faces* (1938), *The Sea Wolf* (1941), *Yankee Doodle Dandy* (1942) and *Mildred Pierce* (1945), amongst many others. His work was nominated for the Best Picture Academy Award on six separate occasions, though ultimately only *Casablanca* would win the coveted accolade. He would also win an Academy Award for Best Short Subject, for his drama film *Sons of Liberty* (1939). The sentimental musical entertainment of *White Christmas* was a somewhat atypical film for Curtiz, who had become widely recognised for his skilful cinematic explorations of complex moral ambiguity. However, upon its release the movie achieved immediate popularity at the box-office, becoming one of the best-known and most financially successful films of his later career.

The narrative of *White Christmas* opens on the Christmas Eve night of 1944, where a division of American soldiers are camped in war-torn Europe. Two entertainers, Captain Bob Wallace (Bing Crosby) and Private First Class Phil Davis (Danny Kaye), are putting on a song and dance show to boost troop morale while enemy bombs explode around them. The division's beloved commanding officer, Major General Thomas Waverly (Dean Jagger), is about to be relieved by a hard-nosed, no-nonsense replacement named General Harold Coughlan (Gavin Gordon). Waverly has obvious affection for the soldiers under his command, and makes use of Wallace and Davis's show to bid them all farewell before Coughlan takes over. As he departs by jeep, the camp is heavily bombarded by the Nazis, causing chaos as ruined buildings begin to topple in the surrounding area. Davis's fast reflexes are all that saves Wallace from being crushed under falling debris, though at the cost of a wound to his arm.

Later, Wallace visits Davis in a field hospital to thank him for saving his life. He adds that if he can ever do anything to help Davis in the future, that he shouldn't hesitate to ask. Davis immediately proposes that he and Wallace become an entertainment double act after the war is over and, although Wallace is highly reluctant (being a successful entertainer in his own right), Davis plays on the officer's sympathy in order to persuade him to agree.

Sure enough, once V-E Day has come about and their division is disbanded, Wallace and Davis return to the United States and make a huge success of their entertainment careers. They soon catch the eye of trade papers such as *Variety*, and after continuing triumph with their stage performances they decide to move into production. They put on a Broadway musical, *Playing Around*, to great acclaim for a two year run, and eventually the production moves to Florida. There, Davis voices his concern that since he and Wallace became producers, Wallace has become a single-minded workaholic – so focused on the success of their careers that he has allowed himself little time for leisure or romance. Wallace responds that he will only entertain the notion of a relationship when the right woman comes into this life; he is unwilling to settle for just any potential partner who might happen by.

Before they are due to leave Florida, Wallace reveals that he has received a letter from a sergeant who they served with in the War, requesting that he and Davis go to a club named Novello's to see a musical performance by his sisters. Davis is highly sceptical about the whole affair, knowing that the letter is essentially inviting them to an audition in all but name, but nevertheless he agrees to go along. The two entertainers in question, Judy (Vera-Ellen) and Betty (Rosemary Clooney) are surprised to discover that Wallace and Davis have actually come to the club; in the dressing room, Betty is amazed that their brother would have written such a letter – he has accepted a job in Alaska and should have been unaware that Davis and Wallace's show would even be taking place in the same area of Florida that the sisters' revue. Sheepishly, Judy reveals that she had written the letter herself, hoping that their brother's old acquaintances would be able to help them with their careers.

Both Wallace and Davis are impressed with the Haynes Sisters' performance, a song and dance number named – fittingly enough – 'Sisters'. After the show, they meet for a drink and an immediate attraction becomes obvious between Davis and Judy. Betty seems rather disappointed that Wallace is unable to offer them any meaningful advice that may aid their professional careers. Later, feeling slightly guilty, she tells him the truth about the letter that brought him there. Wallace laughs, telling her that everyone in show-business always has an ulterior motive, but she is indignant in the face of his cynicism. Meanwhile, on the dancefloor, Judy tells Davis that they will be leaving for Vermont the next day. He is disappointed, knowing that he and Wallace are themselves due to leave Florida for New York later that night.

Davis and Judy enjoy a long dance, which is eventually interrupted by an agitated Betty who reminds her that they must prepare for their next routine. Novello (Herb Vigran), the club's owner, rushes up to the sisters to inform them that a sheriff (James Parnell) has arrived with a warrant for their arrest. It transpires that the pair have been accused by their landlord (Sig Ruman) of causing accidental damage to an expensive rug, but have refused to pay the $200 that has been demanded in recompense. In a convoluted scheme, Davis convinces the sisters to take the train tickets that he and Wallace had intended to use later that night. Smuggling the women out of their apartment with their suitcases, he convinces Novello to stall the sheriff while he and Wallace mime the sister's closing act (using a vinyl record that Davis finds in the pair's apartment) to a puzzled but enraptured audience. As the routine comes to an end, the sheriff and the landlord smell a rat and set off in pursuit of the two beleaguered entertainers. Fortunately the men are able to get their belongings together and escape the club through Judy and Betty's apartment window, boarding a taxi before the sheriff has any chance of catching up with them.

Wallace and Davis only just manage to board the northbound train on time, though Wallace is suspicious when Davis seems unable to find their tickets, forcing him to purchase space on a draughty club car instead. Wallace looks forward to getting back to New York, but Davis tries to persuade him (much to Wallace's confusion) to go to Vermont instead. Eventually the penny drops and Wallace realises that Davis has given away their train tickets to the Haynes sisters. However, before he has the opportunity to confront them the two women come down to the club car to thank Wallace for having agreed to give them the tickets (Davis having convinced them that it had really all been Wallace's idea in the first place). Judy reveals that they are headed to Vermont for the holidays, causing Wallace to recognise exactly why Davis has been trying so hard to persuade him to go there. Betty also attempts to convince him to come along, and Wallace soon realises that any resistance to the idea is pointless.

Some time later, the train pulls in to the town of Pine Tree, Vermont. In spite of much expectation of blizzards and skiing, Davis is disappointed to discover that the temperature seems rather more clement than he'd anticipated – not a flake of snow has fallen since Thanksgiving. Wallace, Davis and the sisters head for the cosy Columbia Inn, which they soon discover to be owned by none other than their old commanding officer, the now-retired Major General Waverly. The general is pleased to see his old military comrades, though it becomes obvious that his inn has been facing hard times due to a lack of custom – guests have been reluctant to visit due to the chronic lack of snow, especially so close to Christmas. The sisters, who have been booked to perform at the inn over the holidays, give their opening show to an audience of barely a dozen people. The inn's housekeeper, Emma Allen (Mary Wickes), reveals that Waverly has invested everything he owns into the business. If the inn should go into decline, as appears to be its fate, then the general will be bankrupt. Wallace immediately springs into action, getting on the phone to New York and having all the sets and costumes from his Broadway show shipped up to Vermont. In spite of the logistical expense, Wallace hopes that their famous act will be able to draw public attention to the Columbia Inn and reverse Waverly's ailing fortunes.

The general appears baffled as the vast amount of equipment required to put on the show begins to arrive at his inn. Knowing Waverly to be a proud man, Davis and Wallace conceal their true intentions from him, telling the general instead that they merely plan to rehearse new elements of their show and are keen to do so in a location other than their usual inner-city venue for once. He is similarly nonplussed when they explain that the change of scene will allow them to try out their new material on a different audience, but the old officer seems to take them at their word – especially once he sees them in action rehearsing a set-piece full of elaborate costumes and intricately-detailed props and staging.

At night, Judy and Davis hatch a plan to get Wallace and Betty to spend more time together. As Betty is unable to sleep, Judy advises her to help herself to a midnight snack, but when Betty heads down into the inn's bar area she finds Wallace playing the piano there. Both unaware that their meeting has been engineered, Wallace offers Betty a variety of refreshments from the bar and they begin to talk. Betty tells Wallace how much she admires his plan to keep the general's business afloat, and they enjoy a brief romantic tryst before Waverly – oblivious to their presence – interrupts the encounter when he enters the room in search of an early-hours snack of his own.

The next day, Wallace arrives back from town when he meets the general sitting outside the inn. He shows him the newly-printed show-bills for the show, but Waverly indicates that he's on to the ruse – he assures Wallace that there is no need to worry about the financial health of his business, as he has applied to rejoin the Army. As it happens, Wallace has just visited the Post Office to pick up the day's mail, and the general's reply from Washington D.C. has already arrived. However, the response makes it clear – in the most diplomatic of terms – that the post-war armed forces no longer have any need for the spirited veteran. Waverly is clearly deflated but puts on a brave face, though his subterfuge is totally wasted on Wallace. Knowing that his old commanding officer has been crushed by the rejection, Wallace catches up with Davis at one of the rehearsals and suggests that they round up as many of their old division as possible. If they were to attend the show in honour of the general, it would show him unequivocally that he remains both respected and needed.

Wallace calls Ed Harrison (Johnny Grant), a high-profile television host in New York City, and asks if he can use his top-rated show to broadcast an appeal in order to encourage as many of the general's old troops as possible to come to Vermont and join him at the inn. Harrison is so enthused by the idea that he tries to encourage Wallace to have the entire show broadcast as a Christmas Eve TV special, and outlines a cynical plan to exploit Waverly's financial woes to gain sympathy with the public. It would also, he suggests, mean thousands of dollars' worth of free advertising for Wallace and Davis. Wallace is not impressed by this plan, rejecting any attempt to take advantage of the general's plight, but neither he nor Harrison are aware that Emma is listening in to the conversation on an extension line. As she is interrupted, however, she only hears a fragment of their discussion and mistakenly comes to believe that Wallace is attempting to exploit the general's situation for his own ends. Disgusted by this apparent turn of events, she makes plain her disdain to Betty. At first Betty does not believe that Wallace would be capable of such a selfish act, but – remembering his earlier comments about everyone in show-business having their own angle – soon even she begins to doubt his good intentions.

Appalled by what she has learned from Emma, Betty angrily rounds on Wallace at a rehearsal. She makes it clear that she regrets getting closer to him the previous night, and tells him that she wants to withdraw from the show. Wallace is hurt and confused by her complete change of heart, particularly as she offers no explanation for it, but he is unable to talk her around. Davis and Judy watch as Betty angrily storms out of the building. As they are also unaware of the reason for her ire, they presume that she is resisting the prospect of a relationship with Wallace due to the fact that she is so protective towards her sister; Judy reasons that until she is engaged herself, her older sister will never consider settling down. Davis is then taken aback when Judy suggests that they should announce their own engagement, in the hope that it will convince Betty that she is free to consider romance with Wallace more seriously. Judy assures Davis that he shouldn't be daunted at the prospect of this union; it is only a temporary measure, she promises him, and they agree to keep the whole thing as low-key as possible.

Waverly organises a cast party at the inn that night, which everyone seems to enjoy with the exception of Betty. Noticing that her sister is still unhappy, Judy hatches a plan with Davis to get her up onto the dancefloor – and into the arms of Wallace. However, at the first opportunity she breaks away and heads off into the furthest corner of the room. Frustrated at Betty's evasiveness, Judy decides that there can only be one thing for it: she persuades Davis to announce their engagement in front of the assembled cast. Everybody is delighted at their happy news, but Betty is horrified and unable to disguise her unease even from Judy. After Wallace has congratulated his long-time friend, Davis suggests that he approach Betty and attempt to reconnect with her. However, Wallace grows increasingly concerned when it becomes obvious that she can barely stand to be in the same room as him; unwilling even to converse with Wallace, she leaves the party abruptly. Later that night, Judy enthusiastically tells Betty that she is now free of responsibility for her younger sister, meaning that she is free to do what she wants in life. Betty offers no reply – Judy believing that she is asleep, but unaware that she is actually too upset to answer.

The following morning, Betty asks the general to drive her to the Pine Tree railway station, where she is due to board a train to New York. She hands him a letter to pass on to Judy, but Waverly advises her to stay, sensing ambivalence in her manner. Betty beseeches the general not to interfere and heads for the train just as it begins to pull away from the platform. As it happens, Wallace is also there, making arrangements with the stationmaster (I. Stanford Jolley) for the arrival of the large number of people that he anticipates will respond to his televised appeal over the holiday season. Wallace spots Betty as the train starts to leave and makes one last attempt to ascertain why she has experienced such a total change in attitude. However, she remains silent on the issue, leaving Wallace upset and bemused in her wake.

Back at the inn, Judy receives Betty's letter and is stunned to discover that she has gone to perform at the Carousel Club in New York. Judy is dismayed that her sister would leave her side so unexpectedly, not least because there had been no discussion of the matter beforehand. Sheepishly, she and Davis approach Wallace and explain their engagement ploy to him. Wallace is annoyed that they would pull such a stunt as a means to bring him closer to Betty, but secretly seems quite touched by their plan. He is also heading for New York, where is due to appear on that evening's edition of *The Ed Harrison Show*. Before he leaves, he tells Davis that he must – at all costs – ensure that the general does not watch the broadcast, so that he remains unaware of the appeal. Davis realises that this is a taller order than it sounds, knowing *The Ed Harrison Show* to be one of Waverly's favourite TV programmes.

As it happens, Wallace is due to meet with Harrison at the Carousel Club, and arrives just in time to catch Betty's act. Betty notices Wallace and becomes reluctant to perform, but after she has delivered her song she decides to bite the bullet and join him at his table. Wallace explains that Judy and Davis had faked their engagement in order to draw the two of them closer together, and Betty appears to reconsider his sincerity when he emphasises that there is no reason to let the matter upset her. However, her attitude turns aloof again when Harrison arrives in a rush and pulls Wallace away so that they will arrive at the studio in good time for the evening broadcast. Wallace tries to arrange a later meeting with Betty, but she is having none of it – dismissively, she brushes off his attempts at rapprochement.

Wallace makes his appeal on national TV as scheduled while, back in Vermont, Davis desperately distracts the general by pretending to have broken his leg (much to the older man's puzzlement). As Wallace asks everyone connected with Waverly's old division to make their way to Pine Tree on Christmas Eve, he stresses the fact that no-one will be benefiting financially from the event in any way whatsoever. Elsewhere in New York, Betty is watching the show on television and becomes tearful as she realises that Wallace's intentions have been altruistic all along.

Sure enough, when the time comes dozens upon dozens of former soldiers descend upon Pine Tree train station and make their way to the inn. But Judy is relieved most of all by one particular arrival – Betty, who returns just in time for the evening's performance. Waverly, meanwhile, is frustrated to discover that Emma has sent away both of his suits to be dry-cleaned, leaving him with no alternative but to wear his old general's uniform to the show. However, when he enters the inn's function room he is stunned to discover so many of his old officers and troops lining up for his personal inspection. Almost overcome with emotion, he warmly greets them before blowing out the candles on a special ceremonial cake to mark ten years since that fateful night back in 1944 when he handed over command of the division.

Waverly sits at the central table as Wallace and Davis perform a complex routine dedicated to their nostalgic memories of army life. Wallace is somewhat taken aback when he discovers Betty's surprise return – the first he knows of her change of heart is when she arrives on stage. After the number is over, one of the general's old aides informs him that it has started to snow. Sure enough, by the time Waverly reaches the inn's front doorway there is already a generous covering on the ground, with flakes continuing to fall heavily. The general is overjoyed, knowing that it is the best possible news for his business.

Wallace and Davis, together with Betty and Judy, then perform their final act of the evening – a lively rendition of 'White Christmas'. Dressed as Santa Claus, Wallace is surprised to discover a gift from Betty in his bag; a model of a knight in shining armour. They embrace, knowing that they have finally overcome the misunderstanding between them. The stage's background scenery is pulled away to reveal snow continuing to fall outside as Davis invites the audience to join him in a toast to the festive season.

White Christmas is a deeply patriotic film: one which celebrates the work of the armed forces without ever glorifying the horrors of war, and which rejoices in the virtues of traditional community spirit while also recognising the challenges manifested in a world which was in the throes of radical social change. Although the film contains few of the distinctive stylistic touches that had come to characterise Curtiz's highly distinctive work in the 1930s and 40s, the glitz and the glamour of *White Christmas* heralded a vital sea-change in the way that Christmas films were perceived by the general public from that point onward. The silver screen charm of *Miracle on 34th Street*'s (q.v.) New York City department store displays and the folksy small-town appeal of Bedford Falls in *It's a Wonderful Life* (q.v.) had been superseded by a new kind of Christmas narrative – one which was vibrant, larger than life and ready to embrace the developing tastes of a country which had hurtled through a multifarious social and cultural transformation since the end of the Second

World War. The end result, as Ray B. Browne and Glenn J. Browne have commented, is secular and patriotic, and ultimately both inclusive and engaging:

> The movie *White Christmas* [concludes] with young girls dressed in fairy-princess costumes performing a ballet. They are surrounded by a large surrogate family (the reassembled World War II regiment) and dance in front of a large Christmas tree. The divine child motif is evoked, without any explicit religious reference. The group is drawn from all faiths. [...] It is a nostalgic representation of Americans assembled into a voluntaristic rather than a biological family, bound together by war. They are now united in a common festival, drawn from a wide variety of sources, the meaning of which is purely human.[8]

The film creates an effective contrast between the fates of Wallace and Davis and their old commanding officer, General Waverly. The younger men, both fresh and energetic professionals, use their ambition, drive and flawless work ethic to rapidly climb the ladder of show-business after their army division is demobilised. For the general, however, life is decidedly less benevolent. Considered surplus to requirements at the Pentagon, he is cast adrift into a country that has changed drastically since he had first entered the armed services. With his business facing closure, and having to deal with the humiliation of being rejected by his old colleagues in Washington D.C., it falls to Wallace and Davis to ensure that Waverly is aware that he has not been forgotten by his old Army subordinates – and, by extension, that his exemplary war service has not been allowed to slip out of the grasp of the national consciousness. The selflessness of Wallace and Davis's gesture, further underscored by the resolution of Betty and Emma's misunderstanding of their philanthropic intentions, is sugges-tive of a wider concern within the film: the way in which long-standing cultural tradition was being challenged by the modernity of the post-war era. To this end, *White Christmas* presents itself as a film which is more secular in nature of many of the Christmas films which had preceded it; there are no particular religious or supernatural undertones in evidence at all, largely because the narrative is concerned more with the ease of access between Americans and a holiday season which is inclusive enough for everyone to engage in, irrespec-tive of the nature of their own personal beliefs. As Marshall W. Fishwick has suggested, the film's appeal has become so widespread specifically on account of its inclusiveness and ac-cessibility: 'Millions of Americans watched *White Christmas*, which became a church service at home in front of the tube. [...] Despite the title, the movie isn't religious at all. [...] The cast is drawn from all faiths (Bing Crosby was a Roman Catholic; Danny Kaye, a Jew). Anyone is welcome, since there is no Christian doctrine or ritual. Even Frosty the Snowman or Rudolph the Red-Nosed Reindeer would feel at home. "The Man Upstairs" would understand'.[9]

Whereas some Christmas films, such as *The Bishop's Wife* (q.v.) and *The Holly and the Ivy* (q.v.), had stressed the ability of Christmas to change lives and attitudes within terms of the religion which had been responsible for the celebra-tion's genesis, the narrative of *White Christmas* instead ex-pressed the view that the festive season was one which had embedded itself so firmly within the American psyche precise-ly because it was a shared celebration of goodwill and mutual understanding, regardless of whether one expressed any faith in the Christian underpinnings of the event. Given the film's key theme of family, specifically the notion that the family unit extends beyond blood ties, the salute to Waverly's military service by his old division – long since disbanded – accentuates the sense that the common purpose of war, which had so profoundly united these men in collective fellowship, has also forged a new America in its wake: an optimistic, hopeful country with both determination and confidence. This sense of common purpose, coupled with the film's unstintingly festive ambiance, was to create a truly arresting cinematic experience. As Martin Liebman has explained:

> Directed by *Casablanca*'s Michael Curtiz and starring several of the 1950s top acts, *White Christmas* represents all that's good and pure about the Christmas movie spectacle, even if the film finds a deeper meaning by using Christmas as but a figurative backdrop rather than an element central to the greater themes the film explores. [...] *White Christmas* is more about the enduring spirit of the season rather than the day and time itself. The picture's bookends are Holiday themed, and through those segments comes the film's structural purpose, but *White Christmas* is far more than its title suggests. The film is about something greater than self, and the characters come to realize as the picture moves along that the best things in life aren't built around the individual but instead a greater whole, whether that's through the benefits of partnership, the bonds of romance, or the unbreakable human spirit that's as much about personal sacrifice as it is personal success.[10]

A film like *White Christmas* lives or dies on the quality of its central performances, and fortunately Bing Crosby and Danny Kaye's undeniable onscreen chemistry meant that the friendship between the two likeable protagonists remains believable and engaging throughout. Crosby's easy-going charm contrasts nicely with Kaye's impeccable comic timing and well-regarded talent for physical comedy, evident most clearly in Davis's constant mischievous manipulation of Wallace by means of highlighting his old war wound, and of course his entertainingly amusing affectation of a broken leg while trying frenziedly to distract Waverly's attention from the Ed Harrison television broadcast. Crosby had remained highly active in film since his appearance as Father O'Malley in *The Bells of St Mary's* (q.v.), making prominent appearances in films as diverse as *Road to Rio* (Norman Z. McLeod, 1947), *The Emperor Waltz* (Billy Wilder, 1948), *Riding High* (Frank Capra, 1950), *Road to Bali* (Hal Walker, 1952) and *Little Boy Lost* (George Seaton, 1953). He was nominated for the Academy Award for Best Actor in 1955 shortly after the release of *White Christmas*, in recognition of his performance in George Seaton's *The Country Girl* (1954). Danny Kaye had been working in the film industry since his appearance in Al Christie's 1935 comedy short *Moon Over Manhattan*. Also a well-regarded actor on the stage, he had given a number of increasingly high-profile performances throughout the forties and fifties which had included *Up in Arms* (Elliott Nugent, 1944), *The Secret Life of Walter Mitty* (Norman Z. McLeod, 1947), *The Inspector General* (Henry Koster, 1949), *On the Riviera* (Walter Lang, 1951), and in the title role of Charles Vidor's *Hans Christian Andersen* (1952). In 1955 Kaye was to receive an Honorary Academy Award for his services to the American film industry.

If the rapport between the two leads was effective, so too was their onscreen relationship with their new-found female companions – the adventurous Judy and feisty, independent Betty. *White Christmas* gave both Vera-Ellen and Rosemary Clooney a golden opportunity to shine, and they match their male counterparts every step – and song – of the way. Indeed, the movie has become known as one of the best-known features in the filmographies of both actresses. (Curiously, while Betty is established as being the older of the two Haynes sisters, in reality Clooney was some seven years younger than Vera-Ellen.) The Hollywood career of Vera-Ellen – real name Vera-Ellen Westmeier Rohe – began alongside Danny Kaye in H. Bruce Humberstone's *Wonder Man* (1945), and from there she would go from strength to strength with appearances in films such as *Carnival in Costa Rica* (Gregory Ratoff, 1947), *On the Town* (Stanley Donen and Gene Kelly, 1949), *Three Little Words* (Richard Thorpe, 1950) and *The Belle of New York* (Charles Walters, 1952). Vera-Ellen would also make numerous appearances on stage and radio as well as on television. Rosemary Clooney had made her first appearance in the film world in the early fifties, and prior to her performance in *White Christmas* she had become known for her work in films including *The Stars Are Singing* (Norman Taurog, 1953), *Here Come the Girls* (Claude Binyon, 1953) and *Red Garters* (George Marshall, 1954). Clooney would later enjoy success on television and as a jazz vocalist, being conferred the Society of Singers Lifetime Achievement Award in 1998.

The film's supporting performances, though in actuality they are relatively few in number, are also robust throughout. Dean Jagger makes an emotional impact as the retired general, nostalgic for the past glories of his career but suffering from his perceived lack of purpose since departing his post. His barely-contained sentiment at the film's climax is truly touching to behold, and is perfectly attuned to the sincerity of the occasion. (Ironically, given his stoic evocation of a war hero in his twilight years, Jagger was actually six months younger than Bing Crosby, who was playing a role much closer to his actual age.) Jagger was perhaps best-known to audiences of the time for his appearance as Lt. Colonel Harvey Stovall in war movie *Twelve O'Clock High* (Henry King, 1949). Mary Wickes also gives a nicely-judged performance as well-meaning busybody Emma Allen, her pernickety fussing over the inn generally – and Waverly's affairs specifically – slowly being disrupted by the arrival of ever more New York stage hands and theatrical paraphernalia as the film unfolds. Additionally, there is a brief but notable appearance by George Chakiris as one of the supporting dancers; Chakiris would, of course, later go on to be presented the Academy Award for Best Actor in a Supporting Role for his performance as Bernardo in *West Side Story* (Robert Wise and Jerome Robbins, 1961).

White Christmas opened to great critical anticipation in the October of 1954, and went on to become the biggest box-office success of the year. Indeed, it was such a commercial success that it eventually proceeded to become the fifth highest-grossing cinematic musical of the decade. Many reviewers praised the film for everything from Sam Comer and Grace Gregory's wonderfully-detailed set design to Irving Berlin's winning selection of songs – including 'Sisters', 'Snow', '(We'll Follow) The Old Man', 'What Can You Do with a General?', 'Love, You Didn't Do Right By Me', and of course the already-famous title song. However, critical praise was far from unanimous at the time of release. *The New York Times* review, for example, approved of the film's production values but was sceptical of its overall effectiveness: 'The confection is not so tasty as one might suppose. The flavoring is largely in the line-up and not in the output of the cooks. Everyone works hard at the business of singing, dancing and cracking jokes, but the stuff that they work with is minor. It doesn't have the old inspiration and spark. [...] Director Michael Curtiz has made his picture look good. It is too bad that it doesn't hit the eardrums and the funnybone with equal force'.[11] By contrast, *Variety* was largely complimentary towards the movie's efficacy as musical entertainment, praising the way in which so many accomplished elements of the production came together to form a satisfying whole: '*White Christmas* should be a natural at the boxoffice, introducing as it does Paramount's new VistaVision system with such a hot combination as Bing Crosby, Danny Kaye and an Irving Berlin score. The debut of the new photographic process is a plus factor complementing the already solidly established draw of Crosby and Kaye. [...] Both Crosby and Kaye are long in the talent department and provide a lift and importance to the material scripted by Norman Krasna, Norman Panama and Melvin Frank. The directorial handling by Michael Curtiz gives a smooth blend of music (13 numbers plus snatches of others) and drama, and in the climax creates a genuine heart tug that will squeeze tears'.[12] *Time* magazine, on the other hand, offered a more balanced appraisal, recognising the artistic aims of the film while expressing some degree of scepticism about the extent of its creative success: '*White Christmas* (Paramount) is a sentimental recollection of the 1942 musical *Holiday Inn*, in which Bing Crosby first sang the song "White Christmas". From the first scene (Christmas 1944) to the last (Christmas 1954), it is blatantly the "big musical", a big fat yam of a picture richly candied with VistaVision (Paramount's answer to CinemaScope), Technicolor, tunes by Irving Berlin, massive production numbers, and big stars. Unfortunately, the yam is still a yam'.[13]

Although some commentators have in more recent years voiced scepticism over the film's perceived virtues, others have made the point that to disapprove of *White Christmas* in narrative terms is pointless, as such censure would surely involve observing the same apparent imperfections that existed right across so many other musicals of the same genre which were popular at the time: namely that plot and characterisation are elements that prove to be subordinate to the musical numbers and dance sequences which make up the bulk of the running time and are, in the eyes of many, what is responsible for making the film's content so popular with audiences in the first place. James C. Robertson, for instance, has observed that: 'For the most part Kaye's talent is not fully exploited in the story of two successful entertainers who save their revered, retired Second World War commander Dean Jagger's failing winter resort. However, to criticize *White Christmas* in other respects is merely to criticize the entire thin plot/song-based genre from a serious artistic standpoint. Certainly none of the finest Curtiz touches is present, but the film remains very good light entertainment and was reportedly his greatest money-maker'.[14]

Robertson has not been alone amongst commentators when it comes to detecting faults within various aspects of *White Christmas*; other reviewers, such as David Krauss, have voiced the opinion that the film's festive charm and nostalgic appeal have repeatedly distracted commentators from what he perceived to be various shortcomings in the production:

I love *White Christmas* and never tire of watching it, but, let's be real; when matched up against such immortal musicals as *Singin' in the Rain*, *Meet Me in St Louis*, *An American in Paris*, and *Gigi*, it pales in comparison. With as much subtlety as a Mack truck (director Michael Curtiz did a great job with *Casablanca*, but he's no Vincente Minnelli), a trite and predictable script (paging Betty Comden and Adolph Green), and, with the exception of the title tune and a few others, a bunch of second-rate songs (sorry, Irving, but your *Holiday Inn* score is far better), *White Christmas* remains very much a typical genre entry, but the enthusiasm and talent of its first-rate cast and intoxicating seasonal allure make it seem far better than it is.[15]

Overall, however, positive retrospective appraisals of *White Christmas* have greatly outnumbered their negative counterparts, with most critics recognising the film's enormous popularity as well as its significance to Christmas cinema in general. Andy Webb, for example, notes that the overall sense of entertainment provided by the film easily compensates for any of its professed shortcomings: '*White Christmas* despite its thin plot and a couple of niggles over repetition and length is a very good musical which deserves its place as a Christmas favourite thanks to its heart warming tale. It's a typical glossy Hollywood musical full of memorable songs and a few memorable dance routines, but also offers up a fair amount of good old fashioned humour. Plus it has good performances from all its main stars making it a warm and friendly movie for the lead up to Christmas, if you don't mind a fair bit of sentiment as well'.[16] Laura Grieve similarly has emphasised the film's ongoing success with audiences which, in her opinion, is explained in part by the timelessness of the production: 'Everything about the entire movie is just right, from the choreography by Robert Alton to the costumes by Edith Head and the cinematography by Loyal Griggs. Everyone's work on this film has stood the test of time, and in fact the film has become a part of many people's holiday traditions. [...] That last scene, with the cast singing *White Christmas* as the stage door is opened to reveal falling snow, always induces happy, nostalgic tears'.[17] Derek Winnert even suggests that the film has become so indelibly etched within the public consciousness as an annual festive treat that it may now be considered virtually synonymous with the Christmas movie genre: '*White Christmas* was 1954's most successful film and it is now perhaps the most famous Christmas movie of them all. With the warm glow of an old Christmas card, it looks lovely in Loyal Griggs's colour (Technicolor) and widescreen (VistaVision) cinematography. [...] The four stars sparkle vivaciously, singing, dancing and clowning expertly and amusingly, while character actors like Sig Ruman, Mary Wickes and Grady Sutton twinkle away in support. And of course it's hip, hip hooray for those tremendous, irresistible Berlin tunes'.[18]

Holding the current record as the highest-grossing live action musical film of all time, *White Christmas* was re-released into cinemas by Paramount some years later in 1961, and has enjoyed plentiful sales on home entertainment formats including VHS, DVD and Blu-Ray. In 2004, a stage adaptation – entitled *Irving Berlin's White Christmas* – premiered in San Francisco. It has subsequently been performed in many locations throughout the United States, including a Broadway production between November 2008 and January 2009. The show's Broadway run was to earn it two nominations for To-

ny Awards. It has also been produced on a number of occasions in the United Kingdom, touring Britain in 2006-08 and
being staged in London's famous West End in 2014.

However, the one aspect of *White Christmas* which
seems destined to be its single most lasting contribution to
popular culture is the Irving Berlin song which was responsible for its genesis. The *Holiday Inn* version of 'White Christmas' had won Berlin the Academy Award for Best Original
Song in 1943, though he would be nominated for a further
seven Oscars throughout his long career. Bing Crosby's performance of the song subsequently became so popular, both
from its use in films and from its widespread general release,
that it is now by far the single best-selling Christmas song of
all time. As David A. Jasen comments, '1942 brought Crosby's
biggest-selling record and best-selling disc of all time, "White
Christmas", which has sold more than thirty million copies.
[...] Crosby was one of the greatest entertainers of the twentieth century, recording more than two thousand songs, selling at total of over five hundred million copies, with "White
Christmas" alone accounting for more than thirty million
discs'.[19] This remarkable achievement is further compounded
by the fact that, as the song became popular amongst performers other than Crosby himself, its commercial accomplishment actually became far greater than is often considered.
Don Tyler makes the astute point that 'Christmas songs are
like money in the bank if they are near the caliber of "White
Christmas". By the mid-fifties, that Christmas ballad had
topped the eighteen-million mark in record sales, of which
Bing Crosby's version accounted for half. Holiday songs return every year and usually sell well for more than fifty years
after their publication'.[20] In actual fact, Crosby's song has remained so popular that even today, 65 years after the release

of *White Christmas* and 77 years since it debuted in *Holiday Inn*, 'White Christmas' remains a regular fixture on Christmas compilation albums and is frequently seen in music video format on television music channels during the holiday season. As Gary W. Tooze has remarked, the song's solid commercial performance in the 1940s and 50s was to be only the beginning of its extraordinary record of success: 'Who doesn't know and love that song? Irving Berlin wrote it in 1940. Bing Crosby first performed it on December 25, 1941, on his CBS radio show. In May 1942 he recorded it, and in August of that year, he could be seen singing it on screen in the hit movie *Holiday Inn*. Soon it was at the top of the charts, where it remained for eleven weeks, and in early 1943 it won the Oscar for Best Song. It hit #1 again in 1945 and 1947 and went on to hold the record as all-time bestselling single for over 50 years'.[21] As Karal Ann Marling has explained, the song became so popular in its heyday that Crosby actually had to re-record it in order to enable further sales of the track: 'Because the first pressing had sold out seven times, the die stamp for the record actually wore out with overuse; in 1947, Crosby, the original backup singers, and most of the other musicians reassembled in Los Angeles, in the old Decca studio on Melrose Avenue, and did it again, exactly as they had in 1942'.[22]

There has been some disagreement amongst analysts in more recent years as to whether 'White Christmas' has been overtaken by Elton John's song 'Candle in the Wind' as the best-selling music single of all time. As Crosby's recording of 'White Christmas' pre-dated the singles charts as the system is recognised today, it is difficult to pinpoint exact sales figures of the song, but they are estimated to be well in excess of 50 million copies. 'Candle in the Wind' has been proven to have sold over 33 million, making it the best-selling music single since the modern singles charts began in the UK and US. However, if versions of 'White Christmas' performed by artists other than Crosby are added into the equation, the song has achieved the truly staggering feat of having sold over 100 million copies in total. Over the years, it has been covered by famous recording artists including Frank Sinatra, Perry Como, Ernest Tubb, Mantovani, Andy Williams, Otis Redding, Michael Bolton, Garth Brooks, Martina McBride, Bette Midler, and a great many others besides.

For his *White Christmas* score, Irving Berlin received an Oscar nomination for his song 'Count Your Blessings Instead of Sheep' in the Best Music: Original Song category at the 1955 Academy Award ceremony, just one of the memorable pieces of music which had been responsible for making *White Christmas* a lasting success amongst audiences. With its unashamed razzmatazz and obvious affection for both America and the entertainment industry, Curtiz's film had made an immediate impact on audiences in the United States and beyond. The cobwebs of post-wartime abstemiousness now assertively blown away, from now on the Christmas film would be concerned with more than just social commentary or issues of spirituality and character transformation. *White Christmas* had demonstrated that motion pictures made for the festive season could boast high-end production values to rival entries in any other genre, and that the commercial interest in this category of film had only continued to grow amongst audiences since the dawning of its golden age in the 1940s. In later years there would be further big-budget Christmas movies and musicals with festive themes, but for sheer entertainment value and wistful charm *White Christmas* remains the film that has set a very high benchmark which other features in the genre still attempt to reach.

REFERENCES

1. Peter Lev, *Transforming the Screen: 1950-59* (Berkeley: University of California Press, 2003), p.120.

2. Luke Bonanno, '*White Christmas*: Diamond Anniversary Edition', in *DVDizzy*, 24 December 2014.
    <*https://www.dvdizzy.com/whitechristmas-diamond.html*>

3. Eric Michael Mazur, 'Going My Way?: Crosby and Catholicism on the Road to America', in *Going My Way: Bing Crosby and American Culture*, ed. by Ruth Prigozy and Walter Raubicheck (Rochester: University of Rochester Press, 2007), 17-34, pp.28-29.

4. Stanley Green, *Hollywood Musicals Year by Year*, 2nd edn, rev. by Elaine Schmidt (Milwaukee: Hal Leonard, 1999), p.186.

5. Jay Nash, *The Encyclopedia of Best Films: A Century of all the Finest Movies: Volume 4* (New York & London: Rowman and Littlefield, 2019), p.3022.

6. Martin Chilton, '*White Christmas*, film review: "warm-hearted"', in *The Daily Telegraph*, 22 December 2014.
    <*https://www.telegraph.co.uk/culture/film/filmreviews/112 99626/White-Christmas-film-review-warm-hearted.html*>

7. Jessica Pickens, 'Christmas Musical Monday: *White Christmas*', in *Comet Over Hollywood*, 15 December 2014.
    <*https://cometoverhollywood.com/2014/12/15/christmas-musical-monday-white-christmas-1954/*>

8. Ray B. Browne and Glenn J. Browne, *Laws of Our Fathers: Popular Culture and the U.S. Constitution* (Bowling Green: Bowling Green State University Popular Press, 1986), pp.163-64.

9. Marshall W. Fishwick, *Popular Culture in a New Age* (Binghampton: Haworth Press, 2002), pp.165-66.

10. Martin Liebman, '*White Christmas* Blu-ray Review: I'm Dreaming of This Great Blu-ray', in *Blu-ray.com*, 29 October 2010.
    <*https://www.blu-ray.com/movies/White-Christmas-Blu-ray/15357/#Review*>

11. Bosley Crowther, 'The Screen in Review: *White Christmas* Bows at the Music Hall', in *The New York Times*, 15 October 1954.
    <*https://www.nytimes.com/1954/10/15/archives/the-screen-in-review-white-christmas-bows-at-the-music-hall.html*>

12. Anon., 'Film Reviews: *White Christmas*', in *Variety*, 1 September 1954, p.6.
    <*https://archive.org/stream/variety195-1954-09#page/n4/mode/1up*>

13. Anon., 'Cinema: The New Pictures', in *Time*, 25 October 1954.
    <*http://content.time.com/time/subscriber/article/0,33009,823619-2,00.html*>

14. James C. Robertson, *The Casablanca Man: The Cinema of Michael Curtiz* (London: Routledge, 1993), p.118.

15. David Krauss, '*White Christmas*', in *High-Def Digest*, 7 November 2010.

<https://bluray.highdefdigest.com/3930/whitechristmas.html>

16.   Andy Webb, '*White Christmas*', in *The Movie Scene*, 2010. *<https://www.themoviescene.co.uk/reviews/white-christmas/white-christmas.html>*

17.   Laura Grieve, 'Tonight's Movie: *White Christmas*', in *Laura's Miscellaneous Musings*, 21 December 2013. *<http://laurasmiscmusings.blogspot.com/2013/12/tonights-movie-white-christmas-1954.html>*

18.   Derek Winnert, '*White Christmas*', in *DerekWinnert.com*, 23 February 2015. *<http://www.derekwinnert.com/white-christmas-1954-bing-crosby-danny-kaye-rosemary-clooney-vera-ellen-classic-movie-review-2207/>*

19.   David A. Jasen, *Tin Pan Alley: An Encyclopedia of the Golden Age of American Song* (New York: Routledge, 2003), pp.96-97.

20.   Don Tyler, *Music of the Postwar Era* (Westport: Greenwood Publishing Group, 2008), pp.45-46.

21.   Gary W. Tooze, '*White Christmas* (Blu-ray)', in *DVD Beaver*, 29 October 2010. *<http://www.dvdbeaver.com/film3/blu-ray_reviews52/white_christmas_blu-ray.htm>*

22.   Karal Ann Marling, *Merry Christmas!: Celebrating America's Greatest Holiday* (Cambridge: Harvard University Press, 2000), p.326.

16

We're No Angels (1955)

Paramount Pictures

Director: Michael Curtiz
Producer: Pat Duggan
Screenwriter: Ranald MacDougall,
from a play by Albert Husson

THOUGH it has become affectionately known amongst many film buffs as 'Michael Curtiz's other Christmas movie', the style and focus of *We're No Angels* is just about as far removed as it is possible to be from *White Christmas* while still remaining in the same genre of film. The extravagant set-pieces and elaborate song and dance acts were gone in favour of a tongue-in-cheek stage adaptation, full of witty dialogue and skilfully depicted characterisation, while the grandeur of VistaVision remained – albeit this time depicting a rather more intimate *milieu*. *We're No Angels* deviated sharply from *White Christmas*'s subtext, which had subtly expounded upon the way in which the traditional meaning of the festive season was beginning to be usurped by more commercial concerns – namely, the many different ways in which notions of Christmas (if not the actual spirit of Christmas) could be packaged and marketed by the entertainment industry. In that earlier film, the audience was reminded that it was people, families and communities which made Christmas what it was, rather than any kind of modern day commodification. With *We're No Angels*, Curtiz returned to a more traditional theme of Christmas as a means of renewal and personal redemption, using a starry cast of actors to advance an age-old premise in the most entertainingly unconventional of ways. In this sense, as James C. Robertson explains, Curtiz was reflecting something of the stylistic cinematic trends of the time: '*We're No Angels* is dominated by the do-good activities of hardened criminals. Contemporary cinematic fashions, the genres involved, and studio policies arguably dictated such material, which appears in other directors' work'.[1] The film, an adaptation of Samuel and Bella Spewack's 1953 stage play *My Three Angels* (which, in turn, was adapted from Albert Husson's earlier play *La Cuisine Des Anges* – translating from the original French as *Angels in the Kitchen*), was a relatively unusual departure for Curtiz, but even more so for lead actor Humphrey Bogart – a man who had played both heroes and villains to great acclaim for almost three decades, but who was very rarely to be found cast in comedy roles. Curtiz had, of course, famously worked with Bogart on the legendary *Casablanca* in 1942, but the pair had also collaborated on many other features over the years including *Kid Galahad* (1937), *Angels with Dirty Faces* (1938), *Virginia City* (1940) and *Passage to Marseille* (1944). As Paul Peterson points out, *We're No Angels* would be Curtiz's 'last Bogart film [[and]] a film that has received mixed responses through the years'.[2]

We're No Angels also marked a different approach for Curtiz in the sense that it combined the technical advances of *White Christmas* with something of the earlier conventions that had typified previous Christmas films. The vibrant colour remained, as did the innovative VistaVision process, but *We're No Angels* signified a return to exploring the transformational power of the festive season, examining the ways in which behaviour could be modified and improved through interaction (indirect or otherwise) with the Christmas spirit. This being said, Curtiz's film is no mere collection of sentimental clichés mixed with a helping of festive good cheer. As Kate Kulzick observes, 'from *A Christmas Carol*

We're No Angels (1955): Paramount Pictures

to *It's a Wonderful Life*, holiday films have long explored the idea of the Christmas Miracle. *We're No Angels* falls into this category and follows many of the standard beats but what keeps it from cliché is its twist. Rather than ghosts or angels, the wish-granters/guardians are recently escaped, admittedly guilty, violent convicts. This is what makes the film work. Yes, it's entertaining and fun, but what elevates it above more standard fare is the underlying sense of menace to the cons'.[3] Just as the sub-tropical setting of *We're No Angel* is an undeniably refreshing change from the conventional tinsel-bedecked domestic backdrop that had been so prevalent in many other Christmas movies of the time, so too were the wry dialogic wit and humorously macabre moments which differentiated it from many of the sentimental narrative tropes which had begun to establish themselves in the genre.

Christmas has come to the infamous Devil's Island penal colony in the winter of 1895. Hiding patiently in the island's harbour are confidence trickster Joseph (Humphrey Bogart) and murderers Albert (Aldo Ray) and Jules (Peter Ustinov), who have recently escaped from the prison complex and are biding their time in the adjacent civilian colony until they can board an outbound ship. They encounter Arnaud (John Smith), a medical officer from a ship anchored off the coast, and pick his pockets when he asks them for directions. Among their ill-gotten gains is a letter addressed to Felix Ducotel, who runs a general store on the island. The men decide to deliver it to him personally, in the hope that he may reward them.

The convicts find Monsieur Ducotel (Leo G. Carroll) to be a friendly, mild-mannered gentleman of advancing years. Believing the men to be prisoners on parole rather than escapees, he offers them each a cigar to thank them for taking the trouble of delivering the letter to him, little realising that they have already been helping themselves liberally to his stock. Noticing that the roof of the store is leaking, Joseph suggests that to Ducotel that he and his colleagues could repair it for him. Despondently, Ducotel tells him that business is so poor he would be unable to pay the men for their efforts, but Joseph – knowing that they will have free access to pilfer from the shop's supplies – assures him that this is no problem. Once the three criminals have made their way to the roof, however, Joseph explains that he intends to raid the shop during the night in order to forge the required documents that they will need to stow themselves aboard the soon-to-depart ship on the coast. He assures them that by the very next day – with a bit of luck – they will all be headed for Paris.

Using the building's roof-level windows as a means to eavesdrop, the convicts listen in on a conversation between Ducotel and his wife Amelie (Joan Bennett). Amelie is concerned for the business, not least as Ducotel's position as manager is contingent on its financial success. Ducotel tries to calm her fears, but Amelie persists, warning that the conniving Andre Trochard (Basil Rathbone) will soon be arriving to inspect the accounts. She cautions her husband that Trochard has taken advantage of him in the past, and that although Ducotel and Trochard are cousins Andre will think nothing of casting him aside if it is expedient to do so. Later, a throwaway remark from a customer, Madame Parole (Lea Penman), about the marital status of the Ducotels' daughter Isabelle (Gloria Talbott) stings Amelie; she dislikes being reminded that her offspring remains unmarried at the grand old age of eighteen years. Having secretly read Isabelle's diary, however, Amelie is vexed that her daughter is in love with Paul Trochard (John Baer), knowing that Paul's uncle Andre is unlikely to consent to a union between the affluent Trochards and the less upwardly-mobile Ducotels.

Isabelle returns from church and tells her mother how much she misses Paris; she wishes that she was back in her native France, of which she has so many happy memories. She also confesses her love for Paul, to which Amelie responds with an unconvincing affectation of amazement. Amelie asks her daughter how she can be certain that Paul returns her affections when he is thousands of miles away, but Isabelle replies that she and Paul had agreed not to correspond by letter, preferring instead to wait for a year to see if their feelings for each other remained. Meanwhile, Ducotel finally opens the letter that the convicts had delivered to him and reacts with shock; his cousin Andre has arrived at the colony earlier than he had expected, and is currently aboard the ship berthed off the island's harbour. It also transpires that Andre's nephew Paul has accompanied him on the journey. As quarantine control prohibits Andre from disembarking, Amelie pleads with Ducotel to leave Andre on the ship until Christmas is over. However, Ducotel resignedly heads for the dock to make arrangements for Andre and Paul's release; after all, the letter states that Andre intends to spend Christmas with the Ducotels, which will give him ample time to inspect their accounts.

Isabelle is elated when she discovers that Paul will be joining her family for the festive season, but becomes so upset when she reads the remainder of Andre's letter that she promptly faints. Joseph, Albert and Jules, who have witnessed the whole episode from the roof, make their way back down into the shop to ascertain the cause of her distress, and discover from the letter that Andre has arranged a marriage between Paul and the daughter of a prosperous shipbuilder. Amelie is initially wary when she finds the convicts surrounding her unconscious daughter, especially on hearing a throwaway remark about Jules having earlier murdered his wife, but she discovers that their intentions are honourable when Albert carefully carries Isabelle through the shop to her bedroom in order to allow her to revive in safety. She is also bewildered when Joseph deals with a rare customer to the shop; a highly gifted swindler, he wastes no time in selling him a silver brush and comb set, in spite of the fact that the man is quite clearly bald.

Ducotel arrives back at the shop with news that the port authorities will be unable to release Andre until the following day. He is confused to discover Joseph poring over his financial ledgers; the convict is appalled that the accounts are so badly audited. Before he can explain himself to Ducotel, another customer arrives, to which Joseph promptly sells a jacket that is much too small for the man's girth. He advises Ducotel to put the cash from the sale in his deposit box, the suggestion being that he later intends to raid it before the convicts leave. As Joseph heads back onto the roof, continuing the pretence of repair work, Ducotel tells him that he is so grateful to the three men for their help that he would like to invite them to Christmas dinner. Touched by the older man's sincerity, the convicts readily agree. Joseph even says that he plans to 'acquire' a turkey especially for the occasion.

Later that day, Jules heads off to the governor's garden to steal some flowers for an arrangement while Joseph smuggles a live turkey into the kitchen, getting ready to prepare it for dinner. Albert is hanging Christmas decorations when he discovers Isabelle surreptitiously trying to escape the house. Awkwardly, she explains that she intends to run away and commit suicide due to the news of Paul's engagement. Albert tells her not to be so rash in her intentions; Paul, he points out, would hardly have travelled thousands of miles to simply tell her that he wanted nothing to do with her, when he could so easily have communicated this fact by letter. Instead, he believes that it is more likely that Paul plans to elope with her against Andre's wishes. Isabelle brightens when she hears this alternative viewpoint, even although she considers it highly unlikely. A shy young woman, she is further intrigued when Albert tells her how attractive he finds her. Even his low-key revelation of how he ended up in prison for murdering his uncle, who had refused to lend him money, does little to temper her fascination with Albert's motivations.

Amelie is puzzled to discover her daughter's greatly brightened mood. Heading into the kitchen, she finds Joseph hard at work preparing the turkey. She quizzes him about how he came to be incarcerated on Devil's Island, and he tells her about his incredible talent for deception and fraud. Totally unrepentant, Joseph assures her that – given the chance – the only thing that he would do differently in his life would simply be to avoid having been captured. Joseph realises that they will need a bottle of fine wine to accompany the turkey, and sets off to find one. As he does so, he brings the Ducotel's Christmas tree – little more than a glorified twig with some modest decorations – through to the dining area. There, Isabelle places a shabby ornament on the top of the tree: three angels, which she explains had belonged to her ever since she had been given her first Christmas tree many years ago. The convicts note that the angels look rather scruffy and unimpressive, but the beaming Isabelle assures them that to her, they look just perfect: their presence is a gift from heaven. The men look stunned as, in turn, she kisses each of them on the cheek.

The Ducotel family are all dressed in their best finery as the convicts invite them to take their places at the Christmas table. Felix, Amelie and Isabelle are greatly impressed by the beautiful flowers, perfectly-prepared turkey and gramophone music as the men unveil a full-size fir tree which has been lavishly decorated. They seem entranced as Joseph, Jules and Albert regale them with a hearty Christmas carol. However, they are all unaware that Andre and Paul have arrived early at the dock and are already making their way to the shop. Following the meal, the three convicts are toasting a fruitful new year when they hear Amelie's beautiful voice as she sings while playing the piano. Entranced, they all stop to listen.

Before they turn in for the night, Ducotel thanks the convicts for having gone to such extreme efforts to create the perfect Christmas dinner for his family. He hands Joseph an envelope stuffed with banknotes as a token of their gratitude, even in spite of their straitened financial circumstances, and the whole family voice their thanks as they head for bed. This presents the three criminals with a huge crisis of conscience: how can they possibly steal from such inherently kind and decent people? However, Joseph is still determined that they must escape the colony at all costs – one way or another. While the convicts wash the dishes, Andre and Paul arrive at the front of the shop and noisily demand entry. Just as anticipated, Andre is conceited and arrogant, while Paul is similarly starchy with a haughty, superior attitude. Furious at having been left waiting for so long on the ship, Andre commands Ducotel to tell him why rooms haven't yet been prepared for his arrival. Ducotel hurriedly moves his family out of their bedrooms to make space for his disagreeable relatives during their visit. Andre is also unimpressed to discover that convicts are being employed on the premises. The three criminals, by contrast, are overjoyed by the new arrivals; Andre's luggage contains everything that they need to gain admission to the ship that remains offshore, including all of the required official documentation.

Noticing that Paul and Isabelle appear pleased to see each other, Andre demands that his nephew immediately go to his room and stay there. Firmly, Andre explains to Ducotel that he will not tolerate any relationship between the pair, believing that Isabelle is scheming her way into a wealthier branch of the family via her ambitions of marriage. Instead, he insists that Paul's engagement to the shipbuilder's daughter must go ahead for the sake of his own long-term fortunes. While Andre continues to harangue his cousin, Jules is rifling through his suitcase unnoticed. Andre confronts Ducotel on the issue of why the business is continually performing at a loss, but Joseph unexpectedly steps in to help, producing receipts to prove that for the past few months they have actually been in profit. Andre appears temporarily placated, but as he heads off to bed he warns Ducotel that they will spend the following day – which is Christmas Day – going through the ledgers.

When Ducotel realises that Joseph plans to doctor the books, he refuses to collaborate on the grounds that he is an honest man and will not be party to a criminal action. However, Jules easily breaks into the business's safe, allowing Joseph to massage the figures to suit himself. Just as he is in the process of setting to work, Andre emerges from his room, suddenly deciding to check over the ledgers before he goes to sleep in advance of his full inspection the next day. Joseph is frustrated by this unexpected turn of events, but Ducotel is relieved; he would rather be judged wanting by honourable means than attempt to be saved through trickery and deception.

Knowing that there is now little to be done to help Ducotel escape his fate, the convicts decide that they will assist Isabelle and Paul with their romance before they leave. Joseph forges a note to Isabelle, pretending to be Paul, urging her to meet with the young man that night. As Albert heads off to deliver it, Jules and Joseph persuade Paul that he must attend this impromptu rendezvous. Paul is very reluctant, pointing out that he does not love Isabelle and is unwilling to feign affection for her. However, with some not-so-gentle persuasion they manage to smuggle Paul out of his room just as Amelie arrives at the door in search of Isabelle. Joseph explains to her about the secret tryst that has been arranged, causing Amelie to voice her trepidation; she knows only too well that Paul is not the right partner for her daughter. Joseph agrees, but tells her that Isabelle must discover this fact for herself. Relieved, Amelie apologises for having ever doubted the intentions of Joseph and his two acquaintances. As she points out, how could she ever have believed them capable of robbing her family when they have acted so honourably? Joseph is silently chastened by her comment.

In the garden, Isabelle makes an impassioned declaration of her love for Paul, who seems supremely uncomfortable. She suggests to him that he could leave France and join her in the colony, making a living there without any need of marrying a financially-convenient partner of Andre's preference. However, they are interrupted by none other than Andre himself, who – discovering the young couple together – angrily demands that Paul return to his room immediately. Isabelle beseeches Paul to make a stand against his dictatorial uncle, but much to her disappointment he meekly acquiesces to Andre's wishes and withdraws. As Paul is leaving, Andre hands him Ducotel's ledgers and advises him to check over them before the morning. Rounding on Isabelle, Andre demands that she make no further romantic overtures to his nephew; he has grown so obsessed by financial gain that he has convinced himself everyone is determined to rob him of his fortune by any means, including marital ties. Isabelle angrily responds that Andre's greed and cynicism has left him with a terminally necrotic view of life, but he brushes off her insults, telling her that she should be more concerned with her father's fate –

he has noted irregularities in Ducatel's finances which could lead to his own incarceration on Devil's Island – as an inmate.

When Andre moves to return to the house, his path is blocked by Jules, Joseph and Albert. Intimidated, he threatens to have their parole revoked by the authorities the next day, but is clearly cowed by their casually threatening behaviour towards him. However, Andre is unexpectedly saved when Paul bursts through a nearby door, momentarily distracting the convicts. Paul insists that his uncle take a look at some details that he has flagged up in the ledgers, which provides Andre with just the opening he needs to escape the fate that the criminals have in store for him. Blustering that he will soon uncover evidence that Ducotel has been leeching cash from his business interests, Andre withdraws into the house (and relative safety) with Paul. Thoughtfully, Joseph considers that one further option is left open to them: Andre can still be eliminated, which would give Ducotel a reprieve from an otherwise very difficult future. The three criminals discuss the issue, trying to devise a foolproof way of sealing Andre's fate. Joseph suggests that he gain employment with Andre's business when he returns to France, with the goal of bankrupting him within the year. However, Albert has a rather more immediate plan – unleashing his poisonous pet snake, Adolph, on Andre instead.

When the convicts make their way back into Ducotel's home, Joseph has a pang of conscience. While Andre is certainly an objectionable character, his sudden death would seem overly convenient given Ducotel's current financial woes. Furthermore, it would be upsetting for Amelie and Isabelle, particularly as none of the men particularly feel like lying through their teeth to them if awkward questions are asked. As they wring their hands over the morality of the issue, Andre bursts into the room, fuming at the missing stock that has been catalogued in the ledger. Noticing Albert's wicker cage on the table, currently containing Adolph, Andre decides that it must be stolen stock from the shop and seizes it from him. The criminals warn him that a snake is inside the cage but Andre refuses to believe them, considering their protestations to be a ruse. Now convinced that something of value is inside, he takes the cage into his room, determined to get to the bottom of the issue. Joseph, Albert and Jules prevaricate in a supremely flippant manner before eventually electing (much later) to warn Andre that the snake is real – and lethal. But to no-one's surprise, Joseph finds that Andre has already discovered this fact for himself... rather too late.

The next morning, Joseph forges a Last Will and Testament for Andre – in the deceased cousin's perfectly replicated handwriting – which divides his estate equally between Paul and Ducotel. Jules smuggles it into Andre's briefcase, which is then carefully placed back into his room. Madame Parole unexpectedly returns to the shop, wishing to complain about a bottle of wine that she has purchased, and Joseph sees the chance to encourage an uninvolved bystander to 'stumble upon' Andre's corpse. However, when it becomes clear that she won't budge from the main shopping area, Joseph instead uses the encounter to recover the funds for her long-unpaid store account. Outraged, she departs the shop seething, but Joseph puts the cash aside for Ducotel instead of pocketing it for himself.

Jules and Albert are concerned: Adolph the snake is still on the loose after biting Andre. The three men search feverishly, but are interrupted by Isabelle who is on the way to early morning Mass at the settlement's church. The convicts try to persuade her to ask Andre if he will accompany her to the service, intending for her to discover the body and thus making them seem blameless, but she remains upset at his attitude from the previous night and refuses to speak to him. After she leaves the shop, the criminals continue their search, but they have barely started looking again when Ducotel appears. Joseph tries to convince him to call on Andre in his room, given their earlier failure to encourage Isabelle, but Ducotel is so relieved that his cousin hasn't yet awakened that he decides not to tempt fate and thus elects to go for a walk instead.

The next person that Joseph encounters is Amelie, but when he is unable to influence her to enter Andre's room – on the pretence of making his bed – he becomes frustrated. While Amelie talks with Joseph, Jules discovers that Paul is now up and about. Paul demands to know why his uncle isn't yet awake, and Jules jubilantly invites him to visit Andre's room and find out for himself. Sure enough, Paul emerges soon after with the shocked announcement that Andre has died during the night. The convicts pretend to be shaken by this declaration, while Amelie is genuinely stunned. Paul, on the other hand, can barely contain his glee – on returning to his own room, he can't stop himself from laughing at his obnoxious uncle's fate, although he quickly sobers up when he discovers that Jules and Albert are observing him. Jules suggests that Paul look through his uncle's papers, just in case he had left any instructions to be enacted after his death – such as, for instance, a Last Will and Testament.

Ducotel arrives back at the house and is staggered by the news of his cousin's death. Amelie suggests that they head for the Board of Health in order to obtain a death certificate for Andre. Just as the Ducotels are leaving, Joseph overhears Madame Parole talking to a gendarme, discussing the convicts' presence at the shop. As the officer suggests that she give a statement to the commandant, Joseph realises that his game is almost up. He heads back into Ducotel's home and tells Jules and Albert that they need to depart as quickly as possible. Meanwhile, Paul is burning the Will that Joseph had forged, realising that as his uncle's next of kin he will inherit Andre's entire fortune if there is no legal evidence to the contrary. Paul goes looking for Ducotel but, when he discovers that Felix is not at home, he attempts to make vague arrangements for Andre's funeral with the convicts. He repeatedly denies any knowledge of Andre having a Will, and makes it clear that he will stand by his uncle's position regarding Ducotel – Felix and his family will only be allowed to continue trading on the island if his stock and accounts are found to be in order.

Livid at Paul's callous treachery, Joseph immediately starts work on forging another Will. However, before he can begin in earnest Paul returns to the room with the news that he has just been bitten by a snake that he accidentally discovered hiding in Andre's pocket. The criminals' mirth is tangible. Realising that he doesn't have long to live, the increasingly delirious Paul is dragged out to the summer house by the convicts and passes away soon after. No sooner has Albert safely recovered Adolph, someone enters the shop's main door – Isabelle, on her return from church. Joseph explains to her that Andre has passed away, and she voices concern over the effect that this development will have on Paul. The convicts choose not to inform her of Paul's demise, but instead try to convince her that Paul really did love her in spite of his earlier protestations to the contrary. She thanks them for their kindness, but tells them that she realises that Paul never had any real feelings for her and, indeed, she knows now – with new maturity – that she wouldn't have returned his affections in any respect.

The three men opine that although Isabelle may seem downcast at the realisation that no romance will be possible with Paul, she will surely find a more deserving love in the future. Albert voices his regret that he can't be the right man for her, and they reflect on the issue of who might take Paul's place in Isabelle's affections. Right on cue, Arnaud the medical officer arrives in the shop and tells the convicts that he has been sent to catalogue Andre's death. He meets Isabelle, and the two show early signs of mutual attraction. Shortly afterwards, Isabelle discovers Paul's corpse in the garden and screams; Arnaud heads to her aid and finds that she has fainted. As the convicts direct Arnaud to take Isabelle to her room, they consider that their work at the Ducotels' home is now done.

A quick change of clothing later, the now-smartly attired trio are just leaving the shop when they meet Ducotel and Amelie on their way back home. Ducotel asks if they are leaving, and the convicts reply to the effect that they have mended more than the shop roof for Felix and his family. They make their way to the docks, knowing that they need only take a short trip across the water to make it to the anchored ship and freedom. But at the last minute they have a collective change of heart. Deciding that prison life really wasn't so bad after all, they determine that they don't want or need the added complication of going on the run. At least, the convicts reason, they always knew exactly where they stood during their incarceration. Besides, Joseph thinks aloud as they begin to head back to the penal complex, if things don't work out for them then they can always try the same scheme again during the following year's festive season.

We're No Angels features two prominent qualities which are immediately apparent throughout the whole of the film: the witty dexterity of the script's situations and dialogue, and the appealing charm of all the performances – most especially those of the three leads. In spite of Curtiz's renowned gift for visual flair, the film never entirely manages to evade its obviously stage-based foundations. This has led to criticism from commentators such as John Howard Reid, who have remarked: 'Lured by the big names of Bogart, Ustinov and Rathbone directed by Michael Curtiz in a movie deemed worthy of the full VistaVision, Technicolor treatment, I expected rather more than the very modestly budgeted, obviously constrained stage play actually presented. I kept thinking that some spectacular set-piece or extravagant climax would come along to lift the movie out of its unpretentious rut. But no such luck. Almost from first and certainly till last, *We're No Angels* is undeniably photographed theatre'.[4] Indeed, the film's narrative takes place almost entirely in one location – Ducotel's shop, which is also his home – but such are the quality and range of the performances (both main and supporting) that the action is never allowed to feel too claustrophobic. Oddly enough, while the tale is supposed to unfold on a civilian colony adjacent to Devil's Island, this leads to something of an unintentional geographical anomaly. A penal colony, Devil's Island had no residential settlement alongside its prison complex on the island itself; part of the Salvation's Islands of French Guiana, the closest civilian outpost was actually at Kourou, which was a coastal town located on the mainland. Even more curiously, Ducotel's shop is actually stated as being located at Cayenne, the capital of French Guiana, which is located some 60km to the south-east of Kourou – also on the mainland – and 48km away from Devil's Island.

The story of *We're No Angels* is among the most deliciously unorthodox of all Christmas tales, with everything from the exotically unfamiliar setting to the eccentric range of characters combining to create a very memorable modern fable that features an eccentric but oddly effective take on the Three Wise Men. Ranald MacDougall's sharp, drolly amusing screenplay actually deviates very little from Samuel and Bella Spewack's original play for the stage, *My Three Angels*; the only noteworthy difference is that the three convicts are formally on parole from prison in the play, whereas the jailbreak aspect of MacDougall's screenplay contributes a modicum of additional dramatic urgency and suspense to the criminals' motivations throughout the film. The Spewacks' play was very successful in its own right; opening on Broadway's Morosco Theatre on 11 March 1953 and directed by José Ferrer, it was performed 344 times before it eventually closed on 2 January 1954. The original Broadway cast included Walter Slezak as Joseph, Jerome Cowan as Jules, and Darren McGavin as Alfred (as opposed to the 'Albert' of the film).

What really cements *We're No Angels* as a truly alternative Christmas classic is the sheer charisma of the three talented misfit protagonists, brought to life perfectly by Humphrey Bogart, Aldo Ray and Peter Ustinov. Each of the trio bring different skills to the team – Joseph's silver-tongued hoaxing and light-fingered agility, Jules's amiable charm and safecracking skills, and Albert's winning mixture of good humour and intimidating muscle. Taken together, their well-observed performances are second to none, both in terms of the comic timing of their delivery and their skilfully-rendered physical slapstick. As Ryan McDonald comments:

> What I really appreciated about the film is that for
> most of the film's length, the trio of escaped cons

are a pretty scummy, disreputable brood. You know they're going to be softened a bit eventually, but thuggish Aldo Ray and even Sir Peter Ustinov still look rather sleazy and filthy, and I kinda appreciated that. The element of danger/sleaze to the characters, and Ray in particular, really lifts this film. Ustinov pretty much steals the show, and relatively thin here he looks remarkably like Tom Hardy. It's a completely unsubtle, constantly mugging performance, but a bloody good one. Although he looks disconcertingly pale, Bogey is pretty good, but for the most part he was the same in everything, wasn't he?[5]

There is much humorous glee in Ray and Ustinov's recurrent 'accidental' battering of the self-important cousin Andre with his own luggage, to say nothing of the gloriously whimsical sequence where the convicts extensively draw out the process of warning Andre about the venomous snake that he has unknowingly wrested from Albert (a course of action which becomes so vastly prolonged that they end up cutting cards to find their nominee, all the while fully aware that Andre has almost certainly been bitten already). There is much wry amusement to be found in the early establishment of Albert's pet snake Adolph, a kind of peculiar twist on the Chekhov's Gun principle, while the halos which appear over the heads of the three convicts in the closing sequence – along with the single, prominent star high in the night sky – proves that although the men may claim to be no angels, and have retained the essence of their jovial criminality even at the end of the play, there is no doubt that their actions have changed the lives of one family infinitely for the better during that eventful Christmas.

Humphrey Bogart was, of course, a solid gold star name in cinemas by the time of *We're No Angels*, due to his legendary performances in films such as John Huston's *The Maltese Falcon* (1941) and *The African Queen* (1951), Curtiz's own *Casablanca* (1942), Howard Hawks's *The Big Sleep* (1946), and Edward Dmytryk's *The Caine Mutiny* (1954). He had been nominated for Academy Awards as Best Actor in a Leading Role for *Casablanca* and *The Caine Mutiny*, winning an Oscar for his performance as Charlie Allnut in *The African Queen*. However, he had appeared in a great many other roles besides; having started his career in Edmund Lawrence's short film *The Dancing Town* (1928), he went on to build himself a prolific and diverse career with appearances in films such as *Bullets or Ballots* (William Keighley, 1936), *The Great O'Malley* (William Dieterle, 1937), *Dark Victory* (Edmund Goulding, 1939), *Sahara* (Zoltan Korda, 1943), and *The Treasure of the Sierra Madre* (John Huston, 1948). Bogart's deadpan delivery had been well established in many of his earlier roles, but rarely did he have such an opportunity to exhibit his full range of comedic skills as he was afforded in *We're No Angels*, or indeed the chance to demonstrate his surprisingly impressive singing voice. Remarkably, *We're No Angels* marked the second time that Bogart was to play an escapee from Devil's Island, having previously portrayed fugitive World War II gunner Jean Matrac in Curtiz's drama *Passage to Marseille* (1944).

Cast against type to great effect, the heady blend of jocular charm and under-the-surface coercion that Bogart brings to Joseph is also mirrored in the complex fusion of sophistication and unruly intensity that comprises Albert's character. Aldo Ray had been active in film since the beginning of the decade, first appearing in Mickey Rooney's romantic crime drama *My True Story* (1951). He had continued to perform regularly in films throughout the fifties, with roles in a diverse range of features such as *Idols in the Dust* (David Miller, 1951), *The Marrying Kind* (George Cukor, 1952), *Miss Sadie Thompson* (Curtis Bernhardt, 1953), and *Battle Cry* (Raoul Walsh, 1955). He had been nominated for the Golden Globe Award for Most Promising Newcomer in 1953, for his performance as Davie Hucko in George Cukor's *Pat and Mike* (1952).

Rounding off the film's central trio was Peter Ustinov's Jules, a character whose beguiling sense of well-spoken refinement offset a hint of danger and ruthless criminal efficiency. Ustinov was, at the time, only at the beginning of a massively successful career as an actor, director, producer and writer, one that had started in the early forties and which would extend into the early twenty-first century. A true polymath in every sense of the word, he was also a dramatist, television presenter, voice actor, director for theatre and opera, humourist, stage designer, radio broadcaster, public intellectual and diplomat, amongst his numerous other skills and professional talents. Ustinov had first appeared in Michael Powell and Emeric Pressburger's *One of Our Aircraft is Missing* (1942), and rapidly built on this well-regarded early performance with roles in films such as *The Goose Steps Out* (Basil Dearden and Will Hay, 1942); *Private Angelo* (1949), which Ustinov co-directed with Michael Anderson; and *The Egyptian* (Michael Curtiz, 1954). Ustinov's cinematic credentials also extended to a directorial career, which included films like *School for Secrets* (1946) and *Vice Versa* (1948). He was perhaps best-known at the time for his well-regarded performance as the Roman Emperor Nero in *Quo Vadis* (Mervyn LeRoy, 1951), which had gained him an Academy Award

477

nomination for Best Actor in a Supporting Role. Ustinov would later win Academy Awards in the same category for his appearances in *Spartacus* (Stanley Kubrick, 1960) and *Topkapi* (Jules Dassin, 1964), with a further nomination (along with co-writer Ira Wallach) in recognition of his screenplay for *Hot Millions* (Eric Till, 1968). Among his many state honours and awards over the years, Ustinov was made a Commander of the Order of the British Empire (CBE) in 1975, received the UNICEF International Prize for Outstanding Services in 1978, was elected to the Académie Française in 1987, and was knighted in 1990.

With such strong performances at the centre of *We're No Angels*, it would have been easy for the supporting players to be overshadowed by the sheer wealth of charm on display. However, quite the opposite is true – all of the film's characters are given ample time to shine, with performers such as Joan Bennett, Gloria Talbott and John Baer all rising admirably to the occasion. Particular note, however, is due to veteran actors Basil Rathbone and Leo G. Carroll for their captivating appearances as Andre Trochard and Felix Ducotel. Rathbone, who had enjoyed a highly successful career in the cinema, was perhaps best known for his performances as Arthur Conan Doyle's Sherlock Holmes in the long-running cycle of popular films which had begun with *The Hound of the Baskervilles* (Sidney Lanfield, 1939) and *The Adventures of Sherlock Holmes* (Alfred L. Werker, 1939). A two-time Academy Award nominee for Best Actor in a Supporting Role (as Tybalt in George Cukor's *Romeo and Juliet*, 1936, and King Louis XI in Frank Lloyd's *If I Were King*, 1938), Rathbone delivers a mesmerising masterclass in creating an unsympathetic character for the screen, accentuating Andre's overweening arrogance and oppressive, bullying demeanour with a haughty, aloof physicality. The reverse side of Andre's coin, of course, is the kindly, bumbling Felix Ducotel, played to the hilt with shambling benevolence by Leo G. Carroll. Known at the time for his prolific appearances in such films as *The Barretts of Wimpole Street* (Sidney Franklin, 1934), *Wuthering Heights* (William Wyler, 1939) and *Spellbound* (Alfred Hitchcock, 1945), Carroll's Christmas film credentials had already been established by his appearance as Jacob Marley's Ghost in Edwin L. Marin's *A Christmas Carol* (1938). Some years later, he would become instantly recognisable to a whole new generation of viewers as Alexander Waverly, the head of the United Network Command for Law and Enforcement, in Metro-Goldwyn-Mayer Television's *The Man from U.N.C.L.E.* (1968-69). The blundering kind-heartedness of Ducotel, a man so clearly adored by his wife and daughter, forms the emotional nucleus of the film, with Carroll's adroit performance communicating the character's noble qualities very ably.

There are many other factors to recommend *We're No Angels*, from Sam Comer and Grace Gregory's excellently observed set decoration (especially evident in the vast array of period knick-knacks on sale in Ducotel's shop) to Mary Grant's first-rate costume design. However, critical reception of the film was decidedly mixed at the time of its release in the July of 1955. *The New York Times*, for instance, gave a distinctly lukewarm appraisal, stating that 'this Pat Duggan production, at the Paramount, is generally a slow, talky affair of elephantine roguishness and a few genuine chuckles. Furthermore, if luscious color tinting seems perfectly appropriate to the content, a gargantuan VistaVision span all but envelops the handful of cozy interiors, not to say the heart and spirit of the predecessor (never mind which). Ranald MacDougall's scenario, and subsequently the camera, ignoring a golden chance for contrast, alludes only vaguely to the near-by penal colony. Director Michael Curtiz merely prods a footlighted script'.[6] *Variety*, on the other hand, seemed largely favourable in its consideration of the movie's merits, though with some reservations regarding its stage-based heritage: 'Light antics swing around three convicts of Devil's Island who find themselves playing Santa Claus to a family they came to rob. At times proceedings are too consciously cute and stage origin of material still clings since virtually all scenes are interiors with characters constantly entering and exiting. However, Michael Curtiz' directorial pacing and topflight performances from Bogart, Aldo Ray and Peter Ustinov point up entertainment values in Pat Duggan production and help minimize the few flaws'.[7]

In spite of critical scepticism, the film went on to be a commercial success for Paramount, with Barbara Paulding, Suzanne Schwalb and Mara Conlon pointing out that *We're No Angels* was an 'edgy Christmas comedy [which was] the movie hit of the season' in 1955.[8] In later years, the film has retained something of a tepid response from critics. Some, such as Derek Winnert, have held to the view that in spite of the rather obvious stage drama genesis of the film, the limited scope of its range of locations can be excused given the calibre of its performances: 'Director Curtiz relies heavily on his stars' charm and sense of humour to compensate for the staginess of screen-writer Ranald MacDougall's adaptation of the French play *La Cuisine des Anges* by Albert Husson. But, with these stars, that proves good enough'.[9] By contrast, others – such as Tim O'Neil – felt that the lack of immediacy provided by a live performance meant that the performances in the film were lacking by comparison: 'As rare as it was for Humphrey

Bogart to take a comedic role, he doesn't betray a hint of unease with the light-hearted *We're No Angels*. That was Bogart's great virtue, after all – he was comfortable in any milieu, whether the Old West, wartime Monaco or the Florida Keys. [...] Bogart, Peter Ustinov, and Aldo Ray clearly relish the opportunity to play against type, but their interaction lacks the snap you would expect to see from a stage production'.[10]

Further underscoring this critical divergence, a number of reviewers have celebrated the inspired character interplay between the three leads while others have felt their chemistry to be unconvincing. On one hand, commentators such as Kulzick have noted that the interactions between the central trio can arguably be considered the highlight of the film: 'Bogart, Ray, and Ustinov play well together as the convicts. They're an odd trio, with very different looks, physicality, and characteristics, yet the actors sell their friendship, or perhaps more accurately, colleague-ship. They balance each other well and are all very believable as bad men still capable of their own brand of good. [...] Curtiz, perhaps best known as the director of *Casablanca*, uses few directorial flourishes and stays out of his actors' way. The early film blocking of the trio on the roof, looking in unseen on the action inside the house, may be an unsubtle reference to their role as unlikely guardian angels, but it's still effective and is a nice visual reminder of the tone and purpose of the film'.[11] On the other hand, reviewers such as Adrian Turner of the *Radio Times* have taken precisely the opposite view, believing that the festive sentiment of *We're No Angels* was an incongruous fit for Humphrey Bogart and that the film's lead performers were an unpersuasive troika: 'Reunited with the director of *Casablanca*, Bogart isn't well matched with his co-stars or best suited to this sort of farce.

And when the script turns all moralistic and gooey (with Bogart dressing up as Santa Claus and singing carols) you start looking around for Bing Crosby'.[12] On balance, however, when considered as a Christmas film there has been a growing sense that the eccentric scenario and sheer curiosity value of *We're No Angels* have lent it considerable appeal amongst aficionados, not least given many of the rather more orthodox features which surrounded it at the time of its appearance in cinemas. As Jessica Pickens has noted:

> The comedic roles are deviations from Ray and Bogart's usual gruff roles, which I enjoy. I love seeing actors perform in different genres. [Vincent Sherman's] *All Through the Night* (1941) is one of the few Bogart comedies, but Bogart played a gruff character with the comedy all around him in that film. [...] The funny thing about *We're No Angels* is that you keep thinking these three chaps are sweet, helpful men until you remember they are murderers and crooks, setting out to murder for money. If I have any complaints, it's that I wish the movie was 10 to 20 minutes shorter. For a slightly off-beat Christmas black comedy in the form of classic film, check this one out. You won't regret it.[13]

While its profusion of star names from the time have meant that *We're No Angels* has retained interest from film enthusiasts since the time of its production, there is little doubting that the high-profile reunion of Curtiz and Bogart has meant that this offbeat slice of festive cinema has achieved greater longevity than may otherwise have been the case. The film was loosely remade by Neil Jordan as a 1989 feature, also entitled *We're No Angels*, which starred Robert De Niro, Sean Penn and James Russo. Concerning three convicts on the run in the 1930s who become mistaken for priests as they desperately attempt to escape over the Canadian border, the film had little more than a superficial thematic resemblance to the 1950s original and in general it did not perform particularly well with critics at the time of its release – especially considering the high esteem in which much of Jordan's other cinema has been held. As Winnert has explained, 'talented Irish director Neil Jordan's 1989 feature *We're No Angels* is a re-imagined remake of director Curtiz's 1954 movie, with the films sharing only common themes, situations, mood and characters. They are distant, but recognisable cousins'.[14] The events of *We're No Angels* were also a major influence on George Gallo's later Christmas movie *Trapped in Paradise* (1994), in which three fugitive criminals find themselves ensnared in a small town full of kindly, helpful citizens when a blizzard over the holiday season unexpectedly prevents them from fleeing the crime scene after a bank robbery.

With its central theme of redemption and character transformation, *We're No Angels* follows one of the most tried and tested of Christmas cinema's core tropes. Yet perhaps just as conspicuous is its quirky celebration of the family unit – juxtaposing the loving, mutually-supportive Ducotels and the aloof, hard-hearted Trochards, and then contrasting them with the camaraderie which exists between the three escaped convicts (themselves an elective family of sorts). By the film's conclusion, it is clear whose outcomes the audience are expected to side with; all Ducotel wants is a stable income to provide for his family, while his treacherous cousin seems so fixated on profit and social standing that he appears incapable of any lasting personal satisfaction. It is ultimately the

Trochards' greed, rather than anyone else's machinations, which leads to their downfall. What made *We're No Angels* seem like a breath of fresh air compared to many other Christmas morality tales of the time was the fact that the trio of criminals use their unlawful skills in rather ethically ambiguous ways in order to achieve good ends, instead of aiming solely to benefit themselves (which had, of course, been their initial aim when arriving at Ducotel's shop). In many ways, it may well be considered that Trochard's violation of the Ducotels' Christmas celebrations is the key transgression which marks out his (and Paul's) true detachment from the ideals of an affirmative and compassionate family unit. In spite of their relative material poverty, the Ducotels enjoy a perfect Christmas dinner thanks to the schemes of the escaped felons, who dedicate themselves to providing all the elements of an idyllic family get-together. (While the outlaws obtain these resources by undisclosed means of dubious legality, Felix underscores his own innocence from criminality by offering Joseph cash the family can ill afford to thank him for his efforts – thus unknowingly shaming the charming con-man, who had earlier sought to rob his kindly host.) When Ducotel not only disregards his cousin's festive celebrations but actively opposes them (by choosing Christmas Day to inspect his financial affairs, potentially ruining him), he most clearly emphasises his elevation of material wealth over familial loyalty. In so doing, he unsuspectingly sets in motion the events that will ultimately lead to his own demise – and that of his equally unscrupulous son and heir. Thus, as in the very best of Christmas-situated tales of ethical conflict, we see justice being delivered – albeit in the least conventional of ways. Not only are the convicts fully aware of the problematic scruples of their actions, but they actually act as their own judge and jury –

while their morally vague exploits eventually achieve good ends, they decide against an undeserved break for freedom (even when one finally seems possible) in favour of a return to the harsh familiarity of life in prison on Devil's Island, thus ensuring that their questionable practices are not seen to go unpunished in the eyes of the audience. Christmas has been seen to profoundly reshape these criminals' attitudes, as had been the case in earlier films such as *Three Godfathers* (q.v.) and *The Lemon Drop Kid* (q.v.), once again underscoring the power of the festive season to rejuvenate and re-moralise. While there may be no concrete guarantee as to the full extent of the trio's rehabilitation, they do at least leave us in no doubt that their new-found ethical refinement is an ongoing process – after all, Christmas comes but once a year, and by mulling the prospect of making an escape attempt a kind of annual tradition it is forever left to our own imaginations as to whether their attempt at breaking out of incarceration was actually an effort to abscond from their self-conscious acknowledgement of their own amoral fallibility. While they prove beyond doubt their ability to escape from the physical confines of prison, it takes the whole film to similarly establish their capacity to shake off the manacles of their psychological propensity towards transgressive actions. Encountering the Ducotels has the potential to reconfigure their expectations about the adaptability of the concept of family and the reciprocal supportiveness of friendship, but it requires the redeeming power of Christmas to truly reform their interpretation of honour and constructive moral integrity, making true emancipation possible – even as they collectively decide to head back to jail.

REFERENCES

1.   James C. Robertson, *The Casablanca Man: The Cinema of Michael Curtiz* (London: Routledge, 1993), p.144.

2.   Paul Peterson, 'Michael Curtiz: The Mystery-Man Director of *Casablanca*', in *Political Philosophy Comes to Rick's: Casablanca and American Civic Culture*, ed. by James F. Pontuso (Lanham: Lexington Books, 2005), 135-52, p.149.

3.   Kate Kulzick, '25 Days of Christmas: *We're No Angels* Puts a Welcome Twist on the Standard Christmas Wish Story', in *PopOptiq*, 14 December 2013.
      <*https://www.popoptiq.com/25-days-of-christmas-were-no-angels-puts-a-welcome-twist-on-the-standard-christmas-wish-story/*>

4.   John Howard Reid, *Movies Magnificent: 150 Must-See Cinema Classics* (Morrisville: Lulu.com, 2005), p.221.

5.   Ryan McDonald, 'Review: *We're No Angels*', in *Shameless Self Expression*, 25 August 2014.
      <*http://ryancmcdonald.blogspot.com/2014/08/review-were-no-angels-1955.html*>

6.   H.H.T., '*We're No Angels* Bows', in *The New York Times*, 8 July 1955.
      <*https://www.nytimes.com/1955/07/08/archives/were-no-angels-bows.html*>

7.   Anon., 'Film Reviews: *We're No Angels*', in *Variety*, 15 June 1955.
      <*https://archive.org/details/variety198-1955-06/page/n133*>

8.   Barbara Paulding, Suzanne Schwalb and Mara Conlon, *A Century of Christmas Memories: 1900-1999* (New York: Peter Pauper Press, 2009), p.74.

9.   Derek Winnert, '*We're No Angels*', in *DerekWinnert.com*, 15 February 2016. <*http://www.derekwinnert.com/were-no-angels-1955-humphrey-bogart-peter-ustinov-aldo-ray-leo-g-carroll-joan-bennett-basil-rathbone-classic-movie-review-3362/*>

10.   Tim O'Neil, '*We're No Angels*', in *PopMatters*, 30 October 2005. <*https://www.popmatters.com/were-no-angels-dvd-2496250344.html*>

11.   Kulzick.

12.   Adrian Turner, '*We're No Angels*', in *Radio Times*, 7 November 2005. <*http://www.radiotimes.com/film/fk6mb4/were-no-angels*>

13.   Jessica Pickens, 'Christmas on Film: *We're No Angels*', in *Comet Over Hollywood*, 24 December 2015. <*https://cometoverhollywood.com/2015/12/24/christmas-with-the-comet-were-no-angels-1955/*>

14.   Winnert.

17

Bell, Book and Candle (1958)

Phoenix Productions

Director: Richard Quine
Producer: Julian Blaustein
Screenwriter: Daniel Taradash,
from a play by John Van Druten

AS one of the final Christmas-themed movies to be released in the 1950s, *Bell, Book and Candle* was to be an interesting hybrid of the traditional and the innovative. It may seem strangely ironic that as this break-through period of festive cinema reached its conclusion, it would end as it had begun: that is, with a film starring James Stewart in the lead role. Yet while the stylistic qualities of *The Shop Around the Corner* (q.v.) may have seemed very dissimilar from the supernatural hijinks of *Bell, Book and Candle*, both films do share one palpable similarity in that they use Christmas not just as an atmospheric backdrop for their action, but also as a means of exploring personal renewal; looking forward to the coming year with not just a new rela-tionship, but also a fresh way of looking at life.

Comedies starring (surprisingly good-natured) witches were not a new concept in popular culture, with films such as *I Married a Witch* (René Clair, 1942) cleverly subverting expectations of the horror genre in ways which would heavily influence later productions such as ABC's long-running situation comedy *Bewitched* (1964-72) and Disney's part-animated, part-live action film *Bedknobs and Broomsticks* (Robert Stevenson, 1971), amongst numerous others. *Bell, Book and Candle* was, however, the first to transpose this kind of supernatural comedy scenario onto a holiday season setting, the inspired clash of styles between the warm sentimentality of Christmas and the playful Halloween-style, carnivalesque paganism of the film's witches creating the kind of effective tonal juxtaposition that would inspire many later films in the genre such as *Gremlins* (Joe Dante, 1984), *The Nightmare Before Christmas* (Henry Selick, 1993) and *Rare Exports: A Christmas Tale* (Jalmari Helander, 2010).

Bell, Book and Candle was based on John Van Druten's three-act stage play of the same name, which had opened on Broadway on 14 November 1950 with Rex Harrison and Lilli Palmer in the lead roles. (The enigmatic title can be traced back to William Shakespeare's 1595 historical drama *King John*, and the line 'Bell, book and candle shall not drive me back' – the items in question referring to a ceremony used in excommunication rites.) The original play shared the Christmas setting of the later film, and was adapted by Daniel Taradash – a veteran screenwriter and playwright who had been active in the entertainment industry since the late 1930s, his script for *From Here to Eternity* (Fred Zinnemann, 1953) winning him the coveted Academy Award for Best Adapted Screenplay. Events leading up to the film's production were complicated, however, and – as Heather Greene has observed – there was an unsettled period of gestation before the film we recognise today began to take form:

Often mistaken for a remake of *I Married a Witch*, *Bell, Book and Candle* was actually based on a play by John Van Druten, which ran on Broadway from November 1950 to June 1951. In 1953, David Selznick purchased the film rights, but he never went forward with production, and sold the property to Columbia Pictures in 1956. Although Columbia was prepared to make the film in 1956, the first screenplay attempt was rejected by the PCA. [...] It was not witchcraft that was the problem, but rather the sexually suggestive elements found in costuming and language. [...] After adjustments were made, *Bell, Book and Candle*'s script was finally approved in November 1956.[1]

Eventually James Stewart and Kim Novak were cast as the film's romantic leads. They had been paired, to great acclaim, in Alfred Hitchcock's legendary film noir psychological thriller *Vertigo* (1958), which had been released in the May of the same year, meaning that there was considerable critical interest in their on-screen reunion when *Bell, Book and Candle* was released on 11 November 1958. However, their casting was not the original choice of the film-makers, as Taradash himself explained in an interview with David Thomson: 'We were going for Cary Grant and Grace Kelly, and we tried to get Alexander Mackendrick to direct. Mackendrick wanted changes we didn't want to make. Grant the same. Then Kelly got married. [...] On *Bell, Book and Candle*, the first couple of weeks [Kim Novak] was playing as if she were a witch. There was none of that old-world chemistry between her and Jimmy [Stewart] on screen'.[2] In spite of these early setbacks, however, the film went on to become commercially successful for

Columbia Pictures and one of the high-points of 1950s Christmas film-making.

Bell, Book and Candle was directed by Richard Quine, a former child actor on stage, radio and screen who turned to directing short features and, later, full-length motion pictures in the 1950s. Also a prolific director and occasional producer for television, Quine's cinematic filmography is especially well-remembered for his creative collaborations with Blake Edwards which included films such as *All Ashore* (1953), *Drive a Crooked Road* (1954), *Pushover* (1954) and *So This is Paris* (1954). By the time of *Bell, Book and Candle*'s production, Quine was considered one of the leading directors for Columbia Pictures, and he continued to helm films and television features into the late 1970s. Among his best-known features for the big screen were *It Happened to Jane* (1959), *Paris when it Sizzles* (1964) and *Hotel* (1967). However, the production of *Bell, Book and Candle* has remained one of his most enduring contributions to popular culture.

In 1950s New York City, art dealer Gillian Holroyd (Kim Novak) owns a store in Greenwich Village which specialises in rare African *objets d'art*. To her customers, she is a

Bell, Book and Candle (1958):
Phoenix Productions Inc./
Columbia Pictures

fashionably-dressed, knowledgeable art expert with an eccentric fondness for walking barefoot whenever and wherever she gets the chance. But little do they realise that Gillian is also a witch, whose supernatural powers are more extensive than any could guess at face value. It is late afternoon on Christmas Eve, and Gillian secretly admits to her Siamese cat Pyewacket that she feels jaded and listless. She tires of seeing the same clientele day after day, and wishes that she could meet someone new and unusual. She then spots publisher Shepherd 'Shep' Henderson (James Stewart), who has recently moved in to the apartment above her shop, and voices her approval to Pyewacket. Wistfully, she asks the cat if he would consider giving her Shep as a Christmas gift.

Upstairs, Shep unlocks the door to his apartment and is surprised to discover Queenie Holroyd (Elsa Lanchester), Gillian's aunt, rifling through his desk. She spins him a rather far-fetched yarn about having discovered the door to be open, explaining that she had only come into the apartment to close the window given that heavy snow is falling. But Shep is far from convinced, knowing that he had locked the door before leaving. He is uncomfortable about the fact that a stranger has quite obviously been reading his private papers and rummaging around his belongings. Shep also asks Queenie if she is an aspiring actress, as every night he can hear her reciting lines from the apartment above him – though he has been unable to hear the actual words she utters. Queenie denies any dramatic ambitions, but rather sheepishly agrees to keep the noise down in future. With forced politeness, Shep points out that he has a number of phone calls to make and emphatically suggests that Queenie should leave. Rather annoyed, she tells him that the theosophist who had lived in the apartment previously had been a much more polite and affable character. Shep seems relieved once she has finally left the apartment, but becomes confused when he realises that he can only hear strange gurgling noises from his telephone receiver – totally unaware that the departing Queenie has cast a spell on it.

Some time later, Shep – now immaculately dressed in a dinner suit – calls on Gillian to introduce himself and ask if he can use her phone, given that his own is 'mysteriously' out of order. She invites him through to her own apartment, which is adjacent to her ground-floor store. As he dials the phone, he spots that she is currently reading a book entitled *Magic in Mexico* by Sidney Redlitch. Revealing that he is a publisher, Shep laments that he hadn't signed up Redlitch as his books are proving to be very popular. However, word has it that the author will soon be looking for a new publishing house and Shep has hopes that his company may be able to sign him up in the future. Gillian is interested to hear of Shep's occupation, but is unimpressed by Redlitch's work; having spent a year in Mexico herself, she considers his research to be full of hoary old legends with no real substance. Nonetheless, she claims that she may be able to arrange, through a mutual acquaintance, a meeting between Shep and Redlitch. Shep readily agrees; while Redlitch has a reputation as an oddball and drunkard, his work is highly profitable. After a while on the phone, Shep reports to the operator that his own line is faulty (explaining that it sounds almost as though it is haunted) and asks for it to be repaired before Christmas. Gillian, who seems to know more about this fault than she cares to admit, listens innocently nearby. She asks Shep to join her for a drink, but he is late for a prior social engagement and has to race off. Before he can leave the apartment, Queenie arrives and asks Gillian to join her at the Zodiac Club. Shep seems intrigued, having never heard of the Zodiac before, and encourages

Gillian to go along, reasoning that nobody wants to stay at home alone on Christmas Eve. He wishes them both the compliments of the season as he departs.

With Shep gone, Queenie remarks that she can detect an attraction between him and Gillian. Her niece replies that she approves of Shep a great deal, but is displeased that Queenie has broken into his apartment to find out more about him – to say nothing of having tampered with his phone. Queenie replies that she would never have stolen anything, but did at least discover one interesting fact from reading Shep's private correspondence – he is engaged to be married. This disappoints Gillian, who feels it would be immoral to involve herself in an existing relationship, but Queenie tells her that with the simple use of a spell Shep would fall madly in love with her, never even suspecting the reason why. Not only does Gillian refuse, but she makes Queenie promise to stop practising magical rites in the apartment block, fearing that her lack of discretion will eventually give away the fact that they are both witches.

At the Zodiac Club later, Gillian's brother Nicky (Jack Lemmon) is playing tom-tom drums with the resident band as Queenie enjoys socialising – not least with her old friend Bianca De Pass (Hermione Gingold), another witch. However, Gillian feels strangely downcast in spite of the festival atmosphere. The club has no trace of traditional Christmas decoration, and Gillian feels that – just once – she would like the chance to hear carol singers and celebrate the season the way that mainstream society does. Queenie tells her that she would find normal life to be crushingly banal, but Gillian replies that sometimes ordinariness is a welcome prospect.

Having been intrigued by Gillian's earlier description of the Zodiac Club, Shep unexpectedly arrives there with his fiancée, Merle Kittridge (Janice Rule). Shep is fascinated with the unconventional venue, but Merle is deeply unimpressed, considering the club to be dingy and downmarket. Gillian immediately recognises Merle as an old college rival; during their student days, Merle had mean-spiritedly written an anonymous note to the faculty dean alerting them to Gillian's predilection for going barefoot everywhere, putting her on probation – a fact that the footwear-hating Gillian has never forgotten. Shep makes every effort to be responsive and sociable, but Merle is aloof and condescending to all present. In response, Gillian silently signals to Nicky to surround Merle with deafening trumpet players. She also reminds Merle that she remembers her phobia of thunderstorms, and points out how amazingly improbable it was that their final year at college together was plagued by ear-piercing storms which lasted for weeks. Merle seems discomfited just by the memory of it. Between that and the raucous music, she grows panicky and bolts from the club – much to Gillian's silent satisfaction.

On the way home, as Nicky – a warlock – amuses himself by psychically extinguishing a block's worth of streetlights, Gillian confides to Queenie that she feels no guilt for her treatment of Merle. She had found the woman to be a deceitful, two-faced sneak in college, and clearly little has changed in the years since. Gillian also reveals that it was she who had conjured the endless thunderstorms back then, reducing the untrustworthy Merle to a nervous wreck by the time they were due to graduate. Because Merle had a reputation for stealing other women's partners, Queenie encourages Gillian to make a move while she still can – her conscience need no longer be troubled. Gillian replies that she has no interest in winning Shep's heart unless she can do so by honest means, but Queenie worries that if she genuinely falls in love with the debonair publisher, she will risk losing her supernatural powers. Gillian considers this to be little more than a legend, but does admit that it is rare for witches to find love.

Back at Gillian's shop, she, Queenie and Nicky exchange Christmas gifts. Nicky reflects sadly that he could never understand why magic-users tend to be perpetually broke when they could presumably conjure money from nowhere, but Gillian warns him that using magic indiscriminately can have negative repercussions on the person casting spells. Gillian has bought her relatives distinctly down-to-earth gifts, but she is intrigued with Nicky's present – a potion for summoning someone. If the mysterious liquid is applied to an image of somebody, and a ritual carried out, the person in question will subsequently feel compelled to travel to that destination. Gillian wastes no time in casting the rite on a photo of Sidney Redlitch so that, as promised, she can entice him from Acapulco to meet with Shep.

Shortly afterwards there is a knock at the shop door, but it isn't Redlitch who has arrived – rather, it is Shep, concerned about the pyrotechnics resulting from Gillian's shop (as a result of the spell). Nicky laughs it off as a Christmas lark, but Shep seems unconvinced by the explanation. Sensing an opportunity to leave Gillian and Shep together, Queenie and Nicky make a hasty departure. Gillian pours her neighbour the promised nightcap, and Shep drops the unexpected bombshell that he intends to marry Merle on Christmas Day. This news dismays Gillian, partly because she knows of Merle's poor character but mostly due to her growing attraction to Shep. With the help of her cat Pyewacket, she casts a love spell on the hapless publisher, leaving him defenceless in the face of her romantic allure. Knowing that he has a big day ahead, Shep tries to withdraw back to his apartment but finds that he is incapable of resisting Gillian's charms. Instantly besotted, they spend the night wandering New York in each other's arms, eventually ending up at the top of the Flatiron Building where they watch dawn break as Christmas Day arrives in New York. Totally spellbound, Shep realises that he is completely in love with Gillian to the point that he has difficulty remembering details of events from mere hours beforehand. But for all her earlier protestations of emotional distance, it is clear that Gillian is falling for him too.

Shep meets with Merle and breaks off their engagement, leaving her speechless as he admits that he is no longer in love with her. He considers her ire to be somewhat ironic, given that she had herself jilted a former partner in order to be with Shep. Merle loses her cool, but – in spite of her fury – her former fiancé skips happily away from her apartment towards a different future. He is unaware that back at the shop, Gillian is feeling guilty about having cast the spell, and develops misgivings about the unethicality of her influence over Shep – especially as he is oblivious to her powers.

After Christmas, Shep returns to his office and informs his personal assistant Tina (Bek Nelson) to cancel all future social engagements he had planned with Merle. But he hardly has the time to remove his overcoat before his office is invaded by a slightly dishevelled stranger – none other than bestselling author Sidney Redlitch (Ernie Kovacs). Shep is amazed to meet the enigmatic writer, especially as he had only been talking about him a few days earlier. Neither realises that Redlitch is only there as a result of Gillian's Christmas summoning ritual, and he seems rather dazed to have made the journey from Mexico so rapidly. Though he is unsure how and why he has arrived in Shep's office in New York, Redlitch explains that he is planning to write a new book about witchcraft in New York. Shep and his business partner, Andy White (Howard McNear), are highly sceptical of Redlitch's claims to have tracked down whole communities of witches and warlocks in Manhattan, but cannot deny the inebriated author's commercial potential. Shep is particularly fascinated when Redlitch mentions that one of the epicentres of supernatural activity is the Zodiac Club, and suggests that he introduce him to some friends of his acquaintance.

Sure enough, Shep takes Redlitch to Gillian's shop, where the intoxicated writer regales Queenie, Nicky and Gillian with his grandiose tales of witches and their customs. They listen, straight-faced, as he points out that he would be able to identify a witch or warlock immediately – in spite of the fact that he is currently talking to three of them without realising it. Shep announces that he will agree to publish Redlitch's book, inferring that – although he doesn't take the subject particularly seriously – there is no reason why it might not still go down well with a wide readership. When Gillian asks Redlitch if he fears reprisals, he explains that he hopes to ingratiate himself with Bianca De Pass, who holds a position of seniority amongst the local witches in the area. This statement causes some unease. Gillian is also silently alarmed when Redlitch points out that cats, such as Pyewacket, regularly take on the mantle of a witch's familiar.

Making the excuse of having to attend a dance with Shep, Gillian breaks up the meeting. Queenie leaves, and as Nicky is in the process of departing Gillian warns him to divert Redlitch as much as possible – it will be vital to keep him away from Mrs De Pass if they intend to disrupt the research for his new book. Stopping only to tell Shep that he expects a healthy advance for his manuscript, Redlitch heads off into the city with Nicky in search of another drink. In spite of

Gillian's warnings, Nicky becomes intrigued when Redlitch says that he would split his book's royalties on a 50-50 basis if he could enlist the assistance of an actual witch or warlock. Seeing a solid business opportunity, he reveals that he is part of New York's supernatural community and even gives the mystified author an example of his powers to prove his authenticity. The next day, Nicky takes Redlitch to an herbal remedy shop where he used to work and reveals that it is secretly a front for the witches of New York. Acting as an inside source, he then apprises the writer with a great deal of privileged research which is quickly committed to paper.

After an entertaining afternoon skating in Central Park, Shep and Gillian retire to her apartment behind the shop. Their evening is interrupted when Nicky phones Gillian to clarify a few facts about the supernatural and, when she grows suspicious regarding why he needs to know such arcane details, he reveals that he is working with Redlitch. Gillian is concerned by his collaboration, but with Shep overhearing the conversation she is unable to enquire any further and hangs up before he can give away their supernatural characteristics. However, that isn't the most pressing of her concerns, as Shep decides out of the blue to propose to her. Though they have only been in a relationship for two weeks, Shep is unable to concentrate on his work and finds that he is totally focused on Gillian and their time together. He is startled when she ducks the question and is confused by her reluctance. Pressing her for an explanation, she tells him that she doesn't feel like the marrying type – given her freewheeling approach to life, there seems to be little room for a long-term partnership. Gillian explains that to marry someone would mean having to sacrifice a great deal of herself, though he doesn't realise the true meaning of her statement – that she risks losing her supernatural powers as a result. Realising that she has come to a cross-roads, Gillian eventually relents and tells Shep that she has made a final decision: she wants to marry him, too.

Later, Gillian visits the Zodiac Club and is vexed when she sees Redlitch feverishly writing at the bar. She meets Nicky backstage and discovers that he, too, is hard at work behind a typewriter. Her brother explains that Redlitch's initial research was full of tall tales and inaccuracies, but that he has corrected it with the unvarnished truth about the supernatural underworld of New York in the hope that extra accuracy will ensure the book's commercial success. Gillian is deeply perturbed; after all the effort she has gone to in order to keep her powers a secret, Nicky's exposé now threatens to blow their clandestine community apart. Furthermore, she is concerned that if Shep discovers the truth about their family, he will be able to deduce that his passionate love for her is actually the result of a magic spell. Nicky is aghast that she has agreed to marry Shep and relinquish her powers as a result. He sees this book as his unexpected ticket to a literary career in the prestigious New York publishing scene, and tells Gillian in no uncertain terms that he has no intention of passing up such a golden opportunity.

Back at her shop, Gillian casts another spell and causes Shep to be biased against the quality of Redlitch's book. Once Shep has struggled his way through the manuscript, he believes it to be devoid of literary merit and calls a meeting with Redlitch and Nicky. He proclaims that the book is unpublishable, far-fetched, and makes it clear that if he were to release it to the public his company would become a laughing stock. Redlitch is perplexed, having only delivered the exact type of book he had promised, but Nicky realises what has happened – his suspicions are confirmed when Shep is unable to give any explicit details of what the book's faults are, as though he were in some sort of trance. Gillian arrives unexpectedly and terminates the meeting, but Nicky makes it clear that he knows the truth behind the book's rejection. A conciliatory Shep tells Redlitch that he can keep the advance, but politely brushes off other book ideas. He also suggests that Nicky take his manuscript to another publisher in the city but he refuses, pointing out that it would make no difference (knowing that Gillian would simply pull the same trick again in order to keep the secrets of their supernatural community from prying eyes).

With the two writers gone, Gillian reluctantly confesses to Shep that she is a witch. However, he is unwilling to believe her as he considers the whole world of magic to be hokum – and Redlitch's book has done nothing to change his opinion. Frustrated, Gillian explains that everything from the problems with the telephone in Shep's apartment to the mysterious appearance of Redlitch have all been the product of witchcraft, but he waves away all of these incidents as mere coincidence. Even once she tells him the attraction he feels for her is down to a love spell, he is so infatuated by her that he simply rationalises it by assuming she is talking about her magnetic allure rather than actual supernatural power. Realising that nothing is going to get through to him, she departs leaving a deeply confused Shep in her wake.

That afternoon, as Shep takes a yellow cab back to his apartment, he begins to seriously ask himself about Gillian and the powers she professes to have. He meets Queenie in the street, who congratulates him on his engagement but also corroborates everything Gillian had told him earlier. However, when she explains about the love spell he mistakenly believes that she had stolen his affections not out of mutual attraction but rather in an attempt to punish Merle for their college-era disagreements. After all, as Queenie points out, love is simply not an option for a witch.

Shep is furious at having been manipulated, especially now that he believes Gillian has no genuine feelings for him. She assures Shep that she really was attracted to him and that her desire to even the odds with Merle was simply the starting point of their relationship, not the overall aim of it. But Shep feels used and tells her that he is leaving and has no intention of coming back – until, of course, the spell compels him to immediately return to Gillian's shop. Now realising the enormity of the truth that faces him, the rattled publisher heads back to his office for a stiff drink. Inspiration suddenly strikes Shep, and he visits the Zodiac Club to enlist the help of Nicky and Redlitch. They suggest that he visit Bianca De Pass, who has considerable powers and may have the means to break Gillian's love spell. After a long cab journey to her house, Shep convinces Mrs De Pass to put him through a rather esoteric ritual in order to rid him of his feelings for Gillian. To this end, she concocts a peculiar potion which he reluctantly drinks.

The next day, Gillian watches dejectedly from her shop as removal men load their van with Shep's furniture. She is angry with Nicky for having suggested that Shep visit Mrs De Pass to have the spell broken, but her brother feels she has no-one but herself to blame for the situation. He departs just as Shep appears. The publisher curtly tells Gillian that one of the preconditions of interrupting the love spell was that he had to confront her one last time, hence his current presence in the shop. Gillian despairs that he had gone to such lengths to dismiss her magical rite, especially when she realises that it had cost him $1,000 (considerably less than the cost of a divorce, as Shep points out). Sarcastically, he tells her that he couldn't depart without giving her a parting gift and produces a new broomstick. Fuming at the prospect of him going back to Merle, Gillian threatens to cast a whole range of problematic spells on her old college nemesis – including making her fall madly in love with the first stranger she sets her eyes on. Shep leaves in disdain, but Gillian is more concerned about the fact that Pyewacket – presumably unwilling to take part in casting a damaging spell on someone – seems to have run away from her apartment.

Shep visits Merle and unsuccessfully attempts rapprochement for his earlier rash actions. However, he meets with an icy response – not least as she doesn't believe a word about his brush with witches and warlocks. Eventually realising that any effort at reconciliation is now useless, Shep withdraws. Back at the shop, Queenie has discovered Pyewacket at the top of the apartment building and returns him to Gillian. However, the cat is singularly unwilling to be party to any attempt to cast a spell on Merle and runs off into the streets of New York. Distraught at the loss of her beloved companion, Gillian realises that she has shed a tear – something that it is supposed to be impossible for a witch to do. Gillian realises that she must genuinely have fallen in love with Shep, as she has lost her powers of magic. Thus Pyewacket wasn't just experiencing an attack of conscience; he no longer considers himself to be her familiar. Queenie is curious about what 'normal' life must feel like, but now that Gillian's link to the supernatural has been severed she feels lost and forlorn.

Months pass by. At the Zodiac Club, Redlitch and Mrs De Pass have struck up a close friendship – the author now intends to write a biography of the unconventional sorceress. Nicky and Queenie discuss their concerns about Gillian. She is depressed and solitary, with even Pyewacket refusing to return home. In spite of realising that her feelings for Shep are genuine, she is too independently-minded to reconcile with him – and she has also forbidden Queenie from attempting to do so on her behalf. Nicky is unwilling to help, pointing out that he has never really believed in either love or interacting with non-magic users. But knowing the extent of Gillian's unhappiness, Queenie resolves to find a way of sorting things out once and for all.

At Shep's office, the publisher is cranky and irritable but discovers that his short temper is being exacerbated by an allergy – the long-lost Pyewacket has come to call, jumping in through the window. Knowing that the feisty cat can be a slippery customer, Shep temporarily contains him within a waste-paper basket and takes the elusive feline back to Gillian's shop. To his astonishment, when he arrives there he discovers that Gillian has completely refurbished the premises. All of the exotic African artefacts have gone, replaced with elaborate floral displays and decorative seashells. Furthermore, Gillian herself has substituted her familiar offbeat fashion sense with much more conventional attire (including, amazingly for her, smart shoes). Shep is taken aback by her transformation and gruffly attempts to return Pyewacket – only to discover that Gillian has transferred ownership of her beloved cat to Queenie. This makes Shep wonder if the inscrutable feline's appearance at his office was quite the coincidence it seemed to be. He confirms that he has not renewed his relationship with Merle, and he grudgingly thanks Gillian for not having cast any spells on her. Shep notices that she is blushing, and later cries – both characteristics that indicate that she has lost her powers as a witch. Realising that she must have genuinely fallen in love with him, Shep assures her that he has retained his feelings for her too – and without the need of any magic spell. They embrace, together once again, and Shep wonders if their love was real from the very minute they first met. After all, magic takes many forms.

For all its scenic snowfall and chilly exteriors, *Bell, Book and Candle* is far from a conventional Christmas film; as Shep himself observes, with its outlandish venues and supernatural ambiance it sometimes feels more like Halloween than the festive season – though strangely enough, it is never less than appealing for it. Now generally considered to be James Stewart's last romantic lead role, the film is highly distinctive in its depiction of the urban nooks and crannies of New York (albeit that the streets of the 'city that never sleeps' often look suspiciously depopulated, even in the daytime). The production does occasionally betray its stage-based roots, but Quine's direction and Taradash's screenplay admirably open up proceedings to many locations beyond the apartment building occupied by Gillian, Shep and Queenie, also skilfully integrating characters such as Janice Rule's Merle Kittridge and Hermione Gingold's Bianca De Pass who are mentioned in the original play but do not actually appear in it. Events are also enlivened by James Wong Howe's impressive cinematography, not least in the way that he captures the atmospheric Christmas morning sunrise over a frosty Manhattan; audiences may momentarily forget that they too are not viewing the city from a vantage point high up on Fifth Avenue's Flatiron Building.

In addition to its playful collocation of Christmas cheer and the supernatural macabre, *Bell, Book and Candle* gleefully satirises the fast-moving publishing business of the time. It is hinted that Shep sometimes seems to value a project's commercial viability beyond its quality or originality, signing up Redlitch with a healthy advance even though he personally has misgivings about the planned book's subject matter. (As we later discover, of course, he still considers overall literary merit to be of paramount importance – though how much of this scrupulous critical integrity is down to Gillian's supernatural interference, warning him off the prospect of publishing Nicky and Redlitch's manuscript, is left to the audience to decide.) Ernie Kovacs turns in a brilliant comic performance as the permanently-sozzled Sidney Redlitch, a prolific writer and researcher whose bulletproof work ethic is balanced by his narcissism and the fact that he always has a bottle of bourbon (complete with a straw) placed next to his typewriter. Even the seemingly easy-going Nicky is willing to put the safety and secrecy of his covert community at risk solely for the opportunity to have a crack at making a name for himself in the ultra-competitive New York publishing industry. In the end, however, there is a happy ending for everyone – and even the egotistical Redlitch's writing career is seen to be undamaged by the rejection of his book, given that he plans to write Mrs De Pass's biography (thus ensuring that his copious prior research will not entirely go to waste).

Bell, Book and Candle is at its best, however, in its depiction of its unexpected urban secrets and its supernatural mysteries hidden in plain sight. There is something supremely likeable about a nightclub that will only admit patrons if their star sign is favourable at the time of their attempted entry, just as there is appeal in the collection of kooky magic-users fraternising to the sophisticated singing voice of Philippe Clay (perhaps best-known as Casimir le Serpentin in Jean Renoir's 1955 film *French Cancan*). The focus on the covert nature of the witches and warlocks' activities – to the point that Redlitch's book pitch seems preposterous to 'outsiders' – has led critics to suggest numerous subtexts over the years. This is particularly palpable in a 1950s setting when, as Gillian tries to

confess to being a witch, Shep assumes that she must be admitting to un-American activities (Communist sympathies),
but other allegories have been posited over the years. As
Graeme Clark notes, 'there have been some interesting inter-
pretations of *Bell Book and Candle* and the subculture it presents; depending on who you talk to they can either represent
Communists having to live in secret in McCarthy's America
or the homosexual underground having to live in secret in a
country where their activities are equally as illegal. But really
they look much more like beatniks to me, with all the perceived pretension that went with that lifestyle, still apart from
"normal" society but looking down on the straights who don't
get it'.[3]

Of all the witches in the film, by far the most prominent is Gillian, and her transformation proves to be – in its
way – just as profound as that which affected misers like
Ebenezer Scrooge or ne'er-do-wells such as the Lemon Drop
Kid. With her ultra-cool fashion sense, ethereal presence, oth-
erworldly voice and penchant for going barefoot, she is a striking figure and clearly possessed of great independence of character. (Though bare feet in public and social situations became
a widespread countercultural fashion in the 1960s and 70s, the
practice was considerably less common in the fifties – especially in large urban areas like New York – thus marking Gillian
out to audiences as being a free spirit with a true bohemian
sensibility.) Taradash carefully foreshadows Gillian's conversion from witch to human by emphasising her languor and
general dissatisfaction with life. On one hand, she longs to be
closer to the mainstream of society; on the other, she resists
the comparative mundanity that comes with an ordinary life
as an average human being. Her gradual realisation that Shep
is not simply drawn to her on account of her spell, but that he

reciprocates a romantic attraction that even she does not immediately recognise in herself, parallels her apprehension that her connection to the world of magic is ebbing away. This transformation is, of course, mirrored in Shep's closing observations that magic can present itself in a variety of forms – not all of them supernatural. As Sanderson Beck observes, 'this romantic comedy portrays witches and a warlock who practice the selfish side of spiritual skills and therefore do not know real love. When the love of the publisher awakens Gillian's love, she realizes that magic has kept from experiencing life in its spiritual fullness'.[4]

Due to the high-profile on-screen pairing of Stewart and Novak as John 'Scottie' Ferguson and Madeleine Elster in *Vertigo* earlier that same year, audiences and critics took a genuine interest in the central romance of *Bell, Book and Candle*, keen to see how this mystical Christmas fantasy would compare to Hitchcock's celebrated thriller. In truth, while the two films were wildly dissimilar in tone and style, the age gap between the two leads seems considerably more apparent in the later feature: Stewart was to celebrate his 50th birthday just after the production of *Bell, Book and Candle*, while Novak was only 25 at the time. Though there was no doubting the acting talent on display, the plausibility of the on-screen love match split the opinion of commentators and continues to divide critical judgements even to this day. Ed Howard, for instance, has remarked that the unconventional pairing was an apposite match for a pleasingly quirky film: 'There's something inherently appealing about throwing together Stewart at his most "aw-shucks" with the icy, glib Novak, a perfect Hitchcock blonde if ever there was one. Sparks fly just putting the two of them together, and there's something urgent and believable about their kisses, an uneasy passion that Hitchcock would channel into something sinister and gripping in *Vertigo*, and which here director Richard Quine uses to much more prosaic effect'.[5] On the contrasting side of the argument, other reviewers such as Jeffrey Kauffman have acknowledged the on-screen age gap while similarly stating that this is but one factor in a larger consideration of the film's winning performances:

> The film never really truly catches fire, and yet there's charm aplenty in the performances. Novak has probably never been more alluring, even if at times she's slightly sinister, especially after she decides to get her way by casting a spell or two. Stewart felt he was too old for a romantic part such as this, and that may be true, but he brings a certain fumbling sensibility to Shep that is well modulated and certainly never as buffoonish as, for example, Darrin [Stephens] usually was on *Bewitched*. [...] Seeing the film now it's a quaint time capsule that captures Novak at the height of her almost alien beauty, and which provides a field day for a number of enjoyable character bits by a host of superb supporting players.[6]

Bell, Book and Candle was treated by Columbia Pictures as one if its most high-profile releases of 1958, and this was certainly reflected in its promotion at the time. The year beforehand, producers Phoenix Productions announced an extensive search for a suitable Siamese cat to play Pyewacket. (The cat's unusual name, appropriately enough, originates from the familiar of an alleged witch who was tried by England's Witchfinder General, Matthew Hopkins, in March 1644 during a trial in Manningtree in Essex.) The promotion was used as an early marketing device for the film, and stressed the fact that it may be necessary to recruit a number of cats in order to perform the various stunts required in the film. The most renowned of the Siamese cats to be cast in the role was Houdini, a particularly sociable feline who was filmed in scenes where close-ups were required or when Pyewacket was handled by the human stars of the film. *Bell, Book and Candle* was also featured heavily in the trade press at the time – most prominently in *Life* magazine, where Novak and Pyewacket appeared on the cover of the 25 November 1958 issue. The film's theme music by George Duning was also featured on NBC's *The Steve Allen Show* (1956-64) around the time of its cinematic release; along with the sound of bongo drums which evoke the Zodiac Club's band, the track also includes a brief refrain of 'Jingle Bells' to emphasise the film's Christmas setting.

James Stewart had remained one of America's most famous stars throughout the 1950s, starting with his Academy Award-nominated performance in *Harvey* (Henry Koster, 1950) where he reprised his role as Elwood P. Dowd from Mary Coyle Chase's original 1944 stage version. As the decade progressed, he became particularly well-known for his appearances in Westerns such as Anthony Mann's *Winchester '73* (1950), *The Far Country* (1954) and *The Man from Laramie* (1956), and thrillers including Alfred Hitchcock's *Rear Window* (1954) and *The Man Who Knew Too Much* (1956). Among his many other prominent performances in this period were roles in films such as *Broken Arrow* (Delmer Daves, 1950), *The Greatest Show on Earth* (Cecil B. DeMille, 1952), *The Glenn Miller Story* (Anthony Mann, 1954), *Strategic Air Command* (Anthony Mann, 1955) and *The Spirit of St Louis* (Billy Wilder, 1957). While the ever-reliable Stewart provides a rock solid performance as the slightly baffled Shepherd Henderson, alongside some of the best-regarded roles of his career the part has actually become one of the more obscure of his 1950s acting appearances – a fact which, in the opinion of critics such as Stuart Galbraith IV, may be attributed to his relative paucity of screen time in comparison to Novak's Gillian, meaning that the potential for character development was essentially quite limited:

> I think the basic problem with *Bell Book and Candle* is that Stewart's character is a passive participant for almost the entire film. For the first three-quarters of the picture, he's completely oblivious to the spell cast on him, and when finally told by Gil for a long time after he refuses to believe her. In short, despite Stewart's top billing the movie's drama and conflicts really have nothing much to do with him, nor does he drive the plot at all. Instead, it's all about her conflicted emotions, of being attracted to and repulsed by mortal notions and consequences of falling in love. For Novak this is an excellent star turn, but Stewart is like a fifth wheel.[7]

Kim Novak achieved fame in the 1950s due to positive reception to a prolific string of appearances in films including *Pushover* (Richard Quine, 1954), *Phffft* (Mark Robson, 1954), *Picnic* (Joshua Logan, 1955) and *The Man with the Golden Arm* (Otto Preminger, 1955), in which she performed alongside Frank Sinatra. While *Vertigo* and *Bell, Book and Candle* are often considered her breakthrough roles, she would continue to perform for many years thereafter, her appearances becoming more sporadic from the mid-1960s onwards as she pursued a number of other professional interests including the visual arts, poetry and writing song lyrics.

While the supporting cast of *Bell, Book and Candle* was not especially expansive, every member gives a compelling performance – most notably Elsa Lanchester (forever remembered in the title role of James Whale's 1935 landmark horror film *The Bride of Frankenstein*) as the delightfully wacky Aunt Queenie and Hermione Gingold – perhaps best-known for her appearance in Vincente Minnelli's *Gigi* (1958) – in her brief but effective appearance as the polite but domineering Bianca De Pass. Jack Lemmon, who was just on the cusp of hitting the big time as Jerry in *Some Like it Hot* (Billy Wilder, 1959) has obvious fun as the zany Nicky, his disdain for 'humdrum' society balanced by his laid-back, quirky approach to life. Janice Rule – famous for film noir crime thriller *A Woman's Devotion* (Paul Henreid, 1956) and Western drama *Gun for a Coward* (Abner Biberman, 1957) – gives a glacially contemptuous performance as Merle Kittridge, Shep's formidable ex-fiancée, but overshadowing everyone around him is the scene-stealing Ernie Kovacs in a faultless comic performance as the conceited alcoholic author Sidney Redlitch. Kovacs was a highly influential comedian and writer, his surreal humour and the originality of his performances eventually earning him Emmy Award nominations and a posthumous star on the Hollywood Walk of Fame.

While *Bell, Book and Candle* was a box-office hit for Columbia Pictures, Quine's film split critical opinion at the time of its release. *The New York Times*, for instance, praised the film's technical achievement but derided the plot as being hackneyed and predictable: 'The gimmick of John van Druten's stage play, which has been used as the basis for this film – the gimmick of a woman endowed with witchcraft – is

really rather silly and banal. And, as Daniel Taradash has reduced it in a screen play directed by Richard Quine, it is not
distinguished by any consistent witchary [sic] or bounce.
However, Julian Blaustein's production of this mildly supernatural romance is as sleek and pictorially entrancing as any
romance we've looked at this year. [...] *Bell, Book and Candle*,
like the stage play, is only so-so sorcery, but it comes pretty
close to magic so far as its color values are concerned'.[8] By
comparison, *Variety* found the central performance and outlandish scenarios to be the film's main shortcomings: 'Richard
Quine's direction gets everything possible out of the screenplay and the cast. But with Kim Novak the central figure, the
picture lacks the spontaneity and sparkle written in by playwright John Van Druten. [...] The hazard of the story is that
there is really only one joke. This was sustained in the play by
Van Druten's witty dialog. It is undercut in the picture by the
fact that the backgrounds are too often as weird as the situations'.[9]

Critical variance over the perceived merits and failings
of *Bell, Book and Candle* has continued until the present day,
with commentators focusing on a range of different aspects of
the production over the past few years. Laura Grieve, for instance, has drawn attention to the film's captivating performances: 'This enjoyable film is distinguished by its cast – you
know you're in good hands when the supporting cast is headed by Jack Lemmon – as well as an evocative score by George
Duning and a distinctive "look" filmed in Technicolor by
James Wong Howe. The movie features Oscar-nominated
costumes by Jean Louis; the Art Direction and Set Decoration
also received a nomination. I especially loved an unusual me-
tallic Christmas tree featured in the opening scenes'.[10] Dave
Sindelar, on the other hand, has bemoaned what he has per-

ceived to be surprisingly conventional plot dynamics which lurk beneath the film's eccentric exterior: 'The cinematography is beautiful, the special effects (the few that exist anyway) are very good, the use of color is stunning, and it has an excellent cast. It's the story that leaves me cold. It was originally conceived as a drama, but only became a comedy when laughter during auditions indicated that it would work better that way. Still, I find very few laughs here, and despite the excellent cast, I simply didn't find the characters interesting enough to bring this overlong but rather ordinary love story to life. And, despite the magic and witchcraft, I think the story is very ordinary – it's one where a woman gives up everything for love, and that's fairly common'.[11]

On the other end of the critical spectrum, many reviewers – Derek Winnert among them – have praised *Bell, Book and Candle* for its skilful combination of talent, from its actors to its production values: 'With Technicolor cinematography by James Wong Howe and [an original score] by George Duning, producer Julian Blaustein's movie looks as smart as it sounds. [...] A really lovely vintage cast lights up this bewitching diversion with a dash of real emotion and a high quota of laughs. Lemmon enjoys himself as Novak's impish warlock brother Nicky Holroyd, and scene-stealing Hermione Gingold and Elsa Lanchester are particularly amusing as daffy sorceresses, Bianca de Passe [sic] and Aunt Queenie Holroyd'.[12] Richard Scheib, by contrast, commended James Stewart's take on the lead performance but lamented the film's lack of visual grandeur when it came to presenting supernatural powers: 'The script is well tuned. The cast is a wonderful light comic ensemble and contains fine comic performances from Jack Lemmon, Elsa Lancaster [sic], Ernie Kovacs and Hermione Gingold. At age 50, James Stewart looks a little too old to seem the eminently desirable bachelor but he gives another engaging variation on the deadpan comic performance he had down pat by this point. The production values are lush [[and]] the film does a reasonable job of shuffling locations around so as to keep the story free of its stagebound origins. It is however surprisingly light when it comes to actual displays of magic – only ever providing a green fire and Jack Lemmon's streetlight trick'.[13] The film does retain its admirers, however, with critics such as Andy Webb extolling the effectiveness of the overall production as an alternative treat from a bygone era of cinema:

> Whilst the storyline ends up disappointing there is much to love about *Bell, Book and Candle*. The naturalness between Kim Novak and James Stewart is one of those things which probably comes from having already worked together on Alfred Hitchcock's *Vertigo*. It almost feels in the scenes where they are falling in love that there is real chemistry, not the sort which sparks off of the screen but oozes warmth. And even in the scenes they do not share they both deliver enjoyable performances, Stewart delivering that comfortable every man performance which he did better than anyone. Whilst Novak racks up the sexiness with an almost cat like performance as Gil, slinking about in such an extraordinarily, beautiful way.[14]

Bell, Book and Candle was nominated for two Academy Awards, in the categories of Best Costume Design and Best Art Direction. Many years later, the film was used as the basis for a TV fantasy situation comedy. Loosely based around the characters from the film, the *Bell, Book and Can-*

dle TV series would have starred Yvette Mimieux as Gillian and Michael Murphy as Shep. The pilot episode aired on NBC on 8 September 1976, directed by Hy Averbeck. However, it was not developed into a full series. In more recent years, a musical cinematic remake of *Bell, Book and Candle* was mooted by the Walt Disney Company in 2006. Actress and music star Alicia Keys was approached to play Gillian Holroyd in a production that was intended to bring the action of John Van Druten's play into a modern urban setting. However, the film was ultimately never made.

With its paranormal whimsy and charmingly offbeat characters, *Bell, Book and Candle* was a very different kind of Christmas film, and one which supplanted the transformative effects of the festive season for a simpler message: that true love can change anyone for the better. For all the trimmings of its holiday setting – Gillian's stylish Christmas tree, yellow cabs driving through New York's slushy snow, and some remarkably off-the-wall gifts exchanged between the Holroyds – the film has nonetheless become more memorable for its overlaying of the mystical and the uncanny onto the comforting conventions of Christmas. Though *Ghostbusters* (Ivan Reitman, 1984) would bring comic supernatural thrills to New York City in an even more immediate manner a few decades later (Reitman's 1989 sequel, *Ghostbusters II*, even featuring a Christmas setting), for many years *Bell, Book and Candle* was to be the Big Apple's definitive unearthly comedy and remains fondly remembered as a cult classic even today.

Being released at the end of the fifties, *Bell, Book and Candle* was a successful movie which was nonetheless produced at a point when the Christmas film was just on the cusp of going out of fashion at the box-office. Although the decade had seen numerous other features which dealt specifically with Christmas themes, including *The Holly and the Ivy* (q.v.) and *Susan Slept Here* (Frank Tashlin, 1954), or which had featured prominent Christmas settings such as *The Lemon Drop Kid* (q.v.), *Stalag 17* (Billy Wilder, 1953) and *Auntie Mame* (Morton da Costa, 1958), gradually dwindling audience interest over the following two decades would witness the genre fade almost to the point of obscurity in cinemas. Yet just as the golden age of the traditional Christmas film in the mid-forties to the early fifties had exhibited a rapid evolution into the glamorous Technicolor modernity of *White Christmas*, this highly flexible film genre still had more than a few surprises in store for the wilderness period which lay ahead.

Due to the thematic foundations of the genre laid down in the 1940s, it seems certain that as long as there is a holiday season there will also be a demand for Christmas films: viewer enthusiasm for classic and modern entries in the genre continue to remain healthy year on year. Due to its key themes of inclusiveness, community, family and personal transformation, the Christmas film has continued to remain relevant even as styles have continually changed and evolved from decade to decade. Yet in a critical environment where realism and verisimilitude remain paramount, the cinema of the festive season's continual brush with the playful and the fantastic annually unleashes a joyful, seasonal world of unabashed imaginative caprice and merriment which has allowed an unerringly cheerful, sanguine approach to fictional scenarios that is quite unlike that of any other category of film. Yet the ability of the various subgenres of the Christmas movie which have rapidly developed since the 1940s have allowed this category of film to constantly reinvent approaches to their central subject matter, all the while remaining true to the invariable core themes of festive film-making. Dramatic realism may faithfully attempt to reflect society as it actually is, but the creative imagination of the Christmas film presents us with a tempting projection of how we would ideally like things to be in our own lives. The achievement of the beatific community life of Bedford Falls may seem like the most implausible of goals in a postmodern age of self-isolation and assertive self-interest, but that does not impede audiences from a genuine desire to believe that such a benevolent, unselfish and civilised existence still remains possible and desirable for each of us. So too, as the world's societal and cultural norms continue to change with ever-greater rapidity, are we left with an irrepressible notion that there is undeniable comfort in a seasonal mythology full of reassuring invariants: a world where transformative self-improvement can always prove possible, where a personal redemption that might otherwise seem impossible suddenly becomes a reality, and where we are all presented with a chance to comfort our fellow human being and disseminate goodwill and compassion.

Though the Christmas movie would experience a renaissance and, eventually, a second golden age throughout the 1980s, the sixties and seventies would be an era which would bear witness to considerable experimentation within the genre, where the thematic conventions which had become established from the mid-1940s onwards would be examined, interrogated, reinvented, pushed to their limits, and ultimately reinforced. The progressiveness felt within the genre during those two decades would test the adaptiveness of the tropes which had been laid down within the golden age of the Christmas movie, but in due course would prove that this versatile genre was creatively robust, full of artistic potential, and ultimately here to stay as an enduring fixture in popular culture.

REFERENCES

1.   Heather Greene, *Bell, Book and Camera: A Critical History of Witches in American Film and Television* (Jefferson: McFarland, 2018), p.110.

2.   David Thomson, 'Daniel Taradash: Triumph and Chaos', in *Backstory 2: Interviews with Screenwriters of the 1940s and 1950s*, ed. by Patrick McGilligan (Berkeley: University of California Press, 1997) [1991], 309-29, p.324.

3.   Graeme Clark, '*Bell Book and Candle* Review', in *The Spinning Image*, 19 August 2002.
        <*http://www.thespinningimage.co.uk/cultfilms/displaycultfilm.asp?reviewid=2739*>

4.   Sanderson Beck, '*Bell, Book and Candle*', in *Movie Mirrors*, 2012.
        <*http://san.beck.org/MM/1958/BellBookandCandle.html*>

5.   Ed Howard, '*Bell Book and Candle*', in *Only the Cinema*, 24 November 2008.
        <*http://seul-le-cinema.blogspot.com/2008/11/1124-bell-book-and-candle.html*>

6.   Jeffrey Kauffman, '*Bell, Book and Candle* Blu-ray', in *Blu-ray.com*, 10 April 2012.
        <*https://www.blu-ray.com/movies/Bell-Book-and-Candle-Blu-ray/39855/#Review*>

7.   Stuart Galbraith IV, '*Bell Book and Candle* (Blu-ray)', in *DVD Talk*, 10 April 2012.
        <*https://www.dvdtalk.com/reviews/57348/bell-book-and-candle/*>

8.   Bosley Crowther, 'Screen: A Witch in Love; *Bell, Book and Candle* at Fine Arts, Odeon', in *The New York Times*, 27 December 1958.
<https://www.nytimes.com/1958/12/27/archives/screen-a-witch-in-love-bell-book-and-candle-at-fine-arts-odeon.html>

9.   Anon., '*Bell, Book and Candle*', in *Variety*, 31 December 1958.
<https://variety.com/1957/film/reviews/bell-book-and-candle-1200419169/>

10.   Laura Grieve, 'Tonight's Movie: *Bell Book and Candle*', in *Laura's Miscellaneous Musings*, 29 January 2011.
<https://laurasmiscmusings.blogspot.com/2011/01/tonights-movie-bell-book-and-candle.html>

11.   Dave Sindelar, '*Bell Book and Candle*', in *Fantastic Movie Musings and Ramblings*, 18 January 2007.
<https://fantasticmoviemusings.com/2017/07/01/bell-book-and-candle-1958/>

12.   Derek Winnert, '*Bell, Book and Candle*', in *Derek Winnert.com*, 1 March 2017.
<http://www.derekwinnert.com/bell-book-and-candle-1958-james-stewart-kim-novak-jack-lemmon-ernie-kovacs-hermione-gingold-elsa-lanchester-janice-rule-classic-movie-review-5091/>

13.   Richard Scheib, '*Bell Book and Candle*', in *Moria: The Science Fiction, Horror and Fantasy Film Review*, 8 January 2001.
<http://www.moriareviews.com/fantasy/bell-book-and-candle-1958.htm>

14.   Andy Webb, '*Bell, Book and Candle*', in *The Movie Scene*, 2016.

<*https://www.themoviescene.co.uk/reviews/bell-book-and-candle/bell-book-and-candle.html*>

18

Other Christmas Films Of the 1940s and 50s

W HILE this book has presented a discussion of some of the most prominent Christmas features to emerge throughout the genre's golden age, several other films dealing with themes or scenarios related to the festive season were produced throughout the 1940s and 50s. In this section, I have listed a number of movies which feature Christmas in one capacity or another, either as a backdrop to the action or as an integral aspect of the plot. (Motion pictures which only include very brief holiday season scenes or references are generally not included unless specifically indicated.)

All That Heaven Allows (1955)
Universal International Pictures
Director: Douglas Sirk
Starring: Jane Wyman, Rock Hudson, Agnes Moorehead

A romantic drama in which an affluent widow finds love with a landscape gardener in spite of the social pressures which bear upon their relationship. Based upon Edna L. Lee and Harry Lee's short story, the film is set in a scenic, snowy town in rural Connecticut and features various evocations of the festive season including Christmas shopping and party planning, frosty midwinter backdrops and – in an suggestion of their emotional distance – the protagonist's children deliberately leaving her alone during the holidays, emphasising their emotional distance and abrogation of family duty. The film opened in Los Angeles on the Christmas Day of 1955, and in 1995 was selected to be preserved in the United States National Film Registry.

An Affair to Remember (1957)
Jerry Wald Productions
Director: Leo McCarey
Starring: Cary Grant, Deborah Kerr, Richard Denning
Based on McCarey's earlier film *Love Affair* (1939), this romantic drama concerns Grant's dashing Nicolo 'Nickie' Ferrante and Deborah Kerr's spirited Terry McKay who meet on an ocean liner heading from Europe to the United States and strike up a budding romance. They agree to meet at the Empire State Building six months later, but Nickie finds himself alone on the observation deck, unaware that Terry has been involved in a car accident and has been badly injured. After numerous misunderstandings, the pair find themselves reunited on Christmas Eve and declare their love for one another. In spite of an uneven critical reaction, *An Affair to Remember* was nominated in four categories at the Academy Awards.

An American Romance (1944)
Metro-Goldwyn-Mayer

Director: King Vidor
Starring: Brian Donlevy, Ann Richards, Walter Abel
Also known by the alternative title *The American Miracle*, this drama involves Brian Donlevy's newly-arrived European immigrant Stefan Dubechek (later renamed Steve Dangos) as he works his way up through the world of industry. Starting in the steel industry, he eventually moves into car manufacturing and – with the outbreak of the Second World War – the aerospace business. The inspiring tale of an ambitious, self-made individual seeking to live the American Dream, the film contains a famous scene where, as the foreman of a steel mill, Steve takes the time to speak individually with each of the workers under his authority as they leave at the end of their Christmas Eve shift, giving each of them a sincere festive greeting for the holidays.

Blossoms in the Dust (1941)

Metro-Goldwyn-Mayer/Mervyn LeRoy Productions Inc.
Director: Mervyn LeRoy
Starring: Greer Garson, Walter Pidgeon, Felix Bressart
Biographical drama focusing on the life of social campaigner Edna Gladney (1886-1961), who fought tirelessly for the advancement of children's rights and – in particular – improved living conditions for children who were living in poverty. Though not concentrated specifically on the festive season, the film does contain a number of appropriate Christmas themes including the need for greater community cooperation to support those in need, and snowy winter scenes feature throughout. *Blossoms in the Dust* won an Academy Award for Best Art Direction (Interior Decoration, Colour), and was nominated in three other categories including Best Actress in a Leading Role for Greer Garson.

Bush Christmas (1947)

GB Instructional Films/Ralph Smart Productions
Director: Ralph Smart
Starring: Chips Rafferty, John Fernside, Stan Tolhurst

A lively family comedy-drama set in the less-than-conventional yuletide setting of the Australian outback. Filmed on location in the Burragorang Valley and the Blue Mountains in New South Wales, the movie concerns the efforts of a band of young friends who team up to thwart the nefarious plans of some villainous horse thieves. The film was remade in 1983, directed by Henri Safran and featuring Nicole Kidman in her first cinematic role.

The Cheaters (1945)

Republic Pictures
Director: Joseph Kane
Starring: Joseph Schildkraut, Billie Burke, Eugene Pallette

Also known by several alternative titles, including *The Magnificent Rogue* and *Mr M and the Pigeons*, this festively-situated screwball comedy and morality tale features an upper-crust family in New York City who scheme to cheat the rightful beneficiary of their late uncle's Last Will and Testament. Complicating matters is a washed-up, alcoholic film star named Anthony Marchaund (Joseph Schildkraut), whose interventions help to restore justice. As if the festive setting wasn't enough to cement the film's Christmas credentials, Marchaund even compares the family's transgressions to those of the nefarious Jacob Marley in Dickens's *A Christmas Carol.* Though treated with critical scepticism at the time of its initial screenings, the film was re-released in 1949 with the revised title *The Castaway*, and went on to become a regular

Christmas feature in festive television schedules for many years afterwards.

Christmas Holiday (1944)
Universal Pictures
Director: Robert Siodmak
Starring: Deanna Durbin, Gene Kelly, Richard Whorf
A *film noir* crime drama adapted from W. Somerset Maugham's 1939 novel, *Christmas Holiday* begins on Christmas Eve in atmospheric New Orleans and is told in flashback. The movie itself is a rather harrowing tale of violence, domestic disharmony and emotional complications, albeit one which has an unexpectedly liberating (if not conventionally 'happy') ending. The film's score by Hans J. Salter was nominated for an Academy Award.

Dead of Night (1945)
Ealing Studios
Directors: Alberto Cavalcanti, Charles Crichton, Basil Dearden, Robert Hamer
Starring: Mervyn Johns, Michael Redgrave, Roland Culver
British anthology horror film, produced by the famous Ealing Studios. *Dead of Night* features an infamous sequence entitled 'The Christmas Party'. Directed by Alberto Cavalcanti from a story by Angus MacPhail, the story centres around a mysterious supernatural confrontation taking place at a children's party at Christmas. Starring Michael Allan, Sally Ann Howes and Barbara Leake, this sequence was cut from the film when it was originally screened in America, though in subsequent years it has been restored. The movie would prove influential to later British horror film-making.

Desk Set (1957)
Twentieth Century-Fox
Director: Walter Lang
Starring: Spencer Tracy, Katharine Hepburn, Gig Young
A romantic comedy adapted from William Marchant's 1955 stage play, *Desk Set* explores the growing romance between television network reference librarian Bunny Watson (Katharine Hepburn) and highly-focused efficiency expert Richard Sumner (Spencer Tracy). Sumner, the inventor of a new computer system named EMERAC, is tasked with integrating this new technology amongst a suspicious staff who are convinced that the mainframe's introduction will lead to their redundancy. Featuring a 1950s-era Christmas party, complete with office Christmas tree and plenty of champagne, the film also involves various festive motifs such as searching for just the right gift and some yuletide-themed general knowledge questions being asked by the in-film reference team.

Destination Tokyo (1943)
Warner Bros.
Director: Delmer Daves
Starring: Cary Grant, John Garfield, Alan Hale
Tensely atmospheric and stylistically influential submarine movie, set during World War II. *Destination Tokyo* was released in December 1943 and features a narrative which begins on Christmas Eve. The film concerns the USS *Copperfin*, a submarine under the command of Captain Cassidy (Cary Grant), which is ordered to take part in intelligence-gathering operations ahead of the 1942 Doolittle Raid on Tokyo. A tense game of cat-and-mouse takes place as Cassidy and the officers under his command must evade the detection of Imperial Japanese forces and marine minefields to achieve their ob-

jectives. For his original story, Steve Fisher was nominated for an Academy Award.

Dillinger (1945)
King Brothers Productions
Director: Max Nosseck
Starring: Lawrence Tierney, Edmund Lowe, Anne Jeffreys
Organised crime drama, which centres on the life of infamous gangster John Dillinger (1903-34), as portrayed by Lawrence Tierney. The film explores Dillinger's drift into the world of crime – in particular his talents for robbery, bank raids and safe-cracking – as well as his subsequent downfall. Though now considerably better remembered for its influence on later gangster movies (albeit that some debate has taken place as to whether it can truly be regarded as a *film noir*), the film does feature a Christmas Eve scene where Dillinger is in hiding over the course of the holidays, toting a Colt New Service revolver in a distinctly un-festive manner. Philip Yordan was nominated for an Academy Award in recognition for the film's original screenplay.

The Glenn Miller Story (1954)
Universal Pictures
Director: Anthony Mann
Starring: James Stewart, June Allyson, Harry Morgan
Biopic of the legendary American musician and band-leader Glenn Miller (1904-44), 'The King of Swing', starring James Stewart in the title role. The film follows Miller's career from his early 1920s performances through to his death during World War II. Famous for its many cameos from leading musicians such as Louis Armstrong, Gene Krupa, Arvell Shaw, Frances Langford and The Modernaires, *The Glenn Miller*

Story's connection with the festive season is rather a tragic one as it culminates in Miller's plane being lost over the English Channel as he made his way to a Christmas concert in the December of 1944.

The Greatest Show on Earth (1952)
Paramount Pictures
Director: Cecil B. DeMille
Starring: James Stewart, Charlton Heston, Betty Hutton
Taking place in and around the Ringling Brothers and Barnum & Bailey Circus, this drama examines the challenges facing the circus industry – and those who work in it – in the precarious post-war economy. Though the film's brush with the festive season is admittedly slight, and by no means core to its narrative, its epic scope in the hands of celebrated director DeMille (who also featured as its narrator) incorporates everything from mystery to romance, as well as numerous circus acts executed by real performers from the aforementioned Ringling Brothers and Barnum & Bailey Circus. The film won two Academy Awards for Best Picture and Best Story, with nominations in a further three categories.

Holiday Inn (1942)
Paramount Pictures
Director: Mark Sandrich
Starring: Bing Crosby, Fred Astaire, Marjorie Reynolds
Now famous as the movie which launched Irving Berlin's song 'White Christmas' (along with eleven other songs written for the film), *Holiday Inn* features Crosby's Jim Hardy retiring from showbusiness during a Christmas Eve performance to move to a farm in Connecticut, which he later transforms into a hotel with its own range of musical entertainment that opens only on holidays. Christmas continues to loom large

throughout the film; Jim meets his future romantic partner Linda Mason (Marjorie Reynolds) on Christmas Day – where he performs 'White Christmas' – and after an eventful year (punctuated by various holiday celebrations such as Easter, Independence Day and Thanksgiving) – the couple are reunited for good during the following festive season. The song 'White Christmas' won Irving Berlin the Best Original Song Academy Award, and the film was also nominated in the Best Score and Best Original Story categories.

I'll Be Seeing You (1944)
Selznick International Pictures
Director: William Dieterle
Starring: Ginger Rogers, Joseph Cotten, Shirley Temple
Emotional romantic drama (adapted from a radio play by Charles Martin) concerning the fates of two social outsiders, the shell-shocked Sergeant Zachary Morgan (Joseph Cotten) and Mary Marshall (Ginger Rogers), who has been convicted of involuntary manslaughter. The pair meet when Mary has been given a temporary furlough from prison for the Christmas holidays, at the same time as Zach has been temporarily discharged from military hospital in an attempt to acclimatise himself to everyday living. During the festive season, both must come to terms with their misgivings over how their lives have played out, and unexpectedly find each other in the process.

Lady in the Lake (1947)
Metro-Goldwyn-Mayer
Director: Robert Montgomery
Starring: Robert Montgomery, Audrey Totter, Lloyd Nolan

Robert Montgomery's debut as director, this *film noir* was adapted from Raymond Chandler's 1943 novel, shifting the summertime backdrop of Chandler's original text to a Christmas setting. Montgomery stars as private investigator Phillip Marlowe, who is tasked with tracking down the wife of publishing executive Derace Kingsby (Leon Ames) during the holiday period. The film frequently contrasts the themes and iconography of the festive season with the bleaker facets of Marlowe's investigation, and to good effect.

Ma and Pa Kettle at Home (1954)
Universal International Pictures
Director: Charles Lamont
Starring: Marjorie Main, Percy Kilbride, Alan Mowbray
The sixth entry in the long-running *Ma and Pa Kettle* series of films, and arguably the most critically successful, this comedy concerns the titular couple (Marjorie Main and Percy Kilbride) as they head out to their family farm in December 1953 when their eldest son, Elwin (Brett Halsey), has his work selected for contention for a college scholarship. Unfortunately for Elwin, his essay concerns the state of an ideal modern farm, and a pair of upmarket judges are on the way to assess the aforementioned Kettle homestead... which in reality is in a state of neglect and disorder. Ma and Pa must therefore help to save the day. With a festive background evident throughout proceedings, including a Christmas Eve party and some specially-composed yuletide poetry, the film exudes warmth and folksy charm.

Man of a Thousand Faces (1957)
Universal International Pictures
Director: Joseph Pevney
Starring: James Cagney, Dorothy Malone, Jane Greer

Biopic of silent movie star Lon Chaney (1883-1930), portrayed here by James Cagney. The film follows Chaney's career from his days in vaudeville theatre through to his emergence into the early cinema industry and eventual stardom. With little more than a tenuous connection to the festive season, the conviviality of Christmas is used as a sharp contrast to the bleak realities of the protagonists' professional and domestic lives. The festivities form a kind of hearth-and-home ideal in the film, as Chaney laments the fact that life in showbusiness is more likely to see him and his wife celebrating the holidays in an impersonal hotel room than a warm and inviting family home. *Man of a Thousand Faces* was nominated for Best Original Screenplay at the Academy Awards.

The Man Who Came to Dinner (1942)

Warner Bros. Pictures Inc.
Director: William Keighley
Starring: Bette Davis, Ann Sheridan, Monty Woolley

An unconventional but heartwarming comedy for the festive season in which a famous but self-important radio personality named Sheridan Whiteside (Monty Woolley) suffers a hip fracture during a lecture tour and decides to recuperate at the Ohio home of Ernest and Daisy Stanley (Grant Mitchell and Billie Burke) – where the accident took place – over the Christmas holidays. Throughout December the entertainingly insufferable Whiteside turns the lives of his hosts upside down, whipping up new-found artistic ambitions in the Stanleys' children and attempting to sabotage a budding romance between his efficient personal assistant and a local journalist. Based on a stage play of the same name by Moss Hart and George S. Kaufman, *The Man Who Came to Dinner* provides plenty of enjoyment from Woolley's scene-stealing performance, some years before his appearance as the similarly larger-than-life Professor Wutheridge in Henry Koster's *The Bishop's Wife* (q.v.).

Meet John Doe (1941)
Frank Capra Productions
Director: Frank Capra
Starring: Gary Cooper, Barbara Stanwyck, Edward Arnold

Starting in December in the run-up to Christmas, this uplifting comedy-drama involves a fictionalised letter printed in a newspaper by a journalist, Ann Mitchell (Barbara Stanwyck), from an (imagined) homeless man threatening suicide on account of his poor treatment by society. However, the letter causes mass public interest, and the newspaper's editor is forced to employ a genuine drifter – one-time baseball player John Willoughby (Gary Cooper) – to pose as its author. Over time this 'John Doe' figure becomes a major celebrity, but his rising star is tainted by others' political ambitions and eventually he plots to carry out the letter's threat of a Christmas Eve suicide in an attempt to highlight the distress suffered by the people that society has left behind. Fortunately there is a happy ending, whereby his life is saved and the machinations of his detractors are exposed. The film's story was nominated for an Academy Award.

The Miracle of Morgan's Creek (1944)
Paramount Pictures
Director: Preston Sturges
Starring: Eddie Bracken, Betty Hutton, Diana Lynn

This wartime screwball comedy stars Betty Hutton as Trudy Kockenlocker, a woman from a small American town who unexpectedly discovers that she is pregnant after an evening of wild partying with some soldiers departing for the front line. However, she has no idea of who the father might be, and many misunderstandings ensue before she eventually gives birth at Christmas, when the town of Morgan's Creek comes together (in the best festive spirit) to show their support and appreciation of the new arrivals. The film's original screenplay received an Academy Award nomination, and in 2001 *The Miracle of Morgan's Creek* was chosen by the Library of Congress for preservation in the United States National Film Registry.

Night of the Hunter (1955)
Paul Gregory Productions
Director: Charles Laughton
Starring: Robert Mitchum, Shelley Winters, Lillian Gish
Tense thriller, adapted from Davis Grubb's 1953 novel of the same name. Based loosely on the story of real-life serial killer Harry F. Powers (1893-1932), the film focuses on the life of Rev. Harry Powell (Robert Mitchum), a duplicitous minister of religion and murderer who justifies his lethal crimes by reasoning that he is ridding the world of sinful figures and using the money they leave behind to further his preaching. While in prison, Powell learns of a cache of stolen funds from another prisoner, who is subsequently executed. Determined to find the hidden money, he tracks down his cellmate's widow Willa (Shelley Winters) and marries her, but things do not go according to plan and Powell's scheming eventually leads to his downfall. The film ends on a Christmas scene as Willa's two children, mistreated by Powell, enjoy the festivities with Rachel Cooper (Lillian Gish) and her family – a movingly positive counterpoint to the dark subject matter of the film's main narrative. *Night of the Hunter* has become hugely influential since its release, and in 1992 it was selected by the Library of

Congress to be preserved in the United States National Film Registry.

O. Henry's Full House (1952)
Twentieth Century Fox
Directors: Henry Hathaway, Howard Hawks, Henry King, Henry Koster, Jean Negulesco
Starring: Fred Allen, Anne Baxter, Jeanne Crain
An anthology film which comprised five disparate stories, all of them authored by short fiction writer O. Henry (1862-1910) and narrated by novelist John Steinbeck (1902-68). The final sequence of the film, entitled 'The Gift of the Magi', was directed by Henry King and starred Jeanne Crain and Farley Grainger as a pair of young lovers – Della and Jim – who are each searching for an ideal Christmas gift to present to the other. One of Henry's best-known tales (said to have been written at Pete's Tavern on New York City's Irving Place) and published in December 1905, the story revolves around Della agreeing to have her hair cut off to raise $20 in order to buy Jim a fob chain made from platinum for his pocket watch. When they later meet to exchange gifts, Jim admits that he had sold the aforementioned watch in order to buy his present for Della – a set of ornate combs. Though both have been given gifts that they cannot use, they realise that their sacrifices were driven by their love for one another – something more priceless than any material gift.

The Painted Hills (1951)
Metro-Goldwyn-Mayer
Director: Harold F. Kress
Starring: Pal (a.k.a Lassie), Paul Kelly, Bruce Cowling
Also known by the title *Lassie's Adventures in the Goldrush*, and based loosely on Alexander Hull's novel *Shep of the*

Painted Hills (1930), this family drama centres around Shep, a collie who seeks justice after her owner – prospector Jonathan Harvey (Paul Kelly) – is murdered by his corrupt business partner Lin Taylor (Bruce Cowling). Though Taylor attempts to poison Shep, his efforts are unsuccessful and the resourceful dog leads the unsuspecting villain onto a treacherous mountain path where the murder meets his demise after falling from a precipice. In spite of its rather stark premise, the film takes place over the festive period and evokes the holiday season in various areas of its rustic frontier setting. *The Painted Hills* was to be the seventh *Lassie* film to be produced by MGM, and would also be the last.

Penny Serenade (1941)
Columbia Pictures
Director: George Stevens
Starring: Cary Grant, Irene Dunne, Beulah Bondi
A romantic melodrama which considers the life of spouses Julie (Irene Dunne) and Roger (Cary Grant), as well as the precarious state of their marriage. In spite of having divergent views over the subject of if and when to start a family, and various other domestic and professional pressures, the pair eventually pull together and start to plan a future that the two of them can agree on. The film features numerous prominent sequences taking place over Christmas and the New Year period, many of which have particular personal significance for the characters. Cary Grant was nominated for the Best Actor Award at the Academy Awards for his performance as Roger Adams.

Remember the Night (1940)
Paramount Pictures
Director: Mitchell Leisen

Starring: Barbara Stanwyck, Fred MacMurray, Beulah Bondi

Romantic comedy, set during the approach to the Christmas holidays. Shoplifter Lee Leander (Barbara Stanwyck) is arrested after stealing from a jeweller's store in New York City, and Assistant District Attorney Jack Sargeant (Fred MacMurray) is assigned as the prosecutor in the case. Sensing that the holiday season might incline the jury to be sympathetic to Lee's case, Sargeant deliberately has the case delayed, but later feels guilty over the prospect of Lee spending Christmas in a jail cell and posts bail. Realising that she has nobody with whom to spend the festive season, Sargeant drives Lee to her family home, but when she is rejected by her embittered mother he feels no choice but to invite her to spend Christmas with his own family. Their feelings grow, and he eventually declares his heartfelt affection for her on New Year's Eve... but as ever, the course of true love never did run smooth.

Santa Claus (1959)

Cinematográfica Calderón S.A.

Director: René Cardona

Starring: José Elías Moreno, Cesáreo Quezadas, José Luis Aguirre

Mexican fantasy film, sometimes known by its alternative title *Santa Claus vs the Devil*, in which Santa (José Elías Moreno) gets ready for his Christmas Eve deliveries – never suspecting that the demon Pitch (José Luis Aguirre) schemes to turn the children of the world against the jolly old elf. In spite of the malevolent character's best attempts, Santa manages to sidestep all of the malicious machinations that are put in his path and ensures that the world's children are still delivered a happy Christmas. The film introduces a number of interesting additions to the Santa Claus mythos, including Merlin (Armando Arriola), the wizard of Arthurian legend, and Santa's workshop being transplanted from the North Pole to somewhere in Earth's orbit. Under the direction of Ken Smith, the film was edited and dubbed into English for American audiences in 1960. *Santa Claus* was to win the Golden Gate Award for Best International Film at the 1959 San Francisco International Film Festival.

Say One for Me (1959)
Bing Crosby Productions
Director: Frank Tashlin
Starring: Debbie Reynolds, Bing Crosby, Robert Wagner
In this film musical, Father Conroy (Bing Crosby) is the priest of a parish situated at the heart of New York's theatre district. This has allowed the cleric to befriend many stage professionals who attend his church services. In the course of his parish duties, Father Conroy manages to act as matchmaker for playboy entertainer Tony Vincent (Robert Wagner) and reluctant showgirl Holly LeMaise (Debbie Reynolds), as well as encouraging the career revival of washed-up songwriter Phil Stanley (Ray Walston). The film culminates with a national Christmas benefit event which is broadcast on television and is arranged by Conroy and other churches located in the district, forming an endpoint to proceedings. For her performance as Chorine, actress Stella Stevens was bestowed the New Star of the Year (Actress) Award at the Golden Globe Awards.

So Proudly We Hail! (1943)
Paramount Pictures
Director: Mark Sandrich
Starring: Claudette Colbert, Paulette Goddard, Veronica Lake

Patriotic wartime movie based on a book by Lt. Colonel Juanita Hipps, focusing on the experiences of three military nurses deployed to the Phillippines during World War II. All of the nurses are depicted as playing their part in the overwhelming difficulties of providing combat medical aid, and individual love stories are transposed with the challenges of their attempts to ensure the reassurance and wellbeing of their patients even in the most rarefied of circumstances. The film contains a noteworthy Christmas party scene where an Army Chaplain (Walter Abel) delivers a rousing speech inspiring onlookers to keep their faith in the virtues that America was founded on and still stands for. Paulette Goddard was nominated for the Best Supporting Actress Award for her performance as Lt. Joan O'Doul at the Academy Awards.

Storm Warning (1951)

Warner Bros.
Director: Stuart Heisler
Starring: Ginger Rogers, Ronald Reagan, Doris Day
Tense *film noir* thriller, where a peripatetic dress model named Marsha Mitchell (Ginger Rogers) witnesses first-hand the bigotry and brutality of a group of Ku Klux Klansmen in a small town and later realises that one of their number, Hank Rice (Steve Cochran), is actually her brother-in-law as well as an accomplice to murder. Marsha teams up with straight-talking District Attorney Burt Rainey (future US President Ronald Reagan), who is determined to achieve justice in spite of constant obstruction, and eventually uncovers the perpetrators amongst the townsfolk. Though its dark subject matter and moody tone are far from festive in nature, the film does feature the Christmas holidays as a backdrop – even if the characters themselves observe the ambiguity of the season

being so proximate to the sinister events that are witnessed throughout the narrative.

The Seven Little Foys (1955)
Scribe Productions
Director: Melville Shavelson
Starring: Bob Hope, Milly Vitale, George Tobias
Biopic of vaudeville stage entertainer Eddie Foy (1856-1928), with the veteran actor being portrayed by Bob Hope. Though determined to remain a solo artist, Foy marries ballerina Madeleine Morando (Milly Vitale), and the couple eventually raise seven children who are destined to follow in their parents' footsteps and enter the world of showbusiness in the wake of Madeleine's tragic death. The conflict between the workaholic Foy and his children is highlighted by its contrast with the warmth and homeliness of the traditional Christmas festivities; the siblings resent being compelled to perform on Christmas Day, and later reject their fathers' presents as a result. Memorably, James Cagney briefly reprises his famous role as George M. Cohan (1878-1942), 'The Man who Owned Broadway', as popularised in the film *Yankee Doodle Dandy* (Michael Curtiz, 1942).

Susan Slept Here (1954)
Harriet Parsons Productions
Director: Frank Tashlin
Starring: Dick Powell, Debbie Reynolds, Anne Francis
Adapted from Steve Fisher's stage play by screenwriter Alex Gottlieb, *Susan Slept Here* involves the complicated life of writer Mark Christopher (Dick Powell) who yearns to make a break from penning trivial entertainment and instead produce a drama about serious social issues. On Christmas Eve, two policemen arrive who had previously worked with Mark

as advisors on an earlier film, where he had been the screen-writer. The cops have a teenaged tearaway named Susan (Debbie Reynolds) in their custody, and reveal an idea they have hatched – they suggest that Mark can learn directly from her about issues of juvenile delinquency for his new play, and in return Susan will be spared jail over the holiday season. Naturally the situation proves to be considerably more com-plicated than either could have guessed. Curiously, Powell was 49 when he played the supposedly 35-year-old Mark, while Reynolds – in spite of playing a 17-year-old – was actu-ally 22 when she appeared in the film. *Susan Slept Here* was nominated for two Academy Awards, in the categories of Best Sound: Recording and Best Music: Original Song (for the track 'Hold My Hand').

Tenth Avenue Angel (1948)
Metro-Goldwyn-Mayer
Director: Roy Rowland
Starring: Margaret O'Brien, Angela Lansbury, George Murphy
Family drama set during the Great Depression. A young girl named Flavia Mills (Margaret O'Brien) lives with her family in a run-down tenement building in New York City in the late 1930s. In spite of having a close family unit, Flavia slowly begins to realise the harshness of life around her as chronic cashflow problems cause major difficulties, emphasising her father Joe's (Warner Anderson) desperation to find a job and her aunt's boyfriend Steve (George Murphy) falling under the influence of mobsters as he tries frantically to find a source of income. The film's emotional conclusion arrives at Christmas Eve where Flavia's mother Helen (Phyllis Thaxter) has an accident and gives birth early, while an unexpected confluence

of events transpire to give the Mills family the happy ending
they have so urgently been hoping for.

Young Man with a Horn (1950)
Warner Bros.
Director: Michael Curtiz
Starring: Kirk Douglas, Lauren Bacall, Doris Day
Adapted from Dorothy Baker's novel of the same name,
which was based loosely around the life of jazz musician Bix
Beiderbecke (1903-31), this drama concerns the life experiences
of the fictionalised Rick Martin (Kirk Douglas), a talented
brass performer who is eventually employed by a big band –
though his tendency to improvise soon sees him come into
conflict with the organisers. Subsequently working for a dance
orchestra in New York, he falls in love with enigmatic, troubled psychology student Amy North (Lauren Bacall), but
their complicated relationship threatens to derail their careers
and eventually even their lives. Rick is shown performing on
his trumpet during a Christmas Eve sequence, though the
film's engagement with the festive season is otherwise mini-
mal.

Filmography

THE SHOP AROUND THE CORNER (1940)

Production Company: Metro-Goldwyn-Mayer.
Distributor: Metro-Goldwyn-Mayer.
Director: Ernst Lubitsch.
Producer: Ernst Lubitsch.
Screenplay: Samson Raphaelson, based on a play by Nikolaus Laszlo.
Original Music: Werner R. Heymann.
Director of Photography: William H. Daniels.
Film Editing: Gene Ruggiero.
Art Direction: Cedric Gibbons.
Set Decoration: Edwin B. Willis.
Running Time: 99 minutes.
Main Cast: Margaret Sullavan (Klara Novak), James Stewart (Alfred Kra-
lik), Frank Morgan (Hugo Matuschek), Joseph Schildkraut (Ferencz
Vadas), Sara Haden (Flora Kaczek), Felix Bressart (Pirovitch), William
Tracy (Pepi Katona), Inez Courtney (Ilona Navotny), Charles Halton
(Detective), Charles Smith (Rudy), Sarah Edwards (Customer), Edwin
Maxwell (Doctor), Charles Arnt (Policeman), Mabel Colcord (Aunt
Anna), Grace Hayle (Plump Customer).

MEET ME IN ST LOUIS (1944)

Production Company: Metro-Goldwyn-Mayer.
Distributor: Loew's, Inc.
Director: Vincente Minelli.
Producer: Arthur Freed.
Screenplay: Irving Brecher and Fred F. Finklehoffe, based on a novel by
Sally Benson.
Original Music: Roger Edens and Conrad Salinger.
Musical Director: George Stoll.
Director of Photography: George J. Folsey.

Film Editing: Albert Akst.
Art Direction: Lemuel Ayers, Cedric Gibbons and Jack Martin Smith.
Set Decoration: Edwin B. Willis.
Costume Design: Irene Sharaff.
Running Time: 113 minutes.
Main Cast: Judy Garland (Esther Smith), Margaret O'Brien ('Tootie' Smith), Mary Astor (Mrs Anna Smith), Leon Ames (Mr Alonzo Smith), Lucille Bremer (Rose Smith), Tom Drake (John Truett), Marjorie Main (Katie, the Maid), Harry Davenport (Grandpa), Henry H. Daniels Jr. (Alonzo 'Lon' Smith Jr.), Joan Carroll (Agnes Smith), June Lockhart (Lucille Ballard), Robert Sully (Warren Sheffield), Hugh Marlowe (Colonel Darly), Chill Wills (Mr Neely, the Iceman).

CHRISTMAS IN CONNECTICUT (1945)

Production Company: Warner Bros./First National Pictures.
Distributor: Warner Bros.
Director: Peter Godfrey.
Producer: William Jacobs.
Executive Producer: Jack L. Warner.
Screenplay: Lionel Houser and Adele Comandini, from a story by Aileen Hamilton.
Original Music: Frederick Hollander.
Cinematography: Carl E. Guthrie.
Film Editing: Frank Magee.
Art Direction: Stanley Fleischer.
Set Decoration: Casey Roberts.
Costume Design: Milo Anderson.
Running Time: 102 minutes.
Main Cast: Barbara Stanwyck (Elizabeth Lane), Dennis Morgan (Jefferson Jones), Sydney Greenstreet (Alexander Yardley), Reginald Gardiner (John Sloan), S.Z. Sakall (Felix Bassenak), Robert Shayne (Dudley Beecham), Una O'Connor (Norah), Frank Jenks (Sinkewicz), Joyce Compton (Mary Lee), Dick Elliott (Judge Crothers).

THE BELLS OF ST MARY'S (1945)

Production Company: Rainbow Productions.

Distributor: RKO Radio Pictures.

Director: Leo McCarey.

Producer: Leo McCarey.

Screenplay: Dudley Nichols, from a story by Leo McCarey.

Original Score: Robert Emmett Dolan.

Director of Photography: George Barnes.

Film Editing: Harry Marker.

Art Direction: William Flannery.

Set Decoration: Darrell Silvera.

Costume Design: Edith Head.

Running Time: 126 minutes.

Main Cast: Bing Crosby (Father Chuck O'Malley), Ingrid Bergman (Sister Mary Benedict), Henry Travers (Horace P. Bogardus), William Gargan (Joe Gallagher), Ruth Donnelly (Sister Michael), Joan Carroll (Patricia 'Patsy' Gallagher), Martha Sleeper (Mary Gallagher), Rhys Williams (Dr McKay), Dickie Tyler (Eddie Breen), Una O'Connor (Mrs. Breen).

IT'S A WONDERFUL LIFE (1946)

Production Company: Liberty Pictures.

Distributor: RKO Radio Pictures.

Director: Frank Capra.

Producer: Frank Capra.

Screenplay: Frances Goodrich, Albert Hackett and Frank Capra, with additional scenes by Jo Swerling, from a story by Philip Van Doren Stern.

Original Score: Dimitri Tiomkin.

Director of Photography: Joseph Biroc and Joseph Walker.

Film Editing: William Hornbeck.

Art Direction: Jack Okey.

Set Decoration: Emile Kuri.

Costume Design: Edward Stevenson.

Running Time: 130 minutes.

Main Cast: James Stewart (George Bailey), Donna Reed (Mary Hatch), Lionel Barrymore (Mr Potter), Thomas Mitchell (Uncle Billy), Henry Travers (Clarence), Beulah Bondi (Mrs Bailey), Frank Faylen (Ernie), Ward Bond (Bert), Gloria Grahame (Violet), H.B. Warner (Mr Gower), Frank Albertson (Sam Wainwright), Todd Karns (Harry Bailey), Samuel S. Hinds (Pa Bailey), Mary Treen (Cousin Tilly), Virginia Patton (Ruth Dakin), Charles Williams (Cousin Eustace), Sara Edwards

(Mrs Hatch), Bill Edmunds (Mr Martini), Lillian Randolph (Annie), Argentina Brunetti (Mrs Martini), Bobbie Anderson (Little George), Ronnie Ralph (Little Sam), Jean Gale (Little Mary), Jeanine Ann Roose (Little Violet), Danny Mummert (Little Marty Hatch), Georgie Nokes (Little Harry Bailey), Sheldon Leonard (Nick), Frank Hagney (Potter's Bodyguard), Ray Walker (Joe from the Luggage Shop), Charlie Lane (Real Estate Salesman), Edward Kean (Tom from the Building and Loan), Carol Coomes (Janie Bailey), Karolyn Grimes (Zuzu Bailey), Larry Simms (Pete Bailey), Jimmy Hawkins (Tommy Bailey).

MIRACLE ON 34TH STREET (1947)

Production Company: Twentieth Century-Fox Film Corporation.
Distributor: Twentieth Century-Fox Film Corporation.
Director: George Seaton.
Producer: William Perlberg.
Screenplay: George Seaton, from a story by Valentine Davies.
Original Score: Cyril Mockridge.
Director of Photography: Lloyd Ahern and Charles Clarke.
Film Editing: Robert Simpson.
Art Direction: Richard Day and Richard Irvine.
Set Decoration: Ernest Lansing and Thomas Little.
Costume Design: Kay Nelson.
Running Time: 96 minutes.
Main Cast: Maureen O'Hara (Doris Walker), John Payne (Fred Gailey), Edmund Gwenn (Kris Kringle), Gene Lockhart (Judge Henry X. Harper), Natalie Wood (Susan Walker), Porter Hall (Granville Sawyer), William Frawley (Charlie Halloran), Jerome Cowan (District Attorney Thomas Mara), Philip Tonge (Julian Shellhammer).

THE BISHOP'S WIFE (1947)

Production Company: The Samuel Goldwyn Company.
Distributor: RKO Radio Pictures.
Director: Henry Koster.
Producer: Samuel Goldwyn.
Screenplay: Leonardo Bercovici and Robert E. Sherwood, from the novel by Robert Nathan.

Original Score: Hugo Friedhofer, Emil Newman and Herbert W. Spencer.
Cinematography: Gregg Toland.
Film Editing: Monica Collingwood.
Art Direction: Perry Ferguson and George Jenkins.
Set Decoration: Julia Heron.
Costume Design: Irene Sharaff.
Running Time: 109 minutes.
Main Cast: Cary Grant (Dudley), Loretta Young (Julia Brougham), David Niven (Bishop Henry Brougham), Monty Woolley (Professor Wutheridge), James Gleason (Sylvester), Gladys Cooper (Mrs Hamilton), Elsa Lanchester (Matilda), Sara Haden (Mildred Cassaway), Karolyn Grimes (Debby Brougham), Tito Vuolo (Mr Maggenti), Regis Toomey (Mr Miller), Sarah Edwards (Mrs Duffy), Margaret McWade (Miss Trumbull), Anne O'Neal (Mrs Ward), Ben Erway (Mr Perry), Erville Alderson (Stevens), Bobby Anderson (Defense Captain), Teddy Infuhr (Attack Captain), Eugene Borden (Michel).

CHRISTMAS EVE (1947)

Production Company: Benedict Bogeaus Productions/Miracle Productions Inc.
Distributor: United Artists.
Director: Edwin L. Marin.
Producer: Benedict Bogeaus.
Screenplay: Laurence Stallings, from a story by Richard H. Landau.
Original Music: Heinz Roemheld.
Cinematography: Gordon Avil.
Film Editing: James Smith.
Art Direction: Ernst Fegté.
Production Manager: Ken Walters.
Set Decoration: Gene Redd.
Running Time: 90 minutes.
Main Cast: Ann Harding (Aunt Matilda Reed), Reginald Denny (Phillip Hastings), Clarence Kolb (Judge Alston), Carl Harbord (Dr Doremus), Joe Sawyer (Private Detective Gimlet), George Raft (Mario Torio), George Brent (Michael Brooks), Randolph Scott (Johnny), Joan Blondell (Ann Nelson), Virginia Field (Claire), Dolores Moran (Jean Bradford), Douglass Dumbrille (Dr Bunyan), Claire Whitney (Mrs Bunyan), John Litel (Joe Bland, FBI Agent), Marie Blake (Reporter),

Dennis Hoey (Williams the Butler), Molly Lamont (Harriet Rhodes), Walter Sande (Mario's Hood), Konstantin Shayne (Gustav Reichman), Andrew Tombes (Auctioneer).

IT HAPPENED ON FIFTH AVENUE (1947)

Production Company: Roy Del Ruth Productions.
Distributor: Allied Artists.
Director: Roy Del Ruth.
Producer: Roy Del Ruth.
Associate Producer: Joe Kaufmann.
Screenplay: Everett Freeman, from an original story by Herbert Clyde Lewis and Frederick Stephani, with additional dialogue by Vick Knight.
Original Music: Edward Ward.
Cinematography: Henry Sharp.
Film Editing: Richard V. Heermance.
Art Direction: Lewis Creber.
Set Decoration: Ray Boltz.
Production Manager: Glenn Cook.
Costume Design: Lorraine MacLean and Willard H. George.
Running Time: 116 minutes.
Main Cast: Don DeFore (Jim Bullock), Ann Harding (Mary O'Connor), Victor Moore (Aloysius T. McKeever), Charles Ruggles (Michael J. 'Mike' O'Connor), Gale Storm (Trudy O'Connor), Grant Mitchell (Farrow), Edward Brophy (Patrolman Cecil Felton), Alan Hale Jr. (Whitey Temple), Dorothea Kent (Margie Temple), Edward Ryan (Hank), Cathy Carter (Alice).

THREE GODFATHERS (1948)

Production Company: Argosy Pictures.
Distributor: Metro-Goldwyn-Mayer.
Director: John Ford.
Producers: Merian C. Cooper and John Ford.
Screenplay: Laurence Stallings and Frank S. Nugent, from a story by Peter B. Kyne.
Original Music: Richard Hageman.
Cinematography: Winton Hoch.

Film Editing: Jack Murray.
Art Direction: James Basevi.
Set Decoration: Joe Kish.
Production Manager: Lowell J. Farrell.
Costume Design: Michael Meyers, Ann Peck and D.R.O. Hatswell.
Running Time: 106 minutes.
Main Cast: John Wayne (Robert Marmaduke Sangster Hightower), Harry
    Carey Jr. (William Kearney, 'The Abilene Kid'), Pedro Armendáriz
    (Pedro 'Pete' Rocafuerte), Mildred Natwick (Dying Mother), Ward
    Bond (Sheriff Buck Sweet), Mae Marsh (Mrs Sweet), Jane Darwell
    (Miss Florie), Guy Kibbee (Judge), Hank Worden (Deputy Curley),
    Dorothy Ford (Ruby Latham), Ben Johnson (Posse Man #1), Charles
    Halton (Oliver Latham), Jack Pennick (Luke), Fred Libby (Deputy),
    Michael Dugan (Posse Man #2), Francis Ford (Drunken Old-Timer at
    Bar), Richard Hageman (Saloon Pianist), Gertrude Astor (Townswom-
    an), Ruth Clifford (Woman in Bar), Jack Curtis (Bartender #1), Harry
    Tenbrook (Bartender #2), Eva Novak (Townswoman), Amelia Yelda
    (Robert William Pedro Hightower, the Baby).

HOLIDAY AFFAIR (1949)

Production Company: RKO Radio Features.
Distributor: RKO Radio Features.
Director: Don Hartman.
Producer: Don Hartman.
Screenplay: Isobel Lennart, based on *Christmas Gift* by John D. Weaver.
Original Music: Roy Webb.
Director of Photography: Milton R. Krasner.
Film Editing: Harry Marker.
Art Direction: Carroll Clark and Albert S. D'Agostino.
Set Decoration: Darrell Silvera and William Stevens.
Costume Design: Howard Greer and Bruce MacIntosh.
Running Time: 87 minutes.
Main Cast: Robert Mitchum (Steve Mason), Janet Leigh (Connie Ennis),
    Wendell Corey (Carl Davis), Gordon Gebert (Timmy Ennis), Griff
    Barnett (Mr Ennis), Esther Dale (Mrs Ennis), Henry O'Neill (Mr
    Crowley), Harry Morgan (Police Lieutenant), Larry J. Blake (Plain-
    clothesman), Helen Brown (Emily, Mr Crowley's Secretary), Frances
    Morris (Mary, the Housekeeper).

THE LEMON DROP KID (1951)

Production Company: Paramount Pictures/Hope Enterprises.
Distributor: Paramount Pictures.
Director: Sidney Lanfield.
Producer: Robert L. Welch.
Screenplay: Frank Tashlin, Robert O'Brien and Edmund Hartmann, with additional dialogue by Irving Elinson, from a story by Damon Runyon and Edmund Beloin.
Original Music: Victor Young.
Cinematography: Daniel L. Fapp.
Film Editing: Archie Marshek.
Art Direction: Franz Bachelin and Hal Pereira.
Set Decoration: Sam Comer and Ross Dowd.
Production Management: Frank Caffey and Richard Johnston.
Costume Design: Sam Levine and Ruth Stella.
Running Time: 91 minutes.
Main Cast: Bob Hope (Sidney Milburn, The Lemon Drop Kid), Marilyn Maxwell (Brainey Baxter), Lloyd Nolan (Oxford Charlie), Jane Darwell (Nellie Thursday), Andrea King (Stella), Fred Clark (Moose Moran), Jay C. Flippen (Straight Flush Tony), William Frawley (Gloomy Willie), Harry Bellaver (Sam the Surgeon), Sid Melton (Little Louie), Ben Welden (Singing Solly), Ida Moore (The Bird Lady), Francis Pierlot (Henry), Charles Cooley (Goomba), Hary Shannon (The Policeman), Tor Johnson (The Super Swedish Angel), Tom Dugan (No Thumbs Charlie).

SCROOGE (1951)

Production Company: George Minter Productions.
Distributor: Renown Pictures Corporation/United Artists.
Director: Brian Desmond Hurst.
Producer: Brian Desmond Hurst.
Associate Producer: Stanley Haynes.
Screenplay: Noel Langley, from the novella by Charles Dickens.
Original Score: Richard Addinsell.
Cinematography: C. Pennington-Richards.
Film Editing: Clive Donner.
Art Direction: Ralph Brinton.

Costume Design: Constance Da Finna and Doris Lee.

Casting Director: Maude Spector.

Running Time: 86 minutes.

Main Cast: Alastair Sim (Ebenezer Scrooge), Kathleen Harrison (Mrs Dilber), Mervyn Johns (Bob Cratchit), Hermione Baddeley (Mrs Cratchit), Michael Hordern (Jacob Marley/Marley's Ghost), George Cole (Young Ebenezer Scrooge), John Charlesworth (Peter Cratchit), Francis de Wolff (Spirit of Christmas Present), Rona Anderson (Alice), Carol Marsh (Fan Scrooge), Brian Worth (Fred), Miles Malleson (Old Joe), Ernest Thesiger (The Undertaker), Glyn Dearman (Tiny Tim), Michael Dolan (Spirit of Christmas Past), Olga Edwardes (Fred's Wife), Roddy Hughes (Fezziwig), Hattie Jacques (Mrs. Fezziwig), Eleanor Summerfield (Miss Flora), Louise Hampton (Laundress), C. Konarski (Spirit of Christmas Yet to Come), Eliot Makeham (Mr Snedrig), Peter Bull (First Businessman/Narrator), Douglas Muir (Second Businessman), Noel Howlett (First Collector), Fred Johnson (Second Collector), Henry Hewitt (Mr Rosehed), Hugh Dempster (Mr Groper), Maire O'Neill (Alice's Patient), Richard Pearson (Mr Tupper), Patrick MacNee (Young Jacob Marley), Clifford Mollison (Samuel Wilkins), Jack Warner (Mr Jorkin).

THE HOLLY AND THE IVY (1952)

Production Company: London Film Productions/De Grunwald Productions.

Distributor: British Lion Films.

Director: George More O'Ferrall.

Producer: Anatole de Grunwald.

Associate Producer: Hugh Perceval.

Screenplay: Anatole de Grunwald, from a play by Wynyard Browne.

Original Music: Malcolm Arnold.

Cinematography: Edward Scaife.

Film Editing: Bert Bates.

Production Manager: Jack Swinburne.

Costume Design: Ivy Baker.

Running Time: 83 minutes.

Main Cast: Ralph Richardson (The Reverend Mr Martin Gregory), Celia Johnson (Jenny Gregory), Margaret Leighton (Margaret Gregory), Denholm Elliott (Michael Gregory), Hugh Williams (Richard Wyndham), John Gregson (David Patterson), Margaret Halstan (Aunt Lyd-

ia), Maureen Delany (Aunt Bridget), William Hartnell (Company Sergeant Major), Robert Flemyng (Major), Roland Culver (Lord B.), John
Barry (Clubman), Dandy Nichols (Neighbour).

WHITE CHRISTMAS (1954)

Production Company: Paramount Pictures.
Distributor: Paramount Pictures.
Director: Michael Curtiz.
Producer: Robert Emmett Dolan.
Screenplay: Norman Krasna, Norman Panama and Melvin Frank.
Lyrics and Music: Irving Berlin.
Cinematography: Loyal Griggs.
Film Editing: Frank Bracht.
Art Direction: Roland Anderson and Hal Pereira.
Set Decoration: Sam Comer and Grace Gregory.
Costume Design: Edith Head.
Casting Director: Maude Spector.
Running Time: 120 minutes.
Main Cast: Bing Crosby (Bob Wallace), Danny Kaye (Phil Davis), Rose-
mary Clooney (Betty Haynes), Vera Ellen (Judy Haynes), Dean Jagger
(Major General Thomas F. Waverly), Mary Wickes (Emma Allen),
John Brascia (John), Anne Whitfield (Susan Waverly).

WE'RE NO ANGELS (1955)

Production Company: Paramount Pictures.
Distributor: Paramount Pictures.
Director: Michael Curtiz.
Producer: Pat Duggan.
Screenplay: Ranald MacDougall, from the play *La Cuisine de Anges* by
Albert Husson.
Original Music: Frederick Hollander.
Cinematography: Loyal Griggs.
Film Editing: Arthur Schmidt.
Art Direction: Roland Anderson and Hal Pereira.
Set Decoration: Sam Comer and Grace Gregory.
Costume Design: Mary Grant.

Running Time: 106 minutes.

Main Cast: Humphrey Bogart (Joseph), Aldo Ray (Albert), Peter Ustinov (Jules), Joan Bennett (Amelie Ducotel), Basil Rathbone (Andre Trochard), Leo G. Carroll (Felix Ducotel), John Baer (Paul Trochard), Gloria Talbott (Isabelle Ducotel), Lea Penman (Madame Parole), John Smith (Medical Officer Arnaud).

BELL, BOOK AND CANDLE (1958)

Production Company: Phoenix Productions, Inc.

Distributor: Columbia Pictures.

Director: Richard Quine.

Producer: Julian Blaustein.

Screenplay: Daniel Taradash, based on the play *Bell, Book and Candle* by John Van Druten.

Original Music: George Duning.

Director of Photography: James Wong Howe.

Film Editing: Charles Nelson.

Art Direction: Cary Odell.

Set Decoration: Louis Diage.

Costume Design: Jean Louis.

Running Time: 106 minutes.

Main Cast: James Stewart (Shepherd 'Shep' Henderson), Kim Novak (Gillian 'Gil' Holroyd), Jack Lemmon (Nicky Holroyd), Ernie Kovacs (Sidney Redlitch), Elsa Lanchester (Aunt Queenie Holroyd), Hermione Gingold (Bianca De Pass), Janice Rule (Merle Kittridge), Howard McNear (Andy White, Shep's Co-publisher), Dick Crockett (Ad-lib Bit), Bek Nelson (Tina, Shep's Secretary), The Brothers Candoli (Musicians at the Zodiac Club), Pyewacket the Cat (Himself).

Bibliography

A.W., 'At the Broadway', in *The New York Times*, 28 November 1947.
<*https://www.nytimes.com/1947/11/28/archives/at-the-broadway.html*>

Agajanian, Rowana, '"Peace on Earth, Goodwill to All Men": The Depiction of Christmas in Modern Hollywood Films', in *Christmas at the Movies: Images of Christmas in American, British and European Cinema*, ed. by Mark Connelly (London: I.B. Tauris, 2000), pp.143-64.

Agee, James, '*It's a Wonderful Life*', in *The Nation*, 20 December 2000.
<*https://www.thenation.com/article/its-wonderful-life/*>

Aldgate, Anthony, and Jeffrey Richards, *Best of British: Cinema and Society from 1930 to the Present* (London: I.B. Tauris, 2002).

Allon, Yoram, Del Cullen and Hannah Patterson, eds, *Contemporary British and Irish Film Directors: A Wallflower Critical Guide* (London: Wallflower Press, 2001).

—, eds, *Contemporary North American Film Directors: A Wallflower Critical Guide* (London: Wallflower Press, 2000).

Altman, Rick, *The American Film Musical* (Bloomington & Indianapolis: Indiana University Press, 1987).

Anderson, Jeffrey M., 'Christmas Peeve', in *Combustible Celluloid*, 19 January 2016.
<*http://www.combustiblecelluloid.com/dvds/christmas_eve.shtml*>

—, 'Clang, Clang, Clang', in *Combustible Celluloid*, 12 April 2004.
<*http://www.combustiblecelluloid.com/classic/meetstlouis.shtml*>

—, 'Going Another Way', in *Combustible Celluloid*, 19 November 2013.
<*http://www.combustiblecelluloid.com/classic/bellsmarys.shtml*>

—, 'Holes in the Holidays', in *Combustible Celluloid*, 25 December 2009.
<http://www.combustiblecelluloid.com/classic/chrisconn.shtml>

—, 'Secret Santas', in *Combustible Celluloid*, 26 May 2006.
<http://www.combustiblecelluloid.com/classic/shoparound.shtml>

—, 'The Turn of the *Scrooge*', in *Combustible Celluloid*, 14 December 2007.
<http://www.combustiblecelluloid.com/classic/christmascarol.shtml>

Anon., '*3 Godfathers*', in *Let's Not Talk About Movies*, 25 December 2012.
<http://letsnottalkaboutmovies.blogspot.com/2012/12/3-godfathers-1948.html>

—, '*A Christmas Carol*', in *Variety*, 14 November 1951.

—, '*Bell, Book and Candle*', in *Variety*, 31 December 1958.
<https://variety.com/1957/film/reviews/bell-book-and-candle-1200419169/>

—, 'Cinema: Import', in *Time*, 3 December 1951.
<http://content.time.com/time/magazine/article/0,9171,889415,00.html>

—, 'Cinema: New Picture: *It's a Wonderful Life*', in *Time*, 23 December 1946.
<http://www.time.com/time/magazine/article/0,9171,793342-1,00.html>

—, 'Cinema: The New Pictures', in *Time*, 16 June 1947.
<http://content.time.com/time/subscriber/article/0,33009,855765-2,00.html>

—, 'Cinema: The New Pictures', in *Time*, 8 December 1947.
<http://content.time.com/time/subscriber/article/0,33009,934178-2,00.html>

—, 'Cinema: The New Pictures', in *Time*, 25 October 1954.
<http://content.time.com/time/subscriber/article/0,33009,823619-2,00.html>

—, 'Film Reviews: *We're No Angels*', in *Variety*, 15 June 1955.
<https://archive.org/details/variety198-1955-06/page/n133>

—, 'Film Reviews: *White Christmas*', in *Variety*, 1 September 1954, p.6.
<https://archive.org/stream/variety195-1954-09#page/n4/mode/1up>

—, '*Miracle on 34th Street*', in *Variety*, 5 June 1947.
<https://variety.com/1946/film/reviews/miracle-on-34th-street-1200415057/>

—, '*It's a Wonderful Life*', in *Urban Cinefile*, 1 August 2002.
<http://www.urbancinefile.com.au/home/view.asp?a=6367&s=DVD>

—, '*The Holly and the Ivy*', in *The Times*, 27 October 1952, p.10.

—, '*The Lemon Drop Kid*', in *Variety*, 31 December 1950.
<https://variety.com/1950/film/reviews/the-lemon-drop-kid-1200416853/>

—, 'The New Pictures', in *Time*, 27 November 1944.
<http://content.time.com/time/subscriber/article/0,33009,796926,00.html>

—, 'The Screen: *Christmas in Connecticut*, With Barbara Stanwyck, Opens at Strand', in *The New York Times*, 28 July 1945.
<https://www.nytimes.com/1945/07/28/archives/the-screen-christmas-in-connecticut-with-barbara-stanwyck-opens-at.html>

Arnold, Jeremy, *Christmas in the Movies: 30 Classics to Celebrate the Season* (New York: Hachette Book Group, 2018).

Arroyo, José, '*The Bells of St Mary's*', in *First Impressions*, 15 July 2015.
<https://notesonfilm1.com/2015/07/15/the-bells-of-st-marys-leo-mccarey-usa-1945/>

Ashby, Justine, and Andrew Higson, eds., *British Cinema, Past and Present* (London: Routledge, 2000).

Attebery, Brian, *Stories About Stories: Fantasy and the Remaking of Myth* (Oxford: Oxford University Press, 2014).

Austin, Joe, and Michael Nevin Willard, eds, *Generations of Youth: Youth Cultures and History in Twentieth-Century America* (New York: New York University Press, 1998).

Babington, Bruce, and Peter William Evans, *Biblical Epics: Sacred Narrative in the Hollywood Cinema* (Manchester: Manchester University Press, 1993).

Baumgarten, Marjorie, '*The Shop Around the Corner*', in *The Austin Chronicle*, 15 July 1999.
<*https://www.austinchronicle.com/events/film/1999-07-15/139751/*>

Beck, Sanderson, '*3 Godfathers*', in *Movie Mirrors*, 2006.
<*http://san.beck.org/MM/1948/ThreeGodfathers.html*>

—, '*Bell, Book and Candle*', in *Movie Mirrors*, 2012.
<*http://san.beck.org/MM/1958/BellBookandCandle.html*>

—, '*Holiday Affair*', in *Movie Mirrors*, 2006.
<*http://san.beck.org/MM/1949/HolidayAffair.html*>

—, '*Miracle on 34th Street*', in *Movie Mirrors*, 2006.
<*http://san.beck.org/MM/1947/Miracleon34thStreet.html*>

—, '*Scrooge (A Christmas Carol)*', in *Movie Mirrors*, 2007.
<*http://san.beck.org/MM/1951/Scrooge.html*>

—, '*The Bells of St Mary's*', in *Movie Mirrors*, 2005.
<*http://san.beck.org/MM/1945/BellsofStMarys.html*>

—, '*The Bishop's Wife*', in *Movie Mirrors*, 2006.
<*http://san.beck.org/MM/1947/BishopsWife.html*>

—, '*The Lemon Drop Kid*', in *Movie Mirrors*, 2007.
<*http://san.beck.org/MM/1951/LemonDropKid.html*>

Berardinelli, James, '*It's a Wonderful Life*', in *ReelViews*, 1 January 2000.
<*http://www.reelviews.net/reelviews/it-s-a-wonderful-life*>

—, '*Scrooge*' in *ReelViews*, 1 January 2000.
<*http://www.reelviews.net/reelviews/scrooge*>

Black, Ace, 'Movie Review: *3 Godfathers*', in *The Ace Black Blog*, 6 February 2014.

<*https://www.theaceblackblog.com/2014/02/movie-review-3-godfathers-1948.html*>

Bonanno, Luke, '*White Christmas*: Diamond Anniversary Edition', in *DVDizzy*, 24 December 2014.
<*https://www.dvdizzy.com/whitechristmas-diamond.html*>

Bookman, Milica, and Aleksandra S. Bookman, *Economics in Film and Fiction* (Plymouth: Rowman and Littlefield Education, 2009).

Bradshaw, Peter, '*Meet Me in St Louis*: Review', in *The Guardian*, 15 December 2011.
<*https://www.theguardian.com/film/2011/dec/15/meet-me-in-st-louis-review*>

—, '*The Shop Around the Corner*: Review', in *The Guardian*, 9 December 2010.
<*https://www.theguardian.com/film/2010/dec/09/the-shop-around-the-corner-review*>

Browne, Ray B., and Glenn J. Browne, *Laws of Our Fathers: Popular Culture and the U.S. Constitution* (Bowling Green: Bowling Green State University Popular Press, 1986).

—, and Pat Browne, *The Guide to United States Popular Culture* (Madison: University of Wisconsin Press, 2001).

Cabin, Chris, 'Blu-ray Review: *It's a Wonderful Life*', in *Slant Magazine*, 17 December 2011.
<*https://www.slantmagazine.com/dvd/its-a-wonderful-life-2172/*>

Cameron, '*Holiday Affair*', at *The Blonde at the Film*, 6 December 2017.
<*https://theblondeatthefilm.com/2017/12/06/holiday-affair/*>

Cameron, Kate, '*It's a Wonderful Life* Lifts the Spirit', in *The New York Daily News*, 21 December 1946.
<*https://www.nydailynews.com/entertainment/movies/wonderful-life-designed-lift-spirits-1946-review-article-1.2916205*>

Camp, Brian, 'Merry Christmas: *Holiday Affair* (1949) with Robert Mitchum and Janet Leigh', in *Brian Camp's Film and Anime Blog*, 22 December 2012.
<*https://briandanacamp.wordpress.com/2012/12/22/merry-christmas-holiday-affair-1949-with-robert-mitchum-and-janet-leigh/*>

Canote, Terence Towles, '70 Years of *It Happened on Fifth Avenue*', in *A Shroud of Thoughts*, 18 December 2017.
<*http://mercurie.blogspot.com/2017/12/70-years-of-it-happened-on-fifth-avenue.htm*>

Carlson, Kristine Butler, '1945: Movies and the March Home', in *American Cinema of the 1940s: Themes and Variations*, ed. by Wheeler Winston Dixon (Piscataway: Rutgers University Press, 2006), pp.140-61.

Carney, Raymond, *American Vision: The Films of Frank Capra* (Cambridge: Cambridge University Press, 1986).

Cátia, '12 Days of Christmas Films: Day 5: *Christmas in Connecticut*', in *Back to Golden Days*, 18 December 2015.
<*http://back-to-golden-days.blogspot.com/2015/12/12-days-of-christmas-films-day-5.html*>

—, '12 Days of Christmas: Day 9: *The Shop Around the Corner*', in *Back to Golden Days*, 22 December 2015.
<*http://back-to-golden-days.blogspot.com/2015/12/12-days-of-christmas-day-9-shop-around.html*>

Chapman, James, 'God Bless Us, Every One: Movie Adaptations of *A Christmas Carol*', in *Christmas at the Movies*, ed. by Mark Connelly (London: I.B. Tauris, 2000), pp.9-38.

Charity, Tom, '*Scrooge*', in *Time Out*, 24 June 2006.
<*https://www.timeout.com/london/film/scrooge*>

Chen, Will, 'FBI Considered *It's A Wonderful Life* Communist Propaganda', in *WiseBread*, 24 December 2006.
<*https://www.wisebread.com/fbi-considered-its-a-wonderful-life-communist-propaganda*>

Chilton, Martin, '*White Christmas*, film review: "warm-hearted"', in *The Daily Telegraph*, 22 December 2014.
<*https://www.telegraph.co.uk/culture/film/filmreviews/11299626/White-Christmas-film-review-warm-hearted.html*>

Christley, Jaime N., 'Review: *The Shop Around the Corner*', in *Slant*, 22 December 2014.
<*https://www.slantmagazine.com/film/the-shop-around-the-corner/*>

Clark, Graeme, '*Bell Book and Candle* Review', in *The Spinning Image*, 19 August 2002.
<*http://www.thespinningimage.co.uk/cultfilms/displaycultfilm.asp?reviewid=2739*>

Clarke, Donald, '*Scrooge* Review: A *Carol* that Hits All the Top Notes', in *The Irish Times*, 15 December 2016.
<*https://www.irishtimes.com/culture/film/scrooge-review-a-carol-that-hits-all-the-top-notes-1.2904075*>

Coe, Richard, '*Fifth Avenue* a Nice Little Film That's Been Gushed About Too Much', in *The Washington Post*, 8 May 1947, p.2.

Cohan, Steven, 'Introduction: Musicals of the Studio Era', in *Hollywood Musicals: The Film Reader*, ed. by Steven Cohan (London: Routledge, 2002), pp.1-15.

—, ed., *Hollywood Musicals: The Film Reader* (London: Routledge, 2002).

Collins, Ace, *Stories Behind the Great Traditions of Christmas* (Grand Rapids: Zondervan, 2003).

Collins, Cindy Ruth, '*It's a Wonderful Life*', in *It's Christmas Time at the Movies* by Gary J. Svehla and Susan Svehla (Baltimore: Midnight Marquee Press, 1998), pp.146-151.

Connelly, Mark, ed., *Christmas at the Movies* (London: I.B. Tauris, 2000).

—, 'Santa Claus: The Movie', in *Christmas at the Movies*, ed. by Mark Connelly (London: I.B. Tauris, 2000), pp.115-34.

Connolly, Joseph, 'Personally speaking *It's a Wonderful Life* spotting all the gaffes', in *The Sunday Telegraph*, 23 December 2007.

Cook, David C., *The Inspirational Christmas Almanac: Heartwarming Traditions, Trivia, Stories, and Recipes for the Holidays* (Colorado Springs: Honor Books, 2006).

Cornelius, David, '*Warner Brothers Classic Holiday Collection*, Vol. 2', in *DVD Talk*, 11 November 2008.
<*https://www.dvdtalk.com/reviews/35677/warner-brothers-classic-holiday-collection-vol-2/*>

Crouse, Richard, *The 100 Best Movies You've Never Seen* (Toronto: ECW Press, 2003).

Crowther, Bosley, '*Holiday Affair*, Tinsel-Trimmed Trifle with Mitchum and Janet Leigh, at State', in *The New York Times*, 24 November 1949.
<*https://www.nytimes.com/1949/11/24/archives/holiday-affair-tinseltrimmed-trifle-with-mitchum-and-janet-leigh-at.html*>

—, 'Literate British Drama Opens', in *The New York Times*, 5 February 1954.
<*https://www.nytimes.com/1954/02/05/archives/literate-british-drama-opens.html*>

—, '*Miracle on 34th Street*, with Edmund Gwenn in the Role of Santa Claus, at Roxy – *Web* at Loew's Criterion', in *The New York Times*, 5 June 1947.
<*https://www.nytimes.com/1947/06/05/archives/miracle-on-34th-street-with-edmund-gwenn-in-the-role-of-santa-claus.html*>

—, 'Screen: A Witch in Love; *Bell, Book and Candle* at Fine Arts, Odeon', in *The New York Times*, 27 December 1958.
<*https://www.nytimes.com/1958/12/27/archives/screen-a-witch-in-love-bell-book-and-candle-at-fine-arts-odeon.html*>

—, 'The Screen: *Meet Me in St. Louis*, a Period Film That Has Charm, With Judy Garland and Margaret O'Brien, Opens at the Astor', in *The New York Times*, 29 November 1944.

<https://www.nytimes.com/1944/11/29/archives/the-screen-meet-me-in-st-louis-a-period-film-that-has-charm-with.html>

—, 'The Screen in Review: Bob Hope a Hapless Race-Track Tout in *The Lemon Drop Kid* Opening at Paramount', in *The New York Times*, 22 March 1951.
<https://www.nytimes.com/1951/03/22/archives/the-screen-in-review-bob-hope-a-hapless-racetrack-tout-in-the-lemon.html>

—, 'The Screen in Review: Dickens' *A Christmas Carol*, With Alastair Sim Playing Scrooge, Unveiled Here', in *The New York Times*, 29 November 1951.
<https://www.nytimes.com/1951/11/29/archives/the-screen-in-review-dickens-a-christmas-carol-with-alastair-sim.html>

—, 'The Screen in Review: *It Happened on Fifth Avenue*, With Victor Moore in Bright, Gay Mood, Opens at Rivoli', in *The New York Times*, 11 June 1947.
<https://www.nytimes.com/1947/06/11/archives/the-screen-in-review-it-happened-on-fifth-avenue-with-victor-moore.html>

—, 'The Screen in Review: *White Christmas* Bows at the Music Hall', in *The New York Times*, 15 October 1954.
<https://www.nytimes.com/1954/10/15/archives/the-screen-in-review-white-christmas-bows-at-the-music-hall.html>

Crump, William D., *The Christmas Encyclopedia*, 3rd edn (Jefferson: McFarland and Company, 2013).

D'Ecca, Artemisia, *Keeping Christmas Well* (Dublin: Phaeton Publishing, 2012).

Davis, Nick, '*Miracle on 34th Street*', in *Nick's Flick Picks*, December 2009.
<http://www.nicksflickpicks.com/mirc34th.html>

Deacy, Christopher, *Faith in Film: Religious Themes in Contemporary Cinema* (Aldershot: Ashgate Publishing, 2005).

Detora, Lisa M., ed., *Heroes of Film, Comics and American Culture: Essays on Real and Fictional Defenders of Home* (Jefferson: McFarland, 2009).

DeVito, Carlo, *Inventing Scrooge: The Incredible True Story Behind Dickens' Legendary* A Christmas Carol (Kennebunkport: Cider Mill Press, 2017).

Dickens, Charles, *The Christmas Books* (Ware: Wordsworth Editions, 1995) [1852].

Dixon, Wheeler Winston, ed., *American Cinema of the 1940s: Themes and Variations* (Piscataway: Rutgers University Press, 2006).

Docker, John, *Postmodernism and Popular Culture: A Cultural History* (Cambridge: Cambridge University Press, 1994).

Duhamel, Brandon A., '*Miracle on 34th Street*', in *TheaterByte*, 22 October 2009.
<*https://www.theaterbyte.com/bluray-uhd-reviews/miracle-on-34th-street-1947-blu-ray-review.html*>

Duralde, Alonso, *Have Yourself a Movie Little Christmas* (Milwaukee: Limelight Editions, 2010).

Ebert, Roger, '*It's a Wonderful Life*', in *The Chicago Sun-Times*, 1 January 1999.
<*https://www.rogerebert.com/reviews/great-movie-its-a-wonderful-life-1946*>

Eliot, Mark, *Jimmy Stewart: A Biography* (New York: Random House, 2006).

Ellis, John, *Visible Fictions: Cinema, Television, Video* (London: Routledge, 1989) [1982].

Erickson, Glenn, '*Meet Me in St Louis*', in *DVD Savant*, 27 November 2011.
<*https://www.dvdtalk.com/dvdsavant/s3740meet.html*>

Eschner, Kat, 'The Weird Story of the FBI and *It's a Wonderful Life*', in *Smithsonian.com*, 20 December 2017.
<*https://www.smithsonianmag.com/smart-news/weird-story-fbi-and-its-wonderful-life-180967587/*>

Everett, William A., and Paul R. Laird, eds., *The Cambridge Companion to the Musical* (Cambridge: Cambridge University Press, 2008).

Eyman, Scott, *Ernst Lubitsch: Laughter in Paradise* (Baltimore: Johns Hopkins University Press).

Fairclough, Norman, *Critical Discourse Analysis: The Critical Study of Language* (Harlow, Longman: 1995).

Felton, Bruce, *What Were They Thinking?: Really Bad Ideas Throughout History*, rev. edn (Guilford: Lyons Press, 2007).

Fishwick, Marshall W., *Popular Culture in a New Age* (Binghampton: Haworth Press, 2002).

Forbes, Bruce David, *Christmas: A Candid History* (Berkeley: University of California Press, 2007).

Fowler, Karin J., *David Niven: A Bio-Bibliography* (Westport: Greenwood Publishing Group, 1995).

Franson, Robert Wilfred, '*It Happened on Fifth Avenue*', in *Troy Novant*, January 2013.
<http://www.troynovant.com/Franson-3/Del-Ruth/It-Happened-on-Fifth-Avenue.html>

French, Philip, '*Meet Me in St Louis*: Review', in *The Observer*, 18 December 2011.
<https://www.theguardian.com/film/2011/dec/18/meet-me-st-louis-review>

—, '*The Holly and the Ivy*: Review', in *The Observer*, 1 November 2009.
<https://www.theguardian.com/film/2009/nov/01/holly-and-ivy-philip-french>

—, '*The Shop Around the Corner*: Review', in *The Observer*, 12 December 2010.
<https://www.theguardian.com/film/2010/dec/12/the-shop-around-the-corner>

Frow, John, *Genre* (London: Routledge, 2006).

Fusion, Marc, '*Christmas in Connecticut*', in *Marc Fusion: King of Twitch*, 20 December 2017.
<*https://marcfusion.com/2017/12/20/christmas-in-connecticut-1945/*>

Gabbard, Glen O., and Krin Gabbard, *Psychiatry and the Cinema*, 2nd edn (Washington D.C.: American Psychiatric Press, 1999).

Galbraith, Stuart, IV, '*Bell Book and Candle* (Blu-ray)', in *DVD Talk*, 10 April 2012.
<*https://www.dvdtalk.com/reviews/57348/bell-book-and-candle/*>

—, '*Miracle on 34th Street*', in *DVD Talk*, 2 November 2009.
<*https://www.dvdtalk.com/reviews/38505/miracle-on-34th-street/*>

—, '*Warner Bros. Classic Holiday Collection*', in *DVD Talk*, 8 November 2005.
<*https://www.dvdtalk.com/reviews/19068/warner-bros-classic-holiday-collection-boys-town-men-of-boys-town-a-christmas-carol-christmas-in-connecticut/*>

Gallagher, Tag, *John Ford: The Man and His Films* (Berkeley & Los Angeles: University of California Press, 1986).

Garrett, Eddie, *I Saw Stars in the 40's and 50's* (Victoria: Trafford Publishing, 2005).

Garrett, Greg, *The Gospel According to Hollywood* (Louisville: Westminster John Knox Press, 2007).

Giddings, Robert, and Erica Sheen, eds, *The Classic Novel: From Page to Screen* (Manchester: Manchester University Press, 2000).

Glavin, John, ed., *Dickens on Screen* (Cambridge: Cambridge University Press, 2003).

Goodman, Walter, 'Home Video: Movies', in *The New York Times*, 25 October 1987.

<https://www.nytimes.com/1987/10/25/arts/home-video-movies-413487.html>

Grant, John, '*Christmas Eve*', in *Noirish*, 25 December 2013.
<https://noirencyclopedia.wordpress.com/2013/12/25/christmas-eve-1947/>

Green, Stanley, *Hollywood Musicals Year by Year*, 2nd edn, rev. by Elaine Schmidt (Milwaukee: Hal Leonard, 1999).

Greene, Heather, *Bell, Book and Camera: A Critical History of Witches in American Film and Television* (Jefferson: McFarland, 2018), p.110.

Grieve, Laura, 'Tonight's Movie: *3 Godfathers* (1948) at the Lone Pine Film Festival', in *Laura's Miscellaneous Musings*, 15 October 2016.
<http://laurasmiscmusings.blogspot.com/2016/10/tonights-movie-3-godfathers-1948-at.html>

—, 'Tonight's Movie: *Bell Book and Candle*', in *Laura's Miscellaneous Musings*, 29 January 2011.
<https://laurasmiscmusings.blogspot.com/2011/01/tonights-movie-bell-book-and-candle.html>

—, 'Tonight's Movie: *Christmas Eve*', in *Laura's Miscellaneous Musings*, 29 January 2016.
<http://laurasmiscmusings.blogspot.com/2016/01/tonights-movie-christmas-eve-1947-olive.html>

—, 'Tonight's Movie: *Christmas in Connecticut*', in *Laura's Miscellaneous Musings*, 27 December 2007.
<https://laurasmiscmusings.blogspot.com/2007/12/tonights-movie-christmas-in-connecticut.html>

—, 'Tonight's Movie: *It Happened on Fifth Avenue*', in *Laura's Miscellaneous Musings*, 25 December 2011.
<https://laurasmiscmusings.blogspot.com/2011/12/tonights-movie-it-happened-on-fifth.html>

—, 'Tonight's Movie: *Miracle on 34th Street*', in *Laura's Miscellaneous Musings*, 27 November 2008.

<https://laurasmiscmusings.blogspot.com/2008/11/tonights-movie-miracle-on-34th-street.html>

—, 'Tonight's Movie: *The Holly and the Ivy*', in *Laura's Miscellaneous Musings*, 7 December 2011.
<http://laurasmiscmusings.blogspot.com/2011/12/tonights-movie-holly-and-ivy-1952.html>

—, 'Tonight's Movie: *The Lemon Drop Kid*', in *Laura's Miscellaneous Musings*, 26 December 2011.
<https://laurasmiscmusings.blogspot.com/2011/12/tonights-movie-lemon-drop-kid-1951.html>

—, 'Tonight's Movie: *The Shop Around the Corner*', in *Laura's Miscellaneous Musings*, 28 November 2017.
<https://laurasmiscmusings.blogspot.com/2017/11/tonights-movie-shop-around-corner-1940.html>

—, 'Tonight's Movie: *White Christmas*', in *Laura's Miscellaneous Musings*, 21 December 2013.
<http://laurasmiscmusings.blogspot.com/2013/12/tonights-movie-white-christmas-1954.html>

Guida, Fred, A Christmas Carol *and Its Adaptations: A Critical Examination of Dickens' Story and Its Productions on Stage, Screen and Television* (Jefferson: McFarland, 2000).

H.H.T., '*We're No Angels* Bows', in *The New York Times*, 8 July 1955.
<https://www.nytimes.com/1955/07/08/archives/were-no-angels-bows.html>

Hales, Stephen D., 'Putting Claus Back into Christmas', in *Christmas: Philosophy for Everyone*, ed. by Scott C. Lowe (Chichester: Blackwell, 2010), pp.161-71.

Hallenbeck, Bruce G., *Comedy-Horror Films: A Chronological History, 1914-2008* (Jefferson: McFarland and Company, 2009).

Hardy, Phil, ed., *The Aurum Film Encyclopedia: Science Fiction* (London: Aurum Press, 1995).

Harrison, Eddie, '*The Bishop's Wife*', in *The Film Authority*, 8 February 2014.
<*https://tensecondsfromnow.wordpress.com/2014/02/08/the-bishops-wife-1947/*>

Heath, Glenn, Jr., 'DVD Review: *The Lemon Drop Kid*', in *Slant*, 18 October 2010.
<*https://www.slantmagazine.com/dvd/the-lemon-drop-kid/*>

Henderson, Eric, 'Review: *Meet Me in St. Louis*', in *Slant*, 8 April 2004.
<*https://www.slantmagazine.com/film/meet-me-in-st-louis/*>

Hill, John, and Pamela Church Gibson, eds, *The Oxford Guide to Film Studies* (Oxford: Oxford University Press, 1998).

Hischak, Thomas S., *American Literature on Stage and Screen: 525 Works and Their Adaptations* (Jefferson: McFarland, 2012).

Hjort, Mette, and Scott MacKenzie, *Cinema and Nation* (London: Routledge, 2000).

Hoffman, Robert C., *Postcards from Santa Claus: Sights and Sentiments from the Last Century* (New York: Square One Publishers, 2002).

Hollows, Joanne, and Mark Jancovich, eds, *Approaches to Popular Film* (Manchester: Manchester University Press, 1995).

Hopper, Briallen, '*Christmas in Connecticut*', in *NotComing.com*, 25 December 2010.
<*http://www.notcoming.com/reviews/christmasinconnecticut/*>

Hornak, Robert, 'Blu-Ray Review: *The Lemon Drop Kid*', in *ZekeFilm*, 6 July 2017.
<*http://www.zekefilm.org/2017/07/06/blu-ray-review-the-lemon-drop-kid-1951/*>

Howard, Ed, '*3 Godfathers*', in *Only the Cinema*, 14 April 2009.
<*http://seul-le-cinema.blogspot.com/2009/04/3-godfathers.html*>

—, '*Bell Book and Candle*', in *Only the Cinema*, 24 November 2008.

<*http://seul-le-cinema.blogspot.com/2008/11/1124-bell-book-and-candle.html*>

—, 'Films I Love #55: *The Shop Around the Corner*', in *Only the Cinema*, 19 October 2011.
<*https://seul-le-cinema.blogspot.com/2011/10/films-i-love-55-shop-around-corner.html*>

Hunter, Allan, ed., *The Wordsworth Book of Movie Classics* (Ware: Wordsworth, 1996) [1992].

Hutchinson, Tom, '*The Holly and the Ivy*', in *Radio Times*, 26 October 2009.
<*https://www.radiotimes.com/film/cfb8n/the-holly-and-the-ivy/*>

Jacobson, Colin, '*Meet Me In St Louis*', in *DVD Movie Guide*, 2 December 2011.
<*http://www.dvdmg.com/meetmeinstlouisbr.shtml*>

Jasen, David A., *Tin Pan Alley: An Encyclopedia of the Golden Age of the American Song* (New York: Routledge, 2003).

Jeffers, H. Paul, *Legends of Santa Claus* (Minneapolis: Lerner Publishing Group, 2001).

Johanson, MaryAnn, '*Christmas in Connecticut*', in *Flick Filosopher*, 11 December 1999.
<*https://www.flickfilosopher.com/1999/12/christmas-in-connecticut-review.html*>

—, '*It's a Wonderful Life*', in *Flick Filosopher*, 1 December 1999.
<*https://www.flickfilosopher.com/1999/12/its-a-wonderful-life-review.html*>

—, '*Miracle on 34th Street*', in *Flick Filosopher*, 11 December 1999.
<*https://www.flickfilosopher.com/1999/12/miracle-on-34th-street-review.html*>

Johnston, Hank, and John A. Noakes, eds, *Frames of Protest: Social Movements and the Framing Perspective* (Oxford: Rowman and Littlefield, 2005).

Jones, Ken D., Arthur F. McClure and Alfred E. Twomey, *Character People* (New York: A.S. Barnes, 1977).

Kaiser, Andy, '*Holiday Affair*', in *Andy's Film Blog*, 21 December 2012. <*http://filmreviewsnsuch.blogspot.com/2012/12/holiday-affair.html*>

Kalaga, Wojciech H., and Marzena Kubisz, eds, *Multicultural Dilemmas: Identity, Difference, Otherness* (Frankfurt am Main: Peter Lang, 2008).

Kamiya, Gary, 'All Hail Pottersville!' in *Salon*, 22 December 2001. <*http://www.salon.com/2001/12/22/pottersville/singleton/*>

Kauffman, Jeffrey, '*Bell, Book and Candle* Blu-ray', in *Blu-ray.com*, 10 April 2012. <*https://www.blu-ray.com/movies/Bell-Book-and-Candle-Blu-ray/39855/#Review*>

—, '*Miracle on 34th Street*: 70th Anniversary Edition', in *Blu-ray.com*, 17 October 2017. <*https://www.blu-ray.com/movies/Miracle-on-34th-Street-Blu-ray/186945/#Review*>

—, '*The Bells of St Mary's* Blu-ray Review: Going Their Way', in *Blu-ray.com*, 19 November 2013. <*https://www.blu-ray.com/movies/The-Bells-of-St-Marys-Blu-ray/84798/#Review*>

Kehr, Dave, '*The Shop Around the Corner*', in *The Chicago Reader*, 27 November 2007. <*https://www.chicagoreader.com/chicago/the-shop-around-the-corner/Film?oid=1051445*>

Kelly, Richard Michael, 'Introduction', in Charles Dickens, *A Christmas Carol* (Peterborough: Broadview Press, 2003).

Knapp, Raymond, *The American Musical and the Performance of Personal Identity* (Princeton & Oxford: Princeton University Press, 2006).

Koller, Brian, '*The Bells of St Mary's*', in *FilmsGraded.com*, 21 April 2008. <*http://www.filmsgraded.com/reviews/2008/04/bellso.htm*>

Krauss, David, '*White Christmas*', in *High-Def Digest*, 7 November 2010. <*https://bluray.highdefdigest.com/3930/whitechristmas.html*>

Krizanovich, Karen, '*It's a Wonderful Life*: Eternally Charming and Fun', in *Little White Lies*, 14 December 2018. <*https://lwlies.com/reviews/its-a-wonderful-life-1946/*>

Kuhn, Adam, '*3 Godfathers*', in *Corndog Chats*, 14 March 2018. <*https://corndogchats.com/2018/03/14/3-godfathers-1948/*>

Kulzick, Kate, '25 Days of Christmas: *We're No Angels* Puts a Welcome Twist on the Standard Christmas Wish Story', in *PopOptiq*, 14 December 2013. <*https://www.popoptiq.com/25-days-of-christmas-were-no-angels-puts-a-welcome-twist-on-the-standard-christmas-wish-story/*>

Langford, Barry, *Post-Classical Hollywood: Film Industry, Style and Ideology Since 1945* (Edinburgh: Edinburgh University Press, 2010).

Leitch, Thomas M., *Film Adaptation and Its Discontents: From* Gone With the Wind *to* The Passion of the Christ (Baltimore: Johns Hopkins University Press, 2007).

Lester, Meera, *Why Does Santa Wear Red?... and 100 Other Christmas Curiosities Unwrapped* (Avon: Adams Media, 2007).

Lev, Peter, *Transforming the Screen: 1950-59* (Berkeley: University of California Press, 2003).

Levi, Ross D., *The Celluloid Courtroom: A History of Legal Cinema* (Westport: Greenwood Publishing Group, 2005).

Levy, Emanuel, '*Meet Me in St. Louis*: Minnelli's Classic Musical and First Masterpiece, Starring Judy Garland', in *Cinema 24/7*, 14 March 2007.

<http://emanuellevy.com/review/meet-me-in-st-louis-1944-3/>

Lewis, Morgan R., '*It Happened on Fifth Avenue*', in *Morgan on Media*, 18 December 2013.
<https://morganrlewis.wordpress.com/2013/12/18/it-happened-on-fifth-avenue/>

Liebman, Martin, '*It's a Wonderful Life* Blu-ray', in *Blu-ray.com*, 3 November 2009.
<https://www.blu-ray.com/movies/Its-a-Wonderful-Life-Blu-ray/6097/#Review>

—, '*White Christmas* Blu-ray Review: I'm Dreaming of This Great Blu-ray', in *Blu-ray.com*, 29 October 2010.
<https://www.blu-ray.com/movies/White-Christmas-Blu-ray/15357/#Review>

Lingan, John, 'Take Two #16: *The Shop Around the Corner* (1940) & *You've Got Mail* (1998)', in *Slant*, 29 March 2011.
<https://www.slantmagazine.com/film/take-two-16-the-shop-around-the-corner-1940-youve-got-mail-1998/>

Loggins, Gary, 'Christmas Confection: *Holiday Affair*', in *Cracked Rear Viewer*, 23 December 2015.
<https://crackedrearviewer.wordpress.com/2015/12/23/christmas-confection-holiday-affair-rko-1949/>

Lopez, Kristen, '25 Days of Christmas: *Holiday Affair*', in *Journeys in Classic Film*, 11 December 2008.
<https://journeysinclassicfilm.com/2018/12/11/25-days-of-christmas-holiday-affair-1949/>

Loukides, Paul, and Linda K. Fuller, eds, *Beyond the Stars: Plot Conventions in American Popular Film* (Bowling Green: Bowling Green State University Popular Press, 1991).

—, eds, *Beyond the Stars: Studies in American Popular Film Volume 5: Themes and Ideologies in American Popular Film* (Madison: Popular Press, 1996).

Lovell, Mitch, '*3 Godfathers*', in *Video Vacuum*, 20 August 2018.
<*https://thevideovacuum.blogspot.com/2018/08/3-godfathers-1948.html*>

Lovell, Wesley, '*The Shop Around the Corner*', in *Cinema Sight*, 22 November 2010.
<*http://www.cinemasight.com/review-the-shop-around-the-corner-1940/*>

Lowe, Scott C., ed., *Christmas: Philosophy for Everyone* (Chichester: Blackwell, 2010).

Lussier, Germain, 'Is Holiday Classic *It's a Wonderful Life* Secretly (or Actually) a Sci-Fi/Fantasy Movie?', in *io9*, 9 December 2018.
<*https://io9.gizmodo.com/is-holiday-classic-its-a-wonderful-life-secretly-or-ac-1830726913*>

Lynch, Jacqueline T., '*Christmas in Connecticut*', in *Another Old Movie Blog*, 10 December 2007.
<*https://anotheroldmovieblog.blogspot.com/2007/12/christmas-in-connecticut-1945.html*>

Magala, Slawomir, *Cross-Cultural Competence* (Abingdon: Routledge, 2005).

Mansour, David J., *From Abba to Zoom: A Pop Culture Encyclopedia of the Late 20th Century* (Kansas City: Andrews McMeel Publishing, 2005).

Marling, Karal Ann, *Merry Christmas!: Celebrating America's Greatest Holiday* (Cambridge: Harvard University Press, 2000).

Mavis, Paul, '*The Bob Hope Collection*', in *DVD Talk*, 7 December 2010.
<*https://www.dvdtalk.com/reviews/45799/bob-hope-collection-the/*>

Mazur, Eric Michael, 'Going My Way?: Crosby and Catholicism on the Road to America', in *Going My Way: Bing Crosby and American Culture*, ed. by Ruth Prigozy and Walter Raubicheck (Rochester: University of Rochester Press, 2007), pp.17-34.

McDannell, Colleen, ed., *Catholics in the Movies* (New York: Oxford University Press US, 2008).

McDonald, Ryan, 'Review: *We're No Angels*', in *Shameless Self Expression*, 25 August 2014.
<*http://ryancmcdonald.blogspot.com/2014/08/review-were-no-angels-1955.html*>

McGee, Patrick, *Cinema, Theory, and Political Responsibility in Contemporary Culture* (Cambridge: Cambridge University Press, 1997).

McGilligan, Patrick, ed., *Backstory 2: Interviews with Screenwriters of the 1940s and 1950s* (Berkeley: University of California Press, 1997) [1991], pp.309-29.

McQuain, Christopher, '*Meet Me in St Louis*', in *DVD Talk*, 13 December 2011.
<*https://www.dvdtalk.com/reviews/51997/meet-me-in-st-louis/*>

Mechling, Jay, 'Rethinking (and Reteaching) the Civil Religion in Post-Nationalist American Studies', in *Post-Nationalist American Studies*, ed. by John Carlos Rowe (Berkeley: University of California Press, 2000), pp.63-83.

Medcalf, Josh, '*Christmas in Connecticut*', in *The Parallax Review*, 17 December 2010.
<*http://www.theparallaxreview.com/on_cable/christmas_in_connecticut.html*>

Mellor, Louisa, 'The Unusual Places *It's a Wonderful Life* Has Popped Up', in *Den of Geek*, 15 December 2018.
<*https://www.denofgeek.com/movies/its-a-wonderful-life/33441/the-odd-places-its-a-wonderful-life-has-turned-up*>

Meredith, 'A Christmas Discovery: *It Happened on Fifth Avenue*', in *Vitaphone Dreamer*, 14 December 2016.
<*https://vitaphonedreamer.wordpress.com/2016/12/14/a-christmas-discovery-it-happened-on-fifth-avenue/*>

Meshman, Gregory, '*3 Godfathers*', in *DVD Beaver*, 20 December 2005.
<*http://www.dvdbeaver.com/film/DVDReviews19/3_godfathers_dvd_review.htm*>

Miller, Toby, and Robert Stam, eds., *A Companion to Film Theory* (Oxford: Blackwell, 2004) [1999].

Mitchell, Jeremy, and Richard Maidment, eds., *The United States in the Twentieth Century: Culture* (London: Hodder and Stoughton, 1994).

Moore, Kenneth, *The Magic of 'Santa Claus': More Than Just a Red Suit!* (Martinez: Ken Moore Productions, 2006).

Munby, Jonathan, 'A Hollywood Carol's Wonderful Life', in *Christmas at the Movies: Images of Christmas in American, British and European Cinema*, ed. by Mark Connelly (London: I.B. Tauris, 2000), pp.39-57.

Murphy, Robert, ed., *The British Cinema Book*, 2nd edn (London: British Film Institute, 2001).

Murray, Noel, '*Meet Me in St Louis*', in *AV Film*, 20 April 2004. *<https://film.avclub.com/meet-me-in-st-louis-1798199532>*

—, '*Miracle on 34th Street*', in *AV Club*, 13 December 2006. *<https://film.avclub.com/miracle-on-34th-street-1798202201>*

Nafus, Chale, 'Holiday Favorites 2012: Chale and the Noir Side of *Scrooge*', in *Slackerwood*, 10 December 2012. *<http://www.slackerwood.com/node/3345>*

Naremore, James, *The Films of Vincente Minnelli*, Cambridge Film Classics series (Cambridge: Cambridge University Press, 1993).

Nash, Jay, T*he Encyclopedia of Best Films: A Century of all the Finest Movies: Volume 4* (New York & London: Rowman and Littlefield, 2019).

Neale, Steve, *Genre and Hollywood* (London: Routledge, 2000).

Neff, Alan, *Movies, Movie Stars, and Me* (Bloomington: AuthorHouse, 2008).

Noakes, John A., 'Official Frames in Social Movement Theory: The FBI, HUAC, and the Communist Threat in Hollywood', in *Frames of Protest:*

Social Movements and the Framing Perspective, ed. by Hank Johnston and John A. Noakes (Oxford: Rowman and Littlefield, 2005), pp.95-101.

Nugent, Frank S., 'The Screen in Review: Ernst Lubitsch Offers James Stewart and Margaret Sullavan in a Genial and Tender Romance in *The Shop Around the Corner* at the Music Hall', in *The New York Times*, 26 January 1940.
<*https://www.nytimes.com/1940/01/26/archives/the-screen-in-review-ernst-lubitsch-offers-james-stewart-and.html*>

O'Neil, Tim, '*We're No Angels*', in *PopMatters*, 30 October 2005.
<*https://www.popmatters.com/were-no-angels-dvd-2496250344.html*>

Orndorf, Brian, '*The Lemon Drop Kid*', in *Blu-Ray.com*, 4 July 2017.
<*https://www.blu-ray.com/movies/The-Lemon-Drop-Kid-Blu-ray/173529/#Review*>

Orypeck, Greg, '*Christmas in Connecticut*', in *Classic Film Freak*, 15 December 2012.
<*https://www.classicfilmfreak.com/2012/12/15/christmas-in-connecticut-1945-barbara-stanwyck/*>

—, 'Remembering WWII, 1947, and *The Bishop's Wife*', in *Classic Film Freak*, 21 August 2009.
<*https://www.classicfilmfreak.com/2009/08/21/remembering-wwii-1947-and-the-bishops-wife/*>

Parkinson, David, '*Scrooge: A Christmas Carol*', in *Radio Times*, 26 November 1999.
<*https://www.radiotimes.com/film/jh5yg/scrooge/*>

—, '*The Shop Around the Corner* Review', in *Empire*, 26 June 2006.
<*https://www.empireonline.com/movies/shop-around-corner/review/*>

Patel, Sonja, *The Christmas Companion* (London: Think Books, 2008).

Paulding, Barbara, Suzanne Schwalb and Mara Conlon, *A Century of Christmas Memories 1900-1999* (New York: Peter Pauper Press, 2009).

Peters, P., 'The Holly and the Ivy', in Moviemail Film Catalogue, November 2009, p.13.

Peterson, Paul, 'Michael Curtiz: The Mystery-Man Director of Casablanca', in Political Philosophy Comes to Rick's: Casablanca and American Civic Culture, ed. by James F. Pontuso (Lanham: Lexington Books, 2005), pp.135-52.

Phipps, Keith, 'John Wayne/John Ford Film Collection', in The Onion A.V. Club, 20 June 2006.
<https://film.avclub.com/john-wayne-john-ford-film-collection-1798201750>

Pickens, Jessica, 'Christmas at Comet's: It Happened on Fifth Avenue', in Comet Over Hollywood, 22 December 2013.
<https://cometoverhollywood.com/2013/12/22/christmas-at-comets-it-happened-on-fifth-avenue-1947/>

—, 'Christmas Musical Monday: White Christmas', in Comet Over Hollywood, 15 December 2014.
<https://cometoverhollywood.com/2014/12/15/christmas-musical-monday-white-christmas-1954/>

—, 'Christmas on Film: The Holly and the Ivy', in Comet Over Hollywood, 13 December 2017.
<https://cometoverhollywood.com/2017/12/13/christmas-on-film-holly-and-the-ivy-1952/>

—, 'Christmas on Film: We're No Angels', in Comet Over Hollywood, 24 December 2015.
<https://cometoverhollywood.com/2015/12/24/christmas-with-the-comet-were-no-angels-1955/>

—, 'Holiday Affair (1949) and interview with Gordon Gebert', in Comet Over Hollywood, 30 November 2018.
<https://cometoverhollywood.com/2018/11/30/holiday-affair-1949-and-interview-with-gordon-gebert/>

—, 'Musical Monday: Lemon Drop Kid', in Comet Over Hollywood, 21 December 2015.

<https://cometoverhollywood.com/2015/12/21/musical-monday-lemon-drop-kid-1951/>

Plath, James, '*The Lemon Drop Kid*', in *Family Home Theater*, 13 July 2017. <https://familyhometheater.com/2017/07/13/review-of-the-lemon-drop-kid-blu-ray/>

Pontuso, James F., ed., *Political Philosophy Comes to Rick's: Casablanca and American Civic Culture* (Lanham: Lexington Books, 2005).

Prigozy, Ruth, and Walter Raubicheck, eds, *Going My Way: Bing Crosby and American Culture* (Rochester: University of Rochester Press, 2007).

Propes, Richard, '*The Bishop's Wife*', in *The Independent Critic*, 22 August 2007. <https://www.theindependentcritic.com/bishops_wife>

Puccio, John J., '*Meet Me in St Louis*', in *Movie Metropolis*, 2 December 2011. <https://moviemet.com/review/meet-me-st-louis-blu-ray-review>

Purves, Barry J.C., *Stop Motion: Passion, Process and Performance* (Oxford: Elsevier, 2008).

Quart, Leonard, and Albert Auster, *American Film and Society Since 1945*, 3rd edn (Westport: Greenwood Publishing Group, 2002).

Rabin, Nathan, '*The Bells of St Mary's*', in *The Dissolve*, 19 November 2013. <http://thedissolve.com/reviews/381-the-bells-of-st-marys/>

Raymond, Nicholas, 'Why the *It's a Wonderful Life* Sequel Was Canceled', in *Screen Rant*, 23 December 2018. <https://screenrant.com/wonderful-life-sequel-movie-canceled/>

Reid, John Howard, *Hollywood Movie Musicals: Great, Good and Glamorous* (Morrisville: Lulu.com, 2006).

—, *Movies Magnificent: 150 Must-See Cinema Classics* (Morrisville: Lulu.com, 2005).

Reuben, Michael, '*Christmas in Connecticut* Blu-Ray', in *Blu-Ray.com*, 9 November 2014.
<*https://www.blu-ray.com/movies/Christmas-in-Connecticut-Blu-ray/109472/#Review*>

—, '*The Bishop's Wife* Blu-ray Review: Bishop Takes Queen', in *Blu-ray.com*, 31 October 2013.
<*https://www.blu-ray.com/movies/The-Bishops-Wife-Blu-ray/77925/#Review*>

Rich, Jamie S., '*It's a Wonderful Life*: 60th Anniversary Edition', in *DVD Talk*, 31 October 2006.
<*https://www.dvdtalk.com/reviews/25017/its-a-wonderful-life-60th-anniversary-edition/*>

Richards, Jeffrey, 'Crisis at Christmas: *Turkey Time*, *The Holly and the Ivy*, *The Cheaters*', in *Christmas at the Movies: Images of Christmas in American, British and European Cinema*, ed. by Mark Connelly (London: I.B. Tauris, 2000), pp.97-113.

—, *Films and British National Identity: From Dickens to Dad's Army* (Manchester: Manchester University Press, 1997).

Robertson, James C., *The Casablanca Man: The Cinema of Michael Curtiz* (London: Routledge, 1993).

Roscoe, J.P., '*A Christmas Carol (Scrooge)*', in *Basement Rejects*, 30 November 2011.
<*http://basementrejects.com/review/a-christmas-carol-scrooge-1951/*>

—, '*Christmas in Connecticut*', in *Basement Rejects*, 30 November 2012.
<*http://basementrejects.com/review/christmas-in-connecticut-1945/*>

—, '*It Happened on Fifth Avenue*', in *Basement Rejects*, 16 December 2013.
<*http://basementrejects.com/review/it-happened-on-fifth-avenue-1947/*>

—, '*Miracle on 34th Street*', in *Basement Rejects*, 4 December 2017.
<*http://basementrejects.com/review/miracle-on-34th-steet-1947/*>

—, '*The Bells of St Mary's*', in *Basement Rejects*, 29 November 2012.

<http://basementrejects.com/review/the-bells-of-st-marys-1945/>

—, '*The Bishop's Wife*', in *Basement Rejects*, 8 December 2011. <http://basementrejects.com/review/the-bishops-wife-1947/>

Rose, Brian Geoffrey, *An Examination of Narrative Structure in Four Films of Frank Capra* (New York: Arno Press, 1980) [1976].

Rowe, John Carlos, ed., *Post-Nationalist American Studies* (Berkeley: University of California Press, 2000).

Ryan, Michael, and Douglas Kellner, *Camera Politica: The Politics and Ideology of Contemporary Hollywood* (Indianapolis: Indiana University Press, 1988).

Samuel, Raphael, The*atres of Memory: Volume 1: Past and Present in Contemporary Culture* (London: Verso, 1994).

Santino, Jack, *All Around the Year: Holidays and Celebrations in American Life* (Champaign: University of Illinois Press, 1994) [1985].

—, *New Old-Fashioned Ways: Holidays and Popular Culture* (Knoxville: University of Tennessee Press, 1996).

Saunders, D.J.M., 'Home Is Not Just for Christmas... or Thanksgiving... or Middle-Class Chaps, However Decent', in *Bright Lights Film Journal*, 25 December 2014.
<https://brightlightsfilm.com/holly-and-the-ivy-christmas-wynyard-browne-play/>

Scheer, Ron, '*3 Godfathers*', in *Buddies in the Saddle*, 19 July 2011.
<http://buddiesinthesaddle.blogspot.com/2011/07/3-godfathers-1948.html>

Scheib, Richard, '*Bell Book and Candle*', in *Moria: The Science Fiction, Horror and Fantasy Film Review*, 8 January 2001.
<http://www.moriareviews.com/fantasy/bell-book-and-candle-1958.htm>

—, '*Miracle on 34th Street*', in *Moria: The Science Fiction, Horror and Fantasy Film Review*, 1 March 2003.
<http://www.moriareviews.com/fantasy/miracle-on-34th-street-1947.htm>

—, '*Scrooge*', in *Moria: The Science Fiction, Horror and Fantasy Film Review*, 5 December 2018.
<*http://www.moriareviews.com/fantasy/scrooge-1951.htm*>

—, '*The Bishop's Wife*', in *Moria: The Science Fiction, Horror and Fantasy Film Review*, 12 November 2001.
<*http://www.moriareviews.com/fantasy/bishops-wife-1947.htm*>

Schochet, Stephen, *Hollywood Stories: Short, Entertaining Anecdotes about the Stars and Legends*, 2nd edn (Los Angeles: Hollywood Stories Publishing, 2013).

Schwartz, Dennis, '*3 Godfathers*', in *Dennis Schwartz Reviews*, 27 June 2004.
<*https://dennisschwartzreviews.com/3godfathers/*>

—, '*Christmas Eve*', in *Ozus' World Movie Reviews*, 25 December 2012.
<*http://homepages.sover.net/~ozus/christmaseve.htm*>

—, '*Christmas in Connecticut*', in *Ozus' World Movie Reviews*, 26 December 2004.
<*http://homepages.sover.net/~ozus/christmasinconnecticut.htm*>

—, '*Meet Me in St Louis*', in *Ozus' World Movie Reviews*, 28 November 2005.
<*http://homepages.sover.net/~ozus/meetmeinstlouis.htm*>

Shail, Robert, *British Film Directors: A Critical Guide* (Edinburgh: Edinburgh University Press, 2007).

Simpson, Paul, ed., *The Rough Guide to Cult Movies* (London: Haymarket Customer Publishing, 2001).

Sindelar, Dave, '*Bell Book and Candle*', in *Fantastic Movie Musings and Ramblings*, 18 January 2007.
<*https://fantasticmoviemusings.com/2017/07/01/bell-book-and-candle-1958/*>

—, '*Miracle on 34th Street*', in *Fantastic Movie Musings and Ramblings*, 8 November 2015.

<https://fantasticmoviemusings.com/2015/11/08/miracle-on-34th-street-1947/>

—, '*The Bishop's Wife*', in *Fantastic Movie Musings and Ramblings*, 2 August 2015.
<https://fantasticmoviemusings.com/2015/08/02/the-bishops-wife-1947/>

Sinnott, John, '*Bells of St Mary's*', in *DVD Talk*, 19 November 2013.
<https://www.dvdtalk.com/reviews/62052/bells-of-st-marys/>

Skinner, Jacob, '*Miracle on 34th Street*', in *Film Write-Up*, 25 December 2012.
<https://filmwriteup.wordpress.com/2012/12/25/miracle-on-34th-street-1947-review/>

Smith, Anthony Burke, 'America's Favorite Priest: *Going My Way* (1944)' in *Catholics in the Movies*, ed. by Colleen McDannell (New York: Oxford University Press US, 2008), pp. 107-126.

Sorrento, Matthew, 'Essential Film Performances 2013 Update: Part 7', in *Pop Matters*, 6 August 2013.
<https://www.popmatters.com/174230-essential-film-performances-2013-update-part-7-2495734419.html>

Staiger, Janet, *Perverse Spectators: The Practices of Film Reception* (New York: New York University Press, 2000).

Stott, Iain, '*Holiday Affair*', in *An Evening Illuminated*, 12 December 2012.
<http://artemisnt.blogspot.com/2012/12/holiday-affair-1949.html>

Strupp, Phyllis, *The Richest of Fare: Seeking Spiritual Security in the Sonoran Desert* (Scottsdale: Sonoran Cross Press, 2004).

Sullivan, Daniel J., 'Sentimental Hogwash?: On Capra's *It's a Wonderful Life*', in *Humanitas*, Vol. 18, Nos. 1-2, 9 January 2012, pp.115-140.

Sunday, Steve, '*The Lemon Drop Kid*', in *Black and White Movies*, 1 January 2017.
<https://black-and-white-movies.com/the-lemon-drop-kid/>

Svehla, Gary J., '*Christmas Eve*', in *It's Christmas Time at the Movies* by Gary J. Svehla and Susan Svehla (Baltimore: Midnight Marquee Press, 1998), pp.18-22.

—, '*The Holly and the Ivy*', in *It's Christmas Time at the Movies* by Gary J. Svehla and Susan Svehla (Baltimore: Midnight Marquee Press, 1998), pp.24-28.

—, and Susan Svehla, *It's Christmas Time at the Movies* (Baltimore: Midnight Marquee Press, 1998).

Thomas, Tony, *A Smidgeon of Religion* (Bloomington: AuthorHouse, 2007).

Thomson, David, 'Daniel Taradash: Triumph and Chaos', in *Backstory 2: Interviews with Screenwriters of the 1940s and 1950s*, ed. by Patrick McGilligan (Berkeley: University of California Press, 1997) [1991], 309-29, p.324.

Thompson, Frank, *American Movie Classics' Great Christmas Movies* (Dallas: Taylor, 1998).

Tooze, Gary W., '*White Christmas* (Blu-ray)', in *DVD Beaver*, 29 October 2010.
<*http://www.dvdbeaver.com/film3/blu-ray_reviews52/white_christmas_blu-ray.htm*>

Tucker, David C., *Gale Storm: A Biography and Career Record* (Jefferson: McFarland and Company, 2018).

Turner, Adrian, '*We're No Angels*', in *Radio Times*, 7 November 2005.
<*http://www.radiotimes.com/film/fk6mb4/were-no-angels*>

Turner, Graeme, *Film as Social Practice* (London: Routledge, 1999).

Tyler, Don, *Music of the Postwar Era* (Westport: Greenwood Publishing Group, 2008).

Van Spall, Owen, '*The Shop Around the Corner*', *Eye for Film*, 20 November 2010.

<https://www.eyeforfilm.co.uk/review/the-shop-around-the-corner-film-review-by-owen-van-spall>

Vienna, '*Christmas Eve*', in *Vienna's Classic Hollywood*, 4 November 2015. <https://viennasclassichollywood.com/2015/11/04/christmas-eve-1947/>

Watt, Kate Carnell, and Kathleen C. Lonsdale, 'Dickens Composed: Film and Television Adaptations 1897-2001', in *Dickens on Screen*, ed. by John Glavin (Cambridge: Cambridge University Press, 2003), pp.201-16.

Webb, Andy, '*A Christmas Carol* (a.k.a. *Scrooge*)', in *The Movie Scene*, 2018. <https://www.themoviescene.co.uk/reviews/a-christmas-carol-1951/a-christmas-carol-1951.html>

—, '*Bell, Book and Candle*', in *The Movie Scene*, 2016. <https://www.themoviescene.co.uk/reviews/bell-book-and-candle/bell-book-and-candle.html>

—, '*Christmas Eve*', in *The Movie Scene*, 2016. <https://www.themoviescene.co.uk/reviews/christmas-eve-1947/christmas-eve-1947.html>

—, '*Holiday Affair*', in *The Movie Scene*, 2012. <https://www.themoviescene.co.uk/reviews/holiday-affair/holiday-affair.html>

—, '*The Bishop's Wife*', in *The Movie Scene*, 2018. <https://www.themoviescene.co.uk/reviews/the-bishops-wife/the-bishops-wife.html>

—, '*The Holly and the Ivy*', in *The Movie Scene*, 2018. <https://www.themoviescene.co.uk/reviews/the-holly-and-the-ivy-1952/the-holly-and-the-ivy-1952.html>

—, '*White Christmas*', in *The Movie Scene*, 2010. <https://www.themoviescene.co.uk/reviews/white-christmas/white-christmas.html>

Weber, Bill, 'Blu-Ray Review: *The Bells of St Mary's*', in *Slant Magazine*, 18 November 2013.
<*https://www.slantmagazine.com/dvd/the-bells-of-st-marys/*>

Werts, Diane, *Christmas on Television* (Westport: Greenwood Press, 2006).

Wickliffe, Andrew, '*The Shop Around the Corner*', in *The Stop Button*, 28 December 2014.
<*https://thestopbutton.com/2014/12/28/shop-around-corner-1940/*>

Willian, Michael, T*he Essential It's a Wonderful Life: A Scene-by-Scene Guide to the Classic Film* (Chicago: Chicago Review Press, 2006).

Wilson, Richard, *Scrooge's Guide to Christmas: A Survival Manual for the Festively Challenged* (London: Hodder and Stoughton, 1997).

Winnert, Derek, '*Bell, Book and Candle*', in *Derek Winnert.com*, 1 March 2017.
<*http://www.derekwinnert.com/bell-book-and-candle-1958-james-stewart-kim-novak-jack-lemmon-ernie-kovacs-hermione-gingold-elsa-lanchester-janice-rule-classic-movie-review-5091/*>

—, '*The Holly and the Ivy*', in *Derek Winnert.com*, 12 February 2019.
<*http://www.derekwinnert.com/the-holly-and-the-ivy-1952-ralph-richardson-celia-johnson-margaret-leighton-denholm-elliott-john-gregson-hugh-williams-maureen-delaney-margaret-halstan-classic-movie-review-8120/*>

—, '*The Lemon Drop Kid*', at *Derek Winnert.com*, 14 July 2019.
<*http://www.derekwinnert.com/the-lemon-drop-kid-1951-bob-hope-marilyn-maxwell-lloyd-nolan-jane-darwell-william-frawley-classic-movie-review-8705/*>

—, '*Three Godfathers*', in *Derek Winnert.com*, 17 August 2018.
<*http://www.derekwinnert.com/three-godfathers-3-godfathers-1948-john-wayne-pedro-armendariz-harry-carey-jr-classic-movie-review-7458/*>

—, '*We're No Angels*', in *Derek Winnert.com*, 15 February 2016.

<http://www.derekwinnert.com/were-no-angels-1955-humphrey-bogart-peter-ustinov-aldo-ray-leo-g-carroll-joan-bennett-basil-rathbone-classic-movie-review-3362/>

—, '*White Christmas*', in *Derek Winnert.com*, 23 February 2015.
<http://www.derekwinnert.com/white-christmas-1954-bing-crosby-danny-kaye-rosemary-clooney-vera-ellen-classic-movie-review-2207/>

Young, Neil, 'July Briefs: *Senna & The Shop Around the Corner*', in *Neil Young's Film Lounge*, 5 July 2011.
<https://www.jigsawlounge.co.uk/film/reviews/july2011/>

Zegarac, Nick, 'Classic Holiday DVDs', in *DVD Beaver*, 23 September 2003.
<http://www.dvdbeaver.com/film/DVDReviews19/holiday_dvds.htm>

Zupan, Michael, '*A Christmas Carol*', in *DVD Talk*, 6 November 2012.
<https://www.dvdtalk.com/reviews/57588/christmas-carol-2012-a/>

Index

594

596

G

N

P

614

T

Acknowledgements

I am most grateful to my family, Julie Christie and Mary Melville, and to my friends Professor Roderick Watson, Amy Leitch, Eddy and Dorothy Bryan, Alex Tucker, Denham Hardwick MBE, David Addison, Ian McNeish, Dr Colin M. Barron, Robert Murray and Dr Elspeth King for their fellowship and encouragement throughout the course of this project.

With special thanks to my dear friends Joe and Mary Moore of the North Pole Press, who keep the Christmas spirit alive all the year round!

About the Author

Dr Thomas Christie has many years of experience as a literary and publishing professional, working in collaboration with several companies including Cambridge Scholars Publishing, Crescent Moon Publishing and Applause Books. A passionate advocate of the written word and literary arts, over the years he has worked to develop original writing for respected organisations such as the Stirling Smith Art Gallery and Museum and a leading independent higher education research unit based at the University of Stirling. Additionally, he is regularly involved in public speaking events and has delivered guest lectures and presentations about his work at many locations around the United Kingdom.

Tom is a Fellow of the Royal Society of Arts and a member of the Royal Society of Literature, the Society of Authors, the Federation of Writers Scotland and the Authors' Licensing and Collecting Society. He holds a first-class Honours degree in English Literature and a Masters degree in Humanities with British Cinema History from the Open University in Milton Keynes, and a Doctorate in Scottish Literature awarded by the University of Stirling.

He is the author of a number of books on the subject of modern film which include *Liv Tyler: Star in Ascendance* (2007), *The Cinema of Richard Linklater* (2008), *John Hughes and Eighties Cinema: Teenage Hopes and American Dreams* (2009), *Ferris Bueller's Day Off: Pocket Movie Guide* (2010), *The Christmas Movie Book* (2011), *The James Bond Movies of the 1980s* (2013), *Mel Brooks: Genius and Loving It!: Freedom and Liberation in the Cinema of Mel Brooks* (2015), *A Righteously Awesome Eighties Christmas: Festive Cinema of the 1980s* (2016), and *John Hughes* FAQ (2019).

His other works include *Notional Identities: Ideology, Genre and National Identity in Popular Scottish Fiction Since the Seventies* (2013), *The Spectrum of Adventure: A Brief History of Interactive Fiction on the Sinclair ZX Spectrum* (2016), and *Contested Mindscapes: Exploring Approaches to Dementia in Modern Popular Culture* (2018). He has also written a crowdfunded murder-mystery novel, *The Shadow in the Gallery* (2013), which is set during the nineteenth century in Stirling's historic Smith Art Gallery and Museum.

For more details about Tom and his work, please visit his website at:
www.tomchristiebooks.co.uk

Also Available from Extremis Publishing

The Spectrum of Adventure
A Brief History of Interactive Fiction on the Sinclair ZX Spectrum

By Thomas A. Christie

The Sinclair ZX Spectrum was one of the most popular home computers in British history, selling over five million units in its 1980s heyday. Amongst the thousands of games released for the Spectrum during its lifetime, the text adventure game was to emerge as one of the most significant genres on the system.

The Spectrum of Adventure chronicles the evolution of the text adventure on the ZX Spectrum, exploring the work of landmark software houses such as Melbourne House Software, Level 9 Computing, Delta 4 Software, the CRL Group, Magnetic Scrolls, and many others besides.

Covering one hundred individual games in all, this book celebrates the Spectrum's thriving interactive fiction scene of the eighties, chronicling the achievements of major publishers as well as independent developers from the machine's launch in 1982 until the end of the decade in 1989.

A Righteously Awesome Eighties Christmas
Festive Cinema of the 1980s

By Thomas A. Christie

The cinema of the festive season has blazed a trail through the world of film-making for more than a century, ranging from silent movies to the latest CGI features. From the author of *The Christmas Movie Book*, this new text explores the different narrative themes which emerged in the genre over the course of the 1980s, considering the developments which have helped to make the Christmas films of that decade amongst the most fascinating and engaging motion pictures in the history of festive movie production.

Released against the backdrop of a turbulent and rapidly-changing world, the Christmas films of the 1980s celebrated traditions and challenged assumptions in equal measure. With warm nostalgia colliding with aggressive modernity as never before, the eighties saw the movies of the holiday season being deconstructed and reconfigured to remain relevant in an age of cynicism and innovation.

Whether exploring comedy, drama, horror or fantasy, Christmas cinema has an unparalleled capacity to attract and inspire audiences. With a discussion ranging from the best-known titles to some of the most obscure, *A Righteously Awesome Eighties Christmas* examines the ways in which the Christmas motion pictures of the 1980s fit into the wider context of this captivating and ever-evolving genre.

Contested Mindscapes

Exploring Approaches to Dementia in Modern Popular Culture

By Thomas A. Christie

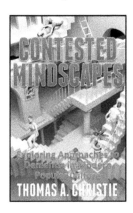

Dementia is a mental health condition which affects an estimated 50 million people worldwide. Yet it has, until recently, been an unfairly neglected subject in popular culture.

Contested Mindscapes considers the ways in which the arts have engaged with dementia over the past twenty years, looking at particular examples drawn from the disciplines of film and television, popular music, performance art, and interactive entertainment.

Examining a variety of creative approaches ranging from the thought-provoking to the controversial, *Contested Mindscapes* carefully contemplates the many ways in which the humanities and entertainment industries have engaged with dementia, exploring how the wide-ranging implications of this complex condition have been communicated through a variety of artistic nodes.

Dying Harder
Action Movies of the 1980s

By Colin M. Barron

The 1980s were a golden age for action movies, with the genre proving popular at the box-office as never before. Across the world, stars such as Sylvester Stallone, Arnold Schwarzenegger and Bruce Willis were becoming household names as a result of their appearances in some of the best-known films of the decade.

But what were the stories which lay behind the making of these movies? Why were the eighties to bear witness to so many truly iconic action features? And who were the people who brought these legends of action cinema to life?

In *Dying Harder: Action Movies of the 1980s*, Colin M. Barron considers some of the most unforgettable movies of the decade, exploring the reasons behind their success and assessing the extent of their enduring acclaim amongst audiences which continues into the present day.

For details of new and forthcoming books
from Extremis Publishing,
please visit our official website at:

www.extremispublishing.com

or follow us on social media at:

www.facebook.com/extremispublishing

www.linkedin.com/company/extremis-publishing-ltd-/